D1552970

Awakening Vocation
A Theology of Christian Call

Edward P. Hahnenberg

A Michael Glazier Book

LITURGICAL PRESS
Collegeville, Minnesota

www.litpress.org

A Michael Glazier Book published by Liturgical Press

Cover design by Ann Blattner. Photo courtesy of Photos.com.

2   3   4   5   6   7   8   9

Library of Congress Cataloging-in-Publication Data

Hahnenberg, Edward P.
    Awakening vocation : a theology of Christian call / Edward P. Hahnenberg.
        p. cm.
    "A Michael Glazier book."
    Includes bibliographical references (p.   ) and index.
    ISBN 978-0-8146-5389-0 — ISBN 978-0-8146-5733-1 (e-book)
    1. Vocation—Catholic Church.   2. Catholic Church—Doctrines.   I. Title.
BX1795.W67H34   2010
248—dc22   2010016695

For our girls,
Kate, Meg, and Abby

Contents

Acknowledgments

This book has been a journey that I have been blessed to share with others. It began in conversations with family members. It took shape through more conversations—with family, with friends, with students and colleagues. As the writing comes to a close, my main hope for the book is that these conversations carry on, and that others join in.

I am deeply grateful for this journey and for all those who have helped so much with this published piece of it. A Pastoral Leadership Grant from the Louisville Institute and a Faculty Development Grant from Xavier University gave me the time and the space to reflect theologically on all the questions these conversations raised. Invitations to speak in a number of different dioceses and to various groups of ministers have given me the opportunity to share what I have been learning—and to learn a great deal in return. In particular, an address at the 2007 National Symposium on Lay Ecclesial Ministry at Saint John's University provided an important early catalyst for my research on vocation. I am thankful for all of these opportunities.

In addition, a number of individuals offered help. Matthew Ashley, Robert Krieg, Robert Lassalle-Klein, Michael E. Lee, Richard Lennan, and Edward Sloane all read portions of this manuscript and offered excellent feedback. I thank them again for their generous responses. My colleagues in the department of theology at Xavier University have been incredibly supportive. They not only provide an ideal context for the theological life but also diverse and challenging models of it. In particular, I thank Ken Overberg, whose offhand comment about Rahner took this project in a wonderfully unexpected direction and whose dependable presence is a source of ongoing support; and Chris Pramuk, whose insightful response to my manuscript has led to one of the richest conversations of the many conversations that are connected to this book. I am grateful for such colleagues and friends.

The team at Liturgical Press has been amazing. Thanks to Peter Dwyer for his early encouragement, to Hans Christoffersen for his generous hospitality and gentle guidance through the publication process, and to Mary Stommes and Stephanie Lancour for their editorial expertise.

Finally, I thank my wife Julie and our three daughters, Kate, Meg, and Abby. In this effort to articulate anew the meaning of Christian discipleship, these traveling companions are not mentioned again. But they are present on every page. In their love, I catch a glimpse every day of that Love that draws us all forward.

Introduction

"Tell me," prompts the poet Mary Oliver, "what is it you plan to do with your one wild and precious life?"[1] Is there any more pressing question? Is there one that cuts more quickly to the heart, gathering up all of our decisions and our dreams and directing them into the future? Stretched out between birth and death lies my one opportunity. What will I do?

Over the centuries, the Christian tradition has asked this question in the language of vocation. And in the years since the Second Vatican Council, Catholics have become more and more accustomed to a broad and inclusive understanding of God's call. Once it was Protestants alone who spoke of work and marriage, farm and family, as callings coming from God—while Catholics confined the category to the realm of priesthood or religious life. Now Catholics too share this wider view: "Everyone has a vocation!" In a line that glosses over a significant shift, Vatican II's Dogmatic Constitution on the Church states, "It is therefore quite clear that all Christians in whatever state or walk in life are called to the fullness of christian life and to the perfection of charity, and this holiness is conducive to a more human way of living even in society here on earth."[2] The universal call to holiness extends to all.

This widening is welcome. But it has not resolved some of the most difficult theological questions that come with the claim that "God is calling me." Does God have a specific plan for each of us, or is it more like general guidelines for all of us? What is holiness? And what does it mean within the particular circumstances of my own individual life? When I face difficult decisions, how am I to know what God wants me to do? Is that even the right way of framing the question? Lying just below the surface of these questions is a thicket of theological problems that are not easily resolved: the relationship of the divine will to human freedom, the nature of providence and predestination, the workings of grace and the limits of spiritual experience. The question of vocation taps into our deepest assumptions about God, ourselves, church, and moral commitment. It offers a concrete way of talking about nothing less than the meaning of life. But for all its potential, the category of vocation has been overlooked by theologians and not well understood by Christians.[3] It has slipped into a silent slumber. The following pages are an attempt to wake it up.

Awakening Vocation argues that what I call "the modern Catholic theology of vocation" is a limited theology that took shape within the context of a dualistic understanding of the nature-grace relationship. That dualistic understanding was abandoned in the middle decades of the twentieth century, and was replaced by a theology of grace that affirms a richer, more biblical and traditional vision of God's pervasive presence in the world. It was a revolution that touched virtually every area of Catholic theology—but its implications for vocation have yet to be thought out. The task of this book is to do some of that thinking. My goal is to reimage God's call in light of this theological revolution, in order to offer a theology of vocation that is intellectually credible, pastorally relevant, and personally meaningful.

What motivates the work is my conviction that the notion of *call* offers a constructive alternative to our contemporary cultural default, namely, *choice*. Choice has become one of our most important ways of framing reality, a lens on all aspects of our lives, including the religious dimension of our existence. A number of commentators have described the predominance of choice in the language of "quest," which functions as a guiding metaphor of contemporary spiritual life. Looking back over the past century of American religious experience, the sociologist Robert Wuthnow notes a fundamental shift in sensibility from religious "dwelling" to spiritual "seeking." If an earlier era located religion within stable institutions, inherited traditions, and clear group identities, then today, spirituality has become a project for the individual, a search for bits of wisdom and insight that might be used to craft a coherent framework for life. Rather than rest secure in the womb of organized religion, today we launch out on our own. We are seekers. Faith is not something given but something for which to strive. External religious forms are less important than the internal spiritual life. Authenticity replaces authority, and wholeness becomes the measure of holiness. Wuthnow concludes, "Spirituality has become a vastly complex quest in which each person seeks in his or her own way."[4]

The individualism inherent in this paradigm and the superficiality of so much of what claims our attention in today's spiritual marketplace have made the culture of religious choice an easy target. Critics accuse it of promoting a trivial, privatized, and self-absorbed spirituality—one that simply mimics a consumer culture in need of its own critique. However, I think it is a mistake to judge the paradigm of choice by its most shallow and stupid forms. It needs critique. But it cannot be written off. To do so would not only miss the larger cultural dynamics at work but also grossly underestimate the motivations of the many spiritual seekers who are looking for purpose, orientation, and meaning in life. Their search—*our* search—cannot be dismissed as selfish. For many, the quest for meaning does not end in self-improvement but extends outward in altruistic behavior, communal participation, and diverse forms of religious practice. Often the rejection of traditional religion and religious institutions has more to do with the failures of those institutions to offer space for the spiritual life than it has to do with the quality of the seekers' own spiritual lives. As Wade Clark Roof acknowledges, people today, particularly young people, are "looking for a more direct experience of the sacred, for greater immediacy, spontaneity, and spiritual depth."[5] This instinct ought to be encouraged. It is a facet of the Christian tradition that stretches back to the beginning. What has changed, perhaps, is that what was once reserved to a few—namely, the quest for a deeper spiritual life—has now become the primary religious stance of most people.[6]

An emphasis on choice in the realm of religion encourages agency and intentionality. It moves people beyond blind acceptance or passive membership. It highlights the personal nature of our relationship with God. However, the principal weakness of choice—as a fundamental framework for the spiritual life—is the way it can so easily short-circuit personal transformation. If religious traditions and religious institutions no longer provide the *context* for the spiritual life, but instead serve as *resources* for our own spiritual constructions, can they ever really challenge us? Despite the sincerity of the search, does Christianity, in the end, become a collection of commodities from which I pick and choose, determining whether or not they fit into my life—a life whose basic pattern is set well before any real encounter with the demands of the Gospel? The framework of choice can neither be uncritically embraced nor flatly rejected. What is needed is a more nuanced engagement—and alternative ways of articulating the concerns of the contemporary spiritual seeker.

Here is where the language of vocation helps. It taps into the deep-seated sensibilities of the quest—integrity, identity, itinerary—but in a way that resists self-absorption. It acknowledges the importance of discernment and decision—the virtues of choice—but recognizes that our decisions come as a *response* to something or someone beyond. To speak of call is to acknowledge a caller, to see that God's gracious initiative precedes all of our projects and our plans, that our individual journeys have a goal. Our freedom does not hover supreme over an infinite number of options (the fundamental paradigm of choice). Our freedom stands under and before the transcendent, always being drawn up and out into the source of our being (the basic pattern of call). How will I respond in love to the God who is love? Unlike the commandments of the moral law, which are meant to mark the floor below which love should never fall, vocation has to do with the wide-open space above.[7] Love has no ceiling, and so my vocation is, quite simply, the way that I will rise. Yet, like picking a point on the dome of the sky, there are an infinite number of ways up. So what will be my unique way of responding to God's loving call? What will be the transcendent trajectory of my life?

It is vocation in this broad and inclusive sense that is the subject of this book. Life—every life—finds meaning when lived as a response to God's initiative. Thus vocation cannot be confined to a few groups, or limited to a certain number of church roles or human occupations. Indeed, one of the particular limitations of the modern Catholic theology of vocation is its tendency to reserve the language of vocation to a few states of life—a deductive and static approach that leaves the particularities of the person and the dynamic nature of human existence undervalued. God calls people in an almost infinite number of contexts. And within any individual life, what we identify as "vocations" might be multiple, interrelated, and overlapping. Vocation implies a deep coherence to life, a consistency in our commitments, but particular vocations can change over time. Thus the category of call applies to lifelong decisions, as well as to particular, more modest ways that individuals respond to God's invitations. Rather than corral the category, I use the word vocation in an inclusive and varied way. The theology developed here is not so interested in deciding what roles or responsibilities are proper to this or to that vocation. I am not trying to determine what careers might be considered callings. Rather, I am searching for a theology that might help each of us navigate with faith our unique, unrepeatable lives as a response to a call from God. Ultimately, I am offering an argument oriented toward discernment: how do I come to know what to do with my "one wild and precious life"?

Awakening Vocation proceeds in two parts. Part 1 explores the historical background to our contemporary understanding of vocation. Part 2 offers a constructive proposal. As I already indicated, one of the keys to understanding the historical narrative is the development of what I call the "modern Catholic theology of vocation." This phrase refers to a certain constellation of assumptions that has taken shape over the past four hundred years and that now needs to be set aside. By "modern," I mean the period of history in the West stretching from the sixteenth-century Reformation to the middle of the twentieth century. By "Catholic," I mean to underscore the important differences between the way in which the Roman Catholic tradition and the various Protestant traditions have talked about vocation during this time. The "modern Catholic" approach is rooted in medieval ecclesiastical structures and early modern conceptions of spiritual experience. It takes explicit form in the neoscholastic manual tradition of the nineteenth and early twentieth centuries. And it continues to operate as a kind of unspoken understanding behind any number of papal documents, bishops' letters, high school textbooks, and prayers for "vocations" offered at Sunday liturgies. The goal of part 1 is to bring this approach into focus, and to identify its significant limitations.

While the language of call goes back to the very origins of Christianity, chapter 1 begins in earnest with Martin Luther. It may seem strange to begin a treatment of the modern Catholic trajectory of vocation with the father of the Protestant Reformation, but Luther's influence cannot be overlooked. And the tradition of reflection he launched sheds important light on contemporary Catholic concerns. Through his critique of the monastery system and his commentary on 1 Corinthians, Luther introduced into Christianity a wholly new way of talking about vocation—one that celebrates the ordinary and everyday occupations of Christians as true "callings" coming from God. In response, Catholics reasserted a more narrow identification of vocation with certain official states of life. While Vatican II opened up a broader view, in postconciliar church documents and in much of the popular Catholic imagination, a narrow and deductive conception carries on.

Chapter 2 turns from the breadth of the callings to the depth of the call by exploring the interiorization of vocation that occurs within the Catholic tradition in the years stretching from Trent to the Second Vatican Council. If Martin Luther stands as the father of the Protestant doctrine of vocation, Ignatius of Loyola emerges as the most influential Catholic voice for a modern spirituality of discernment. As we will see,

Luther's deep insight was later obscured by a secularization of the Protestant notion of vocation. In a similar way, Ignatius's own vision was frustrated by a nature-grace dualism that entered into post-Reformation Catholic theology. Thus the prayerful attention to the subtle movements of God within the soul that was so crucial to Ignatius was transformed by later theologians into an anxious search for some "secret voice" telling the individual what to do. As the supernatural became unhinged from human nature, the "inward turn" became a search for something strange. The end result of the history laid out in part 1 is the modern Catholic theology of vocation: an institutionalization and interiorization of vocation that silences God's call, reserving it to a few and reducing it to a mysterious message hidden in the soul.

In an effort to move beyond this narrowing and burying of vocation, part 2 offers a constructive theological proposal. Chapter 3 ("God Calls . . .") begins by exploring the notion of "God's plan." Drawing on Karl Barth's reading of Luther and his own creative theology of God, this chapter suggests a *theological* foundation for vocation that firmly locates God's plan within the gracious, saving design of God for us, a plan made manifest and actualized in Christ through the Spirit. This preliminary step frees us from a mistaken view of predestination that assumes God prepares a detailed blueprint for every individual life ahead of time—assigning our vocations without ever consulting us. Overcoming such a simplistic view is necessary and helpful, but the alternative, namely, an emphasis on the general, saving plan of God, risks overlooking the particularity of the person. Thus chapter 4 ("Me . . .") takes up the concrete human subject as the center of the vocational dynamic. Here we explore Karl Rahner's reading of Ignatius. Rahner's reflections on vocational discernment begin with Ignatius's startling conviction that each and every person can come to know God's particular will for his or her life. With Rahner's help, we find a way to affirm an inductive approach to discernment that avoids any mechanistic conception of predestination. Leaving behind the nature-grace dualism of the past, this chapter offers a theological *anthropology* of vocation that attends to the unique and concrete particularity of the spiritual subject.

Rahner's work offers one of the most theologically rich treatments of vocational discernment available. What he leaves underdeveloped (but by no means ignored) in his commentaries on Ignatius is Ignatius's own sense that healthy Christian discernment depends on an ongoing process of conversion and discipleship that trains the ear, so to speak, to hear the call of God. The final two chapters of the book attempt to lay out the type of conversion demanded by our present postmodern context. Chapter 5 ("Through Others . . .") turns to the themes of story and community in order to address the context within which conversion takes place. Drawing on insights from narrative theology and postmodern philosophy—and thus bringing into dialogue both identity and alterity—what takes shape is an *ecclesiology* of vocation. This vision is one of participation in an "open church" that schools us in openness to "the other." Precisely through this openness to the other, we become open to *the* Other—the God who calls.

Chapter 6 ("For Others") concludes with the way in which this openness to the other takes shape most powerfully and most urgently today: openness to the other in need. Here is an *ethics* of vocation that is not simply the end or application of Christian discernment but its beginning and foundation. Throughout Christian history, the concept of call has always implied conversion, an often painful confrontation or interruption of one's former way of life. Given the global extent of violence, hunger, and death-dealing poverty today, the conversion demanded by this moment is of a particular form: it is a turning outward, an opening to the suffering other. The various theologies of liberation that emerged over the second half of the twentieth century offer the resources for a spirituality of solidarity. Here we see that discipleship—the necessary context for Christian discernment—is directed. God calls us *for others*.

In this openness to the suffering other—this directed discipleship—we find a corrective to the open-endedness that has plagued broad notions of vocation since Luther, and that threatens Catholic attempts to widen the category today. When vocation spreads out, there is always the danger that it thins out. With expansion can easily come dilution. Over the course of the modern period, the concept of calling has often served as a convenient halo to paste onto any activity, blessing social hierarchies, condoning unjust economic conditions, feeding unhealthy spiritualities, and obscuring the radical demands of the Gospel. Protestant traditions—with their history of "secular callings"—are well aware of this temptation. But I do not believe that Catholics have fully faced the challenge that comes with the "universal call to holiness"—a category more often used to affirm our common baptismal dignity than to confront us with the demands this dignity entails. The response, of course, cannot be a reactionary attempt to pull back the language of vocation—restricting it to a few, the elite, the truly holy ones. Nor can the dilemma be solved by imposing on everyone a cookie-cutter conception of holiness, drawn from past models of ecclesiastical and religious vocations. Rather, we have to find a language of call that speaks to *each* of us and that challenges *all* of us. *Awakening Vocation* is the search for just such a language.

PART ONE

Slipping into Silence

CHAPTER ONE

The Breadth of the Callings

Prince Harry: I see a good amendment of life in thee, from praying to purse-taking.

Sir John: Why, Hal, 'tis my vocation, Hal. 'Tis no sin for a man to labour in his vocation.

—*William Shakespeare*[1]

In his classic study, *The Protestant Ethic and the Spirit of Capitalism*, the sociologist Max Weber famously argued that the theological concept of vocation played an important role in the rise of our modern capitalistic economic system.[2] His thesis was as simple as it was controversial. Weber argued that, by speaking of all occupations as equal callings coming from God, Protestant Reformers gave to the realm of work a newfound spiritual significance. He observed how Martin Luther first broadened the notion of vocation to include all Christians and every state of life. Then John Calvin turned this idea toward industry and commerce. And by the seventeenth century, English Puritans were exhorting their members to obey the commands of God by obeying the demands of their callings, in other words, to show faithfulness to God through fidelity to a job or a trade. For Weber, it was precisely this religious validation of work—a "Protestant ethic" that was inseparable from a particular understanding of vocation—that prepared the ground for the growth of early capitalism. Contrary to the common assumption that the systematically organized economy of modern Europe owed its origins to science, technology, and Enlightenment rationalism alone, Weber argued that this new economic system had religious roots. It sprang, at least in part, from a broadening of vocation.

In the century since its publication, Weber's thesis has been defended, qualified, and outright rejected—with a large body of literature declaring him definitively defeated. But the boldness of Weber's thesis often masks the limits he explicitly set for his project and the rather qualified nature of his conclusions. He was not saying, for example, that Calvinism was the only cause of capitalism's rise, or that these developments were inevitable, that Protestants preached moneymaking, or encouraged greed. His argument was much more nuanced.[3] But that does not mean that he is entirely convincing. How widespread was this "ethic" among early capitalists, or among their workers? How peculiar to Calvinism were certain theological assumptions employed by Weber (such as the doctrine of predestination)? How influential were these religious attitudes given the larger cultural and social forces at work? While interesting in themselves, these questions quickly take us too far afield. Indeed, many of them have to do with what is, in effect, the second part of Weber's thesis, namely, the relationship of Protestantism to capitalism. What interests us is the first part: the relationship between vocation and work. Weber introduces us to an important and indisputable turning point in the history of theological reflection on vocation, a turning point that serves as our own starting point: the expansion of the concept of the calling to include all types of work and every way of life.

This chapter explores the different ways in which Protestants and Catholics have talked about the breadth of God's call, beginning with the Protestant trajectory. Martin Luther launched nothing less than a revolution in his affirmation that every state of life is a calling (*Beruf*) that comes from God. Luther thus stands at the start of modern reflection on vocation. By talking about the work of mothers and fathers, farmers and field hands, as callings from God, Luther wanted to affirm the religious significance of everyday life. However, as the "Protestant doctrine of vocation" evolved, this attempt to sanctify the ordinary led, in an unfortunate reversal, to a secularization of vocation. The concept of calling became associated with the occupations and professions, and in the process lost its reference to its transcendent source. The first part of the chapter surveys this history and concludes by asking what Catholics can learn from the way in which Protestant theologians have recently responded to Luther's legacy. In the second half of the chapter, we consider two paradigmatic attempts by the Catholic tradition to affirm a wider notion of vocation, namely, the devout humanism of St. Francis de Sales and the world-affirming spirituality of the Second Vatican Council. These are exceptions to the general tendency of post-Reformation Catholic theology to reassert the narrow conception of vocation that it inherited from the Middle Ages. During the modern period, Catholicism struggled to find space for a more ordinary sanctity—a vision of holiness for the layperson that comes not by way of exception but precisely by immersion in the life of the world. After centuries of uncertainty, such a broader vision received official endorsement at the Second Vatican Council. And it is this relatively recent widening that sets the context and identifies some of the challenges for a theology of vocation today.

The Affirmation of Ordinary Life

Martin Luther's expansion of call language came in the context of an extended polemic against the spiritual elitism of the monastery system. It was a direct challenge to the two-tiered hierarchy of holiness that marked medieval Christendom. But alongside Luther's critique came a creative and quite positive vision. In laying out this vision, Luther flipped the medieval hierarchy on its head. Life outside the monastery is not lower and lesser. Rather, it has a special dignity. For it is precisely here, in the ordinary tasks and toil of daily life, that God calls the Christian to love. One's station in life—whatever it may be, mother, magistrate, or maid—is a "calling" coming from God. Charles Taylor dubbed this epochal shift in religious sensibility "the affirmation of ordinary life," seeing in Luther and other early Reformers an unprecedented positive appraisal of human existence in the world.[4] By granting spiritual significance to the realm of production and reproduction, the mundane tasks of work and family, the Reformers upset the whole social order of medieval Christendom, and thus helped to usher in the modern world.

As we will see below, Luther believed that his vision of vocation was thoroughly rooted in scripture. The biblical evidence, however, is more mixed. From the very first chapters of Genesis, production and reproduction are ambiguous realities. God placed Adam in a beautiful garden "to till it and keep it" (Gen 2:15); God brought together man and woman in order to "become one flesh" (Gen 2:24). But with the Fall, work became a curse, and the pain of childbirth a punishment. Scripture positively affirms the sacredness of creation, but nowhere do we find the unambiguous association that Luther claimed between the word "call" and ordinary life and work in the world. In the Hebrew

Bible, when God "calls," the word itself evokes a more general appointment, one that both designates and qualifies the recipient to take on a specific task for God. That task brings a new identity. Thus when God calls Israel to be God's people, they become God's people. When God calls particular prophets, they become instruments of God's special purpose. In the New Testament, the various words for vocation—*kalein* (call), *klesis* (calling), *kletos* (called), and their compounds—carry one of two meanings.[5] First and foremost, these words refer to the general call to become a follower of Christ, which Paul interprets as the call to salvation.[6] Second, they refer to the particular call of certain people to some special service on behalf of God.[7] When we look out over the way in which the New Testament uses the word call, what we see is not a distinction between religious vocations and secular vocations. God's call to everyone is always a "religious" call; it always draws one up into the good news of salvation, even as the response to this call takes on a diversity of forms. Indeed, if the various call stories of the New Testament share anything in common, it is this: they all emphasize the initiative of Jesus and the immediate and unconditional response of the disciple.[8] Less is said about the relative value of different ways of living out that unconditional response. And so, as we consider both Luther's notion of vocation and the medieval conception against which he rebelled, we should keep in mind the primary meaning of "calling" in the New Testament, namely, the fundamental call of Christ to discipleship and salvation.

A Hierarchy of Holiness

This primary emphasis on the call to follow Jesus continued on in earliest Christianity. There the most important distinction was not internal to the community. Instead, the most important distinction was between those who were disciples and those who were not. This is not to say that the early Jesus movement was an egalitarian monolith or that all members played the same role. Still, the evolution of early Christianity reveals a gradual separation and subordination within the church community. A hierarchy of holiness develops, and this development significantly narrows the Christian understanding of vocation.

The hierarchy of holiness comes in stages. The first stage was marked by a growing divide, appearing already at the end of the first century, between clergy and laity. Early historical studies assumed that the word "lay"—in Greek *laikos*—derived from the word *laos*, which means "people." The thought was that early Christians adopted "laity" as another expression for the whole "people of God," and used it to designate a sacred people set apart from the pagans.[9] But subsequent scholarship challenged this etymological argument, showing instead that the word "lay" first emerged within Christianity not as a reference to the whole people of God but as a reference to one segment within the Christian community, namely, the ordinary people as distinct from the clergy. Thus the very appearance of the term suggests a separation between two groups. The clergy were those who served as leaders of the community. The laity were those who were *not* clergy, those "who were not consecrated for the service of God."[10]

The twofold division between cleric and layperson was soon complicated by the arrival of a third party, the monk. Disillusioned with the accommodation of church to empire, individual ascetics fled to the desert, where they were soon joined by others striving to live out a more radical way of discipleship—one marked by physical trials, sexual abstinence, and intense prayer. Their exploits became legendary, echoing back to the cities a new model of sanctity. This fuelled a further level of separation. If the laity were seen in contrast to the clergy on the level of leadership and activity, now they were seen in contrast to the monk on the level of holiness. The result was a significant strain on any positive evaluation of the Christian life in the world—which was increasingly presented as a compromise to the monastic ideal.

This monastic model of sanctity was shaped in no small way by the influence of Greek philosophy and its persistent dualism. The Platonic opposition between body and spirit brought with it a disparaging of the material world and the active life that it entailed. The Greeks contrasted *praxis*—which encompassed all of the activities of life oriented toward sustaining life, such as food production, the family, trade and the crafts, even politics—with *theoria*, which referred to the life of the mind that was the philosopher's special prerogative. "The Platonic reading of the spirit/flesh opposition also justifies a certain notion of hierarchy, and this along with pre-Christian notions of renunciation helps to credit a view of ascetic vocations as 'higher.'"[11] Thus, the active life was seen as subordinate to the contemplative life, the layperson subordinate to the monk.

For Christians, this Greek preference for contemplation came into some tension with the Gospel imperative to "love thy neighbor"—a call to charity that implied a certain activity on behalf of others. Saint Augustine struggled to negotiate this meeting of Greek philosophy and

Christian theology. Often accused of uncritically accepting Greek dualism and imposing it on Western Christianity, Augustine in fact sought to balance this philosophical bias toward contemplation with the more complex vision of discipleship presented in the New Testament. For example, in response to the controversy sparked by Jovinian—who was condemned for claiming that virgins and mothers enjoyed an equality rooted in baptism—Augustine charted a middle path.[12] Against Jovinian, he reaffirmed the value of celibacy, contemplation, and the life of withdrawal from worldly affairs. But against St. Jerome, who held a quite low view of married life, Augustine argued that marriage brings with it genuine goods such as children, fidelity, and a guard against concupiscence. When he explicitly addressed the relative merits of the *vita activa* and the *vita contemplativa*, his solution was to locate *both* lives within an eschatological context. Activity in this life, particularly the active love that comes through service to others, *leads toward* contemplation in the life that is to come. This eschatological—and ultimately christological—framework is seen best in his homilies on Martha and Mary, those biblical archetypes of the active and contemplative lives. Augustine wrote, "The kind [of life] Martha was leading, that's where we are; the kind Mary was leading, that's what we are hoping for; let us lead this one well, in order to have that one to the full."[13] For Augustine, neither life can be dismissed, and both are judged by their relationship to Christ, particularly insofar as this relationship is expressed through love for others. Yet, in the end, the active life is temporary, contemplation is eternal. Thus both lives are good, but the contemplative life is our ultimate goal.

As Christianity moved into the early Middle Ages, ecclesiastical authors came to speak of the church as constituted by three groups: clerics, monks, and laypeople. The first group is responsible for the church's ministry, the second is devoted to a life of prayer, and the third strive to follow Christ "in the world." Ezekiel's vision of Noah, Daniel, and Job offered a scriptural symbol for these various states of life (Ezek 14:14). First Origen, then Augustine, and then others took these three patriarchs as representatives of three kinds of Christians: church leaders, contemplatives, and those living amidst the affairs of the world.[14] With some slight variation—for example, Gregory the Great divided Christians into "the pastors," "the chaste," and "the married" (*pastores, continentes, conjugati*)—this triple division of the Christian faithful became a common theme in medieval literature. It continues on in canon law and church teaching up until the present.

Of these three orders, it was the monk who became the paradigm of sanctity. As seen in the popularity of the cult of St. Martin of Tours (d. 397), medieval Christians increasingly looked to the monk as the perfect model of the saint. Under the influence of the monastic ideal, holiness itself came to be defined "in a way that valorized the contemplative life of prayer and study over the active life of works of mercy, virginity over marriage, extraordinary ascetical practices over the faithful fulfillment of duties, and 'leaving the world' over temporal involvement."[15] The ideal of the ascetic flight from the world elevated the monk over not just the laity but the cleric as well. Around the year 1000, Abbo of Fleury drew on the parable of the talents to rank laity, clergy, and monks as, quite simply, good, better, and best.[16] Bernard of Clairvaux (d. 1153) returned to the Ezekiel allegory and placed the "tres ordines Ecclesiae" on a now-standard hierarchy of holiness: "In crossing the turbulent sea of life, Bernard says, the Daniel-like religious use a bridge high above the water; the prelates, following Noah, take a boat; and the Joban laity, the *plebs Domini*, wade and swim."[17] Each group faces dangers, but the laity—so often stuck in the muck of the material world—have the most perilous journey to make.

In the twelfth-century jurist Gratian, whose *Decretum* became the standard canon law textbook of the Middle Ages, the "men of the world" were separated off from the "men of religion"—collapsing the three orders into two. Lay folk "are allowed to marry, to till the earth, to pronounce judgement on men's disputes and plead in court, to lay their offerings on the altar, to pay their tithes: and so they can be saved, if they do good and avoid evil."[18] Life "in the world" was seen as a concession. Its activities stand apart from the sphere of sacred things. By the high Middle Ages a two-tiered hierarchy of holiness had become firmly established, built around states of life and their relation to the temporal world. The counsels of poverty, chastity, and obedience are for those striving for perfection. The commandments are for the rest who are just muddling along.

What we see over this centuries-long development is that the flip side of the monastic ideal was the denigration of lay life in the world. Medievals did not deny that the layperson could attain the heights of sanctity. In fact, some of the earliest monastic writings point to the possibility of individual laypeople matching and even surpassing the monks in personal holiness.[19] But this sanctity usually came by imitating the monks. Those few lay saints recognized in the Middle Ages—mostly kings and queens—led lives that had a distinctly monastic quality.

Hagiographies repeat the common theme of lay saints refraining from sex with their spouses.[20] The world of work, temporal affairs, marriage and family was at best neutral, and more often a hindrance, to sanctity. Most medievals simply assumed if holiness is to be attained by lay folks, it is achieved despite their life in the world, not because of it.

The solidification of this hierarchy of holiness according to states of life provided the context within which the biblical notion of call would be transformed. With the spread of infant baptism and the rise of Constantinian Christianity, the language of call became applied less and less to the call to discipleship, and more and more to the call to enter the monastery. As we will see in the next chapter, in the "Lives" of Anthony and Benedict or in the writings of Basil and Cassian, we find a new consciousness of a personal calling that comes from God to an individual, moving that individual to abandon everything and become a monk.[21] Just as the word *religio* became confined in medieval Latin to the religious order and *converti* to the monk's "turning away" from the world, *vocatio* became narrowly applied to the call of Christ to enter the monastery. The Protestant historian Karl Holl concludes: "The seizure of the title *vocatio* by monasticism prevented for a long time in the West the development of a proper religious evaluation of secular occupations and made it impossible for the word *vocatio* to become customary for them."[22]

This brief history presents the basic paradigm against which Martin Luther and the sixteenth-century Reformers reacted. But before treating Luther's vision, we pause simply to recognize that—even before the Reformation—there were other voices offering alternatives to the medieval denigration of life in the world. We already saw Augustine's attempt to subordinate both the active and contemplative lives to the criterion of love, even as he placed them on an eschatological trajectory that oriented the former to the latter. A more dramatic alternative voice comes in the thirteenth-century mystic Meister Eckhart. In his homilies on Luke 10, we find a radical reversal of the traditional commentary. Rather than elevate Mary over Martha, and thus the *vita contemplativa* over the *vita activa*, Eckhart lifted up Martha, and not Mary, as the model disciple. Eckhart described Martha as both "virgin and wife," the embodiment of both the contemplative and active lives. But in a remarkable move, he calls "wife" the more noble title. His reason: unlike "virgin," "wife" entails fruitfulness.[23] Being "virgin" (contemplation) is necessary to properly dispose the soul, but the soul remains barren if it does not then become "wife" (activity). When Christ called

Martha "careful," he was not condemning her preoccupation with temporal things but affirming her spiritual detachment in the midst of daily life, which was for Eckhart the ideal: "You stand in the midst of things, but they do not reside in you."[24] For Eckhart there is a union with God that comes through certain kinds of loving action in the world that is superior even to contemplative rapture. Thus it is Martha who is the mature Christian, "the one who has reached the end of the mystical itinerary, as far as this is possible in this life."[25]

Eckhart was not alone in searching for an alternative to the two-tiered hierarchy of holiness that privileged contemplation and withdrawal over active engagement in the life of the world. Matthew Ashley describes a millennium-long labor to overcome the philosophical limitations of Greek dualism in order "to more adequately express the complexity of the life of discipleship portrayed in the New Testament."[26] There is just something about Christ's call to love thy neighbor that keeps Christians coming back to the ordinary and the everyday as the concrete space where charity is exercised. Alongside a general attitude of disregard for the lay life, aspects of it were positively affirmed. The canonization of St. Homobonus in 1199 lifted up a lay contemporary (he died in 1197) who was a married man, a tailor renowned for his honesty and almsgiving. It wasn't just avoiding sex with one's spouse that brought lay saints to recognition; they were praised for their charitable works, prayer, patient endurance of various trials, and—particularly in the case of royal saints—faithful exercise of the duties of their station. The rise of the mendicant orders challenged the neat division between the active and the contemplative lives. And lay movements such as the Beguines and Beghards in the thirteenth century or the various movements of the *devotio moderna* in the fifteenth century sought a spirituality for the working classes in the rising urban centers of Europe. These examples provide just a glimpse into some of the forces pushing toward an alternative model of holiness. What Martin Luther brought to these various reforming movements, what is most significant for our purposes, was his explicit and unequivocal embrace of vocation as a primary way to articulate this alternative model.

Luther on Vocation

Martin Luther's almost incomparable impact on Western Christianity can be traced back to a single, central theological insight: we are saved not by any work of our own but by the grace of God. This insight into the nature of justification both calmed Luther's inner anxieties and quickened his call for church reform. By offering a direct relationship with God through faith, Luther tore at the very foundation of the spiritual economy and ecclesiastical system that shaped late medieval Europe. He argued that the institutional church had displaced faith with works, and thus had become an obstacle to God's gift of salvation. Its mediating structures had gotten in the way of the life of holiness that he so earnestly sought as an Augustinian monk. The only response was a thoroughgoing reform of the whole church "in head and members."

It is within the context of Luther's theological vision and his broader movement of reform that the Protestant doctrine of vocation was born. In light of his rejection of works righteousness and his attack on the monastery, Luther argued that through faith all stations of life—all "callings"—are of equal value before God. For Luther, life in the world is not a distraction from the life of holiness. It is precisely the place where we live out our God-given call.

Early into his career as a reformer, Luther became convinced that conditions demanded nothing less than a radical reconfiguration of the ecclesiastical system and the hierarchy of holiness on which it was built. In his 1520 treatise "To the Christian Nobility of the German Nation," Luther proclaimed, "The time for silence is past, and the time to speak has come."[27] Convinced that the clergy had grown indifferent, Luther spoke directly to the laity, spelling out the three "walls" erected by the papacy that he believed needed to come down. The first was the claim that the spiritual power is above the temporal, the second was that only the pope may interpret the scriptures, and the third was that only the pope may summon a council. Of the three, it was the first that was most important. In Luther's mind, what lay at the root of the other abuses was the faulty separation between the spiritual and the temporal estates.[28]

For Luther, "it is pure invention that pope, bishop, priests, and monks are called the spiritual estate while princes, lords, artisans, and farmers are called the temporal estate." The truth is that "all Christians are truly of the spiritual estate, and there is no difference among them except that of office. . . . This is because we all have one baptism, one gospel, one faith, and are all Christians alike; for baptism, gospel, and faith alone make us spiritual and a Christian people."[29] Luther appealed to 1 Peter 2 in order to make his case: Through baptism, every Christian is consecrated a priest—thus taking this cultic term and applying it in its broadest, biblical sense to the whole priesthood of believers. Before long, Luther would make the same move with the word "calling," extending it beyond the narrow confines of the monk or cleric and applying it to all walks and ways of life. But in this early exhortation, Luther leveled the ecclesiastical landscape on which his doctrine of vocation would be built: "It follows from this argument that there is no true, basic difference between laymen and priests, princes and bishops, between religious and secular, except for the sake of office and work, but not for the sake of status."[30]

When Luther turned his critique to the monastery system itself, his deeper theological commitments came to the fore. In his 1521 treatise against monastic vows, Luther condemned the vows for the way in which they challenged the primacy of faith.[31] According to Luther's understanding of justification, all that is required of us in our relationship with God is the response of faith. The fundamental problem with the monastic system was that it injected human works into this relationship, thus attributing saving significance to our own human efforts. By requiring vows—within the monastic ideal—the church had transformed counsels into commands, implying that these works were necessary for righteousness and salvation. For Luther, such a move negated the Christian freedom that is found in faith.

But Luther's condemnation of monastic vows was double-edged. The system of vows not only negated faith but it also threatened a proper understanding of good works. Vows are human works; and, for Luther, works do not belong to the realm of heaven, that upward movement involving our receptivity to God through faith. Works belong to the realm of earth, a downward movement of receptivity to our neighbor in need. The problem with monasticism was that it ignored this downward receptivity. For Luther, monasteries prevented people from loving their neighbors. Withdrawing to the cloister was a flight *away from* the love of neighbor that God commands—not as requisite to justification but as our response to it. Thus the self-defeating irony is that the monk binds himself before God, where faith should make him free. And he frees himself from his neighbor, where love should keep him bound.[32]

> Therefore I advise no one to enter any religious order or the priesthood, indeed, I advise everyone against it—unless he is forearmed with this knowledge and understands that the works of monks and priest, however holy and arduous they may be, do not

> differ one whit in the sight of God from the works of the rustic laborer in the field or the woman going about her household tasks, but that all works are measured before God by faith alone. . . . Indeed, the menial housework of a manservant or maidservant is often more acceptable to God than all the fastings and other works of a monk or priest, because the monk or priest lacks faith.[33]

In the end, it is as much Luther's theology of justification as it is abuses within the monasteries that fueled his attack on the medieval hierarchy of holiness.

The other side of Luther's condemnation of monastic vows is his commendation of life outside the monastery. In his sermons, in his writings on marriage, even in his biblical commentaries, we catch glimpses of the former monk's "affirmation of ordinary life." Luther argued that "all the duties of Christians—such as loving one's wife, rearing one's children, governing one's family, honoring one's parents, obeying the magistrate, etc. . . . are fruits of the Spirit."[34] He praised the mother who gives birth or who cares for the home. He encouraged the father washing diapers, whose friends may ridicule him as an "effeminate fool," to remember that, looking down on him, "God, with all his angels and creatures, is smiling."[35] What matters ultimately before God is not *what* one does. Such confusion takes a person down the path of works righteousness. Instead, what matters is *how* one does it. For Luther, it was important to get the emphasis right: one must act in *faith* before God and in *love* toward one's neighbor. Since *all* Christians are called to love their neighbor, there is in this vision a profound spiritual leveling—which Luther developed through the category of vocation.

In preparing his German Bible, Luther broke with traditional commentaries by translating the Greek word *klesis* (calling) in 1 Corinthians 7:20 with the German *Beruf* and interpreting it in terms of ordinary stations in life.[36] Throughout his letters, Paul used *klesis* (and its various cognates) when speaking about God's call to discipleship in general or about God's call to some task in particular, such as Paul's own call to be an apostle (Rom 1:1; 1 Cor 1:1). But Luther chose to interpret Paul's admonition, "Let each of you remain in the calling [*klesis*] in which you were called," in a different way. He saw this line in light of the verses that follow. These verses speak of the roles and responsibilities of slaves and masters, husbands and wives. Luther used the word *Stand*—"state" or "station in life"—to refer to these roles. Thus he identified these various states as "callings" coming from God.[37]

The implications are twofold. First, Luther's choice of words linked "calling" to his broad conception of the spiritual estate. In medieval German up until Luther's time, *Beruf* (whose root *Ruf*, like that of *klesis*, means "call") had applied only to the priestly or monastic vocations. But here Luther extended it to include the ordinary occupations and stations of life, thus giving to everyday work and responsibilities the religious aura previously reserved to clerics. Vocation is not the exclusive reserve of a select few. It is extended to every Christian. First, all have a spiritual vocation (*vocatio spiritualis*) insofar as every Christian is called to enter into the kingdom of God. This common call is the same for all. But Christians also have an external vocation (*vocatio externa*). This vocation is the call to serve God and one's fellow human beings in and through one's station in life. The application of the word *Beruf* to these ordinary stations in life parallels—both theologically and rhetorically— the way in which Luther extended the category of priesthood to all of the faithful. In 1 Corinthians 7, Luther believed that he had found the biblical basis for a broad conception of vocation.[38]

The second implication of Luther's exegesis has to do not with the scope of vocation but with its shape. In addition to broadening the notion of call, Luther emphasized the importance of *loving others within one's calling*. This emphasis on the love of neighbor is brought out in Gustaf Wingren's classic study of Luther's theology of vocation. Just as Luther criticized the monastic life for separating monks from those in need, so he celebrated the ordinary stations in life as the concrete place where Christians encounter their neighbor. If the love of God is expressed principally through faith, then the love of neighbor is expressed in one's vocation. Living out a calling constitutes the downward receptivity to the needs of others that flows from our justification—it is the love that follows on faith. Wingren summarizes: "God does not need our good works, but our neighbor does."[39] For Luther, it belongs to God's providence that I have *the neighbor that I have*. "As soon as I think of my neighbor, all vocations no longer stand on a common plane, but a certain vocation comes to the fore as mine."[40] To those who wonder whether or not they had a vocation, Luther responded, "Reflect on your condition, and you will find enough good works to do if you would lead a godly life. Every calling has its own duties, so that we need not inquire for others outside of our station."[41] There is no need to go looking for a vocation; it is right there in front of us. Everyone has a calling, for every legitimate *Stand* touches the life of another.

But more than just the arena for Christian activity, one's station is an instrument through which God helps us to do good.[42] As we will see, later Protestant debates distinguished between vocation as a call *to* a particular state or realm of work and vocation as a call *within* one's state or work. For Luther the distinction did not occur. He rejected certain occupations as contrary to faith, but in general it is the faith-filled and faithful exercise of one's station—whatever it be—that marks obedience to God's commands. Luther supported this claim by theologically grounding the doctrine of vocation within the doctrine of creation. He saw the various stations in life that constitute human society as part of God's providential care for the world. Thus it is through these stations that God's loving purposes in creation are fulfilled. Through the milkmaid, God milks the cow, and so sees to it that the cheese is made and the child is fed. Through the judge, God sees to it that justice is upheld and evil punished, and so on. When Luther underscored Paul's injunction to "remain in the calling in which you were called," he was motivated not only by his polemic against the monastic impulse to run off, leaving one's station in order to enter the monastery.[43] He was also motivated by his theology of creation and divine providence.

Later commentators have challenged Luther's doctrine of vocation on precisely this point, seeing in his link between social roles and divine providence a dangerous confirmation of the status quo, a position ill-equipped to deal with social change and impotent in the face of injustice. Indeed, the conservatism of Luther's position—hardened by the peasant revolts of 1525 and the Anabaptist challenge—reflected the medieval social hierarchy in which he lived. *Stand* is itself a feudal concept. And contrary to our modern ideals of freedom and social mobility, Luther's view of society was more static, hierarchical, and patriarchal. While celebrating the dad changing a diaper, he had very definite ideas about the respective roles of men and women.[44] He was, in this way, thoroughly medieval. And yet, there are elements within Luther's doctrine of vocation that suggest a more dynamic and diverse vision. In locating the love of one's neighbor at the center of vocation, Luther highlighted the essentially "local" character of God's call.[45] Because no two people share the exact same constellation of neighbors, no two vocations are exactly the same. This insight lies behind Luther's polemic against the practice of imitating the saints. For Luther, the only saint one could imitate would be the saint who had precisely the same neighbor in exactly the same circumstances, which, of course, is impossible. Imitation is itself a pale imitation of vocation; it can quite easily become a self-centered diversion from the demands of our callings. While changing from one *Stand* to another remains the exception, within one's station, the needs of one's neighbors are constantly shifting. Our life and love must adjust. Thus there are the seeds of a spiritual dynamism beneath Luther's social conservatism.

Finally, in his attention to the neighbor, Luther showed a remarkable sensitivity to the contextualized nature of human experience. But this attention to the particularity of social context is missing from his treatment of the individual herself. The uniqueness that Luther saw marking the outer life of the individual was not matched by similar attention to the uniqueness of the inner life. Within his theology of vocation, less emphasis is placed on individual personality or psychology, to interiority, to the inward movement of the Spirit in recognizing and responding to God's call. Wingren argues that this was precisely Luther's point: "Uncertainty as to whether one is called is often due to regarding oneself as an isolated individual, whose 'call' must come in some inward manner. But in reality we are always bound up in relations with other people; and these relations with our neighbors actually effect our vocation, since these external ties are made by God's hands."[46] In the end, it was Luther's distinction between the realm of heaven and the realm of earth that supported his thoroughly externalized theology of vocation. It is in *faith* that one stands directly and immediately before God, receptive to God's grace (*vocatio spiritualis*). It is in *works*—including the works of vocation—that one stands before one's neighbor, responding to God's command (*vocatio externa*). Here we catch a glimpse of the basic tension that Luther established between heaven and earth—a tension that became the axis on which Protestant reflection on vocation would turn. In Luther, the two poles came together in a creative and powerful synthesis. But whether this synthesis can hold would become *the* question for later Protestant appropriations of Luther's theology of vocation.

Every Work a Calling

Through his doctrine of vocation, Luther gave to Western Christianity the notion that ordinary, everyday work is imbued with religious significance. But it is through those Protestant traditions indebted to John Calvin that vocation took on the purely secular connotation still widespread today.

Luther saw vocation as the call to serve one's neighbor within the context of one's work and life station. Calvin tended to identify it more with the work itself. For the most part, Calvin followed the New Testament by using call language to speak of both God's call to salvation and God's call to ministry. But the growing Protestant sense of ordinary states of life and occupations as "callings" also entered in. God has "appointed duties for every man in his particular way of life. And that no one may thoughtlessly transgress his limits, he has named these various kinds of living 'callings.'"[47] Calvin shared Luther's positive assessment of the ordinary affairs of life. No work, no task is "so sordid and base" that "it will not shine and be reckoned very precious in God's sight."[48] And he shared Luther's disdain for monasticism. But his reasons differ. Commenting on the story of Martha and Mary, Calvin rejected the medieval elevation of the sister who sat and listened:

> As this passage has been basely distorted into the commendation of what is called a Contemplative life, we must inquire into its true meaning, from which it will appear, that nothing was farther from the design of Christ, than to encourage his disciples to indulge in indolence, or in useless speculations. It is, no doubt, an old error, that those who withdraw from business, and devote themselves entirely to a contemplative [life], lead an Angelical life. . . . On the contrary, we know that men were created for the express purpose of being employed in labour of various kinds, and that no sacrifice is more pleasing to God than when every man applies diligently to his own calling, and endeavours to live in such a manner as to contribute to the general advantage.[49]

We can detect in Calvin a subtle shift. For Luther, the problem with the contemplative life was that it removed the monk from his neighbor, compromising his ability to love and serve this neighbor as God has commanded. For Calvin, the problem with contemplation was that it removed the monk from *useful activity*, drawing him instead into "useless speculation." Christ's rebuke of Martha came not because she was working. The rebuke came because she was working at the wrong time. Luther spoke both of charity at work *within* one's calling and of providence at work *through* one's calling. For Calvin, the emphasis shifts to the latter. In Calvin's theology of vocation, less is said about serving one's neighbor directly. Instead, he emphasized how service is offered indirectly. By faithfully fulfilling the duties of one's calling, the individual Christian contributes to the common good of all, and in this way helps his neighbor. Calvin did not dismiss direct charity to those in need. But his concept of call more closely identified obedience to God's call with obedience to one's calling, thus opening the door to the later identification of vocation with one's occupation.

For Calvin, we are born to work. There is an emphasis on activity here that was missing from Luther's account of vocation. Human beings find their model in the creative, providential activity of God—whose omnipotence is "not the empty, idle, and almost unconscious sort that the Sophists imagine, but a watchful, effective, active sort, engaged in ceaseless activity."[50] Like Luther, Calvin presupposed the stable medieval social order of his time. He saw the arrangement and ordering of various callings as part of God's providential plan to calm the "restlessness" and "fickleness" of human nature. To keep us from turning everything "topsy-turvy," God "has appointed duties for every man in his particular way of life."[51] The social status quo is affirmed. And yet Calvin stood at the cusp of a new world. The rural feudalism of the Middle Ages was giving way to the guilds of the cities, to new technologies, and to enormous political reconfiguration. Calvin's own program for Geneva was an effort not just to reform individuals but to reform the whole social order of the city. Thus a certain flexibility, a seminal mobility entered into his theology of vocation. Certain occupations were always off-limits (Calvin saw clearly that being a pimp was not a true vocation). But there was in Calvin the catalyst for a greater voluntarism, the seeds for what Ernst Troeltsch called "a freer conception of the system of callings" in later Calvinism.[52] This can be seen in Calvin's emphasis on the abilities—the talents—that God gives to individuals for the common good. One's vocation is not only discerned in one's station but it is also derived from one's gifts.[53] Thus there is a sense of applying these gifts in the calling most suitable to them. More important, however, was Calvin's clear emphasis on activity and utility in vocation. Comparing Luther to Calvin, Paul Marshall concludes, "While both stressed quiet, unassuming labour and abiding in one's calling, for Calvin, in the heart of a bustling city, the whole tenor of callings was much more aggressive and busy. His readers and hearers were to work, to perform, to develop, to progress, to change, to choose, to be active, and to overcome until the day of their death or the return of their Lord."[54]

It is this emphasis on ceaseless, restless activity that Weber noticed in later Calvinism and that Marshall charts so carefully in his study of sixteenth- and seventeenth-century England. While the terms "vocation" and "calling" appear only occasionally in the earliest English Reformers, still we hear echoes of Luther in William Tyndale's claim that "if thou compare deed to deed, there is difference betwixt washing of dishes, and preaching of the word of God; but as touching to please God, none at all."[55] The Puritan conception of calling came within the context of a spiritual vision that tried to avoid two errors. The first error was to renounce the things of the world—that was the monk's mistake. The second error was to become absorbed in these things.[56] The key was to enjoy things while remaining detached from them. This is the essence of what Max Weber called the "innerworldly asceticism" of the Puritans. Within such a worldview, intentionality loomed large, as captured in the words of the English bishop Joseph Hall: "The homeliest service that we doe in an honest calling, though it be but to plow, or digge, if done in obedience, and conscience of God's Commandement, is crowned with an ample reward; whereas the best workes for their kinde (preaching, praying, offering Evangelicall sacrifices) if without respect of God's injunction and glory, are loaded with curses. God loveth adverbs; and cares not how good, but how well."[57] God loveth adverbs. It is not a particular kind of activity or state of life that marks off the ideal; rather, holiness and godliness consist in the *spirit* one brings to whatever work one does—as lowly as that work might appear.

Within this spiritual framework, Bishop Thomas Becon borrowed Luther's distinction between the spiritual vocation and the external vocation, translating it into language that became standard in later Puritan thought, namely, between the "general" call to salvation and "particular" callings. For Becon, the particular call was "any manner of benefit, office or ministration."[58] Later the particular call came to name all states and occupations, with the call to ministry folded into this category as one vocation among others. In general, the concept of vocation—with its subversive tendency to level out all kinds of work in the world—served the reforming agenda of the more radical Protestants in sixteenth-century England. But it carried its own ambiguity. In tension with the social leveling of call was Paul's injunction to "remain in your calling," which tended to support the established social order. "The result was an uneasy fusion of the medieval hierarchical doctrine of estates with a newer equalitarian doctrine of calling."[59]

This mixed view is exemplified in the work of the sixteenth-century Cambridge theologian William Perkins, who wrote the first classic Puritan treatise on vocation. In it, Perkins drew together various strands of reflection on call, without always resolving the tensions between them. It seems that the practical usefulness of the category was Perkins's chief interest. Perkins defined vocation or calling as "a certain kind of life, ordained and imposed on man by God for the common good."[60] Within this definition lies Perkins's dual conviction that vocation has its source in God and its goal in the good of society, "the benefit and good estate of mankind." For Perkins, "the common good of men stands in this, not only that they live, but that they live well, in righteousness and holiness, and consequently in true happiness. And for the attainment hereunto, God has ordained and disposed all callings, and in his providence designed the persons to bear them."[61] Present in this definition is the more stable conception of life stations that we saw in Luther. God not only ordains the calling itself, "he imposes it on the man called."[62] A vocation seems preordained and fixed—both for society and for the particular individual. But this medieval conception is juxtaposed with the claim that every person must *choose* a calling. In making this choice, Perkins invited every man to "examine himself" according to his affections and his gifts, according to what he likes and what he is good at. "Every calling must be fitted to the man, and every man be fitted to his calling."[63] In his attention to gifts and abilities, Perkins followed Calvin. But in the mobility implied, he went beyond him. On Paul's admonition to "remain in one's calling," Perkins wrote, "it is not the Apostle's meaning to bar men to divert from this or that calling, but he gives them an item to keep them from changing upon every light conceit and every sudden occasion."[64] People can change callings if doing so better serves the common good or, tellingly, if they cannot support themselves in their current occupation.

Taking up Becon's distinction, Perkins exhorted each Christian to join together "the practice of his personal calling with the practice of the general calling of Christianity." Here Perkins's mixed view of vocation is pronounced. At times he described the general calling and the particular calling as existing side by side. At other times, he pictured the particular calling being exercised *within* the general calling to be a Christian.[65] At times, he talked about Christian duties and moral behavior being practiced alongside or within one's occupation. At other times, he spoke of serving God *through* the service that our work provides to others.[66] Perkins did not seem bothered by these tensions. His main point was that Christianity cannot be separated from the ordinary daily life of family and work: "It is not enough for a woman to be virtuous openly to strangers; but her virtue must privately show itself in her subjection and obedience to her own husband. A Schoolmaster must not only be a Christian in the assembly, when he hears the Word and receives the Sacraments, but he must also show himself to be a Christian in the office of teaching."[67] However, by relegating the Christian call to an adjective qualifying one's work, on the one hand, and by imagining Christian duties alongside other daily tasks, on the other, Perkins unwittingly paved the way for later developments in which the adjective was simply removed and the "extra" duties of the Christian were simply dropped, leaving behind a purely secular concept of vocation.

Over the course of the seventeenth century, first Puritans, and then other Anglicans, came to speak of vocation as a trade or occupation separate from any religious element. Marshall notes the "busyness" of the Puritan notion of call. Bound up in their concept of calling was a deep disdain for idleness. Earlier, Perkins had followed Calvin's polemic against monasticism: "every man must have a particular and personal calling, that he may be a good and profitable member of some society and body."[68] But monks do not employ themselves well. They live a damnable life because *they don't do anything.* This emphasis on productivity led to a widespread and rather harsh distinction between the "deserving poor," who through age or deformity could not work, and the "idle poor," who could work but did not. The first deserved Christian charity, the second condemnation. The preoccupation with work and its virtues was intense. And within this context, the whole notion of vocation changed. Whereas the early Reformers spoke of "callings" in terms of relatively stable stations in life, by the seventeenth century the emphasis had clearly shifted to one's *activity.* Luther's *Stand* gave way to employment as the locus of one's call. "The thrust was less on accepting a place in society and more on choosing and pursuing a useful trade."[69] By the middle of the seventeenth century, the words "trade," "employment," "occupation," "calling," and "vocation" became interchangeable.[70]

Together with this emphasis on work came a secularization of the concept of vocation itself. Thomas Watson signaled an important shift when he cast the calling not as a command but as an *allowance* from God: "As if God had said 'I am not an hard master, I do not grudge the time to look after thy calling, and to get an estate—I might have reserved six days for myself and allowed thee but one, but I have given thee six days for the work of the calling, and have taken but one day for my own service."[71] In these lines, one's "calling" during the work-week is set apart from—and even in some competition with—the duty to God due on Sunday. A calling is something that God allows or grants to an individual, not what God expects of him. Thus the distinction between the general calling to be a Christian and the particular calling to one's work became a separation. For Perkins, the two were either closely related or the particular was found *within* the general. But by the end of the seventeenth century they sit alongside one another in Protestant England. One even distracts from the other. In a coming full circle that Luther would have abhorred, William Gurnall argued that "the power of holiness" is manifest when "the Christian's particular calling doth not encroach upon his general."[72] Gone is the dynamic synthesis of faith and works that we saw in Luther. Instead, the religious element was something one must add onto one's work life. Pious duties were set off from one's daily labor. For early Protestantism, the notion of calling had fostered a dedication to hard work that was, quite literally, a religious dedication. But as Sunday split off from the rest of the week, the intense commitment to one's calling remained—only without the religious motivation. Work became a religion all its own.

Luther's Legacy

The great irony of the Protestant doctrine of vocation is that Luther's attempt to highlight the sacredness of work led to a secularization of the concept of the calling.[73] Vocation in Luther took its strength from its source, the command of God. But as duty to God *within* one's station became duty to God *through* one's station, it was only a short step toward seeing vocation as simply the duty *to* one's station—the faithful (but not necessarily faith-filled) exercise of a trade or occupation. What at first rested in the command of God later became based in various configurations of social life and the particular responsibilities inherent in a line of work. The sacred and secular split apart and vocation landed on the side of the secular. Thus God became superfluous to a theory of vocation. The calling no longer needed the caller.

This history conditions the way in which Protestant theologians have come to approach the question of vocation: Can the religious dimension of work be reclaimed? Is "calling" a fruitful category for speaking of the spiritual significance of life in the world? Or does it need to be set aside?

In the twentieth century, a number of voices raised concerns about too closely identifying God's call with human work. Critics argued that work—particularly as it has taken shape in the modern global economy—risks alienation, the instrumentalization of persons, and a dehumanizing abdication to a corrupt status quo. Today, they want to say, the world of work cannot be so easily baptized by the Protestant view of vocation. This was not the first time that the ambiguity of the professions has been called into question. John Calvin confronted the libertines of his own day, who claimed that the concept of vocation freed an individual to pursue any kind of work, "to follow the inclination of his own nature and to work and live according to what advances his profit or pleases his heart." Is every work a calling? Calvin answered no. And he laid out his polemic against those "wretches" who would argue otherwise: "And not only under this guise do they approve of all these vocations, which are repugnant to the truth of Scripture, but also of those which pagans condemn by their natural reason. Let a pimp, they say, do his job! Let a thief rob boldly! For it is right for everyone to pursue his calling. If anyone replies to the contrary how villainous these matters are, and that nature itself teaches us to regard them with horror, they respond that it is enough for everyone 'to remain in his calling.'"[74]

Calvin's argument was straightforward: God's call could never violate God's commandments. Thus if an occupation or activity did not conform to the Bible or natural law, then it could not be a calling. What more contemporary theologians notice is the rather obvious differences between the world of work in Calvin's day and in our own. Today's global economy is not sixteenth-century Geneva. Rather than a few immoral occupations within a divinely ordained social order, contemporary critics point out that we work within a complex global economic system that serves to oppress and dehumanize millions of people in the interest of a few. To put it directly, the libertines have got nothing on neoliberalism. How do we speak of callings within such a world?

The social theorist Jacques Ellul argues that nothing in the Bible allows us to identify work with calling. Work is "an imperative of survival, and the Bible remains realistic enough not to superimpose upon this necessity a superfluous spiritual decoration."[75] He sees Luther injecting into the necessity of work the possibility of service to others, and recognizes the subsequent history as a steady search for some redemptive value within our daily labor. Yet it is precisely this religious validation of work that is so easily abused, as vocation becomes a tool of the bourgeoisie "to maintain the workers in submission and obedience to a divine order."[76] With industrialization and the commodification of labor—what Ellul calls the "capitalism-machinism-technicization" trio—the situation becomes even more ambiguous. Thus Ellul looks for some meaningful calling alongside, or in addition to, the insignificance of one's career. The Protestant moral theologian Stanley Hauerwas underscores even more forcefully the fallenness of work—indeed, the idolatry of trying to make it into something more than it is. For Hauerwas, work offers some benefit—a way to make a living, an opportunity to serve others, a hedge against boredom—but we should not pretend it plays some grand role in the plan of salvation. "Attributing greater significance to work risks making it demonic as work then becomes an idolatrous activity through which we try to secure and guarantee our significance, to make 'our mark' on history."[77]

We see a quite different approach in the theologian Miroslav Volf. Volf sets out not to condemn the world of work but to construct a positive theology of it. In order to achieve such a positive theology, Volf argues, Protestants should abandon the long history of talking about work in terms of vocation, and instead turn to a more pneumatological and eschatological vision—what he calls "work in the Spirit."[78] His proposal includes a strong critique of the Protestant doctrine of vocation. He argues that the notion of secular work as a calling is unbiblical; it remains indifferent toward alienation in work and innocent of the ways in which calling can be abused ideologically to support unjust economic structures or inhumane working conditions; it is too static and hierarchical to speak to our mobile society.[79] But Volf's most insightful observation is his recognition of the ambiguity that lies at the heart of Luther's notion of vocation. "In [Luther's] view, spiritual calling comes through the proclamation of the gospel, while external calling comes through one's station (*Stand*). It has proven difficult for Lutheran theology to reconcile the two callings in the life of an individual Christian when a conflict arises between them."[80] Thus juxtaposed, the worldly calling too often won out over the call of the Gospel. Volf quotes Jürgen Moltmann appreciatively: "The history of Lutheranism as well as Lutheran ethics shows that Luther's bold identification of vocation [i.e., *vocation externa*] with the call [i.e., *vocatio spiritualis*] led again and again to the integration of the call into vocation and vocation into occupation, and thus to the consecration of the *vocational-occupational structure*. 'Vocation began to gain the upper hand over the call; the Word of God on the right (gospel) was absorbed by the word of God on the left (law).'"[81]

What Volf puts his finger on is the fundamentally dialectical cast of Luther's theology of vocation, and the way in which subsequent Protestantism has framed reflection on vocation in terms of a tension between the divine call and human occupations. Too often, he argues, the former loses out to the latter. Sharing this critique was the great Swiss theologian Karl Barth—whose rich treatment of vocation will warrant a chapter of its own below. Barth rejected the subordination of God's call to human vocation, and replied with a forceful reassertion of the transcendence of the Gospel to all human affairs, occupations, and states of life. Yet, as I will argue, there remains an unresolved tension even in Barth—an inability, in light of this stress on the Gospel call, to account for the role that our particular and unique created existence plays in discerning a response to this call. What Volf notices in Luther is what ultimately frustrates Barth, namely, *the location of the doctrine of vocation within the doctrine of creation*. It is precisely this "protological" (having to do with the "first things" or creation) framework that leads Volf to conclude that vocation has to be abandoned as the primary lens for a theology of work. What is needed instead is an eschatological and Spirit-based approach.[82] Thus Volf replaces "calling" with "charism"—choosing not to develop a theology of vocation, and instead offering one of the more creative and thought-provoking theologies of work available.

Is there an alternative to the tension that arises between God's call and human callings? The dialectical cast to this question seems endemic to the Protestant doctrine of vocation, reaching all the way back to Luther's fundamental distinction between heaven and earth, faith and works, Gospel and law. While this distinction opened up a broader notion of vocation, it offers little help when a concrete conflict arises between the call of the Gospel and the demands of a calling. Or, even in the absence of conflict, the distinction still sets up a question that confounds a theology of vocation: how much does who I am and where I am influence what God calls me to be and to do? Recent Protestant theology has acknowledged this dilemma and has struggled to respond to it. Barth underscored the primacy of the divine summons over all human activity. Volf turned to the categories of charism and eschaton. But is there another way to respond to this tension? Can we find a way to talk about vocation that does not set up these pairs in dialectical opposition—*either* God's call *or* human callings, *either* creation *or* justification—but rather discovers points of analogical continuity and challenge? In other words, can we articulate a theology of vocation that affirms *both* human life *and* God's plan, *both* nature *and* grace?

In many ways, the Catholic history of reflection on vocation is the mirror image of the Protestant trajectory. Against Luther's inclusive notion of callings, Catholics restricted the category to priesthood and religious life. Against the Reformation's leveling of sanctity, Catholics reasserted the medieval hierarchy of holiness. Against the Protestant emphasis on external occupations or societal roles, Catholics grew increasingly preoccupied with the internal call of God in the depths of the soul. At the root of these two approaches is a fundamental difference in the "location" of the theology of vocation: Protestants placed vocation within the doctrine of creation; Catholics treated it within a theology of supernatural grace. In this different starting point, we find a different, and less dialectical, approach. To be sure, Catholic thinking on vocation stirs up its own set of problems, as chapter 2 will make clear. But as we turn now to consider Catholic attempts to affirm a more universal call, we keep in mind both the promise and the perils of a broader notion of vocation. What we want to see is how these concerns play out when the primary lens is not the tension between law and the Gospel but the relationship between nature and grace. For, as the rest of the book argues, the success of a contemporary Catholic approach to vocation depends in large part on getting this relationship right.

The Universal Call to Holiness

As the preceding pages show, the broadening of vocation that marks the Protestant trajectory impacted not only the scope of sanctity but also the nature of it. Luther did not just extend holiness to all of the baptized; he also affirmed that this holiness is found precisely in the ordinary and everyday exercise of the duties of one's station. Life in the world is not an obstacle to the full following of Christ; rather, it represents the primary context and medium through which believers respond to Christ's command to love thy neighbor. Thus the broadening of vocation cannot be understood apart from the "affirmation of ordinary life" that would have such a profound impact on the modern history of the West.

Catholics came more slowly to this affirmation of the ordinary. The official response to the Reformation largely reasserted the hierarchy of holiness that had taken shape over the course of the Middle Ages, underscoring the narrow conception of vocation that came with it. The Council of Trent condemned anyone who denied that celibacy or consecrated virginity was superior to marriage.[83] And Catholic apologists, such as Robert Bellarmine, focused their energies on defending what the Reformers had attacked. This meant a vigorous restatement of the monastic ideal in the realm of spirituality and a strong defense of papacy, priesthood, and the clerical system in the realm of ecclesiology. So forceful and frequent were these official voices that we might be tempted to tell the story of the Counter-Reformation as a hierarchical hardening pure and simple—four hundred years of Catholic clergy disparaging lay life in the world along a trajectory that only came to an end with the Second Vatican Council.

Obviously, the story is more complex. We have already seen—in a figure like Meister Eckhart or a movement like the *devotio moderna*—glimpses of medieval alternatives to the two-tiered hierarchy of holiness. Various reforming impulses, bubbling up well before the sixteenth-century Reformation, sought out a more positive appreciation for lay life in the world. Medieval Christendom was not, after all, content to cede sanctity to the elites. And it was this larger trajectory of reform that set the stage for the Reformation and the Catholic response to it.[84] Early modern Catholicism saw the rise of new religious orders, like the Jesuits, experiments in religious education for the laity, the promotion of various sodalities and guilds, the expansion of charitable works. These dynamics all point to an affirmation of the lay condition that is missing from the official, hierarchical theology of the Counter-Reformation period.

Still, Catholicism enjoyed nothing like the explicit history of reflection on the breadth of vocation that shaped the Protestant conversation in the modern period. The term "vocation" was largely restricted to the priesthood or religious life. When theologians engaged the topic, their focus was on the internal dynamics of discernment, rather than external roles in society. Yet that did not mean that the modern Catholic tradition was indifferent to the breadth of the demand that comes with the call of the Gospel. In the remainder of this chapter, we explore two examples of Catholic "broadening": the writings of the seventeenth-century saint Francis de Sales, and the theology of the laity promoted by the Second Vatican Council. In their quite different approaches, these two examples help to transition from the Protestant conversation surrounding call to the particular challenges facing a contemporary Catholic theology of vocation.

Francis de Sales and the Devout Life

No writer of the Catholic Reformation came closer to affirming the religious significance of ordinary life than the nominal bishop of Geneva and later Doctor of the Church, St. Francis de Sales. In his two major works, the *Introduction to the Devout Life* (1608) and the *Treatise on the Love of God* (1616), as well as in his many letters of spiritual direction, Francis offered gentle guidance for the devoted soul striving to live out her or his faith in the world. With an extensive knowledge of the tradition and the confident conviction that he was doing something new, Francis began his *Introduction*: "Almost all those who have hitherto written about devotion have been concerned with instructing persons wholly withdrawn from the world or have at least taught a kind of devotion that leads to such complete retirement. My purpose is to instruct those who live in town, within families, or at court, and by their state of life are obliged to live an ordinary life as to outward appearances."[85] For Francis, "it is an error, or rather a heresy, to wish to banish the devout life from the regiment of soldiers, the mechanic's shop, the court of princes, or the home of married people."[86] His *Introduction* offered an alternative: straightforward advice and simple steps that *anyone* could take to advance along the path of devotion. During this era, others were writing similar spiritual manuals for the literate layperson, but none matched the influence of the *Introduction*.[87] Within ten years of its publication, more than forty editions of the *Introduction to the Devout Life* had appeared in France alone, with translations quickly produced in all the major languages of Europe. The *Treatise on the Love of God*—a much longer, technical, and more theoretical text—was itself translated into English as early as 1630, by then already in its eighteenth French printing.[88]

The orienting idea of Francis's spirituality is the concept of devotion. And he fleshed out this concept in his *Introduction*, an inviting text full of colorful metaphors drawn from nature and concrete examples drawn from seventeenth-century aristocratic life. For Francis, devotion is not occasional acts of piety but a deep love of God that bursts forth into loving action. Love is multivalent. Insofar as love adorns the soul, it is called grace. Insofar as it strengthens us to do good, it is called charity. "When it has reached a degree of perfection at which it not only makes us do good but also do this carefully, frequently, and promptly, it is called devotion."[89] Francis explained with one of his many analogies: Sinners are like ostriches who never fly. Good people are like hens who fly, but slowly and awkwardly. Devout souls are like eagles who ascend to God "with lofty flights." Devotion is nothing other than charity marked by "great ardor and readiness in performing charitable actions." It is love burst into flame.[90]

Francis's approach to the spiritual life was inviting, even disarming—as he encouraged his readers that "the way to heaven is not as difficult as the world makes it out to be."[91] One seventeenth-century synopsis of the *Introduction* was titled *Devotion Made Easy*, which could very well serve as the motto of Francis's work.[92] All of his writings exude warmth and a spirit of gentle familiarity, written like letters from one friend to another, from one heart to another. Michael Buckley observes, "When Francis wrote, he wrote not only about something but to someone, and even his greatest works are but correspondence writ large."[93] The *Introduction* was largely compiled from letters Francis wrote to Madame Marie de Charmoisy, a noblewoman anxious about following the spiritual life amidst the distractions of court. The *Treatise on the Love of God* grew out of Francis's long and important friendship with Jeanne de Chantal, a widowed mother who, together with Francis, would go on to found the Visitation Sisters. Eschewing the harsh asceticism of the monastic ideal, Francis met people where they were, enjoining moderation, balance, and the purification of motives. Spiritual growth comes gradually, through small steps by which one advances from desire to purification to resolution to progressive growth in the life of devotion. And the method Francis proposed was meant for everyone, adaptable to every vocation and each individual. "Devotion must be exercised in different ways by the gentleman, the worker, the servant, the prince, the widow, the young girl, and the married woman. Not only is this true, but the practices of devotion must also be adapted to the strength, activities, and duties of each particular person."[94]

What grounded Francis's inclusive vision was his unmistakable confidence in human nature as redeemed.[95] Many Catholic theologians in Francis's day held a view of divine grace that—despite all the qualifications to the contrary—was not all that different from the doctrine of predestination typically associated with Calvin.[96] The theology of predestination *ante praevisa merita* (predestination prior to one's merit) that was so common at the time seemed to suggest a God who arbitrarily saved some and just as arbitrarily damned others. Early in his life, Francis came face-to-face with the horror of this theology. As a young student at the Jesuit College of Clermont, Francis spent six weeks tormented by the thought that he had been condemned to hell by God and that there was nothing he could do about it. Only by a revelation of love—coming through a small prayer to Mary posted in the church of St. Etienne-du-Grès—did the young Francis break out of his despair.[97] It was an experience he never forgot. And out of it came his clear emphasis on the universal salvific will of God. Parting ways with "the Augustinians, the Banezian Thomists, the majority of Scotists, and the two major Jesuit theologians of the period, Robert Bellarmine and Francis Suarez," Francis insisted that grace is offered to everyone and that whatever damnation did occur happened only *post praevisa merita.*[98] For Francis, God's love for humanity cannot be hemmed in. It spills over, empowering a response in every way and walk of life.

The fundamental theological anthropology that lies beneath the *Introduction* is brought to the surface in the *Treatise.* Here Francis argued, "If there could be found any men who were in the integrity of original justice in which Adam was created, though otherwise not helped by another assistance from God than that which he affords to each creature, in order that it may be able to do the actions befitting its nature, such men would not only have an inclination to love God above all things but even naturally would be able to put into execution so just an inclination."[99] For Francis, we are created from the beginning with a natural drive—a dynamic orientation—toward the love of God. This desire for God is itself a grace, a gift of God's own love. Despite our fall through sin, the human desire to love God remains. It's just that we no longer have within us the power to realize it. "This radical though impotent desire that marks the human is caught up by the universal desire of God and his reach into creation through providence. The whole of the spirituality of Francis falls within these two movements: the surge that is the human being and the outpouring that is the divine providence—the desire and the love of God to transform human beings into his friends, the universal salvific will."[100]

In chapter 2, we will see how the separation of nature and grace in early modern theology came to frustrate a Catholic affirmation of ordinary life in general and a theology of vocation in particular. But in Francis, we have an early creative synthesis. "Grace transforms nature from within, resulting in a single reality that is both human and divine."[101] Theologians may distinguish nature and grace to the point of separating them from one another, but in his own personal and pastoral experience, Francis saw the two united. Even in the most depraved soul, Francis contended, the inclination to love God is there, ready to be awakened. In fact, the conversion that Francis experienced in the Lady Chapel of St. Etienne-du-Grès came at the moment he realized that, even though he felt he might be damned, he still could not stop loving God.

Both in his invitation to a life of devotion "in the world" and in his dynamic sense of graced nature, Francis de Sales offered an alternative to the monastic spirituality of the Middle Ages. Do we have here a

Catholic counterpart to Luther's theology of vocation? Critics have accused Francis of a certain social elitism. The "Gentleman Saint" undeniably moved among the aristocratic upper class of seventeenth-century France. His *Introduction* encouraged a devout life lived quite comfortably amidst the preoccupations of court, with its banquets and balls, hunting expeditions and games of chance. Did Francis too quickly baptize bourgeois values, extolling the appearance of indifference, sociability, polite conversation, and concern for one's reputation? Where *are* we when we hear the bishop say that devout people should always be "the best dressed in a group," even if "the least pompous and affected"?[102] Is devotion made *too* easy for Francis's rich friends already enjoying the finer things of life? The *Introduction* is innocent of those structural issues of injustice so important to our ethical consciousness today. But any critique must not forget Francis's own criticisms of the hypocrisy at court and, more important, the way in which traditional courtly ideals are transformed by his notion of true devotion. While his harmless analogies drawn from nature and his preoccupation with appropriate pastimes may seem trite, they can mask the way in which Francis tried to replace the rigors of physical asceticism with the much more difficult demands of charity. Still, the writings of Francis never fully escape their aristocratic origins. While Francis explicitly stated that the devout life is open to all ranks and stations of life, the elegance of the *Introduction* is a far cry from Luther's earthy call to the Christian day laborer, the peasant mother, and the milkmaid.

If the social location of the *Introduction* sets it at a certain distance from the ordinary daily life of the masses, its spirituality is certainly not out of reach—as evidenced by the enormous popularity of the book from the moment of its publication down to the present. A greater difficulty arises in Francis's treatment of life in the world. Despite his claim that the *Introduction* offers a new way of devotion for those living in town, within families, and at court, Francis signaled at the very beginning a rather traditional ambivalence about life in this world:

> I shall show to such men that just as the mother of pearl fish lives in the sea without taking in a single drop of salt water, just as near the Chelodonian islands springs of fresh water may be found in the depths of the sea, and just as the firefly passes through flames without burning its wings, so also a strong, resolute soul can live in the world without being infected by any of its moods, find sweet springs of piety amid its salty waves, and fly through the flames

of earthly lusts without burning the wings of its holy desires for a devout life.[103]

Devotion is possible in the world, but it is difficult. And the means of strengthening the devout soul often involve withdrawal from its activities. The *Introduction* encourages the reader to set apart an hour a day for personal prayer, preferably in a church—precisely in order to avoid the distractions of town, family, or court.[104] The emphasis on growth in devotion leads from the *Introduction* to the *Treatise on the Love of God*, which Francis wrote for "souls that are advanced in devotion."[105] In this later work, devotion reaches a kind of culmination in mystical contemplation, understood as the highest realization of human love for God. It is not entirely cynical to point to the career of Jeanne de Chantal who, under Francis's direction, "progressed" from a widow struggling to practice piety in the world to a religious foundress, withdrawn from the world within a fully cloistered religious order.[106]

Classic monastic spirituality began by calling individuals out of the world. This external change in the life of the monk was meant to prompt an internal change. Francis insisted that he wanted to reverse this order. It is the internal, interior change in the soul that leads to external changes in one's way of life.[107] True devotion is simply inner love pushed outward in ready and regular charity. His vision of the dynamism of love at the heart of the human is profound. But in the end his understanding of the world beyond the human person seems untouched by this vision, leading his harsher critics to accuse the "external change" brought about in the life of the devout soul as consisting mainly in better manners. Louis Dupré offers a more precise assessment of Francis's limits: "While Francis succeeded in restyling the modern synthesis of nature and grace in accordance with the new type of personhood, he utterly fails to do the same for either cosmos or society. The Salesian synthesis remains a strictly interior one, between God and the soul."[108] Despite all the references to partridge eggs and almond seeds, the *Introduction to the Devout Life* ultimately fails to integrate the natural world; it fails to offer an adequate theological account of how holiness is found not merely *in* one's everyday life but *through* it.

In Francis de Sales, we begin to see the important role played by the nature-grace relationship in articulating a broader conception of vocation. Luther may have been the first to fully realize the magnitude of the problem caused by the late medieval separation of nature from grace. However, as we saw above, the dialectical character of Luther's own thinking kept him from fully overcoming this split. Instead, he offered a kind of dynamic tension between the two.[109] Francis's vision of love as an inner orientation of the human person toward God offered a more unified picture of human nature as graced. Thus his contribution is significant. But it is only in the twentieth century that this fundamental insight into the unity of nature and grace reappears, as Catholic theologians take it and push it out beyond the boundaries of the human soul in order to speak about the graced character of all of creation. This move provides an affirmation of the world itself that stretches the Catholic theology of vocation.

Vatican II and the Laity

In contrast to Francis de Sales's interior synthesis, the Second Vatican Council developed a broader conception of holiness—and thus of vocation—in the context of an explicitly world-affirming spirituality. Ironically, this spirituality emerged not so much out of a positive appreciation for the beauty of creation or an unbridled confidence in human achievement. Rather, it was a spirituality of worldly realities that grew precisely out of deep concerns about where the world was headed.

In the era leading up to Vatican II, the secularization of European society seemed to pose a mortal threat to the historic influence of the church. This secularization can be traced back not only to the intellectual Enlightenment and political revolutions of the eighteenth century but beyond that to the Reformation, Renaissance, and general disintegration of the late medieval world. It posed such a challenge to the church not just because of the anticlerical tone secularism took in post-1789 France but, more deeply, because this process of secularization introduced into the West, for the first time on a wide scale, alternative narratives of meaning. With the rise of humanism, empirical sciences, and newly independent Christian communities, no longer could the church's claim to possess *the* truth be taken for granted. Other stories claimed legitimacy as the ultimate explanation of the meaning of life. In the nineteenth and early twentieth centuries the church slowly came to recognize this new world: It looked out, as it were, on vast segments of Europe that had become "other." Henri Godin and Yvan Daniel's explosive little book of 1943, *France, pays de mission?*, framed the question dramatically: has France become missionary territory?[110] Earlier conflicts between popes and princes had led to medieval treatises on the relationship of spiritual authority to temporal authority, but these debates were ultimately about the locus of power *within* Christendom. Now, temporal authority was no longer "within" the church; rather the secular world stood outside of and autonomous to it.

Feeding these broader philosophical and cultural transformations were dramatic changes in social and economic life. The Industrial Revolution and the rapid urbanization of the eighteenth and nineteenth centuries brought a triple alienation of the Catholic faithful from traditional society, work, and church. The cities separated individuals from past patterns of family and village life. The factories cut off workers from the fruits of their labor. And the church seemed increasingly bourgeois and distant to these workers living in these cities and laboring in these factories.[111] Two world wars would crystallize, in a particularly horrific way, this social upheaval, pressing upon the church the unavoidable question of the world, and the role of the Christian within it. Yves Congar, a Dominican priest and theologian who spent much of World War II in a German internment camp, reflected on the war and its impact on theology:

> Then came the war with its train of fateful events, captivity, the exodus on the roads, the fraternity of distress, the comradeship of the Resistance, all contriving to lead us into the rich but demanding experience of a laity aware of its obligation to active existence in the Church, and to the sense of the immense extent of ignorance of the Gospel as well. The real world of men was much more remote and foreign to the faith than we had thought even after so many searchings. But on the other hand priests and faithful alike had undergone experiences and uncovered tracks which the years of peace had not hitherto revealed.[112]

One might expect, given this sad history, that a spirituality of withdrawal would develop, that the church would respond to all of these threats with anxiety and defensiveness. And surely there is a fair share of this reaction, seen most dramatically in the antimodernist campaign of Pope Pius IX (1846–78). But what is remarkable is that the experiences of secularization, disenchantment, and global war sparked not just resignation and withdrawal but also a spirituality of engagement—an attempt to speak the Gospel anew in this newly independent world. For Catholics during the middle decades of the twentieth century, this spirituality and theology of engagement came to center around the question of what was then called "the layman."

"The upshot," Congar continued, "was that in the euphoric post-war years of liberty regained, 1946–1947, the question of the status of the laity in the Church forced itself upon us in a new way." Following the Second World War there was an explosion of interest within the Catholic Church in all things lay. Major conferences were held at the Vatican in 1951 and 1957, preceded and followed by a seemingly unending avalanche of publications on the topic. Much of this was prompted by the desire to promote at the pastoral level the various lay initiatives grouped under the title "Catholic Action," which were already sponsoring a variety of activities in the 1920s and 1930s. But theologians involved with these groups—from the Young Christian Workers to the various Marion sodalities—also sought out a deeper theological foundation. They were not content to describe these activities simply as the extension of the hierarchy's work out into the world—a way of asserting the church in a place where the clergy could no longer reach. This was the vision of Pius XI, who defined Catholic Action as "the participation of the laity in the apostolate of the Church's hierarchy."[113] Instead, theologians asked how the world itself impacted the life and activity of the laity. In other words, they asked: Is the world simply the arena (or even an obstacle) to the apostolate of the laity? Or, rather, does the world in some way contribute to the distinctive character of the lay apostolate? Is there something positive that needs to be affirmed in the ordinary, daily life of the lay faithful?

The theology of the laity that would emerge in the twentieth century and that would shape Vatican II's treatment of the layperson rested on a renewed appreciation for the value and goodness of the temporal world. New developments in theology fed into this affirmation of the world in a number of ways. Biblical studies uncovered elements of a "realized eschatology" in scripture, pushing Catholic reflection on the "last things" beyond an individualistic concern for heaven, hell, purgatory, and judgment toward a greater emphasis on the unfolding of the reign of God in history. Critical study of early church councils led theologians like Karl Rahner to explore the multiple implications of the incarnation as God's entry into human life. Gustave Thils developed a theology of "earthly realities" in the mid-1940s, anticipating "creation theology" by decades. But perhaps most significant of all was a basic rethinking—fueled by Henri de Lubac's historical studies and Rahner's transcendental philosophy—of the nature-grace dualism that had plagued so much of neoscholastic theology. Fed by these various currents, the theologies of the laity that took shape on the eve of Vatican II shared a fundamental recognition that the layperson's place "in the world" offered the positive content for articulating the layperson's Christian identity and mission. Largely abandoned was the basically negative assessment of the world that shaped centuries of Christian spirituality, theology, and church policy on the laity. Instead, earthly realities were now seen to have a value and goodness that is their own.

Vatican II stands apart from all previous general councils in the amount of attention it gave to the life and activity of laypeople in the church. After centuries of neglect, the laity were brought to the center of the church's consciousness and placed at the heart of its most official pronouncements. Given this historic shift within an institution so shy of change, what is remarkable is how uncontroversial the whole question of the laity was at the council itself. The initial draft of Vatican II's document on the church, which in all other respects was roundly criticized, already contained within it a quite positive chapter on the laity. Though the whole document was rejected and sent back to committee, the original core of the chapter on the laity survived. Throughout the various revisions of this chapter, reactions came mostly in the form of speeches that praised the laity's contributions to the church and the world. Bishops wanted more said about the laity, not less. The final version of the chapter on the laity passed almost unanimously, with only eight negatives out of 2,236 votes cast.[114]

Perhaps this relatively smooth progression came from the fact that Vatican II did not set out to articulate an original theology of the lay state; rather, its goal was to promote the activities of laypeople.[115] And yet, despite that focus, the council could not avoid addressing the theological foundations of this activity. Thus a theology of the laity emerged deliberately and clearly, even if in the end it remained somewhat general. What seems to have unified the council's approach was a widely shared desire to craft a theology of the laity in *positive* terms. This was an approach stressed by Yves Congar in the years leading up to the council.[116] Congar—who became a theological advisor at Vatican II, and thus helped to shape its statements on the laity—argued that over the course of the church's history the laity were defined in a basically negative way. They were either contrasted with the monk in terms of holiness or contrasted with the clergy in terms of authority. This contrast gave rise to what Congar called the "absurdly over-simplified formula, 'Spiritual things appertain to the priest, temporal things to the layman.'"[117] For Congar, the laity are not excluded from the realm of the sacred. They too are ordered to heavenly things. Their religious and spiritual orientation does not come by way of exception. It comes by virtue of their own distinctive state of life and orbit of activity. Laypeople are called to the same end as clergy and monks—union with God, a life of holiness, and participation in the mission of Christ. However, their way of achieving this end differs, which led Congar to his own affirmation: laypeople "do God's work *in so far as it must be done in and through the work of the world.*"[118]

This approach reveals an important but subtle shift from what we saw in the devout humanism of Francis de Sales. In contrast to Francis's interior synthesis, Congar's view of the laity rested on a more robust "world oriented" theology. In fact, so strong was Congar's emphasis here that critics accused him of ignoring the spiritual in his affirmation of the temporal. In reply, Congar argued that nature and grace do not exist in a state of juxtaposition but in an order of relationship to one another. Drawing on Aquinas's notion that grace brings nature to its full destiny, Congar argued that the perfection of things "to which they are called by nature, involves not only the being or the doing that they can attain by the exercise of the energies whose active principle they have, but also the being or the doing that comes to them from their conjunction with a higher principle."[119] It is precisely in his attention to the presence of grace (the "higher principle") in things (the realm of secondary causes, all of creation and the inner workings of the world) that Congar articulated his broader vision. It is the whole world, and not just the human heart, that is directed to God. Francis de Sales began with the inner life, a change of heart that is meant to lead to a change of life. Congar began with the world of secondary causes, created by God and imbued with saving significance. He asked, "Do our interior spiritual dispositions alone signify for that Kingdom? Is the world only the occasion or the background (how often tragic!) of our charitable deeds and spiritual purification?"[120] In his assessment of contemporary movements, Congar answered no. Forms of dualism that he identified in Martin Luther and Karl Barth, as well as the Catholic Louis Bouyer, gave the impression that this earthly ship on which we sail is destined to sink, and that the only hope lies in the lifeboat that is the church. In his own preference for a more incarnational and paschal vision, Congar suggested a different image, an image rooted in God's one plan of creation/salvation: "final salvation will be achieved by a wonderful refloating of our earthly vessel rather than by a transfer of the survivors to another ship wholly built by God."[121]

It is just such a positive appreciation for the secular context of the laity that shaped the initial draft of what would become Vatican II's Constitution on the Church, *Lumen Gentium*. This preliminary text described the laity as "those who must strive after christian sanctity for the glory of God in their own special way, including secular activity. Actively engaged in the concerns of this world, but led by the spirit of the gospel, they courageously fight the evil of this world and even sanctify the world so to speak from within through their christian calling."[122] But concerns were raised that this stress on the secular meant that the document did not say enough to affirm the laity's full membership within the church. Thus the second draft, taken up at the council's second session, shifted its emphasis to the ecclesial dimension of the layperson's identity: "The Holy Synod understands by the name of laity the faithful who, incorporated in the People of God, serve God in the state common to all Christ's faithful, and for their part fulfill the mission of the whole christian people in the world, which includes religious activity, but they do not belong to the hierarchical order nor to a religious state approved by the Church."[123] The second text deliberately tried to correct the first draft's overemphasis on the secular orientation of the laity by highlighting their place within the people of God, the church. And while the revised text goes on to mention the role of the laity in the world, a note added to the text by the drafting commission suggested that this relationship to the secular world is descriptive and thus falls outside the *theological* definition of the layperson.[124]

When this second draft was taken up by the full council, it was for the most part received enthusiastically.[125] But some of the bishops felt that too much had been lost. In locating the laity more confidently within the church, the new text had downplayed their role in the world. More needed to be said about the legitimate autonomy of the temporal realm, and a fuller description of lay life in the world was needed. The drafting commission then faced the challenge of balancing these two approaches: one that began with ecclesial identity, another that began with the secular orientation of the laity. The end result was chapter four of the Dogmatic Constitution on the Church (*Lumen Gentium*), which was debated and approved at the council's third session. The theology of the laity proposed in the final text affirms, first, that the laity belong to the Body of Christ and people of God by virtue of their baptism. Distinct from clergy and religious, the laity share in their own way in the priestly, prophetic, and kingly functions of Christ. But this ecclesial emphasis is balanced by a second affirmation: "A secular quality is proper and special to laypersons." The laity, "by their proper vocation [*ex vocatione propria*], seek the kingdom of God by engaging in temporal affairs and by ordering them according to the plan of God."[126] Thus we see in this final draft an attempt to balance the approaches of the first two: the laity "carry out their own part in the mission of the whole Christian people with respect to *the Church and the world*."[127]

This basic tension between what the laity share with the rest of the church (ecclesial identity rooted in baptism) and what distinguishes the laity from other groups within the church (secular character) helps to illuminate the basic Catholic consensus on vocation to emerge out of Vatican II. Postconciliar magisterial documents speak of two intimately related realities: (1) the one universal call to holiness, and (2) the different ways in which this universal call takes shape in various states of life—various vocations—within the church.

The first claim is articulated most fully in chapter 5 of *Lumen Gentium*, which is dedicated to "The Universal Call to Holiness." The council's desire to speak of the gift of holiness and the pursuit of perfection as extending to all Christians in every state of life was not totally disconnected from its concern to develop a positive theology of lay secular involvement. Even before the council, Pope John XXIII made this link: "No one should make the mistake of supposing that his own spiritual perfection is inconsistent with the tasks of this present life. The two are perfectly consistent. Let no one imagine that he must necessarily withdraw from the activities of temporal life in order to strive for Christian perfection, or that it is impossible to engage in such activities without jeopardizing one's human and Christian dignity."[128] However, *Lumen Gentium*'s chapter 5, on the universal call, emerged not out of debates about the laity but from discussions surrounding religious life. And the text itself grounds the universal vocation not on any convictions about the secular world but with a distinctly ecclesiological claim: "The church, whose mystery is set forth by this sacred synod, is held, as a matter of faith, to be unfailingly holy."[129] Because Christ loved the church, because he gave himself up for it, because he endowed it with the gift of the Holy Spirit, the church is holy. And because the church is holy, all those who belong to it, "whether they belong to the hierarchy or are cared for by it," are called to holiness. It is only within this ecclesiologically conditioned conception of holiness that the call to perfection of various groups and individuals— including married couples and parents, widows and widowers, single people, those who are poor or who suffer—is spelled out.

The second aspect of the postconciliar consensus on vocation, after the affirmation of the universal call to holiness, is the tendency to consider vocational diversity according to different states of life. Despite a more flexible use of call language evident in chapter 4 of *Lumen Gentium* and in many recent church documents, three vocations stand out in postconciliar Catholic teaching as the paradigmatic way of living out the universal call to holiness: ordained ministry, consecrated life, and the lay life. Already in *Lumen Gentium*, we see this tendency, where the laity are described as a "state" (*status*) in the church.[130] The drafting commission explained that it chose the language of *status*, rather than "condition and mission," so that "the laity would be acknowledged to have the honor of constituting a *state* in the Church, at least in a broad sense."[131] It seems that there was a deliberate intention to raise the laity—as a state of life—to a dignity comparable to the ordained and religious lives. This move coincided with a subtle shift in the text of *Lumen Gentium*. The initial draft of paragraph 31 spoke of the layperson living out his or her "Christian vocation" (*vocatione sua christiana*) through active engagement in the secular world. The final draft speaks not of the laity exercising their *Christian vocation* in the world but of the proper *vocation of the layperson* in this world (*Laicorum est, ex vocatione propria . . .*). The change is slight. But what the final text suggests is a further call beyond the call to be a Christian, namely, the call to be a layperson.[132] In the theology and spirituality preceding the council, it was the vowed religious and the ordained priest who had a vocation beyond the call of baptism. *Lumen Gentium* suggests that the laity too have a vocation beyond the call of baptism, a particular call to seek the reign of God through their work in the world. Not simply left behind in the world, the laity receive a positive call *to* it.

This threefold division of the universal call to holiness is hardened in subsequent magisterial documents. While not exclusive, these three vocations—understood as distinct states of life—are nonetheless paradigmatic, evidenced, for example, in Pope John Paul II's three major postsynodal apostolic exhortations on the laity, the formation of priests, and religious life.[133] The late pope's writings, like those of Vatican II, recognize that there is a rich diversity of vocations within the church, and multiple ways of naming them. But, in the end, these three are primary: "The vocations to the lay life, to the ordained ministry and to the consecrated life can be considered paradigmatic, inasmuch as all particular vocations, considered separately or as a whole, are in one way or another derived from them or lead back to them, in accordance with the richness of God's gift."[134] Thus what we have seen in official Catholic theology since the council is a reinforcement of the traditional triad of cleric, monk, and layperson—*pastores*, *continentes*, and *conjugati*, Noah, Daniel, and Job.

What is new to this traditional triad is a theology of the laity that affirms the positive value of life and activity in the world. John Paul II's apostolic exhortation on the laity, *Christifideles Laici*, is full of concrete encouragement and deep appreciation for the many ways laymen and laywomen live out their Christian faith in the context of family, neighborhood, and work. We can celebrate the affirmation of the ordinary that comes with the positive conception of the lay vocation. But we should also note the tensions that remain.

The first tension comes out of the decision to speak of the secular vocation as particular to the laity. Is there a call "to the world" that comes to the layperson over and above the universal call to holiness that comes in baptism? Are not *all* of the baptized called "to the world"— precisely by being incorporated into the mission of Christ to transform creation in the light of the Gospel? Commentators point out that, over the course of the council, there was a gradual development in its treatment of "the world." In the early drafts of *Lumen Gentium* and in the Decree on the Apostolate of Lay People, responsibility for the world falls squarely on the shoulders of the laity. But by the time *Gaudium et Spes* was approved at the last session of the council, the responsibility for transforming society and the world is presented not as the laity's peculiar mission but as the mission of the whole church. "It is as if the Fathers had realized that the task of ordering temporal things toward God, of taking them up to transform them in Christ, and of the recapitulation that involves the whole of the created order is now seen to be *distinctive of the whole Church and not only of lay people*."[135]

Second, despite the council's clear affirmation that *all* Christians "in whatever state or walk in life" are called to holiness, "the fullness of christian life and the perfection of charity," there continues a certain ambiguity about the relative excellence of these different states of life. Vatican II consciously avoided speaking of vowed life as a "state of perfection," as if other Christians were not also called to perfection. And its chapter on religious life comes only after treatment of the universal call to holiness. While the documents commend the evangelical counsels and praise them as a compelling sign of the heavenly kingdom to come, the passages on religious life avoid the disparaging comparisons to marriage and lay life that marked previous church teaching. Still, the Decree on the Training of Priests speaks of the "greater excellence" (*praecellentia*) of consecrated virginity, and *Lumen Gentium* repeats the traditional argument that the evangelical counsels free the individual from "those obstacles which might draw him away from the fervor of charity and the perfection of divine worship."[136] The special witness and symbolic value of religious life reemerged in subsequent teaching, to the point that John Paul II's exhortation on consecrated life, *Vita Consecrata*, states, "As a way of showing forth the Church's holiness, *it is to be recognized that the consecrated life*, which mirrors Christ's own way of life, *has an objective superiority*."[137] Avoiding the problematic tendency within the tradition to conflate the value of the evangelical counsels with the moral status of individuals, the pope very deliberately offered an ontological claim: the "objective superiority" of consecrated life is not a comment about the subjective state of grace of any individual vowed religious; rather, it is a claim about the consecrated life as a particular state of life within the church—a state of life that, as a witness to the holiness of the church, is credited with an "objective superiority." Here we see the continuing hold of a hierarchy of holiness.

Even with all of the necessary qualifications, the recognition of important theological distinctions, and the many positive affirmations of lay life, recent church teaching never really escapes a deductive and ontological approach to vocation. Such an approach has its limits. To continue to frame diversity according to different "states of life" not only grates against our more dynamic and developmental sense of human life and historical existence but it also risks making the descriptive prescriptive—laying out, in a deductive way, models or molds of life into which individuals are forced to fit. "Typical forms and characteristic behavior, which arose historically in response to particular conditions, now are removed from history, ontologized, and made normative for any conceivable set of circumstances, even ones quite different from those in which the typical forms and behavior first arose."[138]

Since the Second Vatican Council, Catholics have settled into a kind of sleepy consensus on vocation. Papal statements and bishops' letters continue a basically deductive approach, repeating Vatican II's distinction between the universal call to holiness and the various vocations within which that call is lived out. Most Catholics still associate the word "vocation" primarily with priesthood or religious life—as do the homilies they hear, the bulletin announcements they read, and the prayers of the faithful they offer at Sunday liturgy. But, if asked, most would readily agree that marriage, for example, is a vocation, or that anyone can feel "called" to a particular way of life, work, or ministry in the church. Theologians might critique the clericalism implied in the church's language, or celebrate the universal call to holiness as a call to equality among all of the baptized. But few have tapped the full potential of this key category for Christian discipleship today. The result of the broadening of vocation language within the Catholic tradition seems to be a kind of vague appreciation for a concept that offers little help in living out the faith. It offers little guidance for discerning Christians. Now that God's call is extended to all, how do I discover my vocation? Lost in this ontological and deductive approach is the concrete Christian—the unique child of God who is not just a member of a class or category of callings but who responds to God in a way never before seen and never to be seen again. Taking Vatican II's broad and inclusive vision as the essential and welcome starting point, the remainder of this book seeks out a more inductive approach to vocation. We will grapple with the difficult question of discernment in order to better appreciate the deep biblical truth that God calls us—all of us and *each* of us—by name.

Conclusion

Martin Luther started something genuinely new when he extended the biblical category of calling to include the ordinary and everyday activities of the faithful Christian. Rooted in his convictions about faith and sharpened by his polemic against the monastery system, Luther's theology of vocation not only radically broadened the notion but also focused it concretely on the law of love. Christ commands us to love our neighbor. But, as the scribe asked Jesus, "Who is my neighbor?" For Luther, the answer is simple: Our neighbor is the one we encounter and serve in and through our daily lives and work in the world. One's station in life—whatever it may be—can be considered a calling because it is precisely here that God invites us to respond to our neighbor in love. One of the things that Luther found so offensive about the monastery was the excuse it offered to avoid the difficult demands of love. For Luther, monks are not following their calling; they are fleeing from it. They are ignoring God's call to love and serve others in the world, in the place and station in life ordained for them by divine providence. Mothers do not have to go looking for God's call; they are already responding to it when they care for their children. Farmers need not seek some higher vocation; they already live it out when they serve others through their work. In Luther's view of vocation, we find a deep affirmation of ordinary life, a positive appreciation for the earthy, embodied nature of human existence as the concrete place where we respond to God's call.

The Catholic tradition came to its own affirmation of the ordinary in its twentieth-century reflections on the laity. However, it followed a very different trajectory than the one launched by Luther. Rather than raise up the secular callings of the laity by putting down the monk or the cleric, Vatican II sought to lift up all of these vocations as various and complementary ways of responding to the one universal call to holiness.[139] The result was a particular recasting of the traditional triad of cleric, monk, and layperson. Postconciliar magisterial documents continue to divide vocation into three broad states of life, each with distinct realms of responsibility: clergy are called to church service, religious are called to witness through their embrace of the evangelical counsels, laity are called to life in the world. While we can surely raise concerns about the neat division of labor implied by this framework, or ask whether there still exists—however tempered or qualified—a hierarchy of holiness implicit in this configuration, nonetheless, it represents a distinctively Catholic attempt to affirm the breadth of God's call.

Beyond these legitimate concerns, the real problem with the postconciliar Catholic consensus is the way in which its deductive approach frustrates a theological consideration of discernment. Protestants face their own difficulties here. With its roots in the medieval *Stand*, and developed within a theology of creation and divine providence, the Protestant doctrine of vocation has emphasized a calling as the place *from which* we respond to God and serve others. As theologians have recently pointed out, this emphasis on "place"—one's place in the world, in society, in a particular role, in a certain occupation or line of work—has helped to dilute the notion of calling itself. Is such a concept of vocation capable of confronting our fallen human condition, able to challenge unjust social structures, or robust enough to call individuals beyond conformity to the status quo? The dilemma of discernment then becomes a question of conflict. How does one negotiate the dialectical tension between God's call and human callings?

Catholic thinking on vocation has a different history. It was born out of the monastic call to leave the world, and it grew within a theology of grace. Thus the Catholic tradition has spoken of vocation not so much as the place *from which* we respond but as the place *to which*

God calls. Thus the problem for discernment is not the same as the Protestant dialectic; instead, the problem is its deductive approach. In other words, too often in the Catholic tradition, the theology of vocation has been reduced to the sorting out of the proper roles and responsibilities of different states of life. Such an approach reduces the *whither* of vocation to the level of the objective, the general, and the detached. What is needed instead is a thoroughly subjective, personal, and engaged theology of vocation that worries less about states of life and looks more to the concrete person—orienting the whole person, who exists in history and among others, toward the future that is God's call. Over the course of the period we have been considering, the place where this more inductive approach was kept alive was in the realm of spirituality, in the context of reflection on the inner life. And so we turn from the breadth of the callings to the depth of the call.

CHAPTER TWO

The Depth of the Call

Whisper in my heart, "I am here to save you."

—*Psalm 35:3*[1]

At the start of the twentieth century, a relatively unknown seminary professor by the name of Joseph Lahitton created a minor sensation in France with the publication of his book *La Vocation Sacerdotale*.[2] In it Lahitton blasted the Catholic seminary system of his day for gathering a mediocre crop of candidates and graduating too few priests truly competent to meet the demands of ministry. This particular charge was not what sparked the controversy—indeed, complaining about the clergy is a venerable Catholic tradition. What caused the uproar was Lahitton's thesis that the crisis of vocations in France was at root a crisis in the very notion of vocation itself. Lahitton argued that the widespread assumption that a priestly calling consisted in the inner movement of God in the soul—a secret voice prompting an individual toward the ministry—had reduced the church to a position of passivity in its vocational efforts. Instead of calling forth the most gifted men for service, those responsible for clergy formation were required to wait. They were to wait for a young man to approach them and announce that he had heard God's call in his heart. Everything seemed to rest on an interior spiritual inclination, an "attraction" (*l'attrait*), that Lahitton worried was overly mystical and ultimately unverifiable.

Lahitton argued that this "theory of attraction" diverged from the teaching of the Council of Trent and the ancient tradition of the church. The only call that mattered for a candidate coming into the priesthood was the call of the bishop that occurred in ordination. It was not the inner experience of the individual but the external mechanics of the institution that determined a vocation. Lahitton's argument prompted a flurry of responses, with the most critical coming from the Sulpicians, who staffed many of the French seminaries and who were most identified with the attraction theory. This intramural debate rose to such a pitch that two years after the book appeared, Pope Pius X convened a special commission of cardinals to examine the issue. Their 1912 verdict vindicated Lahitton and endorsed his central thesis—thus seeming to marginalize the inner experience of vocation. The result left Catholic theologians wondering, well into the twentieth century, just what role the heart does play in hearing the call of God.

"L'affaire Lahitton" introduces us to the interiorization of God's call that marks the second major story line in the development of the modern Catholic theology of vocation. In chapter 1, we noted that Catholics responded to the Protestant expansion of call language largely by reaffirming a narrow identification between vocation and certain states of life. But alongside this narrowing of vocation came a burying, as God's call was increasingly described in terms of a supernatural grace located deep within the soul. Because of the neoscholastic split between nature and grace, vocation came to be seen as an extrinsic force, a kind of secret voice whispering within. Lahitton was right to critique this tradition. However, his historical argument was limited to a survey of scholastic and neoscholastic theological texts. What he overlooked was the explosion of spiritual literature and disciplines of discernment that followed on the Reformation. In these spiritual traditions, we see an interiorization that cannot easily be dismissed. In these movements, we find a creative engagement with modernity and its "turn to the subject" that takes seriously the depth of the personal experience of God.

The following chapter takes up two representative, and deeply influential, trajectories that emerged in the sixteenth and seventeenth centuries: the spiritual vision of Ignatius of Loyola and the French school of spirituality. It then examines the way in which the insights of these traditions became skewed when viewed through the lens of modern Catholic assumptions about grace. In his attention to the subtle movements of God in the soul, Ignatius stands at the start of this story line. However, just as the wisdom of Luther was diluted in later Protestant treatments of call, so too the insight of Ignatius was distorted in subsequent Catholic treatises. As in chapter 1, here we will observe both gains and losses in this history. The goal is to bring into focus the limitations of the modern Catholic theology of vocation in order to prepare the way for a renewed theology that better attends to the mystery of God's call within.

Spiritual Masters

The era stretching from the Council of Trent to the eighteenth-century Enlightenment stands out as one of the most creative, adaptive, and expansive periods in the history of Roman Catholicism. Once dismissing it as a reactionary and negative "Counter-Reformation," scholars today speak of a Catholic Reformation, Early Modern Catholicism, or the Catholic Baroque in order to convey something of the positive initiative of this era.[3] Amidst the disintegration of European Christendom, the Roman Church burst open with new energy, new ministries, and a new missionary impulse. During a time of war, inquisition, and colonization, Catholicism also saw spiritual and religious renewal. "The Baroque spirit brought to the church new theologies and spiritualities, new ministries and arts: these manifested new interplays between personality and grace pioneered by Ignatius Loyola, Philip Neri, Teresa of Avila, and their numerous followers. There was a universality in which Catholicism experienced God in a vastness, freedom, and goodness flowing through a world of diversity, movement, and order. Christ appeared in a more human way, filled with a personal love, redemptive and empowering. This was a time of methods and exercises, of imagination and conversation with the divine."[4] Among all the movements set in motion during this dynamic era, the following pages identify two as particularly germane to our topic, Ignatian spirituality and the French school. In Ignatius we see a distinctive interior turn, one in which the classic discernment of spirits was transposed in a modern key. In the French school we see how this turn came to inform a particular understanding of the call to priesthood—which was the primary context within which Catholic theologians worked out their views on vocation in the period stretching from the seventeenth century to the middle of the twentieth.

Early Openings of an Inner Call

In chapter 1, we saw how the emergence of clerics and monks in early Christianity gave shape to distinct states of life and a clear hierarchy of holiness within the church. At the risk of overstating an important distinction, we could say that, with the cleric and the monk, two dialects developed for talking about vocation. On the one hand, the call of the cleric came through the bishop or the community.[5] This call spoke of office and activity, jurisdiction and power. It was more concerned with service than personal sanctity. Its emphasis was on the external. On the other hand, the vocation of the monk came directly from God. It concerned a way of life that was more about sanctity than service. The call was individual and spiritual. Its emphasis was on the internal. As we saw in chapter 1, there was a great deal of mutual interplay and mutual influence between these two vocations from the fifth century on. Monastic ideals began to shape the priesthood, just as monasteries became increasingly clericalized. But present in the earliest tradition was a basic distinction between cleric and monk that would develop into the separation between secular and regular clergy in the Middle Ages, and that would carry on into the distinction between ecclesiastical and religious vocations that have guided modern treatments of our topic up until the present.

It was the monk who bequeathed to the church the notion of the inner call. The early "Lives" of Anthony, Benedict, or Martin of Tours dramatize the call of Christ through stories of visions and inspirations—sudden conversions of a deeply personal nature that led to a major life change. These individuals were called by God out of the world to live a heightened holiness, a special sanctity, apart from the ordinary realm of human affairs. Of course, concern for the holiness of the clergy was part of the tradition as well, stretching back to the exhortations found in the letters to Timothy and Titus. But, for centuries, the real reflection on holiness surrounded not the cleric but the monk. The monk was the one called by Christ to flee the world in order to pursue a life of spiritual perfection. In the Constantinian church, conversion came to be understood not primarily as a conversion *to* Christianity but as a conversion *within* Christianity—a "turning" toward a more radical form of Christian life. Likewise, Christ's call was no longer just the call to discipleship but that more radical call of disciples to enter the monastery.

The rise of the mendicant orders in the twelfth century added a further layer to this history of the inner call. What came into existence through the activities of Francis, Dominic, and others was a form of religious life lived according to a rule and under vows. But these mendicant movements were not simply a continuation of the monastic trajectory. Their origins lay not in asceticism but in ministry. Thus they complicated any neat division between cleric and monk, or between hierarchical service and personal sanctity. The birth of the Order of Preachers illustrates this point. The ministry of Dominic arose as a direct response to the Albigensian heresy, a world-condemning movement that attacked, among other things, the wealth and lifestyle of the clergy. In order to effectively respond to this threat, Dominic envisioned a countermovement of well-educated teachers and preachers, whose vow of poverty freed them for travel from place to place. "That vow for the Dominicans was not, therefore, simply a continuation of earlier ascetical ideals but had a clear relationship to ministry. By preaching in poverty, the Dominicans had a better chance of being heard."[6] Thus the vocation of the preaching friars was not a call out of the world and into the monastery but a call *into the world* through ministry.

This sense of immersion in the world was central to early Franciscan spirituality as well. The life of Francis tells the story of a deep personal conversion that opened out to God, to others, and to all of creation. Francis's direct encounter with Christ in the poor led him to renounce his family and search out a simple life of service. The ministry flowed from this life story. Those who followed Francis took his attempt to imitate Jesus as their model. His sense of call was an exemplar for their own vocation. Thus early Franciscans drew from the tradition of monastic hagiography that the church had known for centuries, but deeply personalized it around the experience of Francis. If earlier legends inspired a somewhat distant respect for the ascetical feats of the desert athletes, the remembrances of Francis drew his followers intimately into his spiritual experience.[7] Francis's inner call became the inner call of every Franciscan. "Through subsequent propagandistic documents like the *Little Flowers of St. Francis* of the fourteenth century, the idea became widely accepted that the friars were responding to a direct and personal call from God in their life-style and ministry, and that the effectiveness of their preaching was directly related to the holiness of their lives."[8]

This belief in an inner call by God came to shape the self-understanding of the mendicants and strengthened their sense of authorization for ministry. The Dominicans emerged out of pastoral need; the Franciscans were born from personal inspiration. But both distanced themselves from past patterns of priesthood centered on office, benefice, and stability.[9] In fact, these new forms of apostolic life generated strong resistance. Thirteenth-century Paris saw successive ways of antimendicant polemic, which was driven by resentment on the part of the French hierarchy, who saw the friars' freedom to preach, hear confessions, and collect alms as an encroachment on their own rights as bishops. In response to these challenges, both the Franciscan Bonaventure and the Dominican Aquinas rose to the defense. They justified their ministries on a number of fronts, but among these various defenses, the one that stands out for us was their appeal to the mendicant's inner call.[10] For example, Aquinas, in one of his polemical treatises on religious life, defended the practice of allowing boys to enter religious life. Against his opponents, who argued that a young man should enter an order only after long deliberation, Aquinas responded that the call to enter religious life comes directly from God, thus no delay is necessary. In making his case, Aquinas introduced a distinction between God's external call (coming through scripture and the example of Jesus) and God's internal call (the movement of grace): "We have already said that the words of Our Lord, quoted in Holy Scripture, carry the same weight as if spoken by His own lips. But, there is another way whereby God speaks interiorly to men, a way alluded to in Psalm 84, 'I will hear what the Lord God will speak in me.' Now this interior voice is to be preferred to any external speech. . . . If, then, we are bound to obey immediately the audible voice of our Creator, how much more ought we to obey, unhesitatingly and unresistingly, the interior whisper whereby the Holy Spirit changes the heart of man."[11] This distinction between the external and internal call came in the context of a focused polemical argument, on the one hand, and Aquinas's broader theology of grace, on the other. The distinction assumed a significance in later neoscholastic commentators that it did not have in Aquinas, at least as indicated by his other writings on religious life.[12] Nevertheless, this notion of the movement of God's grace in the soul resonates with the broader assumption that the ministry of the mendicants flows out of a direct call from God rather than the external call of the bishop.

This conversation differed significantly from the assumptions of vocation surrounding ordained ministry. There, theological treatments focused overwhelmingly on the juridical and the sacramental, in which the whole notion of an "inner call" seemed to play virtually no role. This focus on the externals of the ministry was connected not just to the canonical dependence of the cleric on the bishop. It also came out of the benefice system of the Middle Ages in which the ministry of clerics was closely tied to the revenue provided by a particular diocese, church, or institution. In such a system, the ability to perform the duties of a particular station outweighed the personal spiritual commitment of the minister. The abuses inherent in such a system and the danger of ignoring the spiritual formation of the clergy were as obvious then as they are now. They played no small part in the Reformation and in the Catholic Church's response to it. However, it would not be until the seventeenth century that a spirituality for the diocesan priest would emerge comparable to the rich spiritualities and deep sense of call permeating the new religious orders. In the meantime, a new form of ministerial life and spiritual discernment bursts onto the scene, leaving a deep impact on the Catholic understanding of vocation.

The Dynamic of Ignatian Spirituality

The idea of a direct and personal call from God that we saw develop among the medieval mendicants took on special significance for the founder of the Society of Jesus, Ignatius of Loyola. So central was Ignatius's belief in God's direct action in the heart of an individual that one commentator concludes, "for the author of the *Exercises*, the idea of interior vocation is not just a predominant idea, it is the axis around which the whole spiritual life revolves."[13]

Iñigo López de Loyola was born to a family of lesser nobility in the Basque region of northern Spain around the year 1491. He received a sparse education and, at the age of thirteen was sent off to the household of King Ferdinand's chief treasurer, where he was trained as a courtier. Though immersed in the local religious culture of his day, Iñigo was not particularly religious. He admitted later that until the age of twenty-six he was "a man given to the vanities of the world." What he enjoyed most "was warlike sport, with a great and foolish desire to win fame."[14] Iñigo's early military aspirations came to an end in 1521, the same year that Martin Luther was excommunicated by Pope Leo X. On May 20, in the midst of the siege of Pamplona, a French cannonball shattered Iñigo's right leg. Carried to the family castle at Loyola, Iñigo survived several operations and a long convalescence. He eventually learned to walk again, though with a pronounced limp.

It was during this time of recovery that Iñigo experienced a profound religious conversion. When he could not find any tales of chivalry to pass the time, Iñigo turned to the only books at hand—a collection of lives of the saints by Jacopo da Voragine titled *The Golden Legend* and Ludolph of Saxony's *The Life of Christ*. Iñigo read about the saints and began to imagine following their example. He daydreamed for hours, fantasizing first about one life—the life of a courtier and successful soldier—and then about another—a life of prayer and penance in imitation of St. Francis or St. Dominic. He noticed something about these daydreams. When he thought about worldly conquests and romantic adventures, he was at first delighted by them, but later he felt dry and dissatisfied. When he thought about imitating the saints, however, he felt consoled and joyful long after the daydream ended. Gradually, Iñigo grew convinced that God was speaking to him through these inner feelings and movements of the spirit. He resolved to change the course of his life and to begin this new life with a pilgrimage to Jerusalem.

Iñigo made it to Jerusalem, but only after a year-long stay in the small town of Manresa, near Barcelona. There at Manresa Iñigo came to see his purpose more clearly. He would not be just a solitary pilgrim, but would work with Christ for the salvation of others. His goal was not monastic but apostolic—he would "help souls." Following his stay in Manresa, and after his brief pilgrimage to Jerusalem, Iñigo turned to study. After time at Barcelona, Alcalá, and Salamanca, he arrived at the University of Paris in February of 1528. There Ignatius (which he began to call himself) drew to himself those first few friends— Francis Xavier, Pierre Favre, and others—who would become the core of the future *Compagnia di Gesù*. For seven years they studied and ministered together in the streets of Paris and surrounding areas. Unable to return to Jerusalem, Ignatius and his friends turned to Rome and offered their services to the pope. They were received well, and on September 27, 1540, Ignatius's "Society of Jesus" was officially instituted by Paul III's papal bull *Regimini militantis ecclesiae*. Ignatius himself was elected the Society's first superior general, a position he held until his death in 1556.

We spend some time on the story of Ignatius's life not only because it illustrates important aspects of his personal spirituality but also because the experience of Ignatius was seen—both by himself and by those who came after him—as paradigmatic for future members of the Society. During his recovery at the castle of Loyola, Ignatius came to believe that God was silently speaking to him through the inner movements of his thoughts and feelings. By attending to these thoughts and feelings, Ignatius discovered God's specific will for his life. This spiritual vision was guided by a profoundly introspective instinct. Of course, this introspective, inward turn was not original to Ignatius, as our previous discussion of the mendicants suggests. Indeed, a concern for interiority touches virtually every strand of the Christian mystical tradition. We see it in Ignatius's younger contemporary Teresa of Ávila, in the flowering of German mysticism that marked the end of the Middle Ages, and in a procession of figures stretching back to that genius of the interior life, Augustine of Hippo. Even Luther shared this with Ignatius: both men had a profound inner experience that they believed was relevant for others.

And yet, while Luther remained in many ways a medieval person, Ignatius stepped into the modern world. His attention to interiority came in the midst of a renewed humanism and a shifting conception of the subject; thus his use of traditional categories took on an original quality. What stands out is his systematic reflection on his experience and his ability to distill it into a method for deepening the experience of others. During his recovery, Ignatius kept a notebook in which he wrote down his thoughts and feelings, recording the meditations that he found helpful and saving the insights he gained. He took these papers with him to Manresa, where he began to see that other people could benefit from what he had discovered. Over those months of prayer and ministry, he continued to write down his ideas, and the pieces of what was to become his most important work, the *Spiritual Exercises*, began to emerge. Though he continued to revise his *Spiritual Exercises* over the next twenty years, most scholars agree that Ignatius already carried the core of it with him in his notebooks when he left Manresa to complete his pilgrimage to Jerusalem.[15]

The *Spiritual Exercises* were published by Ignatius in 1548, eight years after the Society of Jesus had been approved. In its final form, the book represents the culmination of Ignatius's spiritual vision. It is not a treatise on the spiritual life, nor is it devotional reading. It was written as a guidebook, intended to help a guide lead other people through a monthlong retreat. The retreat involves an elaborate program of meditations on the life of Christ whose goal is to draw the individual into the same dynamic of interior conversion and personal commitment that Ignatius himself had experienced. Intended for anyone, the *Exercises* primarily have in mind the person seeking the will of God in the face of a major vocational decision. Thus they became both an important ministerial tool and the foundational experience for those entering the Society. Already at the University of Paris, Ignatius was guiding his first companions through his exercises.

The *Exercises* lay out the program for a retreat of approximately thirty days arranged into four "Weeks."[16] The First Week invites the retreatant to reflect on the purpose of his or her life, the history and horrible effects of sin, and the beauty of repentance. The Second Week

begins with a reflection on the call to follow Christ the King and continues with meditations on Christ's incarnation, childhood, and public
ministry. It culminates in a significant life choice—the "election"—in
which the retreatant responds to the call of the Eternal King through
a concrete vocational decision. The Third and Fourth Weeks reflect on
Christ's passion and the events of the resurrection, respectively, in a
way meant to deepen and confirm this election. In overall structure,
then, the *Exercises* parallel the ancient threefold framework of the purgative (Week One), the illuminative (Week Two), and the unitive (Weeks
Three and Four) ways. The goal of meditating, however, is not meditation itself. The goal is to rid the soul of disordered affections so as to
be able to determine God's will for one's life.[17] The conversion of Week
One prepares the retreatant for the Weeks that follow, in which he or
she comes to recognize and respond to Christ's call. In a way that is
nonprescriptive and adaptable to individual needs, the *Exercises* provide
a structured method for discovering one's vocation.

In guiding the discernment of this vocation, Ignatius was particularly attentive to the role of feeling and the whole affective dimension.
The method of his meditations encourages the retreatant to dwell
within the stories of Jesus by engaging memory, imagination, and
emotion. An important influence here was Ludolph of Saxony's *The
Life of Christ*, one of the books that Ignatius read during his recovery.
This medieval classic, heavily dependent on the earlier *Meditations on
the Life of Christ* once attributed to Bonaventure, introduced Ignatius
to the world of Franciscan piety.[18] Francis of Assisi's unique devotion
to the human Jesus escaped an abstract mysticism by concentrating
love on a concrete person—the baby born in Bethlehem, the son hanging on the cross. In the tradition Francis launched, the universal gave
way to the particular, to narrative and to nature. Not only did Ignatius
literally learn the stories of Jesus from Ludolph (in 1521 Ignatius did
know enough Latin to read the gospels themselves) but he also absorbed a way to meditate on them. Ludolph's goal in presenting these
stories was to stir up love for Jesus. He encouraged his readers to relish
within their hearts the details of Jesus' life:

> Your part will be, if you want to draw fruit from these sayings and
> deeds of Christ, to put aside all other preoccupations; and then,
> with all the affection of your heart, slowly, diligently, and with
> relish, make yourself present to what the Lord Jesus has said and
> done, and to what is being narrated, just as if you were actually
> there, and heard him with your own ears, and saw him with your

own eyes; for all these matters are exceedingly sweet to one who ponders them with desire, and far more so to one who savors them. Although many of these facts are recounted as having taken place in the past, you nevertheless should meditate upon them as if they were taking place now, in the present; for this you will surely experience great delight.[19]

Ignatius heeded Ludolph's advice. He adopted this advice as his own and adapted it for the meditations marking the four Weeks of his *Exercises*.[20] The meditations work by placing the individual inside the narrative of Christ's life, death, and resurrection, inviting the retreatant to vividly imagine each scene, to be open to the emotional pulls of the experience, and to reflect on what these feelings might mean.

If the content of the meditations of the *Exercises* can be traced back to Ludolph's *Life*, the process for interpreting them goes back to that other book Ignatius found in the castle at Loyola, *The Golden Legend*. Dreaming about the lives of the saints, Ignatius found consolation and peace. But fantasies of a more worldly nature left him agitated and empty. Ignatius's breakthrough insight was that these feelings were clues to the workings of good and evil spirits in his soul. From his experience, Ignatius drew the conclusion that powerful emotions need to be taken seriously. Thus the meditations found in the *Exercises* were carefully designed to stimulate these emotions and give the individual an opportunity to reflect on them. Feelings are not to be followed indiscriminately, hence the need for discernment.[21] Still, Ignatius showed extraordinary confidence in the affections. Though we have to avoid overstating the contrast, it seems that according to the *Exercises* God works better through the heart than through the head. John O'Malley offers a more nuanced assessment: "I would stress that the book, and with it Jesuit spirituality, while being rationalistic in its language and arguments, is more profoundly concerned with right affectivity; while being logical in the organization of its parts, it is more profoundly psychological in its movement and design; and while being methodical in the aids it provides to prayer and spiritual discernment, it is more profoundly nonprescriptive in the outcome it foresees for the direct divine intervention that is its basic premise."[22]

But can we place so much trust in our emotions, so much faith in our notoriously fickle affections? Here the total process of the *Exercises* is important. The decision about how one will follow Christ the King, the decision about what shape one's life will take, comes during the Second Week. Here the affections play a role quite different from the one they play in the First Week. In the First Week, the feelings of consolation and desolation are judged according to their overall and relatively obvious orientation toward good or evil; in the Second Week, these feelings themselves become the judge. This is possible because between the two weeks lies a conversion that is nothing less than a radical reorientation of the affections themselves.[23] Before this conversion, the affections are disordered, but through the process and grace of the First Week they become purified and ordered toward the love of God. Only after this conversion do the affections become a reliable guide to the will of God. We can trust our heart because our heart has been purified. With the shift from the First to the Second Week, the retreatant shifts her or his focus: from choosing between good and bad to choosing from among different good options for one's life. In the election, the experience of consolation becomes the signal of God's will. The clear sign that the *Exercises* have achieved their purpose is consolation in the heart of the individual.

For the *Exercises*, one's vocation is recognized within. The "Introductory Explanations" warn the retreat leader not to get in the way of God's action. Better to let God speak directly to the retreatant: "But during these Spiritual Exercises when a person is seeking God's will, it is more appropriate and far better that the creator and Lord himself should communicate himself to the devout soul." The leader should "allow the Creator to deal immediately with the creature and the creature with its Creator and Lord."[24] Ignatius's emphasis on the direct inner inspiration of God led critics to charge him with promoting a dangerous and unchecked mysticism. In 1553, the Dominican Tomás de Pedroche linked these "Introductory Explanations" to Ignatius's comments about consolation and desolation, calling such unrestrained mysticism "scandalous and heretical."[25] Years earlier, while studying at the University of Alcalá, Ignatius had attracted the attention of the Inquisition. He and his friends were accused of being *alumbrados* ("enlightened ones"), a mystical movement originating in fifteenth-century Spain that emphasized visions, illuminations, and special revelations. They were later acquitted, but, as the attack of de Pedroche shows, the rumors of illuminatism continued to circle around Ignatius's ministry.

Perhaps sensitive to these early accusations of heterodoxy, Ignatius incorporated into the *Exercises* a warning against making any rash decisions or hasty promises while on retreat.[26] His mystical vision is hardly untethered. The ecclesial context of the election is brought out in his infamous "Rules for Thinking with the Church,"[27] as well as the presumption that, since the object of the election must be indifferent or good in and of itself, it cannot contradict church teaching.[28] But already we see the seeds of a tension that will play out in the subsequent history of Jesuit spirituality, namely, the tension between a more cautious, methodical, and institutional style of prayer and a more expansive and mystical mode.[29] It is a tension that will also take shape in later debates about vocation, where neoscholastic interlocutors worry about the danger of two extremes, an uncontrolled individualism, on the one hand, and a dead institutionalism, on the other.

What we see in Ignatius is a deep sensitivity to the individuality of the person and to the unique nature of her or his conversation with God. Ignatius placed the human person at the center of his spiritual system. Thus he stands squarely within the humanistic tradition that was reshaping the Europe of his day. Ignatius's sources were medieval, but he was a thoroughly modern person. Not only did he start with the human subject but he also demonstrated a typically modern confidence in the ability to systematically reshape life according to a clear method and well-defined goal.[30] A century later, René Descartes—perhaps influenced by his Jesuit mentors at La Flèche—would display the very same characteristics in his experiment of systematic doubt. But unlike Descartes, Ignatius's method does not end at the self-sufficiency of the *Cogito*. In fact, it presupposes a radical dependency.

Ignatius's own "turn to the subject" and his confidence in the ability to determine one's path can make him sound like an early modern Pelagius, as if one could find and follow the will of God on one's own. But such a judgment would have to ignore Ignatius's most basic conviction that God is at work throughout the whole process of the *Exercises*. It would overlook Ignatius's theology of grace. Louis Dupré argues that, rather than giving in to the modern ideal of self-realization, Ignatius actually inverted it. Grace does not come late to a human nature already well on its way. "Grace must first liberate nature from a state of unfreedom in order to enable it to reach its natural potential."[31] In his emphasis on the primacy of grace, Ignatius sounds a lot like Luther. But against the Reformer, Ignatius maintained the basic integrity of nature, a nature intrinsically restored through grace. As we will see later in this chapter, theology at the time had already begun the "fateful separation" of nature and grace.[32] But Ignatius held the two together, achieving a uniquely modern synthesis. It is possible that Ignatius encountered this deeper and more holistic theology of grace in his study of Aquinas at Paris. But the real origin of his understanding lies in his own mystical experience. Through the process of conversion, he came to see that freedom is not simply the space to pursue one's own agenda. True freedom is "a divinely inspired surrender within which action itself becomes grounded in passivity."[33] Freedom consists in acting under the motion of grace. Thus Ignatius "attaches a particular significance to the capacity to perceive the delicate, highly personal touches of grace and instructs his followers to learn how to distinguish 'the various motions that present themselves in our heart.'"[34] If this is how God speaks—not *to* our fallen nature but *through* our graced existence—then our vocation is not foreign to us, imposed by God from outside. Nor is it simply doing what we want. Our vocation is our unique, outward life of freedom that we can only recognize and embrace through the inner liberation of our affections by grace.[35]

Dupré concludes that Ignatius turned the modern primacy of the subject on its head, offering a radically God-centered view of reality. He filled a new form, namely, modern subjectivity, with traditional content. Thus the *Exercises* are not a Pelagian climb to God. Instead they are a recognition of and a way of responding to God's gift to us. From the opening "Principal and the Foundation" ("Human beings are created to praise, reverence, and serve God our Lord . . .") to the closing "Contemplation to Attain Divine Love" ("I will consider how God dwells in creatures . . ."), we see a descending movement of grace that spills out past the individual retreatant to touch all of creation.[36] Gone is the *contemptus mundi* of monastic spirituality. Instead, the whole world is imbued with God's presence. Like so many Baroque churches in which light descends through a host of mediators, angels, and saints to flood the human stage, grace in Ignatius's vision suffuses the whole human and cosmic drama.[37] The pageant of secular humanism comes to dominate Western political and social thought. But without the divine, Ignatian spirituality seems to say, this play is quite dull. What makes Ignatius's vision so compelling is that this drama is transparent to the presence of God permeating the whole.

In the *Constitutions* for his newborn Society of Jesus, Ignatius encouraged his companions to "find God in all things."[38] Ignatius's notion of the transparency of the world to God explains how the introverted meditations of the *Exercises* burst out into the extroverted activity of the Society. God is at work in the soul and in the world. Jerome Nadal captured the deep unity between the two with his phrase "contemplatives in action." In an earlier era, Thomas Aquinas described his own "active" order as superior to the contemplative life because his Dominicans did not just pray but shared with others the fruit of their prayer. For Ignatius, these two moments cannot be separated and so easily serialized. Apostolic action is itself a form of contemplation. The two are intertwined. Perhaps this deep union between Ignatian contemplation and Jesuit action helps to explain why in some later Jesuit traditions, the election became so tightly tied to entrance into the Society. There was a kind of institutionalization of vocation that occurred alongside the creative adaptation of the *Exercises* to all manner of people and all modes of ministry.[39] At the beginning was Ignatius's contribution. Bridging the medieval and the modern, Ignatius offered a profoundly interiorized notion of God's call that does not slip into either solipsism or stasis. For beneath it pulses a dynamic spirituality of God's extensive and ever-present grace.

Coming into Ministry

The idea of an inner call was central to the self-understanding of the early Jesuits. They spoke often and at length of their call by Christ and their calling as members of the Society. But rarely, if at all, did they speak of a "call to priesthood."[40] As inheritors of the medieval theology of orders, Ignatius and his followers simply took the priesthood for granted. It was not the driving force of their self-identity but a kind of prerequisite for the ministries they undertook. Though a certain priestly spirituality is not missing in the writings of Ignatius and his later companions, the real ground of their ministries and of the Jesuit self-understanding was membership in the Society and the spiritual vision of the *Exercises*.

Thus the Jesuits represent a continuation of the mendicant tradition of the inner call, in which authorization for ministry ultimately rested not on ecclesiastical office or the external call of the bishop but on a personal experience of conversion and entrance into a religious community. Since their emergence, the mendicant orders had fostered this sense of inner call through a more or less standardized process of formation and novitiate. This differed significantly from the model of education followed by the secular clergy. For centuries, priestly formation had followed a loose model of apprenticeship in which a young cleric would attach himself to a master in order to learn the basic functions of the ministry. With the rise of the universities in the twelfth and thirteenth centuries, a more formal and "scholastic" approach began to take hold. This shift had the advantage of regularizing the education of those few candidates who could attend university, increasing the academic content and providing an orderly sequence of study. But it had the disadvantage of separating intellect from affect. Removed to the classroom, theology became disconnected from spirituality and pastoral experience. The mendicants, who took full advantage of the universities from the beginning, overcame this disconnect by establishing their own novitiates and convents near the universities. Thus the academic training of novices was supplemented by a rhythm of prayer, discipline, and liturgy in their residences, modeled, as they were, on the medieval monastery. This rhythm promoted a more integrated spiritual formation for the mendicants, which in turn rested on a shared experience of conversion and commitment to the ideals of the community.[41]

In the differences between the secular clergy and the mendicants we see the emergence of two different trajectories of ministerial formation. After the Reformation, these harden into two separate tracks. The first track, that followed by the secular clergy, took the form of the diocesan seminary, one of the lasting legacies of the Council of Trent. While Trent's decree mandating diocesan seminaries did not revolutionize clergy education overnight, it nevertheless laid the foundation for a distinct model of ministerial formation.[42] The focus of the council seems to have been, first, training seminarians in basic pastoral skills, such as saying Mass and hearing confessions, and, second, providing an environment for healthy moral development. Rather than inner growth, Trent highlighted external moral behavior. The goal was to shelter young men from the seductions of the world and shape them in the habits of devotion. If this fostered the candidate's spirituality or his inner sense of vocation, all the better. But this dimension was beyond Trent's purview.

The second model of ministerial formation following the Reformation was driven by the Jesuits. They adapted the style of education that Ignatius and his companions had learned from the Dominicans and Franciscans in Paris. This entailed a well-structured curriculum divided into disciplines, with a heavy emphasis on the classical humanities. This model kept novitiates and scholastics better connected to "secular" literature and concerns. But at the same time, the Jesuits encouraged a variety of means to help deepen the interior life of those preparing to enter the Society. This spiritual formation took its own unique texture thanks to the deeply interior dynamic of the *Exercises*, which extended to touch the many lay students studying alongside the Jesuits in their schools. External moral behavior was important. But all of the tools employed by the Jesuits—the *Exercises*, retreats, spiritual conversation and direction—served a more important goal: the internalization of the values of the Gospel and of the Society.

Thus the different models of formation for religious and for secular clergy following the Reformation reinforced two different understandings of vocation: the inner call of the religious and the external call of the cleric. As noted, the Jesuits were not indifferent to outward behavior or ecclesial context. Their "Rules of Modesty" instructed students to keep their eyes cast down, their clothing clean, and their every action edifying.[43] Their schools and colleges imposed a discipline that encouraged external moral conformity. But it was really the inner life that led. Likewise, the emerging tridentine seminaries did not ignore the spiritual life. Following Trent, the reforms of Charles Borromeo breathed life into the dry prescriptions of the council. But he furthered a model of education built on cultivating for the clergy a culture that was distinct and separate from the laity. While Borromeo promoted the use of retreats for seminarians, in the seminaries it was the rules of comportment and moral behavior that mattered. A holy clergy—one of the goals of the Catholic Reformation—here meant a moral clergy, not necessarily a spiritual one. During this period, the clerical vocation—and thus the priestly vocation—was an external vocation. This almost exclusive focus was fostered by the very nature of seminary formation, its connection to the bishop, the emphasis on external behavior, and the continuation of the benefice system. It would not be until the seventeenth century that the mystics and reformers of the "French school" would take the interiorization that had been growing among the religious orders and direct it to the diocesan priest. In doing so, the French school gave birth to a new spirituality of the priesthood and a new sense of this particular vocation as a personal, direct, and inner call from God.

The French School of Spirituality

After decades of religious war and political strife, the birth of the seventeenth century brought a rebirth of church life in France. Here mystical depth met pastoral necessity to shape a multifaceted movement of reform. What we call the "French school" grew out of the insights and initiatives of mystical geniuses and energetic pastors like Pierre de Bérulle, Charles de Condren, Madeleine de Saint-Joseph, Jean-Jacques Olier, Jean Eudes, and Vincent de Paul. The spirituality they crafted offered a creative response to the upheavals of a Europe transitioning from Renaissance and Reformation to the Enlightenment and the modern world. This school would shape Catholic spirituality for centuries, and it would have a lasting impact on the Catholic understanding of vocation.[44]

Two dynamics that mark this rich period are of particular interest to us. First, the French school contributes a creative and consequential chapter to the larger story of spiritual interiorization, whose beginnings are difficult to place but whose basic plotline in the modern era is already well established by Ignatius's inward turn. Second, the French school launches a new trajectory in the theology of vocation by taking the notion of an inner call—to this point the preserve of religious life—and applying it to the clerical state. To illustrate these two dynamics, we turn to two giants of the French school, Pierre de Bérulle and Jean-Jacques Olier.

Pierre de Bérulle is rightly recognized as the father of the French school. He was a prolific spiritual writer and a powerful political force—an influential member of court who was often at odds with the formidable Cardinal Richelieu.[45] Named a cardinal himself late in life, Bérulle was instrumental in bringing the Spanish Carmelites into France. He founded the French Oratory and launched an ambitious program of reform for the secular clergy—an agenda taken up by a host of religious congregations that followed in his wake: Vincent de Paul's Congregation of the Mission, Eudes' Congregation of Jesus and Mary, and, most important, Olier's Society of Saint Sulpice. It was largely through the seminaries supported and staffed by the Sulpicians that the spirituality of Bérulle and the French school came to shape the self-understanding of priests in Europe and North America for centuries, lasting up until the eve of the Second Vatican Council.

Bérulle famously reclaimed the Christ of the triune God as the center of the spiritual life. Scholars often style his trinitarian christocentrism as a kind of spiritual rebuttal to the introspection of Renaissance humanism. Instead of focusing on the human person, Bérulle focused on Jesus Christ, the Word Incarnate. However, this did not mean that Bérulle abandoned all concern for the individual or the inner life. But it was the inner life of Christ, not the Christian, that was the center of his mystical vision.

The spiritual journey of Bérulle tells the story of the "christocentric turn" that would become the hallmark of the French school. His earliest spiritual work, *Bref discours de l'abnégation intérieure* (1597), reflected the influence of the "abstract school" of spirituality associated with that remarkable circle of mystical virtuosi gathering in the Paris salons of Madame Barbe Acarie.[46] As the title indicates, the *Bref discours* sought to guide the soul through successive stages of abnegation, leading ultimately to a death of self that makes union with God possible. In Bérulle's early soul-centered spirituality, Christ rarely came up. But in 1602 Bérulle made the *Spiritual Exercises* with the Jesuits at Verdun. The experience clearly moved him. Through these meditations, his various spiritual impulses came together around the person of Christ. Bérulle was especially impressed by the self-humiliation of Christ that took place in the incarnation. The death to self that Bérulle called *anéantissement* (a word that evokes abasement, abnegation, and annihilation) finds a perfect model in the Word Incarnate, who "did not regard equality with God as something to be exploited, but emptied himself, taking the form of a slave" (Phil 2:6-7). In his *Discourse on the State and Grandeurs of Jesus* (1623), Bérulle's shift from anthropocentrism to christocentrism was complete. It was a shift he described as nothing less than a Copernican revolution. Evoking the scientist himself, Bérulle wrote, "An excellent mind of this age claimed that the sun and not the earth is at the center of the world. . . . This new opinion, which has little following in the science of the stars, is useful and should be followed in the science of salvation. For Jesus is the sun that is immovable in his greatness and that moves all other things."[47]

Within such a vision, the human task becomes not devotion or spiritual exercises but *adoration*—the only appropriate response to the grandeur of God Incarnate. "To adore is to have a very high idea of that which we should adore, and a will surrendered, submissive, and abased before the excellence and dignity which we believe or know to be in that object."[48] Adoration is awe and respect for the infinite creator, along with a recognition of the finitude and fallenness of the creature. It is not the work of self-renunciation that leads to God; it is the grandeur of God that reveals the poverty of the human soul. After all, who are we before so great a God? Here the contrast with Ignatius is telling. In the *Exercises*, the self and its affections are purified and strengthened in order to act—a dynamic that pushes the self forward onto the stage. In contrast, the Bérullian self recedes into the wings. Both mystics rejected the narcissism of the modern subject. Ignatius did so through a view of nature intrinsically restored through grace. Bérulle, on the other hand, turned to the categories of adoration, annihilation of the self, and adherence to God. The first fueled the active self; the second was self-effacing.

What has been said so far of Bérulle's spirituality is pretty much standard fare, a variant on the self-denial that has always marked the ascetic tradition. What stands out as Bérulle's truly creative contribution is the way in which he presented the spiritual life as a participation in the "states" (*états*) of Christ. These "states" are the inward dispositions and sentiments of Christ through which he faithfully lived out the mysteries of his life, death, and resurrection. They mark Jesus' own inner life. Bérulle argued that the individual historical events of Jesus' life happened once and for all, thus they are past. However, the attitudes and inner dispositions of Jesus remain present. They are permanent, eternally bound to the eternal Word. Thus they remain available to us even today. "Jesus is at the same time the one who is adored, the means of adoration, and the paradigm of what it is to adore."[49] Bérulle was attracted to a number of these states, including those associated with Jesus' infancy, his relationship to Mary, and his death, but chief among them is the state of *anéantissement* that accompanies the incarnation itself, the utter subjection and sacrifice experienced by the infinite Word who took on finite flesh. Bérulle saw the self-denial of the divine Word as the perfect model for the self-renunciation of Christians, an attitude that ought to mark our most fundamental disposition before God.

In turning to Christ, Bérulle was not ultimately concerned about the historical events described in the gospels or the external behavior of the human Jesus. What mattered most was Jesus' interior life, his own humility, self-effacement, and adoration of the Father. That is what we are to imitate. Our imitation of Christ is itself an interior state, an attempt to put on the mind of Christ, to bring one's will and attitudes into conformity with the will and attitudes of Jesus. Guillén Preckler observes that Bérulle transformed the "essential introversion" of the Rhineland mystics into a christological adoration by state. "His originality is in making the mystic's contemplation a sharing in Christ's exemplary adoration itself."[50] Thus Bérulle's spirituality can be both christocentric and deeply interior, for, as George Tavard points out, while the whole of the spiritual life is Christ-centered, the center *is not exterior to oneself.* "It lies within us by participation in the states of Jesus."[51]

Within this mystical vision, discernment becomes a subtle process of aligning our will to the will of God, exemplified in Jesus' state of *anéantissement*. In other words, it is a matter of attuning our interior life to the interior life of Jesus. We become open to the Father's will through a participation in the Son's self-effacement. Unfortunately Bérulle never developed an anthropology to support this insight into the inner resonance between the soul of the Christian and the soul of Christ.[52] *Anéantissement* mixes with an Augustinian pessimism to give Bérullian spirituality a dark sense of sin and a negative view of the human person. His christology—in which Jesus, from the moment of his conception, is capable of the highest acts of adoration—drifts toward Docetism, presenting little room for human growth. Later appropriations of his thought would transform *anéantissement* into denial, feeding a spirituality that is at the same time sentimental and world-negating. We might sum up by saying that Bérulle raised the profile of the inner life through his attention to the spiritual dispositions and intentions, but he did so without the anthropological framework needed to support this inward turn.

While he was intent on helping individuals grow in spiritual depth and interiority, Bérulle shared the common tridentine assumption that the necessary prerequisite to the reform of souls was the reform of the clergy. Thus he was not only a mystic looking inward but he was also a reformer looking outward. In Bérulle's France, there were too many clerics too poorly prepared for their ministry. Trent issued its decrees on holy orders in 1564. But these decrees remained a dead letter in France well into the seventeenth century. A few seminaries had been instituted, but their impact was mixed and marginal. By and large the formation of clerics continued the rather haphazard and minimalist apprenticeship model of the Middle Ages. Moreover, the continuation of the benefice system meant that a number of clerics took orders at least in part for financial gain, or to improve the social standing of their families, often entering orders at a young age. (Jean-Jacques Olier was tonsured and given his first benefice at the age of eleven.) Secular rulers awarded benefices to political allies, and many clerics piled up multiple benefices in order to multiply their income. It was not without reason that the French clergy at the time was almost universally derided as an uneducated, incompetent, and immoral mass of self-seeking opportunists.[53] Vincent de Paul railed against this state of affairs: "The Church has no worse enemies than her priests. Heresies have come from them . . . and it is through them that heresies have prevailed, that vice has reigned, and that ignorance has established its throne among the 'poor' people."[54]

Even if this language reflects more the rhetoric of the reformer than sober pastoral assessment, still much energy went into improving the formation of the clergy. An early pioneer was Andrien Bourdoise, who established a society for priestly candidates in Paris in 1612, a model that spread to surrounding towns. In 1628, at the invitation of the bishop of Beauvais, Vincent de Paul began giving weeklong retreats to those about to be ordained. These "exercises" consisted of basic instruction in the theology and rubrics of the priest's ministries, with some reflection on mental prayer, the virtues, and vocation—a kind of "crash course" meant to address whatever deficiencies were left over from the candidates' education. Around the same time, de Paul's "Tuesday Conferences" provided a form of continuing education for the elite clergy of Paris. Bérulle himself launched a number of reforming initiatives, most notably founding the Oratory in 1611, which in its early years vigorously promoted seminary education. But just as important as these pastoral initiatives was the emergence of a spirituality distinctive to the diocesan priesthood. Within this new spirituality, the inner call to the priesthood took on a new importance.

Bérulle became interested in the spirituality of the priesthood early on in his career. On the one hand, his christocentric mysticism gave to his system a universal thrust based in baptism: every individual is called to perfection though her or his unique participation in the states of Christ. On the other hand, Bérulle's reliance on the spiritual hierarchy of Pseudo-Dionysius led him to elevate the ecclesiastical state as "the first and the holiest state of the church of God."[55] He saw the ordained priesthood as superior to the religious orders, for the priesthood came directly from Christ and was a participation in Christ's own priesthood. He sought to reunify in the person of the priest three strands that he saw sundered in church life at the time: authority, holiness, and doctrine.[56] Rather than cede sanctity to the monks and teaching to the theologians, Bérulle wanted the diocesan priests ("authority") to be both learned and holy, saints and scholars who would serve the church of Christ. Achieving this synthesis was the goal of the Oratory. Guiding it was a spirituality grounded in the priest's unique participation in the particular *anéantissement* of Jesus as priest and victim. Through Charles de Condren (1588–1641), the second superior general of Bérulle's Oratory, this spirituality took on a heavily sacrificial dimension: the priest was called to an internal participation in the self-sacrifice of Christ. It was this vision that Condren passed on to his spiritual son Jean-Jacques Olier, the founder of the Sulpicians.

Olier was attracted early on to the pastoral initiatives of Vincent de Paul, who visited the Olier home when Jean-Jacques was a boy. After his ordination, Olier joined the saint in his various missions to rural parishes across France. But it was his contact with Condren, who became his spiritual director in 1634, that introduced Olier to the work of Bérulle and so profoundly shaped his own spiritual vision. In Bremond's enthusiastic assessment, Olier's "especial grace and mission was, not exact [sic] to popularise Bérullism, but to present it with such limpidity, richness of imagination and fervour that its apparently somewhat difficult metaphysics are placed invitingly in the reach of most readers."[57] Olier shared Bérulle's christocentric emphasis on interiority—though he spoke less of Jesus' "states" than of the "heart" or "interior" of Jesus: "The interior life [of Jesus Christ] must be always before our eyes as the source and model of all the interior life of our souls."[58] Indeed, Olier's vision of a renewed Christianity was that of "a society of souls filled with the very inner life of Jesus Christ, filled with his sentiments, dispositions, virtues, and habits."[59] In charting the way toward this renewal, Olier shared another important conviction of Bérulle, namely, that to reform souls, you had to reform the clergy.

It was through Olier's reforming efforts that the French school had its greatest impact on the theology of vocation—for in Olier, we see the inner life of the priest lifted up as the primary place for discerning God's call. Olier was one of a number of reformers in midseventeenth-century France calling for better priests and crafting criteria so as to better assess candidates seeking ordination. As we noted above, the benefice system fed a variety of abuses, particularly the tendency to see the ministry as a means to political influence, social standing, or material gain. Because of these systemic problems, most reformers had given up on the clergy already ensconced in their benefices. Instead they turned their attention to forming a new generation of priests, calling the church to raise up only those men who had a "true vocation." But how was this vocation to be discerned? The ancient appeal to the external call of the bishop had broken down under the influence of power and money. So instead reformers turned inward, emphasizing the candidate's suitability for ministry and what his intention, or inner motivation, was for entering the clergy.

What Olier added to the common criteria of suitability and intention was the notion of the soul's "inclination" to the priesthood, which he described as the steady pull of the soul toward this state of life. Indeed, he lifted up this inner inclination as the first of all requirements for ordination.[60] Among his private papers was a passage that was later incorporated into the widely influential seminary manual *Traité des saints ordres*:

> The first thing is to test, in the depths of one's soul, the inclination and movement of God toward the ecclesiastical state. This movement is strong, effective, impervious, powerful, carrying the whole soul and guiding it, not in an impulsive, sentimental, or wavering manner, but in a way that is authoritative, consistent, and immovable in its depths. That is not to say that the soul does not experience attacks from the outside that shake it and disturb it noticeably, but in its depths this disposition and this inclination remain, which shows that it is the Spirit of God living within us who inclines the heart and carries it where it wishes.[61]

In this "inclination" was an early impetus to the "theory of attraction" that would so concern Lahitton. In the later *Traité*, which was attributed to Olier but compiled after his death, great attention is given to the various ways in which one might test the soul's inclinations.[62] The *Traité* counsels that the movement of God in the soul is usually strong, constant, and "smooth." A divine vocation brings with it tranquility and peace. If one experiences turbulence (*turbulente*), haste or impatience, if the inclination is either too weak or too violently felt, embroiling the soul, then the inclination is not a divine vocation but the call of nature or of self-love. In this later text, the candidate's motivation, or intention, is folded within this more primary category of inclination. The *Traité* argues that one should *feel* called for the right reason, namely, to serve the glory of God. If other reasons, such as comfort, pleasure, or money, lead one to the ecclesiastical state, then it is not Jesus Christ who calls the candidate to the height of the priesthood but the devil calling him to the pinnacle of the temple.[63]

The *Traité des saints ordres* first appeared in 1676 and was reprinted in numerous editions up to 1953, with eleven editions appearing in the nineteenth century alone. It had an enormous impact, appearing as it did at the very moment that seminaries were being reestablished across France and spilling over into the New World. In the *Traité*'s treatment of the soul's inclination, we note two things. First, in the *Traité* are the echoes of Ignatius's rules for the discernment of spirits. The constancy and tranquility sought in a true vocation evoke the descriptions of consolation found in the *Exercises*. In Olier, and in the Sulpician tradition in general, we find a typically Ignatian trust in the sentiments, a confidence that one's feelings and affections can be clues to the inner workings of God. But alongside this trust came a deep concern that these affections not lead, as the *Traité* put it, to the pinnacle of the temple. In other words, what is it that prevents love from becoming self-love? Ignatius kept his self-analysis from slipping into solipsism. In some ways, the broader spirituality of the French school was obsessed with avoiding this same fall. But in its advice on the priestly vocation, the *Traité* fails to offer anything like the *Exercises'* rich process of conversion and purification that works to properly order one's affections, and so guards against self-love and inordinate attachments. Instead, what we find is a checklist of appropriate indicators— "marks" or "signs" of a true vocation. The *Traité* talks about the affections and cautions against self-centered loves, but its advice remains disconnected from the larger process of spiritual self-effacement that was central to the French school.

When Olier himself took up the inner inclination that stands as the most important sign of a true vocation, he presumed the larger framework provided by Bérulle's christocentric mysticism. For Bérulle, "adherence" to the triune God is the goal of the spiritual life. This adherence is not mere exterior imitation but a deep unity of life and being whose perfect realization is found in the incarnation. It comes through a profoundly affective experience of participating in the attitudes of Christ—preeminently, a participation in Christ's own adoration of the Father. Such adoration ushers in constancy, tranquility, and deep unity—in a word "adherence." Adherence is simply "adoration as continuous offertory."[64] Michael Buckley captures this sense of spiritual stability: "Through adherence, adoration becomes no longer a series of discrete moments, but a state (*état*), no longer a succession of acts, but a constancy of being in a depth of adherence that can only be effected by God. The hypostatic union is both the archetype and the perfection of human destiny, a destiny that all other human beings share in various degrees of imperfect realization."[65] When Olier spoke of the constancy of the individual's inner inclination toward the ecclesiastical state, he presumed this deeper notion of adherence. Vocational discernment thus depends on a conversion worked by the aligning of one's inner state to the inner state of Christ. Discernment demands a personal conversion understood as adherence. When we hear Olier's description of the tranquility of soul that comes with finding one's true vocation, we are struck not only by its psychological common sense but also by the way in which he evoked this larger spiritual system. The peace of adherence to which all Christians are called serves as a model for the peace that comes to one truly called to the priesthood. Here Olier the mystic and Olier the reformer came together to articulate the first mark of a true vocation. Olier was not limiting himself to the superficial self-assessment of seminarians; instead, he was articulating the core dynamic of their inner life. These marks were not hoops standing between the candidate and ordination; they were an introduction to the spirituality that ought to permeate the whole life and ministry of the priest.

In summary, we can say that Bérulle, Condren, and Olier took Trent's reforming decrees and pushed deeper. For them, it was not enough to have priests who were moral and well trained. This was necessary, but not sufficient. They saw that such external reforms would be fruitless if they were not matched by an internal renewal in the hearts and souls of the ordained. More than moral priests, what the church needed was spiritual priests. Only a spiritual clergy could guide souls in the spiritual life; only priests united to Christ could lead believers to that inner adoration and adherence to God that is the goal of the Christian life. The success of the French school in reforming the French clergy and revitalizing the French church should not be overlooked. But the lasting legacy of the French school of priestly spirituality is mixed. Subsequent centuries saw a decline from that earlier vision. In terms of the spirituality spread by the French school, we see Bérulle's complex vision quickly devolve. The trinitarian christocentrism that was his great contribution was not matched by an anthropology adequate to it. Uncoupled from his system and detached from theology, Bérullian spirituality fostered both the mechanistic moralism and the sentimental devotionalism that would come to characterize popular Catholicism in the eighteenth, nineteenth, and early twentieth centuries. The trajectory of the concrete Christ—launched by St. Francis's devotion to the Jesus of the gospels—was steered by Bérulle toward the inner life of the Son. The effect on later devotions and religious art was to transform the colorful and controversial character of the synoptics into an ethereal and effeminate figure—an unreal Christ whose divinity would overshadow his humanity. The priest was elevated in devotional books and in the popular imagination to similar heights—becoming a sacral, sacrificial figure, one set apart from the world for the things of God, a mediator for humankind who enjoys a more intimate relationship with the divine. Finally, the language of the inner call, now brought to bear directly on the priestly vocation, was increasingly separated from a broader spiritual context. Rather than view vocation through the lens of spiritual masters like Ignatius or Bérulle, seminary personnel and theologians took it up on its own. Read through a growing separation between nature and grace, God's call became a supernatural and secret voice, hidden in the depth of the soul.

The Trouble with the Theologians

In the period that we have been tracing, powerful tributaries came together to shape the landscape that would become the modern world. Renaissance humanism and Reformation theology, the invention of printing and the spread of literacy, massive political reconfiguration and increased participation, urbanization and the rise of commercial guilds—together these currents carved out space for one of the defining features of modernity to emerge: the active subject. In this "turn to the subject," the human person came to stand at the center of a new world.

This newfound subjectivism brought with it a renewal of interest in interiority, which would have a profound impact on Christianity in the modern period. Such an "inward turn" was not new to the tradition, but it now took shape within a very different context. In earlier eras, the cultivation of the interior life was a cultivation of the spiritual life. Augustine observed that God is closer to us than we are to ourselves. And much of the subsequent history of Christian spirituality saw the road inward as the road to God.[66] In the early modern era, introspection continued; but this self-examination led in a different direction. René Descartes' experiment in systematic doubt offers a classic example. Unlike Augustine, who anticipated Descartes' most famous argument by a millennium, Descartes' reflection on his own interior life did not lead to a deeper sense of dependence on God. Instead, his *Cogito* became the ground for a new self-sufficient certainty.[67] If for Augustine, the road inward was the road to God, then for the modern world being born, the journey within ends at the self. Detached from its transcendent source, the subject became itself the source—either as a foundational principle for all reality (e.g., the rationalistic philosophy of the Enlightenment) or as a unique agent of creativity and achievement (e.g., the artistic expression of Romanticism).

As the previous pages suggest, Christians in the modern period did not simply cede the inner life to secularism. They did not give up on the soul, or abandon prayer and contemplation. Through their creative response to this changing worldview, the great spiritual masters of the sixteenth and seventeenth centuries kept alive the divine dynamic at the heart of human existence. In contrast to these spiritual masters, the theologians were far less helpful. In fact, the great irony is that Christian theologians of the late medieval and early modern periods actually helped to foster a split between the human subject and its transcendent source that would ultimately push God out of the world. With roots in Aristotelian philosophy and fed by Nominalist theology, a deficient understanding of grace took hold that separated the natural and the supernatural, the human and the divine. Grace became reduced to a kind of "add-on" to creation, an extrinsic and transient force operating on an independent nature. Within this dualistic understanding of the nature-grace relationship, vocation suffered. For when grace becomes seen as a supernatural gift, an extrinsic power or divine energy transmitted to our soul, then one's vocation becomes detached from one's self. The wise encouragement of Ignatius or Olier to listen for God's call within became, among the theologians, a search for something strange—a secret voice that was hard to hear and always in danger of falling silent.

To understand the modern fate of the theology of vocation, we consider the gradual theological separation of God from the world and the subsequent rise of a dualistic understanding of nature and grace. This background offers the theological context within which the neoscholastic manualists took up the question of vocational discernment in treatises that gave final shape to the modern Catholic theology of vocation.

The Distant God

Louis Dupré argues that the complex constellation of beliefs, values, social patterns, political structures, and basic worldviews that we call modernity emerged as the result of a double breakup: "the one between the transcendent constituent and its cosmic-human counterpart, and the one between the person and cosmos (now understood in the narrower sense of physical nature)."[68] The first separated the world from God; the second removed the human person from this newly independent world. The line of vocation we have been tracing in this chapter speaks of God as present in the depths of the person, thus this double breakup is of prime concern. How can we talk of any connection—how can we talk of God's call—in the face of this split?

Dupré points out how the ancient Greeks held a holistic view of reality, which they affirmed through the notion of the cosmos. All of reality is united in a harmonious, all-inclusive whole. The divine mind permeates, and in some sense is identical with, this organic, cosmic unity. Such a holistic view had been radically challenged by the Christian doctrine of creation, which located the divine creator outside of the cosmos. Yet, rather than fracturing reality by separating the maker from the made, the distinction between creator and creation actually helped early Christians affirm their relationship: God remains immanent in what is not God. In the great theologians of the patristic period, we find a profound sense of the Creator's continuing presence within creation. This had obvious implications for the early church's understanding of human nature. The human person, a creature made in the image and likeness of God, is not from the beginning a closed container. No matter how strong the doctrine of original sin, Christianity in this early period affirmed that humanity is constituted by a fundamental orientation toward and openness to God. Even Augustine recognized in the story of Genesis that the natural and original state of humanity is that of intimate union with God. And thus, he argued, we carry with us a desire for that primal experience. As he put it in the opening of his *Confessions*, "our hearts are restless until they rest in you."[69]

Over the course of the Middle Ages, this rich patristic synthesis began to break down, effectively removing God from the world, and thus setting the terms for the modern separation of nature and grace. Two moments in this theological history were significant. The first was the introduction of Aristotle into medieval theology. Aristotle's writings on logic had survived in Europe over the course of the first millennium, but it was only during the twelfth century that his broader body of work became known to the West. Through contact with Muslim scholars, who preserved the philosopher's writings and passed them on to Latin Christendom, medieval theologians discovered a new worldview, realistic and empirical, one that was quite different from the more participative and essentialistic Platonism that had shaped early Christianity. The paradigm shift was enormous, reshaping a number of theological fronts. But it was ultimately Aristotle's understanding of human nature that would have the most direct impact on subsequent understandings of our topic. In the early church, human nature generally referred to the human person in the concrete context of a creation *already permeated* by God's gracious presence. "Thus Saint Augustine calls the original state of justice 'natural.'"[70] Human nature is already graced nature, open as it is to the indwelling of God. In Aristotle, however, such an open-ended nature is not allowed. Each individual nature is a closed and complete reality, with a clearly delineated purpose or end that is proportionate to its own powers to achieve it. (An acorn becomes an oak, and not something else.) When this conception of nature was applied to human nature, medieval theologians faced a dilemma, for the human person is a finite being oriented toward an infinite end—union with God in the beatific vision. Human nature is pointed toward a goal totally disproportionate to its own ability to reach it. We might achieve a "natural" end, but we require God's grace to achieve our "supernatural" end. This was a logical distinction rooted in Aristotle's notion of nature, but, before long, theologians came to see it as a distinction in reality. Later commentators began to speak of a "pure nature" that was finite and fully constituted apart from God's grace. They argued that, through divine revelation and the work of grace, God chooses to invite human nature to an additional super-natural end—with the implication being that human nature itself could be fully understood apart from this supernatural end. In other words, for these commentators, the definition of humanity did not depend on the human relationship to God.

At the forefront of the medieval encounter with Aristotle was Thomas Aquinas. And it is part of his genius that he was able to draw together into a creative synthesis the Platonic, participative vision of the early church and the newly-recovered categories of Aristotle. Applying Aristotle's notion of nature to human nature, Aquinas did not lock it up within itself.[71] He eschewed any "pure nature" existing apart from God's invitation in grace. Instead, the "natural" end of the human being is always subordinated and subsumed within the more funda-mental end that is the beatific vision. Unlike every other creature, the human being aspires to what totally transcends it: "Irrational creatures do not tend toward the perfect goodness, that is the beatitude; but they attain an imperfect goodness, the natural end that they acquire through the power of their nature. But rational creatures may attain a perfect goodness, namely, the beatitude. To do so, however, they need more than inferior natures require to attain their end. . . . That some-one reaches the beatitude by himself, depends entirely on God."[72] Aquinas's reliance on Aristotle certainly opened the door to a split between the two ends of the human person, with one end correspond-ing to the order of nature and the other to the order of grace. But Aquinas avoided such a separation and instead integrated the two, speaking of a *natural* desire for the beatific vision. Thus in Aquinas, there is to the human person a transcendental openness to grace—a view of nature-as-graced, a view of the human person as always de-pendent on God's free gift. But the very attempt by Aquinas to transpose the patristic heritage into the key of Aristotle left an opening for later misunderstandings. To speak of a natural desire whose fulfillment is supernatural created an almost unbearable tension in later theology, leading ultimately to the rupture between the two orders.

The tension between the natural and the supernatural was exacerbated by a second early modern movement—Nominalism. A philosophical theory that emerged in the fourteenth and fifteenth centuries, Nominalism denied the existence of universal concepts outside of the mind. It marked an intellectual shift away from reason and toward the will as the central theological category—both for understanding the human person and for understanding God. Its effects are seen clearly in moral theology. For if there are no universal moral principles (rooted, for example, in human nature), then what remains are simply individual laws created by the absolutely free (and perhaps even arbitrary) will of God. Morality is not conformity to the rational order of creation but conformity to the will of the Creator. This emphasis on the divine will had distant roots in Augustine's theology of love. It reemerged in Francis of Assisi's experience of God's concrete concern for individual creatures. And it passed through the Franciscan tradition to John Duns Scotus's emphasis on the primacy of the will. In William of Ockham and in the later Nominalists, this emphasis on God's freedom over the world would help push God out of the world. For when creation is determined not by rational order but by arbitrary will, the link between Creator and creature becomes tenuous.

According to Dupré, a key move of the Nominalists was to take the scholastic distinction between what God *can* do (*potentia absoluta*) and what God actually does (*potentia ordinata*) and transform it into two successive moments: "At a first time God possesses absolute power which he at a second time entrusts to secondary causes."[73] The turning over of power to secondary causes—those ordinary interactions of created beings—opened the door for a world that functions well enough on its own. In earlier scholasticism, God did not surrender divine power to natural causes. Instead God's primary causality remained fully operative *in* the secondary causes.[74] In Nominalism, the order of secondary causes became more independent. This newly independent world of secondary causes not only impacted the theological understanding of creation but also affected the nature-grace relationship. "The concept of an unrestricted divine power in the Nominalist theologies of the fourteenth and fifteenth centuries weakened the intelligibility of the relation between Creator and creature. Unconditioned divine power negatively affected any rational a priori for predicting the order of nature, and it had an equally unsettling effect on the theology of grace. Granted by an inscrutable divine decree, grace might be randomly dispensed or withheld regardless of the recipient's moral condition."[75] Not only did this shift introduce an anxiety over the arbitrariness of grace but it also fundamentally changed the relationship of this grace to nature. Once nature (i.e., creation, secondary causality, the world) became an independent entity, a closed system functioning on its own and toward its own end, the order of grace could only be seen as a divine addition, an intrusion or supernatural "add-on" to the order of nature.

The Supernatural

In sixteenth-century commentators on Aquinas, Aristotle's self-contained nature and the Nominalists' all-powerful but distant God mix, producing a wholly new theology of grace. Significant here was one of Aquinas's most influential commentators, the Dominican Thomas de Vio Cajetan. Cajetan dismissed Aquinas's notion of humanity's "natural desire" for a supernatural end, calling it a theological comment, not a philosophical one. In his commentary, Cajetan proceeded to attribute to Thomas what is not there, namely, a conception of the redeemed human person as constituted by two independent orders, nature and grace, each with its own finality. For Cajetan, a pure human nature, fully constituted apart from grace, is not simply a heuristic category, a kind of logical possibility useful for clarification (as it functions in Aquinas). For Cajetan, it is a true reality. Many of Cajetan's contemporaries expressed reservations about this interpretation. But the controversies surrounding two Louvain theologians, Baius and Jansenius, quickly led most theologians to adopt the idea of "pure nature" as a convenient weapon to fight these heresies. When Jansenius denied the possibility that God could have created human beings in a purely natural state, these theologians argued that not only *could* God have done it but that God *did* do it. God allows human nature, with its purely natural end, to coexist with the state of grace. Later theologians hardened this distinction into a separation. Thus grace became a super-nature, "a sort of second story carefully placed on top of a lower nature by the heavenly Architect."[76] Henri de Lubac—whose 1946 study *Surnaturel* exposed this theological devolution—argued that by the nineteenth century the theory of "pure nature" had become so ingrained that to deny it was tantamount to denying the gratuity of grace.[77]

De Lubac's argument was primarily historical: the concept of "pure nature" was a modern innovation that diverged from the patristic and medieval tradition.[78] But he also recognized the philosophical difficulty. To imagine nature and grace as two distinct orders set side by side (or one on top of the other) is to reduce them to two categories within the same genus. Such a move overlooks the totally transcendent nature of grace—a bit like trying to put the finite and the infinite in the same box. By clearly separating grace from nature, neoscholastic theologians believed that they were protecting the transcendence of God's grace. In fact, they radically domesticated it. The ultimate orientation of the human person toward the infinite love of God was reduced to one nature among others, a "super-nature" added onto, but not integral to, human life. For de Lubac, this two-story view of things risked nothing less than a complete separation of faith from life, with a profound impact on all aspects of culture. Philosophy and anthropology no longer needed the divine to explain the human person. Deist thinkers could simply ignore it. And the great nineteenth-century masters of suspicion would find it all too easy to knock off the top floor of this poorly constructed neoscholastic edifice. The theologians not only prepared the way for the cultural alienation of Christianity, by turning God into an external agent and extrinsic force, but they also laid the groundwork for the rise of modern atheism.[79]

For those who hung to belief, all that the theologians could offer was a distant God hovering above the cosmos and a miraculous grace detached from the heart. In an effort to reconnect the human and the divine, the manualists increasingly turned to the category of "actual grace." In an earlier era, actual grace was a relatively minor theological topic. Rather than actual grace, Aquinas's system revolved around sanctifying grace, what he more often called "habitual grace," namely, the effect within the human person of God's saving offer of love. However, Aquinas did acknowledge—against Pelagianism and semi-Pelagianism—that some divine assistance was necessary to help the nonjustified person do good. Following the Council of Trent, this category of actual or auxiliary ("helping") grace rapidly expanded to include the divine assistance needed for any number of particular good actions. Envisioned as an extrinsic and transient force—a power or energy coming from God and granted for this or for that—actual grace came to dominate theological debates and pastoral life.[80] The sixteenth century was lost in a protracted theological debate (the *De Auxiliis* controversy) that broke out between the Dominicans and the Jesuits over the precise relationship of human freedom to these various divine aids. Meanwhile, the church was transformed into a relay station within a vast network of actual graces, directing these bursts of divine help through sacramental rites, appropriate penances, private prayers, pilgrimages, and medals—lighting up everything from miraculous cures and deathbed conversions to ordinary moral acts and major vocational decisions.

Within this world, when theologians reflected on vocation, they brought to that reflection certain assumptions about the relationship of the natural and the supernatural that went largely unexamined. They tended to explain vocation as a kind of actual grace, and they debated, well into the twentieth century, the precise nature of this grace. Not surprisingly, these debates over the nature of vocation replayed the same debates that marked the *De Auxiliis* controversy.[81] But more interesting to us than the intricacies of their differing positions is the basic assumption that they all shared: the grace of vocation was an outside force touching the soul of an individual. As the supernatural became unhinged from human nature, the "turn inward" that characterized the early modern spiritual traditions was radically altered. In the approach to discernment taking shape, the journey within leads to something foreign. I listen for my vocation and hear something strange. It was not the interiorization of vocation alone that caused the problem. It was this interiorization combined with an extrinsic and reified notion of grace. A vocation became some "thing," placed in the individual by God, but difficult to determine. Thus from the seventeenth century on, Catholic theologians writing on priestly formation all struggled with the same question: how do we know when someone "has" a vocation?

The Secret Voice

As we saw in our discussion of Olier, repeated calls for clergy reform in seventeenth-century France ushered in a variety of proposals for better assessing candidates for the priesthood. Theologians increasingly sought out the "marks" of a true priestly vocation—external signs and minimum standards that professors and confessors could use to judge individual seminarians. And soon, these theologians were offering up a dizzying array of such marks. In fact, in the manual tradition that followed, one of the exercises always included was the attempt to reconcile the differing lists of earlier authors. In the seventeenth century, the Paris moralist François Hallier named three marks of a vocation: purity of life, right intention, and the absence of unworthy or deceitful means in seeking ordination. A century later Alphonsus Liguori would offer his own triad: purity of intention, talents, and goodness of character.[82] A manualist by the name of Godeau had listed nine. The *Traité des saints ordres* described four. What these many different lists shared were two commonsensical signs of a genuine vocation: the candidate's suitability for ministry and the proper intention in entering into it. The category of suitability—which could include anything from the absence of canonical impediments to the requisite education to the candidate's personal holiness—seemed to rely on the healthy assumption that if God had intended a man for the priesthood, God would have created him with the gifts appropriate to such an end. The category of intention looked instead at the motivation of the candidate. In various forms we see some configuration of these two elements—external suitability and inner intention—in virtually all treatments of vocation during this period.

The need for adequate criteria for discerning a divine calling took on greater existential urgency as post-Reformation debates on providence and predestination entered into the theological treatment of vocation. Increasingly, theologians tied one's state of life to one's state of grace, thus linking vocation to salvation. The logic was this: if God had predestined a particular state of life for an individual, then God would have prepared for that individual the appropriate graces for that state, and not for any other. Thus to deny one's vocation would be to deny God's grace, and thus endanger one's soul. More than anyone else, it was the Italian saint and moral theologian Alphonsus de Liguori who popularized the notion that God eternally predestines every individual to a particular state of life. Liguori's position on vocation took shape within his broader conviction that holiness is within the grasp of every human being. Every state of life is compatible with sanctity. The key is to discover the state of life that God intended for you.

Liguori began his treatise on the religious vocation with this thesis: "It is evident that our eternal salvation depends principally upon the choice of our state of life. Father Granada calls this choice the chief wheel of our whole life. Hence, as when in a clock the chief wheel is deranged, the whole clock is also deranged, so in the order of our salvation, if we make a mistake as to the state to which we are called, our whole life, as St. Gregory Nazianzen says, will be an error."[83] The person who does not respond to his God-given vocation is like a dislocated limb, "which may be able to perform its functions, but only with difficulty and in an awkward manner."[84] Yet, for Liguori, God has destined each person to a particular state and so has prepared suitable helps and graces for that state. Therefore, to reject one's vocation—particularly a religious vocation—is not just to risk an awkward life but also to seriously imperil one's soul. Liguori repeated as a chorus a line from Augustine to the effect that such a person may run well, but will run in the wrong direction. And his treatise is full of cautionary tales, like the bright young man who leaves the novitiate, falls out of prayer and into the bed of a wicked woman, only to be murdered one night on the way home—expiring on the steps of the very monastery he had abandoned, moments before the priests arrive, too late to administer the last rites![85]

Liguori's treatment of the vocation to religious life is filled with a sense of urgency about responding to this call, the "do not delay" that we saw in Aquinas. He quoted Francis de Sales to point out that the call to religious life does not need an angel to announce itself, nor does it require ten or twelve doctors from the Sorbonne to determine if it is there.[86] But when Liguori turned to the priestly vocation, we see a greater sense of caution. When it comes to the priesthood, one should not rush in. Here was a concern for discernment more characteristic of the French school. No doubt this emphasis reflects Liguori's own experience as bishop of Naples, which in 1762 had far too many priests—and far too many of them uninterested and ill equipped for ministry. Liguori wrote, "To enter any state of life, a divine vocation is necessary; for without such a vocation it is, if not impossible, at least most difficult to fulfill the obligations of our state, and obtain salvation. But if for all states a vocation is necessary, it is necessary in a particular manner for the ecclesiastical state. *He that entereth not by the door into the sheepfold, but climbeth up another way, the same is a thief and a robber.*"[87] The same sense of eternal anxiety about discovering one's vocation pervades his treatment here. The only difference is that instead of worrying about those who do not enter religious life when they should, his concern is now those who enter the priesthood when they should not.

This particular interpretation of predestination passed from the early French theologians, through Liguori, to the great moral and canonical manuals of the nineteenth century. Pietro Scavini and Pietro Gasparri both adopted some version of this predestination theory.[88] In their manuals, a distinct chapter appears on "The Obligation to Follow a Vocation," placed between chapters on the "Nature and Necessity of Vocation" and

"The Marks of a Vocation." Predestination brought with it obligation. Here the earlier distinction between counsels and commands was played off of Alphonsus's tendency to collapse the two. Moreover, the primary responsibility for discerning a vocation moved out of the hands of the bishop and into the heart of the individual candidate, where—with the help of a spiritual director—it was weighed and reviewed as a moral problem. All of this heightened the importance of delineating criteria by which to judge the authenticity of the divine call.

In a theological universe where grace and nature were seen as two distinct orders (*duplex order*), the inner call of God (itself supernatural) could not be known in itself, and the seemingly "natural" standards of suitability and intention did not appear as adequate indicators of it. These natural marks did not seem sufficient to identify the action of God in the soul. Some further assurance was needed. As noted above, the seventeenth century had witnessed the appearance of that assurance, which Jean-Jacques Olier listed as the first sign of a true vocation: the inner inclination of the soul manifested through a strong and steady attraction to the ecclesiastical state. For Olier, the attraction was not the call. This feeling was not the grace of vocation; rather, the attraction was the effect of this grace in the soul. However, in the theological tradition that followed, the two become virtually identified, so that to speak of the attraction was to speak of the call itself.

In the context of the seminary reform movements of 1630s and 1640s Paris, we start to see the notion of an inner call—long associated with the monks and the mendicants—applied to the secular clergy through this category of attraction. This was the world of Olier, newly arrived as pastor of the parish of Saint-Sulpice. It was the world of Vincent de Paul, who in 1631 began leading his famed ordination retreats in the city. It was the world of priest theologians like Godeau, Hallier, and others whose lectures were preserved and where we can still hear their repeated, but undeveloped, insistence on the absolute necessity of an inner inclination to the priesthood. In his two-volume history of French seminaries, Antoine Degert saw a direct link between the seminary reform movements and the development of the concept of the inner call.[89] Certainly, as we have seen, the ecclesiastical climate was right for new ideas and new approaches to emerge. In his *Letters and Conferences*, Vincent de Paul instructed those leading his retreats to introduce the notion of God's call: "On the second day, the lecturer will treat of the vocation to the ecclesiastical state and he will impress upon the ordinands the necessity of having been called by God before they present themselves for Orders.

He will explain to them in what this vocation consists, what are its marks and what the means by which they may correspond with it."[90] The moralist Hallier, who was leading ordination retreats at de Paul's Collège des Bon-Enfants in 1631, offered up a line frequently cited by later manualists: "God gives this call by means of a secret voice whereby He speaks to the soul of the aspirant and invites him to embrace the clerical state. No one should be admitted to sacred orders whom God has not invited to the ministry at least by a secret voice."[91]

Hallier's vivid image of a "secret voice" points to a growing consensus among French theologians that the call to the priesthood was primarily an interior vocation, the whisper of God within the depths of the soul. This secret voice was variously described as a personal revelation, a special inspiration, a more ordinary grace—its precise nature would be debated well into the twentieth century. But what all participants in this debate shared was the common assumption that the "secret voice" came as an extrinsic, supernatural addition to an integral nature: it was something that God places "in" the candidate. Through the lens of the *duplex ordo*, these authors saw vocation separated from personality. Moreover, virtually all agreed that this inner, supernatural call was a necessary prerequisite to ordination. And many of them cited the Council of Trent in support of their position. A passage from the twenty-third session was a key source:

> The holy council further teaches that in the ordination of bishops, priests and other ministers neither the consent nor calling nor authority of the people or of any secular power or functionary is so required that without it the ordination would be invalid. On the contrary, it declares that those who are raised to the exercise of these ministries when called and appointed only by a secular power and functionary, and those who have the temerity to assume such office themselves, are to be regarded one and all, not as ministers of the church, but as thieves and robbers who have not entered by the sheepgate.[92]

Here the council underscored the unique authority of the hierarchy to confer ordination, in direct response to the Protestant claim that the consent of the people was required. The focus of the passage was on the necessity of the external, ecclesiastical call. But in an astonishing reversal of Trent's intent, later theologians like Liguori named as thieves and robbers not those who have been called forth by the people, the civil magistrate, or their own ambition, that is, those without hierarchical approval and valid ordination. Instead, the thieves and robbers were identified as those priests who may have been validly ordained but who did not have a true inner call from God. A similar transformation of texts can be seen in their use of the passage from Hebrews found in the tridentine catechism. To be "called by God as Aaron was" was no longer identified with the call of the bishop. It now referred to those who have heard the "secret voice" in their souls calling them into the priesthood.[93]

Degert argues that Olier's view of the soul's inclination toward the ecclesiastical state was anticipated by Godeau, who was already leading ordination retreats in Paris in the 1630s and who included attraction among his own list of nine marks of a vocation.[94] Still, it was Olier's view of inclination—modified by Tronson in the *Traité des saints ordres*—that launched the Sulpician tradition and gave birth to what would come to be known as the "attraction theory" of vocation. The importance of attraction among the marks of a divine vocation was kept alive by the Sulpician seminary apostolate; it received some impetus as Quietism—with its emphasis on passivity and the soul's abandonment to the movement of grace—moved from Italy into France, and it re-emerged with force in the nineteenth-century manualists, where the "theory of attraction" achieved near-canonical status. Scavini saw "a certain singular attraction for this state" as the first sign of a divine vocation to the priesthood. Such an attraction was recognized as authentic if it was "sweet, constant and strong."[95] Gasparri wrote:

> The ordinary sign of the ecclesiastical vocation is a certain supernatural sense which inclines a man to embrace the clerical state with a view to God's glory and the salvation of his neighbors. God generally does not call a man to the clerical state without inclining him interiorly by a certain supernatural attraction. . . . If this inclination is present and if it is constant and strong; if it is conceived with a right intention; if it is accompanied by the effects indicated (namely, ardent charity, zeal for sacred things and care for things divine); if it is accompanied furthermore by sufficient knowledge and due sanctity; if there is no other impediment; if, finally, the bishop, after examination, admits the candidate and judges him necessary or useful, divine vocation is morally certain.[96]

In the authoritative Gasparri, the attraction itself is called supernatural. It is not one mark among others but the central reality of which all other signs of a vocation are simply manifestations.

In the work of the Sulpician priest and superior of the Grand Séminaire d'Orléans, Louis Branchereau, the theory of attraction reached its high point and its term. In his 1896 treatise, *De la Vocation Sacerdotale*, Branchereau lifted up attraction as the essential and indispensable mark of a genuine vocation. He dedicated the four central chapters of his book to exploring the nature, characteristics, and necessity of *l'attrait*, which he defined as "a strong and permanent inclination that carries us toward an object and makes us desire its possession."[97] He described this attraction as both affective and directive, that is, one experienced both as a "pull" toward a particular state of life and a "push" from within, an imperative imposed by God on the soul. This "secret instinct" is experienced and known by a person through an inclination that is constant, pervasive (*la prédominance*), and marked by humility.[98] While attraction was not the only prerequisite necessary for a vocation, it was the absolutely essential one. Even with all the other personal qualities and characteristics required for the priesthood, without this inner inclination felt deep within the soul, for Branchereau, there is no vocation.

In his widely discussed 1909 treatise, *La Vocation Sacerdotale*, Joseph Lahitton presented Branchereau as a faithful interpreter of the theory of attraction, which Lahitton claimed to be the widely held and commonly assumed position of his day.[99] It was a theory against which Lahitton himself would mount a full frontal assault, attacking it as impractical, untraditional, and dangerous to the life of the church. In *La Vocation Sacerdotale* (a title that mimicked the title of Branchereau's earlier book), Lahitton painted *l'attrait* as a subjective, quasi-mystical theory that, on the one hand, demanded a supernatural revelation of God whispered into the heart of every seminarian and, on the other hand, downplayed the traditional role of the bishop in calling forth ministers. Picking up several of the historical threads we have been tracing, Lahitton presented them as a unified position. According to Lahitton, the theory of attraction abides by the following logic: "One has the right to destine oneself for the priesthood only if God has predestined him to it. Vocation is the manifestation in an individual of this divine predestination. Thus, before choosing the priesthood as a state of life, it is necessary to listen for the voice of God within oneself. This voice of God results in an attraction that is spontaneous, constant, and almost irresistible, carrying one toward the priesthood."[100] According to Lahitton, two consequences follow. First, without this constant, irresistible inclination of the soul, an individual should not even consider the priesthood. Second, if one does in fact feel this attraction, then that person has a right to demand entrance into the seminary and, ultimately, ordination, for to deny him that end would run counter to the will of God and place the immortal soul of the candidate at risk.

Subsequent commentators rightly accused Lahitton of setting up a straw man in his generalizations about attraction. Indeed, no author—not even Branchereau—held all of the positions that Lahitton attributed to the theory. Nevertheless, Lahitton revealed in a rather dramatic way some of the negative consequences of the interiorization of vocation. His primary motivation was to address the deleterious effects certain assumptions were having on the recruitment and training of priests. As a seminary professor, Lahitton believed that an overemphasis on attraction was drawing to the seminary what he called "pious mediocrities" and certain other candidates (the "overly proud," *orgueilleux*) who presumed that their inner calling freed them from any need to learn and grow. Moreover, the theory could easily discourage good candidates, who, even though they were obviously gifted for the ministry and sincerely committed to it, still did not hear the "secret voice" or feel the mysterious pull of grace in their soul, and so faced constant anxiety about whether or not they were truly called. But worse than the admission of mediocre candidates or the discouragement of good ones was the exclusion of the best. Since everyone assumed that God must first work in the soul of a young man, calling him to the priesthood, Lahitton wondered how many truly excellent priests had been lost because no one ever thought to suggest the possibility to them.

Although Lahitton oversimplified the "theory" he critiqued, he accurately observed that something new had appeared in the seventeenth century—an emphasis on the "inner call" to the priesthood and an increased attention to the notion of attraction as the prime factor in discerning this call. Lahitton presented his own position as the traditional one, a position summarized in a line from the tridentine catechism that he selected as the epigraph of his book: "They are called by God who are called by the lawful ministers of his church." Citing St. Paul, John Chrysostom, Cyril of Alexandria, Cornelius a Lapide, Bernard of Clairvaux, Thomas Aquinas, Francis de Sales, Alphonsus Liguori, the Council of Trent, and a host of other witnesses, Lahitton strove to demonstrate his central thesis: "The divine call to the priesthood, formally and properly understood, in the scriptural and canonical sense, is essentially the invitation to receive the priesthood that is addressed to an individual, in the name of God and in virtue of divine authority, by the legitimate minister of the church."[101] At first, Lahitton appeared simply to be harkening back to the earlier distinction between the internal call of the monk and the external call of the cleric. In the first edition of his book, he made it clear that he was not talking about all vocations but only the call to the priesthood: "This little treatise speaks only of the *priestly* vocation. One would be wrong in extending the principles here set forward to other vocations. With regard to religious profession, one is free to think that a divine call is necessary or that one can be carried by one's own choice."[102] But in subsequent editions, Lahitton blurred the issue, indicating that the book's principles could be more broadly applied.[103]

Lahitton's thesis sparked immediate and intense debate within the seminaries of France and beyond.[104] In response to a request for clarification, Pope Pius X appointed a special commission of cardinals to investigate Lahitton's book, chaired by the secretary of state Cardinal Merry del Val. In July 1912, Merry del Val sent to the bishop of Aire a letter, in which he concluded that the work of Lahitton should not be condemned but in fact should be praised for making three important points. First, no one has a right to ordination prior to the bishop's decision. Second, no special interior attraction or invitation from the Holy Spirit is required for ordination. And finally, all that is required for the bishop to ordain is the proper intention together with the suitability that would give a well-founded hope that the candidate would be able to exercise this ministry in a holy way.[105] This verdict, coming with the express approval of the pope, seemed to have settled the matter. At least it closed the door on certain exaggerated interpretations of the attraction theory. Some observers saw in this letter a wholesale endorsement of Lahitton's "external vocation theory," underscoring the juridical and hierarchical dimension as essential to the work of God in calling forth priests. More careful commentators pointed out that the Merry del Val letter was quite circumscribed, rejecting (in most cases) the necessity of an inner experience of attraction or a special revelation of the Holy Spirit, but not in any way denying the role of divine grace in the vocational process. They argued that, having avoided the extreme of a quasi-mystical "secret voice," Lahitton's theory risked the opposite extreme, namely, a pragmatic institutionalism that overlooked the activity of God in the soul.[106]

What frustrated the conversation as a whole was the deficient theology of grace that ran beneath it. Neither side could find a way to talk about the deep intimacy of God's call without presupposing a dualism that ultimately kept this call at a distance. As actual grace, vocation was reified. As supernatural grace, vocation was externalized. Vocation became some thing *in* an individual that was separate *from* that individual. In this theological worldview, the metaphor of the "secret voice" became literalized. And God's call turned into a kind of communiqué—sealed orders squirreled away in the soul, which could ask anything of anyone. Lahitton was right to point out the dangers of this approach. Where he went wrong was in defining vocation without any reference to the inner life. His problem was that he shared with his opponents a theology of grace that was simply incapable of describing the depth of vocation.

Conclusion

In the vision of Ignatius we find a truly modern spirituality—one that embraced the individual and took her or his inner experience seriously. The *Exercises* anticipate modernity's "turn to the subject" but avoid the danger of subjectivism, thanks to Ignatius's dynamic appreciation for the primacy and pervasiveness of grace. It is the rich theological anthropology implicit in his system that serves to link the infinite God with the finite human person, offering nothing less than a method for determining the divine will for each individual, original life. According to Ignatius, one can come to hear God's particular call by listening to one's heart. Affections, emotions, inclinations—these are the clues to the subtle movements of God within. Bérulle too found a path through the affections, even with his more static and pessimistic view of the person. In the correspondence between our inner life and that of the Son, Bérulle opened a way to that identification with Christ and adherence to God that gives meaning to life. And in Olier, we see Bérulle's vision applied in a positive way to the inner attraction that Olier found at the core of the call to the ordained priesthood.

As we charted the subsequent interiorization of vocation in modern Catholic theology, we saw mostly devolution from the insights of these spiritual masters. The conviction that we can connect with God through our inner life remained. Seminary manuals insisted that one can know one's vocation by attending to the inclination or attractions of the soul. But detached from the great spiritual traditions of Ignatius or Bérulle, and marred by a split between nature and grace, the theology of vocation struggled to explain just how this works. Theologians simply did not have the categories to describe a genuine insight, namely, that God speaks to the heart. Thus the voice of God was either restricted to the official channels of revelation and church, on the one hand, or reduced to a mystical illumination or miraculous impulse, on the other. Those who wanted to affirm a deeper experience of call were forced by the nature-grace divide to imagine this call as a kind of external energy sparking one soul but not another. Vocation became a supernatural addition to the person's natural constitution, one that could arbitrarily alter the course of one's life, and which—according to Liguori—you had better get right. Thus it was not the interiorization of vocation that marginalized the concept. It was the interiorization of vocation combined with the extrinsicism of grace that reduced it to a secret, and too often silent, voice.

When the Second Vatican Council broke open the category of vocation with its unequivocal affirmation of the universal call to holiness, all of these neoscholastic debates faded away. But many of the underlying assumptions remained in place. And today, Catholics continue to talk about vocation in ways that are both overly institutionalized and overly interiorized. The modern Catholic theology of vocation still has a hold. So as we come to the conclusion of part 1, it is good to acknowledge the complex legacy of this history. We may rightly critique the way in which, for centuries, Catholicism restricted the category of vocation to the priesthood and religious life, or question the way church documents continue to follow a deductive approach that confines God's call to a few states of life. We may challenge a theology of supernatural grace that reifies vocation or turns discernment into a pseudo-mystical scavenger hunt. However, within this history of the institutionalization and the interiorization of vocation lie, waiting to be recovered, the resources for a broader and more holistic vision. In Francis de Sales's inclusive view of holiness and his graced view of the person, in Ignatius of Loyola's attention to experience and his appreciation for narrative, in Vatican II's world-affirming spirituality and its sensitivity to history, we find the building blocks for a contemporary theology of call. In the last half century, Catholicism has seen a revival, a renewal, even a revolution, in its understanding of God and the human person, in its ecclesiology and its ethics. But the greatest theological transformation is the one that runs underneath all of these—a revolution in the theology of grace. If we are still struggling to talk about the breadth and depth of God's call in ways that are intellectually cogent, spiritually meaningful, and pastorally relevant, it is because we have not yet thought through vocation in light of this grace revolution. Part 2 sets out to do some of this thinking.

PART TWO

Awakening Vocation

CHAPTER THREE

God Calls . . .

There are many types and kinds of vocation, but the core of the experience is always the same: the soul is awakened by it, transformed or exalted, so that instead of dreams and presentiments from within a summons comes from without. A portion of reality presents itself and makes its claim.

—Hermann Hesse[1]

And those whom he predestined he also called; and those whom he called he also justified; and those whom he justified he also glorified.

—Romans 8:30

A theology of vocation begins with the God who calls. What does God have in mind for me? What does God want for me? What is the will of God for my life? To speak of vocation as a call from God implies that there is in God some intentionality, some orientation or direction, some purpose or plan that invites me in and moves me forward. To speak of vocation is to see that the most important thing about *me* is my existence within this wider plan of God.

Providence is the name that theologians give to this divine plan. It is the claim that God not only creates the world, but cares for it. God remains continually present to us, guiding all of creation to its goal. Providence is at root a comforting belief. It proclaims that God is not an arbitrary tyrant, and the world is not a random mess. Rather, what seem to be the haphazard—and often disappointing—events of life are in fact all part of a master plan crafted by a loving parent. If God feeds the birds of the air and clothes the lilies of the field, surely this God must care for us as well. The doctrine of divine providence has always hovered around theological discussions of vocation, and so we cannot avoid it here. Indeed, we take it up first, for vocation is ultimately about the plan of God as it takes shape in an individual life. For all that we will have to say about this individual life—the subject who stands at the center of vocational discernment—we must begin by recognizing that it is not simply my drives and my desires that lead to my vocation. No matter how much it flows through me and is a part of me, my vocation originates beyond me. The summons comes from without. It is God who calls.

At the start, we recognize that providence has its problems. The comfort of knowing that "God has a plan" can quickly give way to a foreboding question: what is that plan? For all its centrality to the life of the believer, God's plan is remarkably inconspicuous. It is frustratingly inaccessible to us. We have a hard time knowing just exactly what God wants us to do. It seems to me that those who speak most confidently about the unfolding of providence in their lives see it best in retrospect—the failed project that opened new avenues, the chance meeting that blossomed into a lifelong commitment. God's plan is harder to see in front of us. There are always a few individuals who feel in the present moment that God is clearly calling them to something very particular. Most of us, however, lack that kind of clarity. We yearn to know what God wants. Such is the reality of human beings caught up in the designs of the divine. From our perspective, the problem with the plan is that it is hidden.

This hiddenness becomes all too evident when the smooth course of life is interrupted by personal tragedy, disillusionment, or significant and difficult decisions. Here we face a crisis, a moment of response, a consequential choice. We may even face the breakdown of meaning itself. Where is God in this? Indeed, looming at the edge of our consciousness are a host of interruptions that threaten to break in and upset any comfortable notion we may have of God's providence: whole continents of peoples abused and misused, unending war and ongoing cycles of violence, so much suffering alongside so much affluence, and our slow, stupid march toward ecological self-destruction. Where is God in *this*? Are we so sure that God is not a tyrant, that the world is not a mess? Martin Luther looked out on a suffering world that was sadly similar to our own and admitted that only faith keeps us from wondering, If there really is a God, can this God be just?[2] In the face of suffering on a global scale, we are right to suspect that there is something deeply unsatisfactory about any simple appeal to "God's plan."

This chapter explores the notion of providence, but its goal is not to begin building a theology of vocation on it. Chapter 1 already noted some of the difficulties of just such an approach. Rather, the goal here is to clear the ground—to confront head-on the notion of "God's plan" in order to overcome some of our limited conceptions about it. Doing so will raise impossible theological questions concerning the problem of evil and the relation of human freedom to divine sovereignty—problems that this chapter does not pretend to solve. Yet, alongside these theoretical difficulties is a more immediate, existential, and ethical question for which we do want some clarity: what is the will of God for my life? The following pages explore the relationship of vocation and divine providence with this question in mind. They acknowledge God's plan but take its hiddenness—in individual lives and in our world—seriously.

While there are many ways to approach this topic, we take our point of departure from the work of the Reformed theologian Karl Barth. Not only did Barth produce a classic commentary on the Protestant trajectory of vocation, thus culling insights from the tradition we met in chapter 1, but he also took up directly the question of divine hiddenness. Barth's massive theological project was, in part, a response to the predicament brought on by the unknown plan of a hidden God. What he helps us to see is that the proper starting point for a theology of vocation is not the plan of God, but the God whose plan it is.

The Plan of God

Karl Barth is best known for his public opposition to the Nazi regime and for his theological emphasis on the utter transcendence of God. These two facts are closely related. For Barth, theology's forgetfulness of the God of Jesus Christ had diluted its ability to confront human evil in general, and the idolatry of the Third Reich in particular. Thus he rejected both the modern myth of human progress and the subjectivism of liberal Protestantism. Instead, he directed his readers back to God as the proper subject matter of theology. Suspicious of forms of analogy that sought points of contact between God and humanity, Barth stressed God as "wholly other"—one whom we can only approach thanks to God's initiative in becoming "God for us" in Jesus Christ.

Barth's doctrine of God and his prophetic witness are well known. What is less well known is that Barth authored some of the twentieth century's greatest paragraphs on vocation. His treatment of this topic stands as a historical and theological tour de force that, despite whatever reservations we might raise about Barth's larger system or his final conclusions, demands serious consideration. In the pages that follow, we enter into Barth's theology of vocation through the question of divine providence and predestination. This approach reveals his attempt to situate all human callings within the one divine call that comes from God in Jesus Christ.

Catholic Vocations and Protestant Callings

In part 1, we charted the quite different trajectories of vocation emerging out of the Reformation. Put bluntly, Catholics largely kept vocation within the sacred sphere of religious life or ecclesiastical ministry. Protestants extended calling into the secular world of work and family. Recall, for example, Alphonsus Liguori's uncompromising exhortations on religious vocations. Remember too Luther's equally uncompromising antimonastic polemic. Along these two different trajectories, and in very different ways, both traditions struggled to explain how divine providence plays out in the process of vocational discernment.

The eighteenth-century saint Alphonsus Liguori stands as a classic exponent of the modern Catholic theology of vocation. Saint Alphonsus is usually remembered for his sane and humane moral system. His life had been deeply touched by Francis de Sales's spirituality of God's universal saving will. It was a vision that—along with Liguori's own pastoral experience—helped move the Neapolitan bishop beyond the negative rigorism of his youth. The basic premise of Liguori's mature ascetical works is that God's call to holiness extends to all people and every way of life. But this emphasis stands in somewhat surprising contrast to his more rigid treatment of vocations to the priesthood and religious life. Here the emphasis shifts from God's love to our response. In encouraging young men and women to enter religious life, Liguori ratcheted up the eternal significance of this life decision and, with it, the anxiety that comes with such a choice. For Liguori, choosing a state of life is of the greatest import. It is the chief wheel on which the whole of life turns. To make a mistake about one's vocation is a greater danger than that of any individual sin, for if a person "violates a particular command, he may rise from his fault, and begin again to walk in the right path; but he who errs in his vocation mistakes the way itself."[3]

More than any other figure, Liguori shaped a certain Catholic assumption about vocation, namely, that God, in an eternal decision before all time, selects out a particular state of life for each individual. God's plan is a very specific blueprint for each person. And vocational discernment is the rather perilous process of trying to discover that hidden plan. Liguori used the analogy of a great king who calls a poor shepherd to join his court. How great would be the offense if the king were to be refused? How much greater would be the offense against the Lord of all were his call to join in his service to be ignored? "God knows well the value of his graces, and therefore he chastises with severity those who despise them."[4] What links a "missed" vocation to divine chastisement is providence. Liguori argued that God allots particular graces to particular lives according to divine providence. Missing your vocation in itself is not what cuts you off from eternal salvation; rather, by missing your vocation, you miss out on all those "abundant and efficacious helps" that God has designed precisely for you *in this state of life.* Without these graces, salvation is virtually impossible. His proof-text came from Paul: "God gives to every one his vocation, and chooses the state in which he wills him to be saved. And this is the order of predestination described by the same apostle: *Whom he predestinated, them he also called; and whom he called, them he also justified, . . . and them he also glorified.*"[5] By interpreting Paul's *kletos* ("called") in this passage as the call to a particular state of life, Liguori conflated this particular vocation with the general call to salvation that Paul saw coming to the elect through Christ.

The simple fact that the call of Christ is not as clear as the call of an earthly king fueled among later commentators a frantic search for "signs" of a vocation. In chapter 2, we saw Catholic treatises on religious life transform vocational discernment into a minefield of spiritual risk. God's plan was kept secret, buried deep in the heart, elusive in prayer. Yet it was absolutely essential to one's salvation. This hiddenness of God's sovereign decree left the destiny of each human being in the dark. Thus the individual fell into a desperate search for some sign to relieve the almost unbearable tension of not knowing whether the next step would bring the possibility of salvation or the certainty of eternal damnation.

Protestants came at the question of vocational discernment from a quite different direction. Luther's critique of the monastery system, together with his deeper convictions about God's grace, led him to broaden the notion of *Beruf* to include various social roles and manners of life. These can all be callings coming from God. Luther not only broadened the notion of vocation but he also specified it by focusing on *Stand*, one's state or station in life. *Stand* was central because it is precisely in one's station that the Christian is called to serve God and neighbor. It is *there* that we love. We need not look elsewhere, fleeing to the monastery or hiding in the convent. In fact, this flight may actually be a sinful attempt to escape the particular responsibility that God has assigned.

Over the course of the modern period, Catholics writing on vocation were preoccupied with the call to religious life and priesthood. Thus their emphasis was on choosing and changing one's state of life. In contrast, Protestants were guided by Luther's gloss on St. Paul's exhortation to "abide in your calling." Seeing the various realms and functions of society as God-given, Protestant preaching tended to emphasize not the call to change but the virtue of staying put. Within this trajectory, the plan of God was not some mysterious secret or silent voice. God's plan was simply the way things were. Running just below the surface of these treatments of vocation were the strong currents of providence and God's predestinating will. One's path in life was preordained no less for the Protestant proponents of vocation than it was for their Catholic counterparts. But with the emphasis on social conformity, the shape and expectations of one's vocation were easier to see. If there was a danger in this Protestant trajectory, the danger was not the unknown of a hidden call. It was the seduction of the status quo. And while Luther's medieval world passed away, his words remained. In later times, in the face of greater social mobility, Luther's theology of vocation supported a certain conservatism. This conservatism appeared in those Protestant preachers who encouraged the faithful to accept their lot in life, and not to flit from place to place or to meddle in other people's affairs. The exhortation to "remain in your calling" also meant to stay within it, not to transgress its boundaries or seek to reform the larger social order.[6] This binding of providence to a divinely ordained social order continued on into the twentieth century, reappearing in a sophisticated and nuanced way in a contemporary of Barth's, Emil Brunner.[7]

Brunner linked the idea of calling to divine providence directly. But he was very much aware of the danger that the notion of providence brought with it. By threatening to justify the status quo, providence has the potential to paralyze the moral will.[8] So Brunner distinguished between the past, on the one hand, and the present that leads into the future, on the other. God may determine the concrete and definite "place," the sphere within which I act (past), but I still have to act and take responsibility for that action (present-to-future). It is the "place," the context for action, that is God-given; this is the decree of providence that is my calling. But we are still free to act within it. Here, it is important to underscore the "within." For Brunner, we act within a divinely established social order. For that reason, he criticized those who see "the reform of life as a *principle*." Such a person "feels himself called upon to 'clean up' these places within the world before he can decide to live in them himself." This attitude "produces a way of living which ignores real life."[9] For Brunner, this was the classic monastic mistake. Instead he advocated a Lutheran vision of vocation as "the thankful acceptance of the place, at which I am now set, from the hands of Providence, as the sphere of my life, as the place in which, and according to the possibilities of which, I am to meet my neighbour in love."[10] His conservatism comes through in his conclusion on vocation: "The idea of the Calling makes us free from all feverish haste, from bitterness, and from the—finally inevitable—hopeless resignation of the reformer; at the same time it keeps the door open for me to undertake such reforming work when it is the duty appointed to me in the exercise of my particular 'office.'"[11] Brunner did not close the door on the work of social reform, but such reforming work is appropriate only when it comes within the bounds established by one's particular calling. We respond *within* our God-given vocation.

Barth on the Divine Call

Barth's own historical assessment of vocation named the shadow sides of both the Catholic and Protestant trajectories. He faulted the medieval church for taking the universal call that is heard in scripture—namely, the call to become a Christian—and reducing it to the narrow call to become a monk. This in effect separated Christians into two classes: those who had a call (the monks) and those who did not have a call (everyone else). For Barth, it was one of the triumphs of the Protestant concept of vocation to overturn this medieval hierarchy of holiness and assert that the divine call comes to *all* Christians.[12] However, the Protestant emphasis on the given social order, human stations, and, ultimately, the world of work carried its own price: forgetfulness of the primacy of the divine call over all human callings. Barth argued that the narrow, technical meaning of vocation as a career or sphere of work that has dogged so many Protestant treatments is nowhere present in the New Testament. Instead, the biblical word for calling, *klesis*, always refers to the divine summons to become a Christian and to take up the duties corresponding to this new life.[13] This is true even in 1 Corinthians 7:20, in which Paul encourages his readers to "remain in the condition in which you were called." Thus Barth confronted Luther directly and explicitly rejected his exegesis.

Barth also responded to Brunner. Barth agreed with Brunner that "faithfulness in vocation must exclude any intention of radically re-forming life." We must not become people for whom "no place in the world is good enough."[14] For Barth, Luther's doctrine of vocation offers a helpful critique not only of medieval monasticism but also contemporary "pessimistic or over-optimistic fanaticism" that sets out to overturn everything.[15] Yet Barth critiqued Luther on this point as well, thus distancing himself from Brunner, by showing that Luther never indicated how it is that we come to that particular place of activity that is pleasing to God. He acknowledged that Luther was working within the medieval world, with its "well-known order of superiority and subordination which is established and obtains for all higher and lower stations." One deleterious consequence of this, according to Barth, was that the Lutheran tradition came to align the call of God too closely with the duties of one's vocation. Barth then asked a series of questions that get at the heart of his own theology of call:

> What about the superiority of the divine calling over all the other prescribed stipulations of the human sphere of operation? Is not its freedom forfeited again if it must coincide *ipso facto* with the well-known limits of a human station and vocation? Does not this again bind man's obedience to a law which is different from the calling itself, except that now this is the law of the world and its historical and transitory order instead of that of the cloister? Ought not the divine calling and man's obedience necessarily to entail the trans-formation and new definition and form of the sphere of operation? Finally, what right have we to exclude the possibility that the divine calling and man's corresponding obedience might one day transfer him altogether from his present sphere to another?[16]

Beyond a critique of medieval hierarchies or static social roles, Barth's questions point to his central thesis: the divine call to be a Christian transcends all human callings.

Earlier in his treatment, Barth had distinguished between calling as a *vocation* (*Beruf*) and calling as the *divine summons* (*Berufung*) to the Christian life. "In the latter sense, calling is the imperative revela-

tion and making known of the special, electing, differentiating will of
God in His Word and command as given to man, i.e., to this man. It
is the summons to his special freedom, the claiming of his special
obedience. . . . Calling in this sense is the new thing which is added
to what man already is before God, not merely in the form of a further
divine decree in the context of His rule as Creator and Lord, but in
the manner of command, freedom and obedience."[17] For Barth, it is
this calling, the divine summons to Christian life, that is primary. This
divine summons is the *klesis* from above; it comes with a sovereignty
that cuts across all human spheres and activities. Unfortunately, according to Barth, the Protestant tradition of vocation tamed this divine
summons. It reduced God's call to a person's work, and subordinated
the divine summons to the duties attached to a profession. Barth
praised Luther for freeing the divine call from the monastery and
extending it to all Christians, but he criticized the subsequent tradition
for diluting this call along the way. "Protestantism successfully expelled
monasticism by recalling the fact that *klesis* is the presupposition of all
Christian existence. But it lost sight of the divine grandeur and purity
of this *klesis*, which were always in some sense retained even by
monasticism."[18] Escaping the Charybdis of monasticism, calling was
caught in the Scylla of secularism.

By underscoring the divine summons to faith, Barth sought to free
God's call from the constraints of some social order or any simplistic
assumptions about divine providence. In fact, by emphasizing the
divine summons (*Berufung*), Barth turned away from providence and
turned instead to its long-suffering cousin, predestination. It is this
shift that set the context for everything that Barth had to say about
vocation. Hans Urs von Balthasar called predestination—understood
as God's loving election in Christ—"the heartbeat of Barth's theology."[19]
It was the pulse of his theology of call. Thus, before exploring more
deeply Barth's contribution to vocation, we must take up this traditional category and see what Barth did with it.

The Hidden God of Predestination

As we have seen, the doctrine of divine providence articulates a
basic conviction that runs throughout the tradition, namely, that God
does not simply create the world and then leave it to its own devices.
Rather, God remains lovingly present to the world that God has made.
Creation is not a onetime event. The universe, with all its galaxies and

life-forms, requires God's ongoing support in order to survive. Without it, the world would simply cease to be. But there is more—and this "more" is what raises so many questions for our understanding of human nature and free will. God not only creates and sustains the universe, God moves its many actors toward their individual and corporate destinies. For free beings, that means that God moves us through our freedom. But if God truly guides our freedom, are we truly free? If not, is God truly free?

The word providence—literally, "foresight"—rarely appears in the Hebrew Bible. However, the notion of God's presence and constant care permeates the biblical narrative. From the creation of the world to the call of Abraham, from the exodus to the exile, from the gift of the covenant to the words of the prophets—the Hebrew Bible tells of a wise and loving God who guides the history of Israel. Indeed, as the voice speaking to Job out of the whirlwind makes clear, the sovereign direction of God touches the whole created order. It also touches the individual heart, as the psalmist sings:

> O LORD, you have searched me and known me.
> You know when I sit down and when I rise up;
>   you discern my thoughts from far away.
> You search out my path and my lying down,
>   and are acquainted with all my ways.
>
>   . . .
>
> Where can I go from your spirit?
>   Or where can I flee from your presence?
> If I ascend to heaven, you are there;
>   if I make my bed in Shē'ōl, you are there.
> If I take the wings of the morning
>   and settle at the farthest limits of the sea,
> even there your hand shall lead me,
>   and your right hand shall hold me fast. (Ps 139:1-3, 7-10)

When we turn to the New Testament, we hear of a kingdom prepared by God for the faithful "from the foundation of the world" (Matt 25:34). And in Jesus of Nazareth, we meet this God who cares and who answers our prayers, who forgives sin and invites all people into eternal life.

For human beings, salvation stands at the end of God's providential plan. This comes through clearly in the Pauline corpus—letters that locate Jesus Christ at the center of God's salvific will. "Blessed be the God and Father of our Lord Jesus Christ, who has blessed us in Christ with every spiritual blessing in the heavenly places, just as he chose us in Christ before the foundation of the world to be holy and blameless before him in love. He destined us for adoption as his children through Jesus Christ, according to the good pleasure of his will, to the praise of his glorious grace that he freely bestowed on us in the Beloved" (Eph 1:3-6). For Paul, God's plan is our destiny, a destiny that lies in conformity to Christ, through whom God brings us to salvation. "For those whom he foreknew he also predestined to be conformed to the image of his Son, in order that he might be the firstborn within a large family. And those whom he predestined he also called; and those whom he called he also justified; and those whom he justified he also glorified" (Rom 8:29-30).

Predestination is perhaps the most misunderstood doctrine in the Christian tradition. But for Paul, it is quite simple. Predestination is God's loving plan in Christ for the salvation of human beings. Thomas Aquinas placed predestination under the umbrella of divine providence as the special direction God gives intelligent creatures toward their final goal. Predestination is providence for people.[20]

Barth, however, was deeply suspicious of any attempt to subsume predestination under divine providence. For him, providence belongs to the order of creation, while predestination belongs to the order of redemption. Predestination is God's election, God's decision to save all of humankind through Jesus Christ. Thus Barth might have agreed with Aquinas's distinction; however, he would have rejected any attempt to use such a distinction to place priority on creation over redemption.[21] For Barth, God's saving election in Christ always comes first. Providence must follow and presume this prior predestination.[22] In order to make a case for the absolute priority of election, Barth had to confront the tradition of predestination he inherited, a tradition that too often had reduced God's universal love to an arbitrary decree, one in which God picks some for salvation and others for condemnation. What ought to be good news had become just the opposite; in the doctrine of predestination, the Gospel had gotten lost in God's hidden and inscrutable plan.

We return then to that puzzle that offers up no easy solution: how does God's infallible will meet my inviolable freedom? Does God's choice leave us free to choose? If God already knows what I will inevitably do, is it really me doing it? And if God has a plan, am I called to bow down in resignation before it? Or am I a partner in this plan? Catholic theologians after Aquinas addressed the interplay of dependence and independence between creation and Creator through a distinction between primary and secondary causality. God acts (primary cause) *in and through* our actions (secondary cause). God's freedom is exercised *in and through* the exercise of our freedom. But the question becomes more difficult when the talk turns to salvation. The too-quick answer is to appeal to free will: God makes an offer of salvation and we are free to accept or reject it. That solution simply dodges the question. For if there is one thing Christians assert about salvation, it is that salvation is not something we can achieve on our own. We cannot turn ourselves toward God. In the fourth century, Pelagius argued that we could. But most of the Christian tradition has been suspicious of such confident claims in the ability of human beings to climb up to God. We rely on God not just for the offer of salvation but also for the grace necessary to accept it. Along these lines, Pelagius's great opponent Augustine emphasized the impotence of human freedom. He argued that original sin had so radically wounded human nature that God's grace was absolutely necessary to enable fallen human beings to respond to God in love. But Augustine so stressed God's initiative, the necessity of grace, and the human dependence on this grace that it became difficult to see how human freedom and self-determination could be preserved. Even though he affirmed the necessity of human cooperation in the work of salvation, Augustine constantly insisted on the sovereignty of God. And at times he spoke of God determining—prior to any consideration of their choices or efforts—some persons for salvation and others for damnation.[23]

Our common associations with the concept of predestination owe much to Augustine's pessimism.[24] In the Augustinian friar Martin Luther, we see some of this pessimism emerge in an account of predestination that appeals directly to the hiddenness of God. In his stinging rebuttal to Erasmus, *The Bondage of the Will*, Luther returned to Augustine's primal insight into the sole initiative and agency of God in bringing about salvation. For Luther, the question as to why some people accept the Gospel and others do not cannot be answered simply by appealing to free will. Indeed, the appeal to free will misses the point. It is not human beings who choose God; it is God who chooses human beings. We depend on God not only for the offer but also for the ability to respond to this offer. Since it always takes God to move the impotent human will toward salvation, the real question to ask is, why does God move only some to accept salvation and not others? To this more difficult question—on which the whole doctrine of predestination revolves—Luther responded in the only way that he could: we simply do not know.

At one point in his argument, Luther confronted a challenge that came in the words of Ezekiel: "I desire not the death of a sinner."[25] Can this passage be affirmed while at the same time claiming that God wills both salvation *and* condemnation? In response, Luther introduced a distinction. Here Ezekiel was "speaking of the preached and offered mercy of God, not of that hidden and awful will of God whereby he ordains by his own counsel which and what sort of persons he wills to be recipients and partakers of his preached and offered mercy."[26] Back, behind revelation, Luther suggested, lies the hidden will of God that predestines some for glory and others for wrath. The whole notion of the hiddenness of God (*Deus absconditus*) and of the divine will was not a new theme for Luther. In his earlier lectures on the Psalms, in his Heidelberg Disputation of 1518, and elsewhere in *De servo arbitrio*, Luther spoke of a God who reveals Godself *precisely as hidden.*[27] This is part of the saving paradox of Luther's theology of the cross—God hides life under death, light under darkness, power under suffering, mercy under wrath. God veils Godself in order to elicit our faith. This notion of God hiding Godself *in* the revelation of Christ is what Brian Gerrish names (accurately, if not artfully) Hiddenness I.[28] But in reflecting on the line from Ezekiel, Luther introduces a quite different notion of God's hiddenness—not God's hiding *in* revelation, but the hiddenness of God *behind* revelation. Gerrish calls this Hiddenness II.

Of this second hiddenness, out of which comes God's predestinating will, Luther cautioned restraint: "This will is not to be inquired into, but reverently adored, as by far the most awe-inspiring secret of the divine majesty, reserved for himself alone and forbidden to us."[29] This "awful will," this secret space of the divine majesty, is not our concern. It is truly inscrutable, and that is all we can say about it. "It is enough to know simply that there is a certain inscrutable will in God, and as to what, why, and how far it wills, that is something we have no right whatever to inquire into, hanker after, care about, or meddle with, but only to fear and adore."[30] At times Luther so contrasted God's revealed will with God's hidden will, that we are tempted to suspect two gods behind them. "We have to argue in one way about God or the will of God as preached, revealed, offered, and worshiped, and in another way about God as he is not preached, not revealed, not offered, not worshiped."[31] Erasmus's mistake was that he did not distinguish between "God preached and God hidden," between "the Word of God and God himself."[32] For Luther, the distinction is in fact on our side and not an inner contradiction in God. Yet the tension—even contradiction—between the two wills is so intense that it finally culminates in the image of Jesus, the incarnate Word, weeping and wailing over those damned souls sent to perdition by the eternal will of the hidden God.[33]

At this point Luther's doctrine of God teeters on the brink of collapse into self-contradiction. He admitted that this portrait of God poses a real challenge, a genuine offense to human sensibilities. "And who would not be offended? I myself was offended more than once, and brought to the very depth and abyss of despair, so that I wished I had never been created a man."[34] Gerrish is right in pointing us toward the depth of Luther's own experience of horror before the divine majesty. "It is impossible to read him and not to recognize that there was a terror in his encounter with the hidden, predestinating God and that the emotional, religious, or spiritual content of the experience burst the limits of the merely rational and conceptual."[35] But—and this is crucial—Luther talked about this despair in the past tense: "I myself was offended more than once. . . . before I realized how salutary that despair was, and how near to grace."[36] Though he held to the hiddenness of God, it no longer held him. For in his advice not to preoccupy our minds with the inscrutable designs of God lay a dynamic—a movement from Hiddenness II to Hiddenness I. We flee *away from* the hidden God and *toward* the revealed God of the incarnate Word. For Luther, the hiddenness of God gives to faith an ongoing urgency. Even after the gift of grace, God's hiddenness maintains something of the awesome and awful mystery that is God. Thus, even though the abject terror is past, Luther did not abandon this predestinating God. The fear of God was something behind him, even as it was always before him.

Later Lutheranism distanced itself from Luther on predestination. The same cannot be said for the Reformed tradition, which confessionalized the theology of predestination found in Luther's younger contemporary, John Calvin. Because of this ecclesial endorsement, later commentators within the Reformed tradition imagined in Calvin's own treatment of predestination a prominence that simply was not there.[37] Calvin took up the topic, articulating a doctrine of double-predestination (God not only predestines salvation for the just but also

positively predestines condemnation for the wicked) that was not all
that different from Luther's basic position. But Calvin never gave
predestination a central doctrinal position. It did not follow on Calvin's
understanding of the divine nature; instead it emerged out of his experience: some people accept the Gospel, others do not. Convinced
as he was that not all people are ultimately saved, Calvin reasoned that
God's eternal plan must select out those who are saved. And if God
freely chooses some for salvation, it necessarily follows that God freely
chooses others for condemnation. "Election itself could not stand
except as set over against reprobation."[38] Calvin believed that predestination had mainly pastoral value. The doctrine was meant to offer
comfort and encouragement to believers, particularly those who were
suffering persecution for their faith. The problem, however, was that
it often failed to provide the peace that it promised.[39] The hiddenness
of the divine decree transformed comfort into anxious worry: Am I
among the elect? Am I truly saved? How do I know if my fate has been
decided for salvation or eternal damnation?

As William Placher points out, when Calvin took up the question
of predestination, his rhetoric raised every possible warning flag.[40]
"Human curiosity" renders the discussion of predestination dangerous,
for we strive to wander along "forbidden bypaths," seeking out the
secrets of God and the "sacred precincts of divine wisdom."[41] He cautioned his readers to curb their curiosity and adopt a posture of humility, for God's designs are hidden to us. "Secret" is one of Calvin's most
characteristic descriptions of God's plan. Yet there is a wonder in the
unfolding of divine providence over the course of human history that,
for Calvin, is not far from dread.[42] While those who live in the Word
may find comfort, those who are unsure face incredible anxiety.

> But the point which must not be overlooked is that, for Calvin,
> the hiddenness of God in the world order is subjectively appre-
> hended as a sense of terrifying contingency—apart from the Word
> of God. He could portray the threatening insecurity of human
> existence (its "ultimate anxiety and dread") with quite extraordi-
> nary power. Life itself is "enveloped with death." "Half alive in
> life, [man] hardly dares to draw an anxious, feeble breath, as
> though he had a sword perpetually dangling over his neck." Igno-
> rance of providence is therefore the ultimate of all miseries.[43]

This "terrifying contingency" confronted later Calvinists above all in
the doctrine of double predestination, what Calvin called that "horrible

decree" by which the hidden will of God foreordained some to salvation and others to condemnation. At times, Calvin appealed to a distinction, similar to Luther's, between the "revealed will" and the "secret will" of God: "But it may be asked, If God wishes none to perish, why is it that so many do perish? To this my answer is, that no mention is here made of the hidden purpose of God, according to which the reprobate are doomed to their own ruin, but only of his will as made known to us in the gospel."[44] Like Luther, Calvin insisted this was a distinction only from our earthly perspective. God in Godself has only one will and it is united. Still, in his effort to harmonize the two, he risked reducing the revealed will of God's universal mercy to mere appearance.[45] We have no real reason to doubt that the hidden God is different from the God revealed in Christ, but we can never be sure. By placing predestination within God's hidden wisdom, considered apart from salvation history, Calvin accentuated the contingency—the arbitrariness—of the divine plan and the abstractness of the God whose plan it is.

As the examples of Luther and Calvin illustrate, no one confession held a monopoly on predestination in the early modern period. Indeed, the franchise extended into the Catholic world as well. The Council of Trent saw itself as rejecting the Calvinist claim that God positively predestines some to condemnation. For Trent, predestination is single, not double. God desires the salvation of all, even as God leaves individual human beings free to reject the divine plan. But that hardly settled the issue of how human freedom relates to the eternal plan of God. In the second half of the sixteenth century, a vigorous debate broke out between the Dominican theological establishment and the upstart Society of Jesus. The question of predestination was at the center: Does God predestine individuals to salvation prior to God's knowledge of the choices these individuals will make in their lives (*ante praevisa merita*), or does God predestine people consequent upon knowledge of what they will do (*post praevisa merita*)? The Dominicans, claiming the mantle of Thomas Aquinas, championed the first position, and thus emphasized the sovereignty of God, whom they argued could in no way be influenced by the actions of human beings. The Jesuits, despite the objections of two giants within their own order, Robert Bellarmine and Francis Suarez, came to advocate the second, thus stressing the human contribution to God's saving plan. Each view laid its own particular burden on the human psyche, and thus left its own particular legacy.

The first and by far the more popular theology of the time, predestination *ante praevisa merita* was hard-pressed to distance itself from the negative reprobation that seemed to be implied by God's eternal decree. If God predestines one person to salvation prior to any consideration of her merits, then doesn't it follow that God equally wills another to condemnation? Michael Buckley captures the classic Jesuit critique when he concludes that this view, "after all the distinctions had been made, was not so different from the theories of Calvin."[46] Hidden in the darkness of the divine decree, the individual's eternal destiny is a mystery. And, it seems, there is nothing one can do about it. On the other hand was predestination *post praevisa merita*, which found a spokesman in the Louvain Jesuit Leonard Lessius (whose 1610 treatise *De gratia efficaci* so moved Francis de Sales that it prompted a letter of appreciation from the Gentleman Saint). This minority position, given space by Paul V's 1607 papal decree, lit a slow renewal in the Catholic understanding of divine providence that Buckley sees spreading from Francis de Sales to Alphonsus Liguori to Karl Rahner to the Second Vatican Council, a renewal that drew new attention to the human and a broadening of God's salvific will.[47] But its emphasis on human agency, even if it escaped the Dominican accusation of Pelagianism, nevertheless brought with it a certain pressure to perform. While it may have freed folks from the absurd contingency of a stingy God, the implications of grace *post praevisa merita* meant for some that greater psychic weight rested on human freedom to get it right.

The God of the Plan

There is a sad irony in the fact that the notion of providence, with its soothing claim that God has a plan for each person, often brought anxiety instead of comfort. Looming behind the gift of the Gospel was the ever-present danger of condemnation. The hiddenness of God's plan always threatened to transform love into fear. Faithfulness was fraught with the prospect of failure. Over the course of the early modern period, Catholics and their various Protestant counterparts offered very different ideas about vocation. Catholics lifted up religious life and the evangelical counsels as the superior path. This was the ideal against which other lives seemed a mere compromise. Luther rejected that ideal and set up another standard. He encouraged conscientious Christians to serve God and neighbor in the midst of whatever station in life God had assigned to them. But the clarity of the ideal—whether Protestant or Catholic—did not remove the fear of falling short. Despite their differences, what these Christian communities shared was the assumption that there was a standard by which human life would be judged. The quest for the meaning of life was not their concern. The meaning of life was all too clear. Rather, their concern was how to meet the heavy demands laid down by the moral and spiritual universe within which they lived. This was the source of their anxiety.

We live in a different world today, with a different kind of anxiety confronting us. Our great fear is not the threat of guilt and condemnation but the prospect of meaninglessness.[48] Before, the fear was one of failing to meet the demands laid down by a universal and unassailed framework of meaning. Today, the fear is that there is no framework, that the whole thing has come undone. This unraveling began with the Reformation itself and accelerated under the social, political, and economic localization of late modernity, leaving our present era with a deep suspicion toward any "master narrative" that attempts to impose universal meaning on human life. "Salvation" and "sin" hang on as important categories for many, but they can hardly be said to shape our corporate consciousness, never mind serve as the unquestionable framework for human action. In short, our present problem is not the fear of failure but of never finding our way. The weight of the *command* has been replaced with the burden of *choice*. Floating free of any grounding narrative, we are continuously presented with the task of creating meaning for ourselves from the various pieces left behind when the older frameworks broke apart. Thus our existential predicament is very different from that of condemnation; it is almost its opposite: "the world loses altogether its spiritaul [sic] contour, nothing is worth doing, the fear is of a terrifying emptiness, a kind of vertigo, or even a fracturing of our world and body-space."[49]

Within this context, the hiddenness of God's plan takes on a different tone. The question, what is God's plan? may no longer evoke the anxiety of eternal damnation en masse. Instead the ambiguity surrounding any answer raises worry about missing the meaning of our lives. Facing a plethora of options, we ask, what *is* the point? Earlier, easier answers simply do not satisfy. Luther's exhortation to "remain in your calling" seems a world away from our mobile society and rather naïve in the face of our global economic system. The older Catholic assertion that religious life and virginity are always better does not fit with our current appreciation of baptism and marriage. A theology of vocation has to take this contemporary experience of ambiguity seriously. But before it can do so, it has to confront the legacy of the doctrine of providence. It has to overcome some of the dead ends associated with the appeal to the plan of God.

The older paradigm of command and condemnation may have forever lost its hold. But that does not mean that the language of "call" is completely foreign to people of faith today. Many experience their faith as a genuine response to a transcendent reality, and not merely a convenient or self-constructed worldview. Finding our way, the search for meaning, discovering our path—these are the themes of a contemporary theology of vocation. For people of faith the quest takes shape as a response. So we turn to the source of the call, and explore the dynamic by which our search to discover the plan for our lives leads us back to the author of that plan, the God of Jesus Christ.

The God of Jesus Christ

Karl Barth was keenly aware of the anxiety brought on by the emptiness of modern subjectivity. In many ways, his project can be seen as a positive reply to the drift of a theology detached from its source. His writings wrench his reader's gaze away from the human subject and direct it to the "theological object," which is nothing other than the God of Jesus Christ. When Barth came to the question of the plan of God, he suggested that the anxiety accompanying it ultimately comes from the way in which the question itself is framed. Instead of asking, What is the plan of God? we ought to ask, Who is the God of the plan?

Barth's doctrine of God began with the conviction that God is not at our disposal. Any knowledge we have of God follows principally and exclusively from the miracle of God's choosing to reveal God's self to us. Revelation enjoys such primacy in Barth's thought that his *Church Dogmatics* places the doctrine on the Word of God prior to the doctrine of God itself. With this emphasis on revelation came a strong polemic against so-called "natural theology"—that effort among apologists and philosophers to describe the divine according to human reason alone. Barth acknowledged the reasons why such an effort has appeared again and again over the course of Christian history. But he argued that natural theology always involves a fatal concession to unbelief. To seek a neutral common ground between believers and unbelievers is to bracket—and thus cede—one's faith in the Gospel.[50] It is not only an artificial enterprise but also a terrible way to witness. What is tragic about natural theology, according to Barth, is that it so easily becomes another human attempt to climb up to God. It risks forgetting the absolute dependence of sinners on God's grace.

For Barth everything we know about God is known through God's revelation. Even God's *hiddenness* is revealed to us. "The hiddenness of God is the content of a statement of faith."[51] Here Barth embraced Luther's notion of God's hiddenness in revelation (Hiddenness I). Here he played with the paradox of the cross, of the infinite becoming incarnate, of life coming through death, of the wholly "Other" God drawing near. "It is because the fellowship between God and us is established and continues by God's grace that God is hidden from us. All our efforts to apprehend Him by ourselves shipwreck on this. He is always the One who will first and foremost apprehend and possess us."[52] The crucial point is that God reveals this hiddenness to us; we cannot come to it on our own. Thus Barth flatly rejected Luther's notion that there is to God a hiddenness somehow separate from revelation (Hiddenness II). For Barth, there can be no mysterious will, hidden plan, or "horrible decree" behind God's revelation of love in Christ. God is as God reveals Godself to be.

Barth saw Luther bound up in medieval debates over the "absolute power" (*potentia absoluta*) of God. The category of *potentia absoluta* (God's power to do whatever God chooses to do, including what God does not actually choose to do) is a helpful category if it serves as a reminder of God's freedom and power. However, for Barth, the category is harmful if it ascribes to God a capacity *different* from what God has revealed. In late Nominalist treatments of the *potentia absoluta*, Barth saw the emergence of an arbitrary, indifferent, and abstract God who could just as easily act against us as for us. Barth knew that Luther knew that if what the Nominalists understood about the *potentia absoluta* was correct, then there could be no assurance of salvation. "At bottom there could never be more than a restless seeking and asking for God's true capacity, and on high or in the depths it could actually be quite different from and even contradictory to the capacity with which we might assure ourselves on the basis of His work."[53] This made Luther's appeal to the *Deus absconditus* of Hiddenness II all the more troubling for Barth. And he wondered if Luther really thought that the tension between the hidden God and the revealed God could be so easily overcome by his advice not to think about it.[54]

Barth avoided the clash between the wrathful, hidden God and the merciful, revealed God by rejecting the first as the conclusion of human reason, the end result of natural theology.[55] Only Jesus Christ reveals the true God, the God of revelation and the Word, the God of mercy and love. The centrality of Jesus Christ within Barth's system is unambiguous. All our anxiety about God, salvation, and the meaning of life has its source in forgetfulness of Christ. Thus Barth could acknowledge the helpful christological reference in Luther but question "the equally definite reference to a divine decision which took place apart from Christ, a decision hidden and unsearchable, but not on that account any the less real."[56] To imagine a secret will or a hidden God behind revelation leads us to look elsewhere for insight into the meaning of life. It also destroys our confidence in the saving work of Jesus Christ. "How can there be any confident turning to the *Deus incarnatus,* when behind Him and above Him another and different *voluntas maiestatis* is always laid down and maintained?"[57] Neither the abstract God of providence nor the arbitrary God of predestination can serve our present search for meaning. Neither has a place in a Christian theology of vocation. "We found previously that the doctrine of election must not begin *in abstracto* either with the concept of an electing God or with that of elected man. It must begin concretely with the acknowledgment of Jesus Christ as both the electing God and elected man."[58] For Barth, God's plan for us is all about God's plan in Jesus Christ.

The Best of All Words

It has been said that Karl Barth's greatest achievement was his reworking of Calvin's notion of predestination.[59] Indeed, Barth's doctrine of election, or electing grace—which was his way of talking about predestination—is the centerpiece of his entire system. He calls it the "sum of the Gospel." What was his achievement? On first glance, it appears that Barth's revolutionary move was to replace Calvin's double predestination with a universal election. In other words, in place of the assumption that God predestines some for salvation and some for reprobation, Barth affirmed that God elects all of humanity for salvation. But on closer inspection, it becomes quite obvious that Barth was far less interested in the question, Who are the elect? than he was with the question, Who is the God who elects? It is his response to this second question that marks Barth's contribution—providing both the necessary context for his theology of vocation and the most important insights for our own.

As we have seen, the traditional Reformed doctrine of predestination followed as a corollary to the doctrine of justification by faith. If the assurance of salvation comes not by relying on one's own merits but by looking upon the mercy of God, then it helps to know that God's mercy is reliable, that it rests in God's eternal plan of salvation. But this plan has implications. For Calvin, if God chooses some, God must reject others. This twofold choice is the basis for the doctrine of double predestination that followed. It was a doctrine that, for all its logical consistency, failed to serve its primary pastoral purpose: offering comfort to the elect.

Barth was well aware of this history. For him, it was a tragedy that the notion of God's predestinating grace should serve as a source of anxiety or despair. It was tragic because, for Barth, this grace is the sole source of hope for sinful humanity. God's election is nothing less than God's decision to save all of humankind through Jesus Christ. It is Gospel, pure and simple—not just a good word for humanity, but the best of all words.

> The doctrine of election is the sum of the Gospel because of all words that can be said or heard it is the best: that God elects man; that God is for man too the One who loves in freedom. It is grounded in the knowledge of Jesus Christ because He is both the electing God and elected man in One. It is part of the doctrine of God because originally God's election of man is a predestination not merely of man but of Himself. Its function is to bear basic testimony to eternal, free and unchanging grace as the beginning of all the ways and works of God.[60]

In this opening thesis, Barth both emphasized the importance of the doctrine of election and indicated where he would go with it. In the pages that follow, he pushes his readers to move beyond the mysterious decree of providence and toward the concrete plan enacted in Christ. In the view of predestination that he inherited, the hiddenness of God's plan suggested a hidden God, whose nature seemed abstract and whose actions seemed arbitrary. "How can the doctrine of predestination be anything but 'dark' and obscure if in its very first tenet, the tenet which determines all the rest, it can speak only of a *decretum absolutum*?"[61] In the face of God's inscrutable will, Barth argued that election needed to be brought out into the open. This unveiling happens in light of God's self-revelation in the incarnate Word. In Christ—and only in Christ—we come to see the living God whose plan this is. "If God is truly revealed to us, then not only the content of the divine election, but the identity of the God who elects can no longer be left hanging—as tended to be the case even in thinkers like Calvin. Not an abstract providence or all-powerful Will, Barth argued, but the *triune* God is the God who elects."[62]

Barth rightly acknowledged that he was not the first to draw attention to the centrality of Jesus Christ in God's election of humanity. Indeed it is a thoroughly biblical doctrine, proclaimed unambiguously in the opening chapter of Ephesians: God has "blessed us in Christ," "chose us in Christ before the foundation of the world," "destined us for adoption . . . through Jesus Christ, according to the good pleasure of his will" (1:3-5). Barth noted that all the great early proponents of the doctrine point to the centrality of Jesus—though he faulted Aquinas for ignoring Christ in his formal treatment of predestination and only introducing the link later in his christology. The Reformers and the Protestant confessions contain ample reference to our election in Christ, but after a lengthy historical survey, Barth remained unsatisfied: "Is it the intention of these thinkers that serious theological attention should be paid to the assertion that the election is to be known in Jesus Christ? Does this assertion contain the first and last word on this matter, the word by which we must hold conclusively, and beyond which we must not conceive of any further word?"[63] In the end, Barth argued that none of these voices confronted the dangerous separation—rooted in the *potentia absoluta* of Nominalism, the *Deus absconditus* of Luther, and the "terrible decree" of Calvin—between the divine decision and Jesus Christ.

Because divine election is more about the God of Jesus Christ than about us, Barth treated it within his doctrine of God, rather than, for example, in his doctrine of creation or his doctrine of reconciliation.[64] The second part of the second volume of his *Church Dogmatics* sinks deep into theology proper in explicating a vision of God as the *electing* God. But this is not merely an exercise in philosophical speculation. Indeed, avoiding precisely this kind of speculation is the whole point of Barth's presentation! The God of the philosophers has nothing to do with the God of Jesus Christ. And whenever the Christian theological tradition slips into this kind of speculation, Barth raised his critique. In this critique lies the point of departure for Barth's split with the classical Reformed doctrine of predestination.

Reformed theologians of the seventeenth century taught that God's decree to elect some people and reject others *precedes* (logically, not chronologically) the decree to effect election through Jesus Christ.[65] Von Balthasar explains how, for Barth, it is precisely the opposite: "The source and wellspring of election is Jesus Christ alone. In him God chooses himself, but in the form of a creature. On him, the merciful mediator and redeemer, all creation was established before the foundation of the world. This one person, and he alone, is the primeval object of the Father's election. . . . This primeval election is the foundation for the whole epic of divine providence, and the doctrine of divine providence must be regarded as part of the more comprehensive doctrine of election. To reverse the relationship between these two doctrines is to distort the true picture."[66] Surely the seventeenth-century Reformers would have agreed that salvation comes through Christ. But Barth argued that if the decision to save comes before the decision to save through Christ, then the God of this decision can too easily be detached from Jesus. The logical implication of such a move is that the incarnation is not essential to the identity of the Word, the Logos of God. It is simply something that the Second Person of the Trinity does—a role that does not determine God's fundamental identity. Thus the incarnation ultimately tells us nothing about the essential nature of God. We turn elsewhere for information. And what we end up with is the God of the philosophers, an abstract deity who could just as well be a tyrant or a terror as the loving parent of Jesus Christ. In the face of an arbitrary predestinating God, Barth insisted that God elects us *in Jesus Christ*. But he took it a step further, and so confronted head-on the idolatry of the abstract God. For Barth, Jesus Christ is not only the object of election but he is its *subject* as well.[67] By this Barth meant that there is no abstract Logos that exists independent of the eternal determination for the incarnation.[68] In other words, in Jesus Christ we get back as far as we can go in God's election. Behind him there is no inscrutable plan, abstract God, or undetermined Logos—for he is the electing God himself. The plan—in both object and subject—is a person.

By calling Jesus Christ—the historical person crucified outside Jerusalem—the subject of election, Barth opened up the very being of God to history, not confusing time and eternity but declaring that the eternal God "makes room" in God's very self for the cross. The covenant that is sealed on Calvary enters into God's own self-definition. The radical implications and potential difficulties of this claim for trinitarian theology cannot occupy us here. Instead, we highlight the crucial move that Barth made with regard to divine election: by the eternal act of election, God not only predestines humanity, God predestines God's very self. The act of election is God's eternal determination to be God *for us*, to be the loving, merciful, saving God of Jesus Christ. "The electing God, Barth argues, is not an unknown 'x.' He is a God whose very being—already in eternity—is determined, defined, by what he reveals himself to be in Jesus Christ; viz. a God of love and mercy towards the whole human race. . . . What Barth is suggesting is that election is the event in God's life in which he assigns to himself the being he will have for all eternity. It is an act of Self-determination by means of which God chooses in Jesus Christ love and mercy for the human race and judgment (reprobation) for himself."[69] In order to disperse the shadow that had fallen over the classical doctrine of predestination, Barth repeatedly underscored the point that the doctrine of election is "definitely and unequivocally" Gospel—good news for the whole human race. It is not some erratic mechanics of destiny that alternates between yes for some and no for others. Election is altogether for everyone yes.[70] Thus Barth marvelously recast Calvin's doctrine of double predestination. The "elect" and the "reprobate" are not two groups of people who are assigned their fate before all time by God. God's twofold decree does not split the whole of humanity; instead, it cuts through the very heart of God. For on the cross, Christ becomes the reprobate, the rejected one. In God's eternal yes to humankind—the act of election in Christ—God chooses to be rejected so that we might be saved. God chooses to die so that we might live.

Contrary to the popular image of Karl Barth as a dour Calvinist suspicious of human initiative and fearful of all points of contact between God and the world,[71] we find in his doctrine of election a generous and liberating vision of God who is *God for us*. The transcendent God—Barth's great concern—is not the unknown God, but the one whom we come to love through the biblical testimony to the covenant realized in Jesus Christ. "When Holy Scripture speaks of God," Barth wrote, "it does not permit us to let our attention or thoughts wander at random until at this or that level they set up a being which is furnished with utter sovereignty and all other perfections, and which as such is the Lord, the Law-giver, the Judge and the Saviour of man and men."[72] Instead, the scriptures focus us on the God who "in the first person singular" speaks to the patriarchs and Moses, the prophets and the apostles. Above all, the Christian scriptures direct us to Jesus Christ. It is in Jesus that we know who God is, for God is the Word Incarnate, whose very being is determined by the eternal decision to be with us and for us in Jesus. This God is the subject matter of theology and the center of the Christian life.

In the face of our questions about God's plan for our lives, Barth's doctrine of election offers not answers but a different question. Looking at Barth's massive volume on divine election, Joseph Mangina notes, "The whole train of reflection that extends over the 800 or so pages of II/2 is intended to help us change the subject. Instead of asking about ourselves . . . we find ourselves asking about God."[73] What is God's plan? This is a legitimate question to ask. But it fades in the face of the more important question, who is the God of this plan? Once we begin to ask this primary question and genuinely enter into it, the secondary question of our particular place within this plan tends to work itself out. Leaving behind fearful or frustrating images of God as the divine tyrant or inscrutable mystery, and turning instead to the story of Jesus, we find a God of care and concern who not only invites us into friendship but is also willing to die for the sake of that friendship. What kind of worry can there be for those whose lives are in the hands of the God made known to us in Jesus Christ? For Barth this is the good news of the doctrine of election, a doctrine that bears basic testimony to God's love and grace "as the beginning of all the ways and works of God."[74]

The Call and Callings

This confidence in the God of the plan—the triune God revealed to us in Jesus Christ, the God for us who loves in freedom—helps to explain why Barth did not seem particularly troubled by the difficult questions faced by those trying to discern their vocation. The cosmic plan of God in Christ infallibly unfolds across creation and over history. This is true. But I still have to decide what I will do with my life. Barth saw the choice of the field of one's everyday activities as significant, for it affects the whole direction of a person's life in a distinctive way. "It obviously means that calling and vocation stand here from the very outset and continually in the most direct interrelation."[75] But at the same time, "choosing a vocation" is secondary to that primary obedience in freedom that constitutes our response to the divine summons of God. The choice of a vocation can never be more than a preparation for or a consequence of the true and decisive choice for God.[76]

Barth's subordination of the traditional notion of human vocation did not discourage him from dedicating several hundred dense paragraphs of his *Church Dogmatics* to the question![77] Earlier, we noted how Barth distinguished the divine summons (*Berufung*) from the human vocation (*Beruf*). But, as the previous paragraph indicates, he also saw these two callings as intimately related: one's vocation is the "place" where the divine summons comes to an individual. Evoking Brunner, Barth spoke of vocation as the "old thing" that a person already is—what he has behind him, what she brings with her—when the new thing that is the divine summons comes. He cited Dietrich Bonhoeffer's definition of vocation as "the place of responsibility" where we respond to God. It is "the *terminus a quo* of all recognition and fulfillment of the command, the status of the man who is called to freedom by the command."[78] Implied in these statements is a notion of human vocation that is broader than employment, broader than a particular state of life or sphere of influence. For Barth, vocation is "the whole of the particularity, limitation and restriction in which every man meets the divine call and command, which wholly claims him in the totality of his previous existence, and to which above all wholeness and therefore total differentiation and specification are intrinsically proper as God intends and addresses this man and not another."[79] In other words, my vocation is not my profession; it is my person—seen as a unique creation placed by God in a particular time, at a particular place, and gifted with particular abilities, disabilities, experiences, and associations. God issues the divine summons to *me*, and my response to this summons cannot but be a response that comes out of the various particularities that together shape my context and constitution. While Barth disagreed with Luther on everything from the hiddenness of God to the stasis of *Stand*, in his treatment of vocation as our "place of responsibility," we see a creative use of Luther's insight that we are called by God to serve God and neighbor precisely where we are.

The category of limitation emerges as key to Barth's understanding of vocation. He set up his treatment by discussing the "unique opportunity" that is the individual human being. Each of us has a unique existence that is determined by the very limitations imposed on us by the Creator. We do not choose our parents or genetic makeup. And we live our lives within the confines of two dates we do not control: birth and death. The fact that God wanted *me* means that God does not want me to be someone else, living in some other place in some other time. In our limits (I cannot be a medieval peasant or the premier of China), we catch a glimpse of God's plan for us. "In the very limitation in which every man is what he is according to the divine will and decree, there is also declared the special determination which he is given by God, the special intention of God as this is made known in the divine command and to be fulfilled in the free act of his obedience."[80] What God commands by means of the divine summons, God commands "with the special intention indicated in the limits which He has already set him as his Creator and Lord."[81] There is a freedom in this limitation, the freedom to be *me*, marked as I am by all the particularities of the existence granted to me by God.

For all of Barth's problems with the modern Protestant trajectory of reflection on vocation, he nevertheless held up its emphasis on the particularity of the person as one of its great contributions. For the divine summons is not something strange to the one who is called, as if it were a "hermetically sealed ball" that has nothing to do with the individual. It concerns him. It is for her. "If Jesus Christ is the One who calls, and if His call goes forth to man as he is, then what the man called by Him is as such cannot be a matter of indifference or unconcern to the One who calls. Christ finds man precisely as the man he is; and He is found by the man who is obedient to His call."[82] This is what Luther realized. Instead of a generic and general call that assumed the monastic life was best for everyone, Luther argued that God's call meets a person in a particular state of life, and that one's response to God must take shape within that context, within that calling. Barth expanded calling, or vocation, to include not just one's *Stand* but the whole complex of particularities, limitations, and restrictions that constitute one's created existence. In this broader context, he remained faithful to Luther's insight. The Word of God, the summons that is the divine call, is not a general invitation but a well-aimed shot that hits me where I am and prompts me to respond precisely in this context. Playing on the interrelation between the biblical *klesis* (the divine call) and *ekastos* (the particular person, "each man"), Barth wrote, "It is this indispensable relation to the *ekastoi* that the concept of *klesis* is revolutionary, shaking what is worldly or human. Men are *ekastoi* before they become *kletoi*, and they remain *ekastoi* even when they are *kletoi*. If their *klesis* is their allotted disclosure of one and the same truth beside which there is no other, the truth is not a general truth, but a special truth for each."[83]

Still, for all his careful attention to *ekastoi*, Barth radically subordinated it to *klesis*—to the divine summons. We can be obedient to this summons only from within our own humanity. If we do not obey here, then we do not obey at all. But our obedience is not split. *Klesis* and *ekastoi* cannot simply be balanced against one another, as if they were equal partners clamoring for our attention. We are to be obedient to

God, not to our vocation. Returning to his more fundamental claim about human limitation as God-given, Barth cautioned that the uniqueness of the human person is only the dependent clause that introduces the main sentence, namely, "that in this way man is pointed directly to the grace of divine calling, that he is orientated on the covenant which God has made with man, that he is disposed for participation in the salvation history which proceeds from this covenant and which constitutes the fulfillment of the particular decree and Word and work which form the internal basis of creation and the centre and meaning of the whole cosmos and history."[84] Our limitation, and thus our unique particularity, and thus our vocation (*Beruf*), is seen clearly only in light of the divine summons (*Berufung*) that is, after all, the primary call.

When Barth turned to consider criteria for judging faithfulness to the divine summons in choosing a vocation, he asked two basic questions.[85] First, what are the needs of my particular historical situation? It is not enough for a possible career or life choice to appear interesting or enticing. It must also meet a genuine need and offer a real service. Second, what are my own gifts and dispositions? I am constituted by God in a certain way. And, somewhere between the modern permissive chorus to "Do as you will" and the old pietistic maxim "What we take ill, is God's will," Barth found a place for attending to one's inclinations and aptitudes in discerning a vocation. Yet, in the end, neither of these criteria is decisive. Neither "the external nor the internal world is the authority which can genuinely summon him with a direct and absolute claim to his obedience."[86] God alone is the one who gives these voices authority. We must listen to these voices, but we must obey only the voice of God. Even the God-given limitations of age, historical context, personal aptitudes, and sphere of activity are confronted by the call from above. We are to respond to God's call according to our age or life stage, but we are not bound by biology. God calls us with the gifts that we have, but God can also call us beyond our abilities. The stuttering Moses comes first in a long list of biblical examples that demonstrate Barth's point. While he shared Brunner's view of vocation as the "place where" we are called, Barth put greater stress on the power of God's call to transform this place, and ourselves as well. The great help that reflection on our created limitations and particular existence can give to guiding our response to God remains only a help. It is just the beginning. Indeed, we cannot begin anywhere else. But we can only begin there. "Man is in no sense responsible to his vocation; he is wholly responsible to God alone. He must not omit to glance at his vocation in the question of obedience. . . . Such a glance is a help towards orientation in the required reflection upon man's being as the *ekastos* whom the command concerns. This glance, however, must not become even a side-glance at an imposed law. It can be a help only toward this necessary orientation."[87]

Thus relativizing the discernment of vocation based on one's context or constitution, Barth concluded with a casual (or faithful) confidence that things will work out: "If he lets God speak to him in His witnesses, and if he prays that He Himself will make him an active hearer, he will always have enough awareness both outwardly and inwardly to be on the right way to the decision for this or that sphere of operation, to the vocation corresponding to his calling."[88] Such simple faith regarding such major life decisions could seem like a rather frustrating conclusion, but only if we forget that this choice—like every choice—always already falls within the larger context of God's loving choice in Christ. Barth was constantly trying to draw our gaze away from ourselves and our plans, and toward the God whose plan has already been made marvelously clear in the life, death, and resurrection of Jesus. It is not that we don't have to make big decisions, but, Barth seemed to suggest, we should relax a little. Focusing on Christ puts everything else in perspective.

Conclusion

The theology of Karl Barth provides one way to reflect on what is the starting point of vocation: the God who calls. His thoroughly christocentric, trinitarian doctrine of God dispels the specter of an abstract deity and removes any fear of an arbitrary plan imposed on our lives from above. At a minimum, this chapter moves us away from some rather simplistic assumptions. In our vocational search, we should not expect a detailed blueprint for our lives drawn up in the mind of God. Nor should we simply equate our calling with the givens of creation. Our vocation is not to be divined in the tea leaves of the soul or discovered in conformity to the given social order. God's plan is neither so secret nor so obvious. Somewhere in between we find God drawing us toward the meaning of our lives.

In that search, Barth suggested we take our first cue from the particularities and limitations of our particular and limited God-given existence. God has not, as Rowan Williams observes, cast us a role before any audition.[89] Rather, God calls us as we are. For Barth, each of us has—each of us is—a "unique opportunity." I am placed here and now as the person that I am. What does the world around me need? What am I able to provide? Frederick Buechner described vocation as "the place where your deep gladness and the world's deep hunger meet."[90] But does vocation end at my individual aptitude or assessment of the world? Barth's only—and crucial—gloss on Buechner is that this place is the place *from which* (*terminus a quo*) God calls us. As important as they are in guiding our vocational search, the cues given in our gifts remain only cues; we glance at them but should not stare. God can always call us to transcend our context and our personal limitations. The call to faith and obedience cuts across all human spheres. Faith is our first and greatest calling. All other vocations follow.

In the end, Barth leaves us with an unresolved tension between the human vocation (*Beruf*) and the divine summons (*Berufung*). Despite his incredible effort to link up the two—and so reignite the Protestant tradition of vocation with the flame of evangelical theology—his treatment remains conditioned by a dialectical understanding of creation and redemption. In his effort to correct the Protestant trajectory, Barth overcorrected, threatening to divorce God's call from the created order altogether.[91] We are left wondering, What can we really learn from our own context and constitution? What can spiritual direction or attention to the signs of the times really tell us about what God is calling us toward? Can our whole created existence, our unique individuality and rich life story, really be reduced to the "dependent clause" of a transcendent imperative? As Brunner put it so sharply, "in Barth Creation comes off badly compared with Redemption."[92] Barth's emphasis on the divine summons that cuts across all human spheres may evoke the challenging call of the Gospel more radically than *Stand*, social status, or professional commitments. But in its "either/or," it is no less arbitrary than the secret voice of the *duplex ordo*. At the least, it makes vocation just as difficult to discern for the individual facing a consequential choice. The divine summons comes to the particular person that I am. But my particularity fades in the face of this transcendent call, and we are left with the question with which we began: what is it that God is calling me to do? Like neoscholastic treatises on vocation, Barth offered practical suggestions for discerning one's call. But the theological link between *who I am* and the God who calls remains weak.

What we need is a more holistic anthropology—a theology of grace that, without denying the reality of sin, affirms God's pervasive presence across human history and within the human heart. We need to affirm both *God* and *me*, both grace and nature, as deeply intertwined realities in the vocational dynamic. If who I am is infused with God's grace, then can we really separate creation from redemption, the human vocation from the divine summons, *ekastos* from *klesis*? In the next chapter, we reflect on how changing conceptions of the nature-grace relationship in twentieth-century Catholic theology help to illuminate these questions. But we take with us the gains of Barth's impressive treatment. With him, we leave behind the hidden God whose designs for us are unknown, whose will for the world is indifferent. Revealed in Christ is a God *for us*, the electing God who elects to be for us a God of mercy and love, extending salvation to all through Jesus Christ. There is, then, a kind of therapy in this theology. Barth's whole project serves to turn us away from worry about our own lives to wonder over the life of Christ. It is an encouragement to let go of that anxiety and ambiguity that so often goes along with the human quest for meaning. Rather than worry about God's plan, we should rest in the comfort of the God whose plan it is.

CHAPTER FOUR

Me . . .

As kingfishers catch fire, dragonflies draw flame;
   As tumbled over rim in roundy wells
   Stones ring; like each tucked string tells,
      each hung bell's
Bow swung finds tongue to fling out broad its name;
Each mortal thing does one thing and the same:
   Deals out that being indoors each one dwells;
   Selves—goes itself; *myself* it speaks and spells,
Crying *Whát I do is me: for that I came.*

— *Gerard Manley Hopkins*[1]

For me to be a saint means to be myself.

—*Thomas Merton*[2]

God calls . . . *me.* It is not selfish or self-centered to affirm the profoundly personal dimension of vocation. Even Karl Barth—that prophet of the transcendent God—acknowledged that the greatest achievement of the Protestant doctrine of vocation was its emphasis on the particularity of the individual Christian. Against the generic ideal of monastic life, Luther argued that Christ calls each of us to serve God and neighbor where we are, as we are. It is a specific person, and not a state of life, that Christ addresses. The plan that is divine providence stretches out across all of human history, touching billions of individuals—each with her or his own history and complex psychology, each with a story that is unique. To speak of the God who calls without at the same time attending to the person who hears this call is to distort the divine-human dialogue. It misses something central to vocation.

But do we need a whole chapter on the human subject? Chapter 3 taught us that our attention should not be focused on our life plans but on the God of the plan—the triune God whose fundamental choice is to be salvation for us in Jesus Christ. There is a liberation in that realization. In light of God's gracious and universal election, do we need to worry so much about who we are and what we ought to do? On the question of vocation, shouldn't we simply conclude that things will work out for those who have faith, that in the light of Christ, the path forward will become clear? Chapter 3 explored two options. The first imagines vocation as a detailed blueprint laying out the design of my life before I actually live it. The second sees this plan in a more general sense, as a kind of generic call establishing broad parameters within which I am free to move. Despite the attractiveness of the latter over the former, both options are problematic. While the first might obscure the freedom of the individual, the second risks washing out the particularity of the person. Does the reality that is *me* disappear in the light and love of God?

Any individual vocation falls within the broader saving purpose of God, the God of Jesus Christ, the God of love and concern. This reminder is a necessary first step. It challenges the anxiety brought on by past conceptions of a distant God whose inscrutable decree imposes an arbitrary plan on unsuspecting people. It says instead that God's plan is always positive for us—bound up as it is in God's loving election in Christ. But to say that a theology of vocation begins with God does not imply that it ends there. Indeed, before a theology of vocation attends to the personal dimension of God's call, it has not yet asked the really hard questions. It is far easier to rest with a rather general notion of vocation. It is easier to say that God calls the individual in a generic way, and that one's specific choices—so long as they stay within the bounds of the moral law—are all equally good ways of responding to this call. But it is much more difficult to defend the claim that God calls the individual to something *in particular*. It is a difficult claim to defend, but one that needs to be taken seriously. Without attention to the particular will of God, the doctrine of providence quickly becomes meaningless, transforming the Lord's Prayer that "thy will be done" into an empty abstraction. Without attention to the personal dimension of vocation, what would we do with the example of the saints, whose lives testify to the conviction that God had something very particular in mind for them? What would we do with those believers today who feel called by God to their specific work or way of life? Are all these men and women delusional? Are they simply projecting their own desires onto God, blessing their own projects with a pious phrase? Maybe so. But even if we admit that church history is full of delusional people, that such projection and self-serving rationalization has occurred many times over, unless we are willing to rule out *all* claims to such a divine call, we have to attend theologically to its possibility. Over against the hiddenness of God's plan is the reality of an *experience*—the experience of God's call to move, to choose, to live one way and not another. It is this experience that prompts us to spend some time on the human being who is called.

There is another way to make a case for the concerns of this chapter. It comes not from the experience of God's call but from the experience of its absence. Often enough in life, the conscientious Christian encounters a significant or difficult decision for which neither the divine imperative contained in the Bible nor the moral law communicated by the church is of much help. Jean-Paul Sartre recalled the story of a student who, during the Nazi occupation, was torn between his desire to join up with the French Resistance, on the one hand, and his duty to stay home and care for his mother, on the other. Christian doctrine, Sartre remarked, offered the young man no guidance in choosing between these conflicting demands; it offered no help in choosing between these two goods. The advice he got depended on the priest he asked. Sartre used the story to lay bare what he saw as the inadequacy of Christian ethics. His reply to the student was a kind of existentialist creed: "You are free, therefore choose—that is to say, invent. No rule of general morality can show you what you ought to do: no signs are vouchsafed in this world. . . . we ourselves decide our being."[3]

Sartre's example dramatizes something we all see: that in some of the most important decisions of our lives, the general call of the gospel simply fails to offer a clear way forward. The Bible, it turns out, is not an answer key, an instruction manual, or a winning recipe. As attractive as these metaphors are in preaching, they quickly break down in real life. For Sartre, Christian doctrine says, "Act with charity, love your neighbour, deny yourself for others, choose the way which is hardest, and so forth." He then asked, "But which is the harder road? To whom does one owe the more brotherly love, the patriot or the mother? Which is the more useful aim, the general one of fighting in and for the whole community, or the precise aim of helping one particular person to live?"[4] The fact that these choices are choices among various goods hardly lessens their import. I imagine we can all think of examples of people we know for whom a poor choice among "goods" in the realm of career or marriage was far more detrimental than that more isolated choice for evil that the church condemns as sin.[5] For Sartre, the dilemma demands that the Christian moral framework be set aside. The following pages come to a different conclusion. In the problem that Sartre posed, we see not an indictment but an invitation. We see an opening to reflect on the individual, existential dimension of the divine call. Does God speak *to me*? That is the difficult question that any adequate theology of vocation must address.

A World of Grace

To explore the dynamism of the personal call, we turn from Karl Barth to another Karl, the German Jesuit Karl Rahner. Rahner was one of the most influential Catholic theologians of the twentieth century. He was a university professor who also advised the bishops of the Second Vatican Council. He was an accomplished speculative theologian who also wrote hundreds of pastoral essays, prayers, and retreat reflections—including several significant pieces on vocation. Though he was a contemporary of Karl Barth, Karl Rahner lived in a different theological universe. Barth was a Reformed theologian who shaped his constructive project in response to humanistic, liberal Protestantism. He sought to reclaim for the churches the priority of God's transcendence. Rahner was a Jesuit priest who articulated his system in the world of dogmatic, neoscholastic Catholicism. He found fresh insight in the transcendental analysis of the human subject. In terms of starting point and method, it is tempting to see the two thinkers as leaders of two opposing schools of thought—standard-bearers in a battle between the dialectical and analogical imaginations.[6] But neither Barth nor Rahner can be so easily pegged. There are real differences between their approaches, but their individual projects are multifaceted and nuanced. We have already seen how, alongside his stress on the utter transcendence of God, Barth attended carefully to the particularity of the person. For Rahner, the transcendental analysis of the human subject comes within a profound theology of grace—a theology that allowed him to talk about vocation in a new and creative way.

As a young Jesuit, Rahner encountered the vocational theory of Joseph Lahitton through his professor of moral theology at Valkenburg, Franz Hürth.[7] As we recall from chapter 2, Lahitton had attacked what

he took to be the common view of his day, namely, that a priestly vocation rested on some mysterious and supernatural "attraction" felt deep
within the soul of an individual. For Lahitton, this view was hampering
the church's ability to identify and educate candidates for the priesthood—putting church leaders in a basically passive position, waiting
for candidates to come forward and announce their calling. Lahitton
argued that a vocation is not constituted by some inner experience but
rather by the external call of ecclesial authority: "The call of a person
to the priesthood by the legitimate ministers of the Church does not
presuppose the presence of a vocation in the person concerned, because this very call itself creates the vocation within him."[8] Rahner
took issue with Lahitton's conclusion, convinced that it too quickly
dismissed the spiritual experience of the individual. Rahner admitted
that Lahitton had raised a legitimate concern of canon law: bishops,
seminary professors, and religious superiors depend on external criteria
to judge the readiness of candidates for ordination. But too much is
lost if vocation is confined to the external, the rational, and the deductive. Rahner wrote, "Even though we should not dispute the practical
usefulness of Lahitton's theory—the usual theory in the Church for
the past forty years—about the choosing of a calling and the requirements for being called, especially where ecclesiastical functionaries are
concerned (and not the person making the choice), we may nevertheless ask ourselves whether this theory is really quite correct theoretically
and in particular where it is a question of the one who asks himself
about his being called."[9] Lahitton's stress on the external may be helpful to the canonist, but it is not so helpful for the individual trying to
discern his or her own vocation.

If Rahner rejected the deductive logic of Lahitton, he did not retreat to the magic of a mystical "attraction." His own experience of
Ignatian discernment, and his early research on Gregory of Nyssa,
Evagrius Ponticus, and Bonaventure, fed Rahner's conviction that the
mystical experience of God—a kind of direct contact with the divine—is real and needs to be taken seriously by theologians.[10] However,
this "immediate experience of God" (*unmittelbare Gotteserfahrung*),
which Rahner gradually came to see as the root of his entire theological
project, is not the exclusive preserve of the mystic; rather, Rahner
argued, it is a broad and basic dimension of all human experience. The
trouble, Rahner recognized, was that the neoscholastic theology he
had inherited was simply incapable of talking about this experience in
an intelligible way. Caught up in a dualism between nature and grace,

the theologians had forced on vocation a false dichotomy: either vocation was a miraculous and mystical illumination or it was simply the
external recognition of one's ability and aptitude for a particular state
of life. Rahner sought out a middle way.[11]

The Experience of God

Sharing the confidence of Ignatius of Loyola, Rahner believed that
it is normal for God to reveal God's will to individuals.[12] This will is
not simply the general exhortation we find in scripture; it is a particular
imperative—a call that comes to each person, inviting and expecting
each individual to choose something specific. For Rahner, this conviction implies some *experience* of God. For if we are meant to respond
to a particular call, we have got to be able to hear it.

How does the divine call come? To answer that question, we first
have to consider Rahner's larger theology of grace and the human
person. For Rahner, the experience of God is real and truly possible.
However, rarely is it found in a miraculous announcement. We have
little evidence that God regularly works through dramatic visions or
supernatural signs. We have little reason to expect divine instructions
spelled out in the clouds or written in the icing of a cinnamon bun.[13]
Yet, if the call of God is not bound to the paranormal, neither can it
be reduced to what reason reflecting on revelation would tell us anyway.
For Rahner, God reveals God's particular will through a kind of individual "inspiration" that falls somewhere in between miraculous intervention and rational deduction. It is a kind of communication more
concrete than general norms but more ambiguous than a vision. It is
more like a "sense" or an "awareness" of something that is both within
us and beyond us. Rahner called this "sense" of ourselves and of God
"transcendental experience"—a philosophical phrase he borrowed
from Immanuel Kant:

> We shall call *transcendental experience* the subjective, unthematic,
> necessary and unfailing consciousness of the knowing subject that
> is co-present in every spiritual act of knowledge, and the subject's
> openness to the unlimited expanse of all possible reality. It is an
> *experience* because this knowledge, unthematic but ever-present,
> is a moment within and a condition of possibility for every con-
> crete experience of any and every object. This experience is called
> *transcendental* experience because it belongs to the necessary and
> inalienable structures of the knowing subject itself, and because

> it consists precisely in the transcendence beyond any particular
> group of possible objects or of categories.[14]

In the process of coming to "know" something, there is present in us
both a knowledge of the particular object or idea we are considering
(Rahner called this the "categorical" level) and, simultaneously, an
awareness of ourselves as a knowing subject. That subjective sense of
ourselves cannot really ever be put into words; it always remains implicit, unthematic, nonconceptual, indefinable. But still, it is not entirely empty. For what we *sense* about ourselves as subjects is that we
are always open to more. We seem aimed at an unlimited horizon. We
are finite beings oriented toward the infinite.

For Rahner, that infinite horizon of the human person is nothing
less than the mystery of God. What grounds our knowing (as well as
our choosing and our loving) is neither an unending emptiness nor
absolute Being. It is the God of Jesus Christ. God is the horizon that
opens up the landscape and encircles our lives, calling us forward even
as it continually recedes before us.[15]

> There is present in this transcendental experience an unthematic
> and anonymous, as it were, knowledge of God. Hence the original
> knowledge of God is not the kind of knowledge in which one grasps
> an object which happens to present itself directly or indirectly from
> outside. It has rather the character of a transcendental experience.
> Insofar as this subjective, non-objective luminosity of the subject
> in its transcendence is always orientated towards the holy mystery,
> the knowledge of God is always present unthematically and without
> name, and not just when we begin to speak of it.[16]

We begin to see the space that Rahner opened up for talking about the
experience of God. Since the transcendental is the ever-present horizon
or backdrop against which ordinary "categorical" realities are known,
loved, and chosen, the transcendental itself can never be the explicit
object of reflection. We cannot "know" the mystery of God in the same
way we know ordinary objects. And yet—in a move central to his
theological project—Rahner argued that this horizon can be "known"
in another way: not through an explicit, categorical delineation but
though an implicit, preconceptual awareness. We have a "sense," a
"consciousness," of our infinite openness to God and of God's gracious
presence to us. Rahner's word is *Erfahrung*, "experience," which (unlike the German *Erkenntnis*, "knowledge") evokes a sense of ongoing
contact with reality, a feeling of something deep, real, but not always

expressed.[17] God's presence is glimpsed, as it were, out of the corner of our eye. When we focus in on it as an object of study, we replace God with the categorical—and the transcendent reality itself slips off to the side, remaining the mystery that surrounds our lives. As the above quote indicates, we always carry with us this "sense" of God. Whenever we know, whenever we love, whenever we choose, whenever we do anything, we feel—even if we do not attend to it or acknowledge it—this divine presence. The experience of God is something that we all share—a sense of silent mystery swirling within and around us. It is through this silent swirling that the call of God comes. To put it more directly, for Rahner, the key to vocational discernment is for each of us to grow more conscious of this transcendent presence within ourselves, to sink more deeply into it. The result is that each of us comes to understand ourselves more fully, and to make important decisions more freely.

A Personal Presence

As the last paragraph indicated, for Rahner, the question that is the human spirit does not fade out across an infinitely receding horizon into a silence saying life is absurd. The horizon itself rushes toward us—even anticipates our questioning. In his theology of God as grace, we see the necessary complement to Rahner's transcendental analysis of the human person. His theology of grace is about the God who creates us and comes to us, the God who lives within us. If grace is a gift, then the gift and the giver are one. Rahner called grace the "self-communication of God" (*Selbstmitteilung Gottes*). But that common English translation sounds too cerebral, as if God were passing along some kind of divine information. What Rahner was getting at is something far more personal: "self-communication" is "self-sharing." God gives God's very self to us, opening up the possibility of an intimate, shared life between human beings and the triune God. What saves us, what completes us, what constitutes us at the very core of our being is not some idea or energy bar dropped down from heaven. What saves us is a friendship. God offers God's self to us in love, and invites us to respond in kind.

On our own, we can only approach God asymptotically, that wonderful mathematical metaphor of a line racing toward another line that it will never meet. It is only God's free decision to be grace that brings the two together. Our transcendental orientation toward the infinite meets the transcendent God who already comes to us. We see this most clearly in Jesus. The incarnation is the definitive inbreaking of the divine horizon into history. In Jesus Christ, God's offer is definitely accepted in a way that makes union with God possible for the rest of us. The incarnation—the "God-Man"—is an event unique in human history; but even so, it is not a bolt out of the blue. The incarnation reveals that God and humanity are free from any kind of a zero-sum game: "Because in the Incarnation the Logos creates the human reality by assuming it, and assumes it by emptying *himself*, for this reason there also applies here, and indeed in the most radical and specific and unique way, the axiom for understanding every relationship between God and creatures, namely, that closeness and distance, or being at God's disposal and being autonomous, do not vary for creatures in inverse, but rather in direct proportion."[18] In every human life, the mystery that is "me" meets and grows in union with the mystery that is God. As Rahner looked out over human history, he concluded that the incarnation is not a divine afterthought or a contingency plan activated to clean up human sin. The world was created precisely with the incarnation in mind. God wants to be close to us, and so creates us in order to make that possible. From the start, it is love that leads.

But even with the radical closeness brought on by God's self-gift, God remains God. The mystery is not removed by intimacy. Rahner took "mystery" primarily in a transcendental, not a categorical, sense. Unlike categorical mysteries, which we work out through investigation (we discover a friend's hidden motives or find the missing car keys), God is a mystery that deepens the closer we get. The mystery of God is not like a puzzle, but more like love. The more we grow in love, the more we are amazed and humbled by it, the more we see that we cannot totally capture it with our words or exhaust it by our categories. It strains our language to the breaking point. Even in the intimacy of grace, God remains mystery—not due to some deficiency on our part but to the sheer incomprehensibility, beauty, depth, and awesomeness that is God.[19]

How did Rahner choose to talk about this mystery of God coming close, the mystery of transcendence in immanence, the mystery of grace? Ironically, to articulate his belief about the personal presence of God, Rahner turned to two quite impersonal distinctions drawn from scholastic theology. The first is the distinction between created and uncreated grace, the second, between efficient and formal causality. Both distinctions help us better appreciate the theological context for Rahner's discussion of vocation. In scholastic theology, *created grace* referred to a gratuitous gift from God, which was distinct from God, that led to a positive change within the human person. *Uncreated grace* referred to God Godself, the indwelling of the Trinity in the human soul. Rahner argued that the neoscholastic theologians of the modern period had ignored their biblical and patristic heritage by stressing created grace over uncreated grace. For these theologians, created grace was generally seen as a precondition—a change in the person that preceded and disposed that person for the Spirit of God to come and dwell within.[20] Hence the priority they assigned to it. Against this tradition, Rahner argued that scripture emphasized the divine indwelling instead. Rahner effected a profound shift within Catholic theology with his simple insight that what is primary is not a precondition but the gift itself, the gift of God's very self. For Rahner, you cannot think of the former without the latter: "there does not exist even the beginning of a possibility of thinking of created grace apart from uncreated grace."[21] God does not demand that we first change (created grace) before becoming present to us in love (uncreated grace). God becomes present to us in love, and that love prompts the change within us. Peter Fransen turns from scholastic categories to the analogy of interpersonal relationships to capture this inversion of created and uncreated grace: "The moment God loves us, we are forthwith attracted to Him from within. We feel urged toward Him. His love wakens in us a hunger for His presence, a thirst for His life. *And that precisely is created grace.* It takes its rise, grows and lives thanks to His presence. As St. Augustine said, '*Quia amasti me, fecisti me amabilem*,' 'Because You have loved me, You have made me lovable.'"[22]

In all of this, God is not working against who we are. By the priority and universality of God's self-gift, we are made lovable from the very moment of our creation. We are born with a hunger for God's presence, a thirst for God's life. This orientation toward union with God constitutes our very existence as human beings. Thus Rahner described grace as more like a formal cause than an efficient cause. According to Rahner, generations of neoscholastic commentary on Aquinas had, in effect, reduced God's presence in grace to a mode of *efficient cause*, that is, a type of cause that is external to the effect it produces (like a potter who molds a vase). Rahner saw something more in Aquinas: grace is not primarily an extrinsic reality pushing people from outside; it is an inner constitutive principle of the human person; it is a type of *formal cause*. By calling grace a type of formal cause, Rahner meant to evoke this sense of grace as the "shape" or inner principle of the human person. God "does not originally cause and produce something different from himself in the creature, but rather . . . he communicates his own divine reality and makes it a constitutive element in the fulfillment of the creature."[23] Thus formal causality better captured Rahner's notion of grace as the "self-communication" of God.

These scholastic categories gave greater precision to Rahner's conviction that God does not simply send us something (created grace) from outside (efficient cause). God comes in person (uncreated grace) to dwell within us (formal cause). Rahner clearly wanted to avoid compromising either the integrity of the human person or the transcendence of God. Thus he added a qualifier, calling uncreated grace a *quasi-formal* cause of concrete humanity. The inner presence of grace does not blur the lines between God and humanity; indeed, it implies "the highest degree of unity in the fullest distinction."[24] But in all of this, Rahner realized that he was seeking out philosophical language to describe an ultimately indescribable mystery, namely, God's decision to come and be with us, within us. In a wonderful essay to his fellow Jesuits written late in life, Rahner called this divine decision the "incomprehensible miracle which overshoots all your metaphysics."[25]

The Particular Person

Rahner's treatment of formal causality points to his sense of the *constitutive* nature of grace. Grace is part of who we are as human beings. In the essay just cited, Rahner described the immediate experience of God emerging within. The dawn of such experience "is not the indoctrination of something not previously present in man, but a more explicit awakening of and to the self . . . this is the grace in which God himself dwells in all his immediacy."[26] In a letter to a depressed but deeply perceptive sixteen-year-old, Rahner wrote, "We cannot select our life according to our pleasure and according to the arbitrariness of our problematic whims and wishes. We must accept ourselves as we are. But when we do this really honestly, courageously and hopefully, we accept God himself."[27] This ability to see grace in the self, this perception of the transcendent God in the transcendental subject, is a dynamic that permeates Rahner's theology and his spirituality. It also raised for him a difficult question: If grace is so intimately tied to who we are, can it really be gratuitous? Is it a gift if it is already ours by nature? In responding to this question, Rahner coined one of his best-known categories, the "supernatural existential," a category that introduces us to Rahner's view of the particular person—the one who stands at the center of vocational discernment.

Rahner's work was part of a broader movement in twentieth-century theology to overcome the extrinsicism of grace that had handicapped Catholic thought since the Reformation. As we saw in chapter 2, Henri de Lubac had argued that neoscholastic attempts to protect divine transcendence had ended up splitting reality into two orders, the natural and the supernatural. Such a split severed faith from real life, effectively banishing God from the world. In response to such an impoverishment of the tradition, de Lubac set out to recover an earlier, Augustinian understanding of the human person: grace is not an add-on but immanent. God lives within our hearts. De Lubac argued that the image of God bestowed in creation gives to the human person a natural desire for union with the divine. Thus all human beings have by nature a spiritual orientation toward God.

The difficulty with this formulation centers on the phrase "by nature." Critics of de Lubac and the *nouvelle theologie*—including Pius XII—believed that if the disposition toward grace belonged to the very nature, or essence, of human beings, then the specific gratuity of grace would be lost.[28] If we are disposed toward God by our very nature, then the gift of grace is reduced to the gift of creation. Union with God becomes something owed to us by God by virtue of the way we have been made. To this charge, de Lubac protested that the absoluteness of our natural desire *for* God in no way compromises the gratuity of this desire as a gift *from* God. Others remained unconvinced.

In response to this controversy, Rahner developed his first substantial treatment of the "supernatural existential."[29] With it, Rahner sought to walk a middle ground between two poles: the standard neoscholastic view, which seemed to compromise the immanence of grace, and the view of de Lubac and his defenders, which seemed to compromise its transcendence.[30] Rahner sought out space between the manualists of the *duplex ordo* and the theologians of the *nouvelle théologie*—attempting to affirm both the relevance of Christianity and the absolute gratuity of grace.[31] He did so by turning from scholastic theology to modern philosophy, creatively appropriating Martin Heidegger's category of the "existential."[32] If "nature" refers to the general, abstract essence of a thing, then Heidegger's "existential" refers to the specific, concrete horizons within which a particular being lives. These existentials are inescapable aspects of my personal existence, horizons or "worlds" within which I move. Rahner added to Heidegger's list of existentials (such as historicity or sociality) a *supernatural* existential: the offer of grace in the depths of the human person.

Just as we live as concrete beings in history and in relationship to others, so we live as concrete beings within the offer of grace. But this offer is not just the stage on which we act—it constitutes our very identity as actors.[33] The supernatural existential is part of our fiber, part of ourselves as the actually existing beings that we are. In the category of the existential, Rahner found another middle ground, this time between human nature (essence) and the individual contingencies that follow from our human choices (Heidegger called this level the *existentiell* to distinguish it from the *existential* that exists prior to free activity). The offer of grace comes not by way of *essence* or *existentiell*. It is neither owed to us nor earned by us. The offer of grace comes as an *existential*. It is a facet of our personal existence—without being our personal achievement. This balance allowed Rahner to call God's self-offer absolutely gratuitous, deeply personal, and totally universal. "What we said about God's self-communication being supernatural and unmerited is not threatened or called into question by the fact that this self-communication is present in *every* person at least in the mode of an offer. The love of God does not become less a miracle by the fact that it is promised to all."[34]

But such a universal offer is not extended by way of a general, impersonal invitation, like an announcement pinned to the bulletin board or the always-open door of a counselor's office. It is a specific and unique event of love. And as such it touches, indeed constitutes, the particular person as the unique child of God that he or she is. For Rahner, the person has a unique individuality, first, because she is a material being, second, because she is a spiritual being, and, finally and most important, because she is a child of God through grace.[35] Thus—and this is key for the theology of vocation taking shape in these pages—our unique particularity follows not just on the fact of our creation (I was born at a certain time and place, with a certain life history, physical attributes, psychological constitution, etc.). It also flows from the unique offer of grace extended in love by God. It is the gift of grace that marks our "highest and finally determining individuality."[36] Rahner offered different names for this gift of God—uncreated grace, a quasi-formal cause, the supernatural existential—but what he was really talking about was a relationship. God's love is what makes each of us special.

Rahner wrote, "But if God's love for the individual man is thus, in each case, divinely unique; if his gift of himself is not something general, as though he were the same for everyone, equally accessible and universally distributed; if God's act of self-communication to the individual man is rather, in each case, a fresh, exceptional, ever unique miracle of utterly personal love, divinely radical and divinely unique— then through this love the beloved himself is truly someone absolutely unique. It is indeed true that God has called each one by his name."[37] No two loves have ever been alike. This is all the more true when the lover is the infinite God, who loves me in a way never seen before and never to be seen again. In doing so, God makes me *me*—a unique and beautiful individual who has never been seen before and will never be seen again. As Augustine prayed, "Because You have loved me, You have made me lovable."

In a universalistic vision that appeals to universal structures within the human subject, Rahner surprisingly rests his case on the specific. He left behind the essentialism of past debates over grace and instead embraced the human being in her or his lovable, concrete existence. It is not a general human nature that supports his system but the particular person that is "the event of God's absolute self-communication."[38]

Here we see an emphasis on particularity that moves beyond Barth's creative appropriation of the Protestant doctrine of vocation. For Barth, the particularities of the individual subject—those "limitations" that constitute each of us as a "unique opportunity"—are dimensions of our created existence. Our individual vocations follow, in very important ways, on how each of us was made. But even as he made this claim, Barth cautioned against the idea that we can deduce our calling from the facts of birth, biology, interest, or aptitude. Thus, while he stressed the importance of these created limitations, he radically subordinated them to the call of God, which cuts across every human sphere. Thus, there is an unresolved tension in Barth's treatment of vocation between creation and redemption, leaving the individual uncertain as to when she might be called to "remain in her calling" and when she might be called to transcend her own particular limitations in responding to the Lord. Rahner approached the issue quite differently by insisting that our unique individuality flows not only from nature but also from grace. Philip Endean notes the significance of this point for vocational discernment: "God is present, not merely as creator, but also as self-giver—a distinction which can imply a difference in our obligations. Moreover, God's gracious presence differs between individuals: hence the consequences of God's grace for our practice cannot simply be deduced."[39] The realization that God loves each of us individually, that God is lovingly present within each of us in a unique way (supernatural existential), serves as the foundation for Rahner's radically inductive approach to vocational discernment—an approach he said he learned from his spiritual mentor, Ignatius of Loyola. If I cannot deduce God's will from the outside, then I have to turn within, discovering the mystery that is my vocation in the mystery that is me.

Decision and Discernment

Part 1 of this book charted the unfortunate split between nature and grace within modern Catholic theology. This split came in stages. At the end of the Middle Ages, Nominalist theologians absolutized divine power, and in the process pushed God up and out of the world. Following the Reformation, Catholic polemicists sought ways to protect the gratuity of grace, and thus set off "nature" as a closed system to which the "super-natural" could only come as an outside addition. In the years leading up to the Second Vatican Council, neoscholastic manualists became preoccupied with the mechanics of actual grace, unwittingly reducing God's activity to an external force that occasionally interrupted the life of a believer. By the time Rahner began his theological career, he would have found firmly in place a fairly consistent picture of the divine-human relationship: a distant God acted on an integral nature through an extrinsic grace.

Within such a theological world, vocation suffered. The interior dimension of God's call—long a part of the Christian spiritual tradition—was read through this extrinsicism of grace. The result was that the metaphor of the "secret voice" became literalized. This "voice" of vocation was presented as a kind of communiqué (extrinsic grace) that was in me but foreign to me (integral nature), that, in the end, could say anything (distant God). Since supernatural grace was considered to be inaccessible to the human mind, the voice truly was a secret. This frustrating realization fueled a frantic search for "signs" of a true vocation, clues or signals that something was there.

Rahner left behind this world of assumptions with his simple claim that an "immediate experience of God" is possible and widely available. And much of his life's work revolved around offering an alternative to the deficient theology of grace he had learned in his seminary textbooks.

Thanks in large part to his work, the Catholic understanding of grace underwent a revolution over the course of the twentieth century—touching virtually every area of theology, from ethics and ecclesiology to liturgy and eschatology. If we are still waiting for a thorough rethinking of vocation in light of this revolution, it is Rahner himself who leads the way. His treatment of grace as God's unique self-gift to each individual laid out an itinerary for coming to a deeper appreciation for the particularity of God's call; and in his several essays on the *Spiritual Exercises* of Ignatius of Loyola, Rahner took the first steps. In the world of Ignatius—a world where God can be found in all things—Rahner recognized that discernment is not a search for some hidden plan; it is the discovery of one's unique and deepest identity.

Rahner and Ignatius

In an interview late in life, Rahner reflected, "I think that the spirituality of Ignatius himself, which one learned through the practice of prayer and religious formation, was more significant for me than all learned philosophy and theology inside and outside the order."[40] Over the course of his career, Rahner wrote occasional essays on Ignatius and the *Spiritual Exercises*—at least one of which was truly groundbreaking. But it was a short, passionate piece that he wrote in the persona of Ignatius himself, titled "Ignatius of Loyola Speaks to a Modern Jesuit," that Rahner called his last will and testament, "a resumé of my theology, in general, and of how I tried to live."[41] Rahner saw Ignatius as an original genius, whose insights had by and large been overlooked by subsequent theologians—including many of the most important Jesuit commentators of the past four hundred years! Just as Karl Barth returned to Luther in a critical and constructive mode in order to correct the later Protestant tradition of vocation, so Rahner returned to Ignatius to advance a rich alternative to what he saw as the thin theological treatment of vocation in his own Catholic world.[42]

For Rahner, the *Spiritual Exercises* of Ignatius is a characteristic document of the modern world.[43] He saw here an effort to incorporate into the heart of Christian mysticism the core of a new worldview: the human subject. It was not that the church or theology had ignored the human person before the birth of modernity; it was more a question of how the person was understood. In the medieval world, the human being was placed within a realm of universals and universal norms.

There the objective realm was a given; in Rahner's words, the human person "thought and lived on God and the world." What marked the passage to modernity was that the individual subject came to stand over and against this unified cosmos. The self became separated from the many mediating structures of medieval life, rising up before God and the world as an individual. No longer one part within an organic whole, the modern subject stood free to accept or reject, appropriate or ignore what was once simply presumed. According to Rahner, the *Exercises* made this "turn to the subject" in a spiritual key. Born out of Ignatius's own subjective experience, the *Exercises* encourage a process of self-discovery before God, a process in which the creature dialogues directly with the Creator.[44] Thus, for Rahner, the individual subject that leads the emerging modern world stands at the center of Ignatian discernment.

The *Exercises* are also modern in that the self-discovery they encourage has a practical orientation. The subject faces a decision. The *Exercises* are aimed at execution. At the heart of these meditations is a fundamental, lifelong choice in which the retreatant responds to the call of Christ by committing to a concrete course of action. Ignatius called this choice the "election." And he sincerely believed that, through the process of the *Exercises*, God would reveal directly to the retreatant what he or she ought to do. Rahner found this remarkable. He saw that the process of Ignatian discernment is not merely the application of general human, Christian, or ecclesiastical norms to a specific case. It is the discovery, within these norms, of one's "unique, individual destiny willed by God which transcends all general norms."[45] Ignatius seems to have seen—long before Sartre—that universal moral norms are not always that helpful in individual cases. But that does not mean they are invalid.[46] It simply means that universal norms have to be complemented by a way of discovering those particular imperatives that God directs to each individual. "The will of God is not, therefore, simply and entirely transmitted through the objective structures of the world and the Church. The subject goes beyond what is universally valid and seeks through his choice his own unique truth."[47] The whole point of the *Exercises* is to help the individual find that particular imperative, to help him or her uncover the unique truth that God calls each human person toward.

This practical and particular dynamic of the *Exercises* is the link that Rahner forged between the Ignatian tradition he had inherited and the theology of grace he was in the process of constructing. In 1956, Rahner published a lengthy essay on the *Spiritual Exercises* titled "The Logic of Concrete Individual Knowledge in Ignatius Loyola."[48] In it, Rahner brought his theology of grace to the *Exercises* in an effort to illuminate the process of Ignatian discernment through the categories of transcendental philosophy. Rahner took Ignatius's rich and complex process of conversion and commitment and focused on what he believed to be its core: the moment of individual vocational choice, the election.

As we recall from chapter 2, the election comes within the Second Week of meditations laid out in the *Exercises*. It is the moment that the first two Weeks are meant to prepare and that the last two Weeks are meant to confirm. As he explained this moment of vocational choice, Ignatius described three "times" for making a good election.[49] The first time, or occasion, involves a free decree of God that comes to an individual by way of a special revelation, as was the case, for example, with St. Paul or St. Matthew. The second involves individual reflection on the inner movements of the spirit—those experiences of consolation and desolation that serve as clues to the inner workings of God. The third involves a more detached, even rational, weighing of pros and cons associated with a particular decision. Rahner argued that, though the three times should not be too sharply separated, it is nevertheless the second occasion that was for Ignatius the norm—the normal way of making a vocational choice.

Rahner's interpretation contradicted the prevailing view, and he recognized that. In fact, he argued that both Ignatius's detractors and his defenders missed the saint's key insight. It is precisely here that the "astonishing originality" of the *Exercises* breaks through.[50] Early opponents saw Ignatius as another *alumbrados*, another prophet of private revelations. They wrongly read the *Exercises* through the lens of the first occasion. In response, later Jesuit commentators, anxious to defend the orthodoxy of their founder, stressed the third occasion, thus highlighting the deductive and the rational. For Rahner, something more significant and creative is going on in the *Exercises*. In his second "time" for making an election, and in the rules for the discernment of spirits that go along with it, Ignatius was pointing to a way of "knowing" the will of God that begins with the concrete choices before us, moves through our emotions and affections, and ends at the God who lives at the very core of our being. God's voice is not a trumpet or a textbook but a kind of presence pulsing through us, silently, invisibly, but no less real. In the second occasion for making an election, Rahner saw Ignatius working in the realm of the transcendental. He saw in

Ignatius a recognition that, in some of the most vital decisions of life, God speaks not through miracles or moral norms but through *me*—through the dynamism of my own personality and inner life.

Ignatius simply took it for granted that the human soul is pulled in different directions. As he lay in bed recovering from his battle wounds, Ignatius found himself drawn to different lives and ways of living. In trying to choose one life over another, he discovered that his feelings could help. The affections and attractions of the heart emerged as central to the process of discernment—demanding careful attention to what Ignatius called the consolations and desolations of the soul. The standard procedure for Christians facing such mixed emotions had traditionally been to examine the *object* of the attraction: Is this life better than the other? Is this course of action more virtuous than that? The goodness of the object would indicate whether the attraction was from God or not. What Rahner saw as truly revolutionary in Ignatius was that this logic was reversed. Instead of looking at the moral goodness of the choice in order to determine the origin of the attraction, Ignatius suggested that we look for the origin of the attraction in order to determine the goodness of the choice.[51] He instructed us not to look at the fruits of our feelings but to search for their seeds. The sources of our affections are what are significant. Thus the *Exercises* offer practical advice for a retreat leader to help an individual recognize where her or his feelings are coming from.

In the *Exercises*, Ignatius split such impulses into those that come from oneself and those that come from without, either from a good or an evil spirit.[52] Rahner recognized that modern men and women might not be so comfortable with such a simplistic psychology, or so quick to attribute inner influences to God or the devil: "It is much more likely [a person today] will think of hormones, effects of the weather, hereditary factors influencing character, repercussions of the unconscious, complexes and innumerable other things than that the idea will occur to him that God, his guardian angel or the devil is at work."[53] Still, Rahner saw no trouble in demythologizing Ignatius's psychology, while at the same time retaining the kernel of his spiritual insight. For unless we are willing to reduce the human spirit to an organism totally determined by environment and genes, we have to find room for freedom. We have to account for the way in which the human spirit freely responds to the depth of her own being, a depth that Christians believe is nothing less than the indwelling of the triune God. Unless everything is mechanistically predetermined, the human person will have to negotiate the moral realm;

he will have to decide where his loves will lead. Key to arriving at this decision is sorting out just exactly where these "loves" come from—whether they are in fact the result of genetic predispositions, cultural conditioning, the lingering repercussions of past trauma, or whether through all of these factors and even against them there is not some other wholly transcendent source calling.

To guide retreat directors and retreatants through this thicket of conflicting feelings, Ignatius proposed two sets of "Rules for the Discernment of Spirits." In taking up particular choices, Ignatius encouraged retreatants to pay close attention to the experiences of consolation and desolation connected with each. Feelings of peace, tranquility, and clarity could be clues to God's call, while feelings of agitation, dissonance, and emptiness signal the opposite. Often the emotional landscape is mixed, and so his various "Rules" were meant to help navigate the terrain. But Rahner asked an important question: If these rules provide a kind of map, is there a North Star? Is there some criterion guiding these rules, a kind of first principle that grounds them and assures their reliability? Here we zero in on the heart of Rahner's theological argument. For Rahner, the key to the whole process of discernment laid out in the *Exercises* is a few confusing sentences buried within Ignatius's second set of "Rules for the Discernment of Spirits." In the second rule for the Second Week, the experience of grace comes to bear on vocational discernment:

> Only God our Lord can give the soul consolation without a preceding cause. For it is the prerogative of the Creator alone to enter the soul, depart from it, and cause a motion in it which draws the person wholly into love of his Divine Majesty. By "without [a preceding] cause" I mean without any previous perception or understanding of some object by means of which the consolation just mentioned might have been stimulated, through the intermediate activity of the person's acts of understanding and willing.[54]

Of this passage, the great Baroque commentator Francisco de Suárez candidly admitted, "I do not find it easy to understand these words."[55] Rahner described the passage as "a masterpiece of brevity but not of clarity."[56] Still, Rahner went on to argue that these lines were the key to the *Exercises* as a whole.

What is this "consolation without preceding cause" (*consolación sin causa precedente*)? The history of Jesuit commentary reveals no consistent interpretation, other than a tendency to dismiss it as a rare and esoteric mystical experience. Contemporary theologians have given the concept more attention, but they have hardly come to a consensus.[57] What launched this new debate was Rahner himself, who pulled the notion out of obscurity, first, by arguing that the consolation without cause is central to the *Exercises*, and, second, by making the case that the concept refers not to a rare and privileged moment but to an ordinary and widespread experience. For Rahner, the consolation without cause is simply the experience of transcendence emerging into our awareness. In the consolation without cause, the ever-present pulse of God that ordinarily exists at the periphery of our consciousness moves more into the center. It is the transcendent becoming thematic, an experience of self-awareness in which we "see" ourselves as we truly are: children of God, friends of Christ, and temples of the Holy Spirit.

What makes this consolation different from other feelings of consolation explored in the *Exercises* is that it is "without preceding cause." Rahner interpreted "without cause" as "without object." Usually, when we turn our attention to God, we focus on *concepts about* God. The transcendent reality that is God slips out of sight, staying as the horizon hidden behind these concepts that occupy our brains. However, there can be times when, while focusing our minds on a particular idea or conceptual object, the object itself begins to fade and the reality of God's love shines through, almost to the point of causing the object itself to disappear. That is how Rahner described the "consolation without preceding cause." It is an experience of pure transcendence emerging into awareness. It occurs when that silent presence—which everywhere permeates our existence, which always accompanies our categorical knowing as a kind of implicit awareness—moves into conscious focus *without being clouded by concepts.*

> The conceptual object which in normal acts is a condition of awareness of this transcendence can also become more transparent, can almost entirely disappear, remain itself unheeded, so that the dynamism itself alone becomes more and more the essential. If this transcendence is present in this way in its purity and as itself the focus of awareness, without being mediated by the conceptual object and so hidden, and if this occurs not only in cognition but also as the pure dynamism of the will in positive affirmation and receptivity, in love that is to say, then we have the lowest stage of what Ignatius is probably referring to, without metaphysical and theological terminology when he speaks of the consolation *sin causa.*[58]

The consolation without cause is an awareness of one's own transcendence that fades into total openness toward God, an openness in which the soul is drawn wholly into divine love. It is a "consolation without conceptual object in the actual concretely personal, radical love of God."[59]

Rahner believed that previous Jesuit commentators had marginalized Ignatius's insight because they refused to acknowledge that supernatural grace could be experienced.[60] Their epistemology was too limited, trapped as it was in a dualism that assumed either you knew something in clear and distinct ideas, or you did not know it. For Rahner, the wisdom of Ignatius reveals that we can "know" ourselves in a deeper and more intimate way than clear concepts allow. Subsequent scholars have questioned whether Rahner's interpretation of the consolation without cause is allowed by his own epistemological assumptions.[61] In Rahner's early philosophical writings, the transcendental is always mediated by the categorical. And throughout his career, he maintained that reality is fundamentally symbolic. Is it possible, then, for transcendental experience to exist "without object"? Can there be such a "pure" experience, free of the categorical realm through which we ordinarily know anything? Rahner's own rhetoric is not always helpful. At times he suggested that the categorical is simply left behind in the experience of fundamental consolation; at other times he emphasized not the relinquishing of the conceptual object but its becoming *transparent* to the love of God. In the 1956 essay, Rahner's language was tentative. Though he underscored the "non-conceptual" aspect of the consolation without cause, when he described the conceptual object, he said it can "become" more transparent, that it "almost entirely" disappears. When he explicitly asked the question about the absence of the object in the consolation without cause, he responded by underscoring the positive content of the experience as utter receptivity to God.[62]

Part of the trouble is simply the tension that arises from Rahner's attempt to articulate the mystical experience of Ignatius in the vocabulary of transcendental philosophy. The underlying issue is Rahner's belief that we can move toward greater and greater awareness of who we are before God precisely by freeing ourselves from that self-deception that is tied to our limited and often mistaken ideas. Ignatius wrote that "when the consolation is without a preceding cause, no deception can be present in it, since it is coming only from God our Lord."[63] For Rahner, it is precisely the "thinness," or transparency, of the conceptual object that guarantees the authenticity of the experience. When we introduce human concepts to speak about God or grace or ourselves, we introduce limits. We vainly try to delineate the infinite, to cordon off mystery. Thus we distort the reality of God and deceive ourselves. "But transcendence pure and simple cannot deceive. . . . Pure openness and receptivity is always genuine and can miss nothing because it excludes nothing but includes all."[64] The fundamental consolation saves us from the idolatry of our ideas, offering a more direct contact with the graced depth of our own being. Freed from the clutter of our concepts, we can touch the living God within. This contact is thus not an ephemeral emptiness but a sinking into the depth of God's love. For Rahner, consolation without cause is the experience of "utter receptivity to God, the inexpressible, non-conceptual experience of the love of the God who is raised transcendent above all that is individual, all that can be mentioned and distinguished, of God as God. There is no longer 'any object' but the drawing of the whole person, with the very ground of his being into love."[65] This experience bears its own warrant.

All of this might sound like the language of the mystic, a flight into the apophatic, some special trance or rarified state of self-abandonment. While Rahner took the experience of the mystic seriously, he did not see the mystic as a special case. The mystic stands on a continuum of consciousness that we all share. For Rahner, the experience of transcendence that is the root of all mystical experience is fundamental to and coextensive with all human knowing, loving, and acting. The trouble is that most of us often miss it. We all have some implicit "sense" of ourselves as an open subject oriented toward mystery, but we can be more or less conscious of it. Particular situations or regular practices can trigger moments of self-awareness, fostering that fundamental consolation that makes the transcendental thematic in a wordless but very real way. Thus each of us can grow in our awareness of our transcendental horizon. We all have the opportunity to be mystics—not spiritual virtuosi but folks who strive to understand our experience of life, and so to work out our basic sense of ourselves and stance toward the world.

Personal Vocation

For Rahner, consolation without preceding cause is the experience of transcendence emerging into awareness. It is coming into a deep recognition of God's presence within ourselves as a unique gift of love (supernatural existential). This unique presence of God within me is what makes me the unique individual—the special child of God—that I am. Thus, consolation without cause is at the same time an always-more-honest sense of myself, an always-more-honest discovery of who I am. It is both a receptivity to the God who made me and an openness to the me whom God has made. As Philip Endean explains, "In the Ignatian Exercises, therefore, Rahner saw a process of discovery essential to Christian discipleship. To summarize it in anticipation: the self can be led to focus on its 'transcendence,' and the basic features of consciousness which are normally just the tacit accompaniments and enabling conditions of particular mental acts can become 'thematic.' The Exercises foster such moments. The effect can be to transform our reflective self-understanding, and the patterns of significance and value that shape our perceptions—a transformation with practical consequences."[66] Coming to feel God's love *for me* changes the way that I look at the world, and the way that I live within it. This experience is the necessary condition for authentic vocational discernment.

The practical payoff to Rahner's exegesis of Ignatius's consolation without cause is the role it plays in decision making. Rahner repeated the observation that, in many of the most crucial life decisions, Christians get little help from a deductive approach that starts with general principles of the gospel and then tries to apply them to a particular situation. What Rahner saw in Ignatius was a more inductive approach. Ignatius focused on the concrete choice facing an individual. He invited that individual to reflect on the feelings surrounding this choice, and argued that, by tracing these feelings to their source, the will of God would be revealed. This will comes "as a summons to man as the precise individual he is, not simply as the general vocation by which anyone is 'drawn wholly into God's love.' It constitutes those concrete individual calls in which a definite state of life, a definite, limited, circumscribed object is chosen in an 'Election.'"[67] How does this work? What is the process that links our "sense of ourselves before God" to the concrete and difficult decisions we have to make throughout life?

For Rahner, the process of Ignatian discernment works by taking the consolations associated with a particular choice and placing them before that more fundamental consolation, the consolation without preceding cause, in order to see if they are in harmony:

> By frequently confronting the object of Election with the fundamental consolation, the experimental test is made whether the

two phenomena are in harmony, mutually cohere, whether the will to the object of Election under scrutiny leaves intact that pure openness to God in the supernatural experience of transcendence and even supports and augments it or weakens and obscures it; whether a synthesis of these two attitudes, pure receptivity to God (as concretely achieved, not as a theoretical principle and proposition) and the will to this limited finite object of decision produces "peace," "tranquility," "quiet," so that true gladness and spiritual joy ensue, that is, the joy of pure, free, undistorted transcendence; or whether instead of smoothness, gentleness and sweetness, sharpness, tumult and disturbance arise.[68]

What we are looking for is a resonance between our basic sense of ourselves before God and the concrete choice before us. Does the decision to follow this particular path preserve or even deepen fundamental consolation? Does it strengthen the peace of heart that we feel when we stand openly and honestly before God? Or does it disturb the peace, jar against our basic self-understanding, feel inauthentic or untrue to our relationship with God? Answers to such questions cannot simply be deduced; they probably won't be miraculously revealed. Instead, Ignatius "has in mind an attempt, undertaken by an individual himself by way of test, at a synthesis of his fundamental innermost attitude, acquired by experience and certainly effected by God, and a definite object proposed from without as a possible matter for a decision of this kind."[69]

If this seems like a technical exposition whose relevance is restricted to a small group of specialists, Rahner himself pointed toward broader implications. At the very end of his 1956 essay, Rahner asked the question, If the second "occasion" for making an election is the normal way in which God speaks to an individual, then what about all those people who are unable to make the *Exercises*? Are these people excluded from the divine call? Does God only speak to Jesuits? Clearly, for Rahner, the answer was no. Appealing to the universal dynamic of transcendental experience, Rahner concluded, "It may be said too that nearly everyone in grave decisions makes a choice more or less exactly in the way Ignatius conceives it, just as the man in the street uses logic without ever having studied it."[70] Most people—even those who are not particularly religious—make big decisions by seeking harmony between the choice they face and their "fundamental global awareness" of themselves. For Rahner, the "man in the street" will decide not entirely on the basis of a rational analysis "but by whether he feels that something 'suits him' or not. And this feeling will be judged by whether the matter pleases, delights, brings peace and satisfaction."[71] Like the student who discovers that she has been speaking prose her whole life, the study of Ignatius's method simply makes explicit what everyone is doing already.

It is important to keep in mind that, in this test of congruence between our fundamental religious attitude and a particular choice, we are not comparing the *object* of the choice (a specific act or series of actions) and the *object* of our fundamental attitude (God, or our conception of God). Such an understanding would simply revert to a deductive method that judges the appropriateness of an action according to general norms. Ignatius was not particularly interested in that approach. He presumed from the start that the object of the election was already something good or indifferent in and of itself. Discernment—as distinct from moral decision making—is always a choice among *goods*. The question is not, what is the good? The question is, what is the good *for me here and now*? The real genius of the *Exercises* is that the reflection takes place not at the level of the objective but at the level of the subjective. We are looking for harmony within ourselves, patterns of coherence among our emotions and affections. Such harmony cannot be deduced but only experienced—hence the trial and error method of meditation proposed by Ignatius.

Through decision, the particular person discovers herself. A year before his major essay on the *Exercises* appeared, Rahner published a set of retreat reflections originally given to seminarians at Canisius College in Innsbruck.[72] In these remarks, Rahner repeated in more pastoral terms his conviction that the *Exercises* are about the election, and the election is about a particular act of freedom. Ignatius did not start with universal norms but with the question, what am I to do? While we owe our existence to God and while we act under the power of grace, still, in a very real way, we craft ourselves. Rahner wrote, "It is in action, in that being which is doing, not in the static being and mere words of conceptual objectivity, that a man arrives at that special individuality which he is meant to have . . . it is really by his own free decision that a man rises from being a mere particular instance of his species to unique, individual personality."[73]

Through activity, we arrive at individuality. By freedom, we become unique. Unlike every other creature, the human person is called. God loves me in a way never seen before and never to be seen again. My unique response to this love gives concrete shape to the vocation that is my life. The fundamental vocation of grace can only be accepted in and through a personal vocation, which can only be arrived at through freedom. However, this exercise of freedom is liable to miscarry; my individuality may morph into a frustrating mass of missed opportunities or a particular constellation of guilt. How is one to find that summons, to hear that call that saves me from being "a source of deathly weariness and desolation" to myself? Appealing to the wisdom of Ignatius, and the broader tradition he inhabited, Rahner replied, look within. The wonder of vocation is the simple fact that this call is me, even though it is not mine.

> Though it does indeed come from one's inmost centre, it is precisely not one's own in the sense of coming from one's own resources, but one's own in the sense of being given; that which is most one's own, because it is God's. In other words, we discover the personal only as we go out to encounter that image of us which God has made for himself, the picture of us which he holds before us and by which we, imperfect as we are, are always simultaneously cast down and delighted, because we recognize in it both ourselves and our God.[74]

The danger in these lines is not a creeping subjectivism that elevates our response over God's call. Rather, the danger is to transform the dynamic subject into a static given—to freeze the metaphor of movement into a still shot, and reduce our vocation to what God *already* had in mind. Such a move misses Rahner's basic point about freedom and overlooks the genius he saw in Ignatius.

Ignatius was about decision. He was about freedom and activity. Pulsing through Rahner's occasional remarks on vocation is a vision of the person as original and creative, as unprecedented and always open to the future. There is a particularity to the human person that cannot be captured by the variables of circumstance, psychology, or genetic makeup alone. It is the individuality that is continually born out of our free decisions. Thus the divine plan does not lie behind us in the mind of God; it lies out ahead of us in our actions lived in harmony with the gift of grace. That is why Rahner could say that God calls each of us to something very particular—without saying anything very particular about it! Our response is yet to be written. Empowered by grace in the core of our personality, we freely shape our own individuality. What God is calling me toward, what God wants for *me* is to be *myself*—to live out that freedom in love that opens into a new and never-seen future. Indeed, what faith-filled people are saying when they say that they "have been called" to this or to that is not that they have found the plan but that they have felt a profound resonance between their deepest sense of themselves before God and this particular path forward.

Rahner's "forward-looking" view of vocation highlights another important difference between his approach and that of Karl Barth. Both Rahner and Barth emphasized the loving initiative of God and the indispensable role of Christ in calling all people to intimate union with the divine life. However, Barth spoke of vocation as the "place of responsibility" where the divine summons meets us. This place is not just a profession but is also the whole context within which a particular person lives. He associated vocation (*Beruf*) more with the particularity of creation than with the new creation that comes with grace. Thus vocation is "where we are" when the divine summons comes, the place "from which" (*terminus a quo*) God invites us to discipleship. Against Barth's *whence* stands Rahner's *whither*. For Rahner, vocation is less about where we are called *from* and more about what we are called *toward*. The divine call does not so much cut diagonally across the human vocation as it is wound up with it. As we have seen, there are historical roots behind these two different emphases. Barth was the heir of Luther's view of estate (*Stand*) as calling. Rahner received impetus from Ignatius's emphasis on apostolic activity. However, ultimately, it is differing anthropologies and theologies of grace that separate the two approaches. For Barth, the divine call confronts a fallen creation. For Rahner, this call comes within and through a grace-soaked world: God calls us to respond by carrying forward our deepest identity—to be saints by being ourselves.

As attractive as that may sound, the response around which Rahner's view of vocation revolves is as deep and mysterious as the human person. In the end, Rahner's interpretation of the Ignatian election suggests that there is no quick and easy formula for finding our vocation. Such a process takes time. It demands going over things again and again, trying this out and then that, testing possible paths over against a sense of oneself before God that, to serve as a reliable guide to discernment, requires brutal honesty and ongoing conversion. In his remarks at Canisius College, Rahner placed the discovery of one's vocation within an eschatological context: "We can do no more than move towards it; it is only slowly revealed, and never wholly in this life. While we are still pilgrims, it is not only God but we ourselves too that we can know only in reflections and likenesses; it is only *then* that we shall know ourselves, too, even as we are known."[75] In the meantime, we can only catch a glimpse of ourselves, "of that special uniqueness which is the grace of God, who gives to everyone that which is uniquely his own and which makes him worthy to exist for ever." That glimpse is got, Rahner concluded, "in the unity of love with God." In bringing our lives before that love—which Rahner elsewhere described as transcendental experience, the preapprehension of mystery, a consolation without preceding cause, a sense of "something more"—we find our vocation. Rahner saw in the meditations of the *Exercises* a kind of playacting, or "make-believe," by which we imagine ourselves in certain lives and then pause to reflect on how it feels. This quiet, slow process of self-discovery—more improvisational than scripted—was the way Rahner described his own life. A year before he died, Rahner shared his story with a group of German schoolgirls: "I must confess honestly that I do not recall any such lightninglike illumination, or a sudden, perhaps mystical, experience in my calling. No, in my case it did not happen so dramatically. Of course there are people who feel called in an entirely different way. . . . Such sudden experiences, which come like bolts of lightning, are entirely possible. Whoever has had such experiences is to be congratulated. However, there is another way of being called, in quiet reflection, and in a prolonged process of discernment and making one's way toward a definite decision for one's calling in life."[76]

Becoming Free to Be Me

In an appreciative early essay, Avery Dulles noted that Rahner's 1956 treatment of Ignatian discernment worked through a series of systematic "reductions." Rahner first reduced the *Exercises* to the election, then the election to the "second time," the "second time" to the rules of discernment of spirits, and, finally, the rules themselves were reduced to the "first principle" of consolation without preceding cause. For Dulles, these reductions are "startling in their illuminative power" and serve to clear up a whole set of problems associated with the *Exercises*.[77]

However, for all the illuminating gains, there is a potential loss that comes with Rahner's systematic reductions. What Rahner would no doubt admit—but what has not been emphasized in our treatment so far—is that the consolation without preceding cause, which stands at the heart of his treatment, is not a given. *The offer of grace* is a given—it is extended to every human subject. But not every person accepts this gift or sees past the distractions of the categorical to embrace the transcendental truth that constitutes our own truth. We do not always have an honest sense of ourselves before God. For Rahner, discernment works by placing the concrete choice before the fundamental consolation, a consolation that grows, more or less, according to our consciousness of and receptivity to God in our lives. We are looking for harmony between the two, but resonance means little if the tuning fork is bent. It is precisely for this reason that Ignatius located the election in the Second Week—*after* the purification of the affections that occurs during the First Week. Authentic discernment occurs only after a conversion that comes through immersion in the story of Jesus.

Rahner's theological system cannot be reduced to his Ignatian "reductions." Indeed, the freedom of the human response to God is essential to his theology of grace. The "supernatural existential" is grace in the mode of *offer*. Amidst changing conversation partners over the course of his career, Rahner struggled to give a precise definition of this existential.[78] But what consistently runs through his many essays is a sense of the supernatural existential as the *beginning* of God's self-communication. If grace *is* God's self-communication, the supernatural existential is a partial realization of this grace, even a "deficient mode" of grace.[79] Once this offer is accepted (which is an act made possible by the offer itself), then the offer becomes the grace of self-communication in all its fullness. This distinction between God's initial offer and its fulfillment underscores the reality of human freedom. Unlike every other creature in the universe, the destiny of the human person is not imposed on us, but comes to us by way of vocation. God calls us to our supernatural end. We have to respond. As spiritual beings, we move toward—or away from—our destiny freely.

Another mystic of ordinary life, Thomas Merton, evoked this theological point in more poetic language:

> For me to be a saint means to be myself. Therefore the problem of sanctity and salvation is in fact the problem of finding out who I am and of discovering my true self.
>
> Trees and animals have no problem. God makes them what they are without consulting them, and they are perfectly satisfied.
>
> With us it is different. God leaves us free to be whatever we like. We can be ourselves or not, as we please. But the problem is this: *since God alone possesses the secret of my identity, He alone can make me who I am* or rather, He alone can make me who I will be when I at last fully begin to be.[80]

Unlike cats or conifers, we have to choose whether we will be who God chooses us to be. In Rahner's theology of the supernatural existential, there is a vision of the individual human person as inescapably constituted by an offer that is not an automatic entitlement but a loving invitation waiting for a response.

This sense of graced humanity did not blind Rahner to the reality of sin. Indeed, for all his attention to the activity of human freedom, he also recognized freedom's profound passivity. Our freedom is always exercised within the context of internal and external forces that influence us for good or for bad. In an early essay, Rahner took the traditional notion of concupiscence, usually seen as the human proclivity toward sin, and transformed it to describe all those premoral structures that shape how our moral decisions are made.[81] These circumstances and situations, these spontaneous appetites, these particular associations or psychological scars—these are facets of our finite existence that impact our freedom. They put to rest the modern myth of the totally autonomous agent, the free subject who escapes all particular limitations. In his later *Foundations*, Rahner revived the category of original sin. Freeing it from past biological or sexual—and ultimately impotent—interpretations, Rahner spoke of original sin as the reality of having to act within a history of sin and guilt.[82] Horrible things have happened, and we are not untouched by them. Through our own failures, we contribute to them. The ubiquity of oppressive structures, vast histories of dehumanization, and ongoing injustices bind us to other sinners in a shadowy solidarity. "In order to arrive at a real understanding of original sin, we begin with the fact that the situation of our own freedom bears the stamp of the guilt of others in a way which cannot be eradicated."[83] This history of sin does not just flow around us; it flows through us. Sin exists too as an existential of our concrete humanity.

Thus the process of vocational discernment that Rahner recommended depends on personal conversion. The fundamental decision that constitutes the "unique truth" for an individual "can only be chosen in a free decision as what is here and now important and subjectively accepted by a person, *if his subjectivity is set free*."[84] To choose freely, our subjectivity must be set free. It must be set free from our attachment to that false self that hides who we really are and obstructs our relationship with God. This freedom is the prerequisite to the process of discernment that Rahner recommended. And in the remaining two chapters of this book, we will turn our attention more explicitly to the kind of conversion that is needed today in order to find that freedom, the freedom that opens up our ears to hear the call of God.

As we do so, we keep before us that deep biblical truth: where sin grows, grace overflows (Rom 5:20). In Rahner's proclamation of the good news, sin is at a decided disadvantage. For the human person does not stand in some neutral ground, poised between sin and salvation. In a world of grace, "yes" and "no" are not parallel possibilities. The whole world is already graced by God's self-offer, and to say no through sin is simply a rejection of reality, a kind of self-destruction. Stephen Duffy summarizes Rahner's point: "Against a graced horizon, sin is less lost innocence than betrayal of the dynamism of one's being, alienation, incompleteness, the measure of one's distance from Christ and authentic selfhood."[85] Opposite authentic selfhood is what Merton called the "false self"—the ego that we set up as ultimate but is really just an illusion.[86] Thus sin is real but abortive. It is a turning away from the deepest truth of our identity. It is a denial of ourselves. For Rahner, every one of us comes into existence positively directed toward God's loving offer and predisposed to accept it. We slant that way. The supernatural existential so shapes us that even if God's invitation is rejected, the supernatural existential remains. It continues to constitute us in our concrete humanity. (Who would say that God stops loving us just because we choose to be unloving?) Thus, to answer yes to God is not to accept a gift alien to us but to strike a resounding chord rising out of our innermost depths.[87] It is to feel that profound consolation that Ignatius described. In the end, the question of sin and salvation *for me* is the question of whether I choose to go with the grain of my being or to grate against it. I can be myself or not, as I please.

Conclusion

Karl Rahner tapped into a rich tradition of reflection on the inner call and reinterpreted it in light of a revitalized theology of grace. The result is a vision of vocation that takes seriously the concrete particularity and freedom of the human subject. For Rahner, God calls the individual toward that future that is felt in the resonances between the right choice and one's fundamental spiritual orientation. In other words, I hear my vocation in the harmony between the path that is before me and the mystery that is me. Thus in Rahner, we find a creative translation of Ignatian spirituality into the transcendental and existential categories of late modernity—a theology that allows God to speak to the heart, without the muffled extrinsicism of past accounts of vocation.

But if the subject stands at the center of a theology of vocation, this subject does not stand alone. One of the reasons that Rahner could so confidently lift up transcendental experience as the touchstone of the Christian life is to be found in his own formation within the heavily categorical world of preconciliar Catholicism. His many pastoral and theological essays are various attempts to move out of a closed neo-scholastic system. Against intellectual dogmatism and institutional rigidity, Rahner offered reflections on God as mystery, grace as personal, mysticism as ordinary, salvation as universal. It makes sense that this was the orientation and emphasis of his theology. It also helps to explain what Rahner left out. What his approach simply assumed was that the very ability to name the experience of transcendence as an experience *of grace* relies on some degree of theological inheritance and ecclesial socialization. It is a larger narrative and community of meaning that enables Christians to recognize the experience of transcendence *as a vocation*, to identify it—and even to experience it—as a call coming from God.

In many ways, Rahner could take that narrative for granted. But such is no longer the case. Transcendental experience, sensed in particular moments of self-awareness, tragedy, or joy, is a constitutive dimension of human existence. However, such depth experiences are no longer automatically perceived as experiences of God. Rahner was not unaware of this epochal shift in religious sensibilities. In remarks on "The *Exercises* Today," Rahner recognized that the fundamental relationship of immediacy to God cannot be presumed to be given either theoretically or existentially in today's society. Thus he recommended a longer and more explicit introduction to the *Exercises* before embarking on them.[88]

Such "formation" is not merely preliminary; it is integral to the process of the *Exercises* itself. Ignatius did not leap to the "consolation without cause" or imagine it as floating free from the larger dynamic of the retreat. Rahner's systematic analysis allowed him to focus his remarks on this one piece, but such a move might mask the broader context of Ignatius's vision. The *Exercises* never allow the individual retreatant to become an autonomous modern subject, alone with her or his transcendental experience. Subjective feelings become a guide to God's will only through a process of purification and conversion that marks the transition from the First to the Second Week. The discernment of spirits is firmly located within a series of meditations on the life of Jesus. The election takes the form of a personal response to the concrete call of Christ. The whole thing works by embedding the individual within a set of practices, a particular narrative, and a historical community that revolves around Jesus. Profoundly personal, the call of Christ is nevertheless mediated. Though Ignatius warned the retreat director not to get in the way of the individual retreatant and God, still it is significant that he did not write a work of personal piety. He wrote a guidebook. The very existence of the *Exercises* implies that it takes another person to bring us before God. It takes another person to help us hear our vocation.

In the next chapter, we turn to reflect on what it means to say that God calls us *through others*. It will serve to build on what we have learned from Rahner by highlighting the communal and contextual nature of the Christian vocation—in some ways by making explicit what is implicit in his work, in other ways by going beyond it. But what we have gained from Rahner is significant. He has turned our eyes toward the experience of God as the North Star of the vocational journey, steering us clear of an impersonal call and a generic plan. God calls. And God calls *me* toward a future that is unique. The chapters ahead consider the questions of identity, narrative, and practice that have taken on special urgency in light of the institutional and cultural recession of Christianity in the West. But as we move forward, I argue that the human subject remains at the center of a contemporary theology of vocation.

Rahner famously remarked that the Christian of the future will be a mystic or will not be anything at all. This mystic is not the spiritual virtuoso or the esoteric visionary. This mystic of the future is "one who has 'experienced' something." She is one whose faith can no longer rely on widespread assumptions or cultural conventions but whose faith demands "a personal experience and a personal decision."[89] To respond to the decline of those social and cultural structures that helped support Christian identity for so long in Europe and North America, we should not attempt the absurd task of recreating the past. For Rahner, the future lies not in enforcing faith from the outside in but inspiring faith from the inside out. Thus our ecclesiology must shift from doctrines to story, from institutions to community. Fostering a renewed sense of the Christian call will require "a genuine experience of God emerging from the very heart of our existence."[90] In the concrete choices and life decisions that confront us, there is a chance for initiation that is as much mystagogy as mission, a chance—in this moment—to listen for God's call already echoing within us.

CHAPTER FIVE

Through Others . . .

Each Christian vocation comes from God and is God's gift. However, it is never bestowed outside of or independently of the Church. Instead it always comes about in the Church and through the Church because, as the Second Vatican Council reminds us, "God has willed to make men holy and save them, not as individuals without any bond or link between them, but rather to make them into a people who might acknowledge him and serve him in holiness."

—John Paul II[1]

I wonder what sort of a tale we've fallen into?

—J. R. R. Tolkien[2]

Fortunately for us, we don't have to figure out life on our own. We have help on the path of vocational discernment. To say that vocation is neither a distant plan (chap. 3) nor a generic invitation (chap. 4) is not to reduce it to a solitary search. As we saw in the last chapter, Ignatius of Loyola rests his *Spiritual Exercises* on the deeply personal relationship between the individual and God. But he never lost sight of the ecclesial dimension of call. The very existence of the *Exercises*—written not as a book of personal devotion but as a guide for guides—reveals Ignatius's profound intuition that each one of us comes to our calling through the help of another. Permeating Ignatius's spirituality, and the Catholic tradition more broadly, is a sacramental sensibility suggesting that the vocation that comes from God is always mediated. God calls me *through others*.

This insight into the call of God that comes to us through others helps to introduce us to the necessary prerequisite to discernment, namely, conversion. Drawing on Karl Rahner, I argued above that discernment is the search for resonance between a particular choice and one's fundamental spiritual identity. In other words, I hear my vocation in the harmony between the path that is before me and the mystery that is me. But even as we underscore the centrality of "me" within the dynamics of discernment, we have to acknowledge that this "me" often messes things up. We do not always have that honest sense of ourselves before God that the process outlined by Rahner (and before him, by Ignatius) demands. Discernment requires of us an ever more clear recognition of our true selves, an acceptance and understanding of the unique child of God that each of us was graciously created to be. We cannot hope for harmony if our basic sense of ourselves is skewed—which is so often the case. Too often I confuse who God made me to be with who *I* want me to be. And our choices suffer.

Discernment, then, depends on conversion. It demands an ongoing process of personal transformation that frees us from our attachments to a false sense of ourselves, our needs, and our plans. The great spiritual traditions have spoken of this conversion as the realization of an inner freedom, and have named it in a variety of ways—poverty of spirit, indifference, loving surrender, the purgative way. In this chapter, I argue that a particular kind of conversion is demanded today, namely, the conversion that comes through openness to "the other." This openness, so widely assumed in postmodern discourse, is actually one of the great challenges of our present moment. Spending some time reflecting on it sheds light on our questions surrounding vocation, helping us to see that it is precisely through openness to the other that we learn to hear more clearly the call of God.

Chapter 5 explores, then, the relationship between the traditional call for conversion and our contemporary concern for "the other." The first half of the chapter explores the creative tension between identity and alterity ("otherness"), suggested by Lieven Boeve's notion of the "open narrative." Narrative is a category that encompasses our own individual stories and the larger stories of which we are a part. Thus it provides a helpful way to talk about the context within which individual discernment occurs. What is it that we learn through the Christian narrative? And what does this tell us about what Christians are called to be and to do? Here we discover that one of postmodernity's most important contributions to ecclesiology is its call to respect the other, its demand that we hold our narratives open to the narratives of others. Taking with us this insight, we turn in the second half of the chapter to consider how the Christian narrative is embodied in the Christian community, the church. In the end, what the chapter articulates is an *ecclesiology* of vocation—a vision of an "open church" in which the faithful are continually trained to be open to others, so that, slowly, we might grow more and more open to *the* Other: the God who calls.

Narrative and Vocation

By emphasizing "the other," I mean to situate the modern focus on the human person within a more postmodern appreciation for the contextual nature of human existence. In constructing a contemporary theology of call, the problem is not emphasizing the individual. The problem is isolating her—forgetting the many ways in which each of us interacts with the people, cultures, institutions, traditions, and stories that constitute the context of our lives. The human subject will always remain at the center of vocational discernment. But our postmodern consciousness looks with suspicion on the Enlightenment ideal of the detached subject, who hovers free from influence and all authority, constructing meaning from a neutral point of pure rationality. Instead, today we are more aware of the many ways that we are shaped and socialized by our surroundings. There is no observation deck, no *tabula rasa* or purely objective point of view to engage the question of vocation, or any question for that matter. We always come to the question within the context of overlapping communities and commitments. I see things a certain way because I was born male rather than female, white rather than black, wealthy rather than poor. As Sam wisely reminded Frodo, in the Tolkien passage cited above, people fall into their stories. They land on paths already laid for them. A number of contexts—a number of narratives—already inform and influence the way each one of us looks at the world. And it is amidst all these stories that we strive to sort out our own story.

Vocation is my story amidst other stories, as all of these stories unfold within the story of God. The theology of vocation taking shape in these pages places great importance on the uniqueness of the individual human person. But, as we have noted, there is a danger that this emphasis on particularity might lead to isolation: I am unique by being distinct, an individual identified and defined apart from others. This view of the person is precisely what we want to avoid. "I" am not a discrete dot but a line arcing from the past into the future, stretched wide and richly textured, thanks to my connections and my commitments. My unique identity takes shape in the depth of my inner life, but it also depends on the length of my history and the breadth of my relationships. And it is story that holds together these dimensions of my identity.

My Story

In his classic work *After Virtue*, the philosopher Alasdair MacIntyre introduced the category of narrative as a way to reclaim the unity of the moral life against what he described as modern moral fragmentation. According to MacIntyre, modern moral theory came to treat human life "atomistically," that is, it broke up human actions into discrete entities, unconnected episodes that were then evaluated independently.[3] This approach was a far cry from the ancient tradition of the virtues, which, by definition, cannot be so easily compartmentalized. MacIntyre argued that virtues (like justice or prudence), if they are to have any meaning, cannot apply to just one part of life; they have to apply to the whole of life. They offer an ethical approach based on a richer vision of the human person, one in which life is conceived and evaluated as a whole, and not merely as the sum of its parts. In order to return to the virtues, and so articulate a more holistic moral framework, MacIntyre turned to narrative.

MacIntyre began with a concrete example. Imagine looking out the window and seeing your neighbor digging vigorously in the backyard.[4] What is he doing? In order to answer that question, and thus understand this action, we need a narrative. Such a narrative depends, first, on the context or setting within which the action occurs. We may know, for example, that every year this neighbor plants a garden in this spot in his backyard. He may have also mentioned once how much his wife loves freshly cut flowers and ripe tomatoes, or commented on the exercise he gets from working in the yard. All of these contexts are the different settings for the action itself, and each setting has a history (the annual tradition of turning the soil, the years of married life, and so on). It is only in light of these histories that what you see outside your window starts to make sense. But a full understanding of the action requires a further layer, namely, the intentions of the neighbor. What is he doing? digging? gardening? exercising? pleasing his wife? He may have one reason for going outside on this day with a shovel; he may have more than one reason. The point is that to truly understand what he is doing, we have to attend to both context and intention. It is precisely narrative that links the two, rendering the action intelligible.

Moreover, any such narrative of a particular action takes place and takes on meaning in the larger context of the narrative that is one's whole life, unitary and unique. Stories are not simply ornaments that we hang on a static life; for MacIntyre, life itself is narrative in form. Thus he proposed "a concept of a self whose unity resides in the unity of a narrative which links birth to death as narrative beginning to middle to end."[5] Enlightenment thinkers like John Locke and David Hume defined the human self apart from physical attributes, social location, or historical context, thus reducing personal identity to a kind of inner, mental state. The problem is that such an approach, by excluding history and intention, ignores precisely those contexts that allow us to understand a person and her actions in the first place. For MacIntyre, human life is better understood as an enacted narrative, a story that is lived before it is told. "Narrative is not the work of poets, dramatists and novelists reflecting upon events which had no narrative order before one was imposed by the singer or the writer; narrative form is neither disguise nor decoration."[6] Indeed, narrative is the basic form of life. While this claim may be contested, MacIntyre noted that the reality of our existence in the time between birth and death suggests otherwise. It is perhaps why we human beings so naturally speak in stories.

In the expanding circles of stories that guide MacIntyre's argument here, he made a crucial move: if the story of an individual action falls within the longer story that is my life, then my life story, in turn, falls within the larger context of other stories. Indeed, my story may not be as discrete as the preceding discussion suggests, for I am at once involved in a multitude of narratives being lived out by many people (and while I may be Hamlet in my own story, I am more likely Gravedigger in yours).[7] Moreover, there are corporate stories, shared narratives that are internally complex but nevertheless shape my individual story. MacIntyre noted:

> I can only answer the question "What am I to do?" if I can answer the prior question "Of what story or stories do I find myself a part?" We enter human society, that is, with one or more imputed characters—roles into which we have been drafted—and we have to learn what they are in order to be able to understand how others respond to us and how our responses to them are apt to be construed. It is through hearing stories about wicked stepmothers, lost children, good but misguided kings, wolves that suckle twin

boys, youngest sons who receive no inheritance but must make
their own way in the world and eldest sons who waste their inheritance on riotous living and go into exile to live with the swine,
that children learn or mislearn both what a child and what a parent is, what the cast of characters may be in the drama into which
they have been born and what the ways of the world are. Deprive
children of stories and you leave them unscripted, anxious stut-
terers in their actions as in their words.[8]

To note the formative influence of stories is hardly noteworthy, but it
is helpful to point out how foreign this view is to modern individualism. Against the Enlightenment claim that "I am what I freely choose
myself to be" comes a more postmodern recognition: "I am someone's
son or daughter, someone else's cousin or uncle; I am a citizen of this
or that city, a member of this or that guild or profession; I belong to
this clan, that tribe, this nation."[9] For MacIntyre, what is good for me
"has to be the good for one who inhabits these roles. As such, I inherit
from the past of my family, my city, my tribe, my nation, a variety of
debts, inheritances, rightful expectations and obligations. These constitute the given of my life, my moral starting point. This is in part
what gives my life its own moral particularity."[10] I am a character as
much as I am an author of the drama that is my life.

Here MacIntyre concluded that "the story of my life is always
embedded in the story of those communities from which I derive my
identity."[11] It is a conclusion that introduces the concept of tradition,
and so prepares the way for the next stage of his argument. For our
purposes, we pause in order to point out the light this account might
shed on a theology of vocation. Clearly, MacIntyre's use of narrative
to illustrate the unity of human life resonates with the Christian instinct
that vocation speaks not to one part of life but the whole of life. However, it is MacIntyre's point about the contextual nature of our individual lives—my story within other stories—that interests us here. For
MacIntyre, the stories that matter are the various traditions of moral
philosophy that have shaped ethical discourse in the West. For us, and
for a theology of vocation, the story that matters is the Christian story,
the Christian narrative in all its complexity.[12]

Our Story

In chapter 4, we explored the experience of transcendence as the
touchstone for vocational discernment. In moments of self-awareness,

of deep sadness or unexpected joy, we may sense "something more"—a boundary or mystery, the limit of ourselves and the possibility of some Other. Such moments stretch across human history and around the world: they are truly universal experiences. However, today we cannot simply assume that these boundary experiences will be automatically perceived as experiences of the divine. We know that not everyone recognizes God's call. The radical plurality of our postmodern world means that any experience of depth will always be open to multiple interpretations. For as much as we want to emphasize the personal experience of God, we have to recognize that this experience is always an interpreted experience. Thus, I only recognize such experience as the experience *of God* because I have been shaped within a context in which the concept of God is meaningful. For me to see my experience as a *religious* experience means that I must have some prior exposure to religion. I only know that the stirrings within my heart come from Christ because of some connection I have to Christianity, no matter how weak that connection might be. In other words, God's call requires a context. Vocation needs a narrative.

This is not to say that God depends on our stories. Grace is always at work in the world, even among those innocent of the Gospel or indifferent to the church. Lives are touched, people are transformed. The call is always and everywhere extended. It is not that God needs a narrative—we do. We need narrative precisely in order to recognize the experience of transcendence *as vocation*, to name it and embrace it as a call coming from God.

One of Karl Barth's significant contributions was his introduction of a narrative sensibility into twentieth-century theology. His project of retelling the biblical narratives over and over, from a variety of different perspectives, provided an early catalyst for various postcritical approaches to biblical hermeneutics and represents something of a precursor to the later rise of "narrative theology" among Protestant theologians.[13] Barth's approach to the biblical text was motivated, in part, by the desire to avoid two problematic tendencies of modern scriptural interpretation. One was a literalism that treated the text as a factual report of events. The other was an expressivism that reduced the biblical text to "mythological pictures" illustrating universal themes.[14] The false choice between these two options revealed, for Barth, the real limitations of modern biblical study. Whether the tools of historical criticism were used to show the continuity between the words and the events they describe (literalism) or whether they were used to show discrepancies (expressivism), the very methodology dangerously subsumed the biblical narrative under an external criterion—a prior set of intellectual values and commitments that served to judge the scriptural story.

For Barth, such a move misses the point of the Bible. Barth did not reject the tools and the results of modern historical criticism; rather, he saw all of it as secondary. Even at its best, Barth would suggest, the historical-critical interpretation of scripture is essentially external to the theological task. The subject matter of theology is, by definition, beyond its purview. Doctrines such as creation *ex nihilo*, the incarnation, and the resurrection are inaccessible to historians, beyond the reach of their scientific tools of investigation.[15] This realization implies a radically different approach to the theological task, one less focused on interpretation and more focused on "re-description." As a function of the church, theology is not a search for contemporary relevance or points of contact with "the world." It is Christian self-description through re-description of the biblical narrative—a deepening of identity through retelling the stories of scripture. In chapter 3 we saw Barth's aversion to natural theology in his polemic against apologetics and any attempt to "prove" the reasonableness of the faith. Here is another manifestation of the same concern: neither the discipline of philosophy nor the discipline of history is to set the agenda and terms for theology. To do so risks bracketing belief and forgetting our absolute dependence on the grace of God revealed in the biblical narrative.

Barth recognized that the Bible was not always read through the lens of modern historical-critical analysis. In earlier eras, Christians naturally found their identity by locating themselves within the overarching story of the Bible, a story that stretches from the creation of the world to the return of Christ who will judge the living and the dead. But, according to Hans Frei, over the course of the eighteenth century, a shift took place that displaced this overarching narrative. A developing historical consciousness and the surprising success of new tools of scientific research led many modern theologians to encompass scripture within "a larger framework or category of explanation."[16] For Frei, "It is no exaggeration to say that all across the theological spectrum the great reversal had taken place; interpretation was a matter of fitting the biblical story into another world with another story rather than incorporating that world into the biblical story."[17] Frei judged these developments as a loss. For him, the narrative form of scripture and its meaning are inseparable. Thus any transposition of the text into "an alien conceptual scheme" would always bring distortion.[18] Echoing Barth, Frei spoke of the Bible not as a source to be used but as a narrative within which one must dwell.

This concern for the primacy of the Christian narrative is one of the key family resemblances marking the various forms of postliberal narrative theology that emerged after Barth's death. The postliberal trajectory underscores this commitment to the Christian narrative as the "world" within which Christians are meant to live. George Lindbeck's "cultural-linguistic" model offers a vision of theology as an intratextual enterprise focused on the peculiar grammar of the Christian faith.[19] Stanley Hauerwas calls out the ecclesial and ethical implications of this narrative, arguing that the modern myth of liberation from normative tradition only separates Christians from those resources needed to live an authentic moral life.[20]

These postliberal approaches have their limitations. Chief among them is the temptation to idealize and isolate the Christian narrative—cutting it off from all other narratives and any significant internal critique. There is a tendency to contrast the Christian story with other stories—another version of the dialectical tendency we saw in Barth's contrast between the divine call and human vocations. Our question is this: Does identity have to come at the cost of alterity? Or, is there a way to acknowledge both, to discover a deeper relationship between the two? In postliberal approaches, we find a helpful emphasis on the particularity of the Christian narrative, and the individual Christian's embedment within that narrative. They remind us that God's call *through others* cannot be reduced to the invitation coming from individual voices, no matter how important these voices may be. God's call is mediated not only through individuals but also through a community and a tradition. It is this community and this tradition—this church—that passes on and pulls us into the narrative of Christ. To be drawn into the narrative of Christ is what marks the first step on the path of discipleship. It is the necessary prerequisite to vocational discernment.

But what kind of a story are we being drawn into? The story of Christ is rich and multifaceted. It is less "a" story than it is many stories. The four gospels mark just the beginning of a diversity of ways this story has been told and retold over the course of centuries. Every era finds a form through which this story can speak; every time translates it into language and images that are meaningful for people in that period. What I want to suggest below is that the particular story needed today is that of the *open narrative*. Unfortunately, the appeal to narrative in theology, which ought to alert us to the importance of context, too often closes the Christian conversation off from others. In its more extreme forms, a narrative approach can too quickly dismiss—or even display hostility toward—the "worlds" beyond the Christian narrative, fostering an insular, superior, and separatist spirit. This danger, lurking around the largely Protestant postliberal conversation, can also be seen in the rise of Radical Orthodoxy and various movements of "neoexclusivism" within the Roman Catholic Church.[21]

Thus in lifting up the category of narrative, we have to resist the temptation to close off and shut in. The concern for Christian identity in a world of permeable boundaries is a legitimate one. But it is a mistake to seek security through isolation or to promote identity by ignoring alterity. If we are really going to take the context of God's call seriously, then we cannot simply place the individual life story within the story of Christianity. We have to go one step further, and attend to the many other narratives (sometimes friendly, sometimes unfriendly) around which and within which the Christian story unfolds.

Open Stories

Today, narrative needs to be qualified: it must be an *open* narrative. This move implies a different posture toward postmodern culture than the approaches described above. It suggests that the church can learn a lot from the radical plurality that shapes our contemporary consciousness. Like the postliberals, the Louvain theologian Lieven Boeve is searching for a theological approach to identity that avoids the extremes of fundamentalism or nostalgic traditionalism, on the one hand, and relativism or uncritical adaptation, on the other. But unlike them, Boeve discovers identity through a much more deliberate dialogue with postmodern consciousness. Whereas in Barth or in Frei, apologetics occurred only in an occasional, ad hoc manner, for Boeve, it is the heart of his project. His numerous essays—part of an ambitious collaborative research project—always come back to a fundamental question: to what extent can the Christian faith still offer meaning to people living in a world marked by such radical plurality?

For Boeve, Christian identity is found not in some internal grammar, a doctrinal or ritual language that is described and redescribed. Instead, identity is found and maintained precisely through engagement with the larger contexts within which the Christian lives. Theology is not redescription but "recontextualization." This methodology recognizes that every tradition is embedded in a specific historical and cultural context. When the context shifts, the tradition develops. If it does not, the tradition dies—fading off into the inaccessible and the implausible. For Boeve, such a recognition does not mean that the Christian narrative simply adapts itself to its surroundings. "What it does imply is that every time and context challenges us to give shape to the message of God's love revealed in Jesus Christ in a contemporary way. If we do not accept this challenge we run the risk of sliding into inauthenticity."[22]

If our present context is marked by the sheer multiplicity of different worldviews and fundamental life options, then, Boeve predicts, the traditions that will stay alive are those that can become "open narratives." Jean-François Lyotard famously defined postmodernity as an "incredulity to metanarratives," that is, a deep suspicion toward any universal, all-encompassing explanation of reality—a "big story" that claims to say "how it is" for everyone everywhere.[23] This suspicion grew out of the twentieth-century failure of such overarching explanatory schemes: the Enlightenment myth of human progress was blown away by the violence of two world wars, our optimism about human liberation was crushed by economic systems that oppress on a global scale. But the rejection of metanarratives also arises out of a more positive engagement. Encounters with "the other"—those who think, act, and imagine in a way radically different from the way I think, act, and imagine—have given many contemporary people a profound appreciation for diversity. Through communications, migration, and travel, we meet more and more different people than we have ever met before. It has injected into our cultural consciousness a certain humility for any story we might tell or explanation we might offer for "how it is."

All of this carries serious implications for religion. It demands brutal honesty about the radical contingency that permeates contemporary consciousness—including Christian consciousness. "In a situation of plurality and conflict, people learn to consider their own fundamental life-options and the sources of meaning and identity in their lives—in short: their own narratives—as particular, unique, bound to place and time, and limited in perspective."[24] This radical contingency is felt by every young person who awakens to the realization that she is a Christian largely because of when and where she was born. There is something unsettlingly accidental about it all. True, we remain free beings; we know that we can choose. But even if I am someone who came to embrace the Christian faith as a free adult—making it truly my own through a deliberate and independent act—still, I cannot escape the haunting suspicion that it all would have been very different had I been born in Riyadh or Tianjin instead of Austin or Evanston. We postmoderns carry that awareness with us; it is inescapable.

This radical pluralism seems to pose a mortal threat to traditional Christianity, a decline into relativism—or worse, indifference. And yet, what Boeve finds so remarkable is that people continue to tell stories.[25] Not all postmodern Christians see their faith as simply one option among others. In fact, the postmodern Christian is more likely to say, there are many options, but not *for me*. Most of us Christians recognize that, because of my own particular story (the narrative that begins when and where I was born), the Christian narrative has a claim on me that no other religious narrative has. I can't simply bracket my belonging. I can reject this faith, but it still continues on as part of my story—even if only as what I left behind, the page that I turned. "The fact that our narrative is always *our* narrative and that we cannot abandon our narrative and withdraw to the observer's post, already implies an important and unavoidable distinction between our narrative and other narratives."[26] People continue to tell their stories. But they are more modest stories. Truth is tempered by contingency. We seem to see that *my* commitments take shape amidst the very different commitments of others. This is the complicated space of the Christian faith today.

And so when we tell the Christian story, it too is a more modest one. A postmodern Christian narrative recognizes that there are other stories; it sees that even "the" Christian story comes in many shapes and sizes, each telling of it shaped by a particular history and a concrete context. Today Christianity achieves intelligibility, plausibility, and authenticity as an open narrative, not by monopolizing the microphone or by ceding the stage but by sharing it. Or, to shift the metaphor, "traditions that have the capacity to transform themselves into open narratives in our postmodern world cease to be shutters which block out the view, as is the case in various strands of traditionalism. On the contrary, they become windows that allow men and women to observe and to live in the colourful multiplicity of postmodernity."[27]

All of this fosters a renewed appreciation for alterity—for "otherness" as such. To acknowledge difference brings with it a demand to let the other stand. We cannot absorb all other narratives into our own. To do so is to destroy the other as other, to make "you" into some version of "me." Boeve writes, "Recent sensitivity towards the otherness of the other has drawn the attention of a significant number of postmodern thinkers, philosophers who point out that a different kind of sensitivity has emerged in the midst of our awareness of irreducible multiplicity. Indeed, this irreducible multiplicity implies otherness as such, irremovable otherness that cannot be reduced to a single narrative nor subsumed within a particular totalising perspective. Whatever we do to encompass otherness within a single narrative, it will always place itself beyond our grasp."[28] It is precisely the presence of this uncontrollable other and the disorientation of diversity that have fueled the resurgence of fundamentalism and neoexclusivism in almost every sector of our postmodern world. But for Boeve, the proper response to relativism cannot be a fundamentalist flight to the fiction of a sure and certain metanarrative. Rather, the appropriate response is the open narrative itself.

Thus Boeve pushes legitimate postmodern concerns about identity toward alterity. The "essence" of Christianity lies precisely in its openness to the other. Here he touches the mystery that lies at the heart of the Christian narrative. For, at the end of the day, is not the Christian claim to truth in fact a truth that is only imperfectly grasped by limited people? For Boeve, truth is a question of "living in the truth," of relating to the elusive other who surprises, challenges, and always escapes the confines of our particular, limited narrative. Running throughout the Christian tradition is a history of reflection on God's incomprehensible otherness, and the limits of our language to name it. "In other words," Boeve reflects, "truth is a matter of relating appropriately to the intangible Truth, of giving witness to this Truth in the full awareness that it is ultimately inexhaustible, incomprehensible and inexplicable."[29] We cannot capture ultimate mystery. We cannot contain "the Truth." Precisely because Truth transcends our narrative, our story must remain open.

In this final point, we see the central insight of Boeve's recontextualization project. It is not postmodern political correctness that motivates his work, nor is the open narrative simply an accommodation to the times. Instead, Boeve makes the case for Christianity as an open narrative on specifically Christian terms. It is a model that rises up out of the Christian tradition itself. "A legitimate recontextualization can only be achieved when there are *profound theological grounds* for it."[30]

These grounds are found, first and foremost, in the biblical narrative. There the "interruptive otherness" of God serves as the reading key linking these stories that stretch from creation to the end of time.[31] From the call of Abraham to the condemnation from the prophets, from the exodus to the exile, from the annunciation to the resurrection—Christians follow a story continually broken open by God's interruption. "The Christian narrative is one of a God who calls us to continual conversion and to the rejection of every form of sin, suffering and oppression. Upon closer inspection, it would almost appear that the Christian narrative exists *by grace of* boundary experiences and experiences of alterity. In the very experience of alterity, the believer recognises the elusive God who always beckons further."[32]

The paradigmatic example of, and the ultimate source for, the open Christian narrative is the open narrative of Jesus of Nazareth. At the heart of Jesus' story are the stories he told: the parables of the reign of God. These short stories were and remain open stories—not tight definitions or the final word but an invitation, a question, a challenge. These narratives of seed scattered, landowners and laborers, yeast, pearls, kings, and banquets were intended to unsettle and upset the closed narratives of Jesus' listeners. They were meant to stimulate discipleship, to call for conversion, and to awaken an audience to the surprising realization that, perhaps, God cannot be so easily contained by our narrow definitions and miserly expectations. In the story of the prodigal son, for example, we are "suddenly confronted with the possibility that another father exists, a father characterised by intense goodness, incredible compassion and unending solicitude. This is a decisive discovery which Jesus himself had also experienced: God is different, God *is love* (1 Jn 4,8)."[33]

Beyond his words, Jesus' whole life embodied a critical-liberative praxis that burst open closed and repressive narratives, transforming them into open narratives directed toward God.[34] The woman caught in adultery was condemned by the logic of the law. But Jesus broke open this logic. His conversation with the Samaritan woman, his encounters with the Pharisees, his cleansing of the temple, his many miracles—these actions broke open oppressive, closed narratives, and restored to dignity and communion those whom these narratives had excluded. Sensitive to the complex layering of the Gospel traditions, Boeve argues that not only did Jesus enact an open narrative but also that his earliest followers interpreted him in this way. Thus the New Testament itself—the foundational text of the Christian narrative—is an open narrative. The fulcrum on which the entire open narrative of Jesus bends is its climax, the resurrection. There God shatters "the hegemonic narrative of rejection and death," revealing a God who interrupts death on behalf of life and who confronts sin with the promise of salvation, a God who will not allow the narrative of Jesus to close.[35]

Boeve links the liberating praxis of Jesus to his fundamental contemplative attitude, "an openness towards the Other who is revealed in moments of interruption."[36] Boeve follows Schillebeeckx in associating this attitude with Jesus' "*Abba*-experience," which was not only an experience of profound intimacy with God, but at the same time, an awareness of the obligation to "do God's will."[37] This linkage of praxis, openness, and attention to God's will offers rich soil for cultivating a contemporary theology of vocation. Drawing together these themes will be the task of the final chapter of this book. At this point, we can only signal where that task will lead.

As "paradigm" of the open narrative, Jesus challenges all those who wish to follow him to abandon their closed narratives and enter into the praxis of the open narrative. Through this praxis, we come to accept and cultivate within ourselves that "fundamental contemplative attitude" that guided Jesus' own actions. We become free to live with the kind of freedom with which Jesus himself lived. Coming to such inner freedom is a process of conversion, mentioned at the beginning of this chapter, which is nothing less than a growing in openness to the will of God. This openness is the necessary condition for authentic vocational discernment. We grow in this openness to God—who is *the* Other—precisely by growing in openness to others.

This vision is far from the open-ended pluralism that inhibits so much of contemporary postmodern thinking. David Tracy argues that the deconstructive project of postmodernity implies a determinate claim—an ethic of resistance, "Respect the other!"—that jars against its own reflections on the impossibility of any determinate claims.[38] If postmodernity cannot provide the imperative, for Boeve, the Gospel can. Find Christ in the neighbor, love God by loving others—these are the claims of faith, not of philosophy. As Matthew 25 reminds us, we meet the mystery of God in the mystery of the other. The interruptive otherness of God is the fundamental insight of Christianity, springing forth not only from the gospels but also throughout the tradition in its theology and spirituality, its doctrine and liturgy. Liberating praxis, negative theology, Jesus as human and divine, sacramental rites of passage, apocalyptic—these are motifs from within our own Christian narrative, motifs that challenge us whenever we try to box God in or elbow others out, motifs of God opening up closed narratives, getting involved in history but never getting caught by it.[39] If the Christian narrative is to be true to itself, it must be an open narrative.

A Community of Call

Stories are told by people. They take shape in community. If all of this talk about narrative begins to sound overly abstract and disembodied, we should remind ourselves that it is primarily a conversation about ecclesiology, not epistemology. We are interested in reflecting on how the call of God comes to each of us through the mediation of people—the Christian community, a community both called and calling.

At the dawn of the twentieth century, the French canon Joseph Lahitton argued that the church plays an essential role in extending God's call to the individual.[40] But in his mind, "the church" meant the hierarchy, preeminently, the bishop who approves and ordains. Thus Lahitton's theology of vocation was limited not only by his theology of grace but also by his theology of church. He placed the individual over and against an institution. This chapter suggests a deeper ecclesiology, one consonant with the vision of the Second Vatican Council and cultivated in dialogue with our postmodern context. It is an ecclesiology of the "open church." In light of my previous remarks, I hope it is clear that the model of the open church proposed here is not the prelude to a content-less Christianity afraid to offend, or a sloughing off of boundaries for the sake of inclusivity. Rather, the "open church" is meant to articulate, in a postmodern idiom, what is in fact the ultimate and difficult demand of the gospel: love thy neighbor.

Vocational discernment—discovering my particular and unique way of loving my neighbor—requires openness to God. But as Ignatius knew so well, this openness to God follows on conversion, which he described as a purification of the affections and a transformation of consciousness that comes by stepping into the story of Christ. Today, the narrative we step into is the open narrative of Christ, a narrative that demands a particular kind of conversion. It is a conversion understood as a turning outward, an opening up to "the other," a willingness to be interrupted by those who exist on the edges of our dominant narratives. In the paragraphs below, we explore the ways in which God interrupts us—and thus calls to us—through the experience of alterity. This experience, in turn, invites reflection on an ecclesiology of the open church. An open church is a community that calls its members to open themselves up to self-criticism, to new insight, to different ideas and different people—particularly those who are marginalized, ignored, or even oppressed by the stories we so often tell ourselves. All of this is intended to offer a vision of church that fosters an appreciation for vocation in this postmodern world. In short, an open church is a church that trains us in openness, which is the *sine qua non* of vocational discernment. By learning to be open to "the other" in our midst, we grow more and more open to *the* Other, the God of Jesus Christ who interrupts our lives and our plans with that loving gift that comes to us as a vocation.

God's Interruption

If ecclesiology is going to speak to the contemporary Christian, it has to begin with the spiritual experience of the individual. We do not have the luxury of undoing the Enlightenment or reversing the modern turn to the subject. People come in to Christianity along a variety of paths, but everyone today understands this path as his or her own. As we alluded to in the book's introduction, never before has "my experience" been so central to the spiritual life and the world of religion. Of course there are plenty of problems with this starting point. But, as Louis Dupré reminds us, there is no real alternative. The only way to overcome the limitations of starting with human experience is from within—not by ignoring modern subjectivity but by living our way through it.[41] At the end of *After Virtue*, Alasdair MacIntyre looked out over the moral fragmentation of modernity. Searching for new forms of community amidst this new Dark Ages, communities within which civility and the intellectual life might be sustained, MacIntyre concluded that we are not waiting for Godot but for "another—doubtless very different—St. Benedict."[42] Dupré replied to this evocative but incomplete ending that, before Benedict, we first need a new Augustine.[43] For Dupré, Augustine was a master of the interior life, one who opened up a journey into the soul that led the soul beyond itself. Benedict, too, was a master of the interior life, and it was this turn inward that kept the retreat into the monastery from turning into a simple flight from the world. "In part because of Augustine the Benedictine monastery became the heart of medieval culture, the spiritual force that motivated the building of a new civilization."[44] Similarly today, renewal has to begin within. And any effort to revitalize Christianity that ignores this fact—such as the restorationist attempt to reestablish authority and impose orthodoxy—sadly misses the moment. Such attempts seek renewal from the outside in. But as Rahner's mystic of the future reminds us, what is needed is a revival from the inside out.

This book emerged out of the conviction that awakening the notion of vocation can serve this revival. The first four chapters argued that a healthy theology of vocation demands a robust theology of the experience of grace—an argument that culminates in Rahner's appropriation of Ignatius's insight into the particular will of God. The reflections of this present chapter push this argument into more direct conversation with our contemporary postmodern context. In light of this context, we see that the experience of grace today takes on a particular form, both widespread and urgent. It is the experience of alterity. In other words, a postmodern theology of vocation may start with me, but it has to open out to "the other."

When we speak about the experience of grace, we all too often assume that we are talking about a spiritual "high." We associate it with some deeply moving event, a "mountaintop experience" or a moment of peace, that alerts us to the loving presence of God in our lives, which ordinarily exists only on the edge of our awareness. The church can even come to see its role as enabling such experiences, seeking ways to provide opportunities for people to get in touch with God. These moments are important. These moments are real. But these moments are always in danger of being subsumed within a larger framework of psychological need, and thus falling alongside all those other intense experiences we look for in life. Lieven Boeve talks about the culture of "the kick," a phrase he borrows to name moments of intense emotional and psychological stimulation, moments of exciting thrill or deep catharsis that so many people today seek out in order to "feel alive." Though he cites a range of such "highs," it is bungee jumping that emerges as Boeve's example par excellence. The kick, he believes, is one response to the emptiness of contemporary culture. It is "an effort to hold on to one's own identity in the midst of fractured multiplicity . . . a here-and-now endeavour to obtain assurance amidst insecurity and stability in the midst of instability."[45] As such, the kick is an experience of fulfillment and confirmation, a moment of ego affirmation ("I exist! I am alive!") that—in a deep irony—does not last. Thus the kick needs to be repeated, always at greater and greater levels of intensity.

Not everyone jumps off a bridge in order to feel alive. The extent of the culture of the kick can be questioned. But in a world in which identity is no longer guaranteed by community or clan, many of us hunger for experiences of self-affirmation and self-assurance. Is the role of the church to facilitate such experiences? Is it supposed to promote spiritual moments in order to shore up religious belonging? Are our churches to become enclaves of identity, stable and safe places protected from the swirling winds of the postmodern world? Is this the way that religious tradition needs to meet the individual? I think not. Indeed, more often than not, the church community has a responsibility to critique those spiritualities that end in the confidence of tight boundaries or the comfort of self-assurance. A more authentic experience of grace today comes not through identity but through alterity—the experience of "otherness" as such. "These are experiences in which the ego senses itself to be approached by the other, experiences of being called away from the acquired certitudes of one's own narrative, experiences of a breakthrough, interrupting the ongoing security of one's personal narrative."[46]

Boeve uses the language of *interruption* to name this encounter with "the other." He recognizes that "the other" meets a narrative already unfolding—and often comes uninvited. I do not choose to think about the innocents killed in war or the children abused by priests or the atmosphere polluted by carbon. I do not choose to think about them; they confront me. They interrupt the narratives that mark my life. They burst into the stories I tell myself about the virtue of my country, the holiness of my church, or the level of my consumption. They burst in and upset, forcing me to rethink things. "This basic attitude expresses itself in our capacity to be open to strangeness, otherness, the unexpected. It implies that we are attentive to boundary experiences, interruptive events, marginality, experiences that reveal that our particular narrative is not all-inclusive. It likewise implies that we must learn to open our eyes to discontinuities, to what is going on at the boundaries of our particular narratives, serving to interrupt them. It calls for an attitude of trusting submission, as it were, which runs counter to our absolute desire to secure and insure ourselves against the unexpected."[47]

For Boeve, an interruption is not a random array or a radical rupture. It is not a breakdown. It is a break-in—a breaking in to *something*. Here is the key difference between Boeve's more analogical notion of interruption and Barth's more dialectic sense of confrontation between the divine call and human vocation. For Boeve, the deeply disturbing force of the interruption presumes a deeper and more primary continuity. An interruption cuts into a story already being told. It presumes a context, a context that continues after the break.[48] Thus an interruption is not destructive. It is transformative—if we are open to it. Our stories go on, but they go on changed.

Life constantly confronts us with the other; it constantly invites us to be open to interruption. This happens at the global level. It also happens at the personal level. A life story is interrupted when a child becomes terminally ill, when a spouse proves unfaithful, when a friend takes her own life. How do we respond when our fundamental confidence in life is so fundamentally shaken? Do we see God calling us through these experiences?

We all sense that there is something inauthentic in a quick and overly confident response to such interruptions. To go on as if nothing had happened, to fold this interruption into our story in a way that leaves that story unaffected, strikes most people as unhealthy. We close ourselves off to the experience itself when we force it to fit within our previous narrative. What makes the experience of "the other" so powerful—what makes it a moment of grace—is precisely our inability to tame it. It confronts us to change. It challenges us to grow. It asks us to open ourselves to what is beyond ourselves. Alterity evokes an *irreducible* otherness, an "other" that cannot be reduced to my story but that calls me to open up my story to new insight and new relationship.

It is important to remember that the interruption—both global and personal—that we are describing here does not come only in negative form. Alterity can be experienced in positive interruptions as well. Here we are not talking about ego affirmation but rather a genuine challenge to the self that comes through the goodness of life. A person's narrative or worldview can be just as upset when she encounters in friendship someone from another culture or religious tradition. A father's certitude and security can be just as threatened when the birth of a child opens up his heart to an experience of love and vulnerability never before felt. In the face of these interruptions—global and personal, negative and positive—we are called through ourselves and our experiences, through others and their very different experiences, toward *the* Other, who also always escapes our grasp.

In attending to the spiritual experience of the individual, the church community is not intent on fostering moments of self-affirmation and identity. Rather, the community seeks to help its participants respond to those interruptions that life inevitably brings and to help open up space within each individual's personal narrative to experience "the other." This is key to the development of discerning disciples in a postmodern world. Too often, our "vocational efforts"—whether that is trying to recruit more seminarians or to motivate more of the faithful to take their Christian calling seriously—are efforts at identity enhancement. We elevate the status of the clergy or underline the distinctiveness of the Catholic vision. And we lose sight of the truth that Christian identity lies precisely in openness: priesthood finds meaning in service, discipleship is lived out in mission. Vocation expects an openness to God that is impossible without an openness to the other. It is this openness to God-through-others that the Christian community strives to cultivate. To do so, it needs to acknowledge its own identity as an open church.

An Open Church

In our recent ecclesial history, we find a model par excellence of this open church in the Second Vatican Council. As indicated above, metanarratives are closed narratives, stories that shut off divergent views or minority voices in their all-encompassing attempt to explain "how it is" for everyone. A closed church is the social embodiment of this closed narrative. Such a church pretends to be a "total cultural environment"—essentially changeless, superior in truth, monolithic in form, and separate from the world beyond its clearly delineated boundaries.[49] Rigid authority and a uniform doctrinal language serve to sustain this vision of ecclesial life, a vision that, in many ways, captures the style of the Roman Catholic Church on the eve of Vatican II. If Vatican II was experienced as an event of significant change, it was primarily a change in attitude, a turn away from the closed church of the preconciliar period and a turn toward a more open and participatory church. In contrast to its recent history, the church at Vatican II affirmed and embodied the characteristics of an open church. These characteristics, which continue to challenge us today, include (1) historical awareness, (2) epistemological humility, (3) internal diversity, and (4) an appreciative engagement with others.

Close to the end of Vatican II, John Courtney Murray said that the development of doctrine was "*the* issue under the issues at Vatican II."[50] Murray was talking about the council's teaching on religious liberty, which he played no small role in helping to advance in a way that was indeed a development—even a significant shift—from previous church teaching. But his comment indicates that he saw a larger question facing the council as a whole: can the church change? More than any previous council, Vatican II was shaped by the church's awareness of its own historicity. Some of the most important theologians at the council—Marie-Dominique Chenu, Yves Congar, Henri de Lubac—were leaders of the *ressourcement* movement, a "return to the sources" that was rooted in the nineteenth- and early twentieth-century resurgence of historical research. Thanks to the renewed historical consciousness such research fostered, those bishops who came to be the council's leading voices knew that the church had changed in the past. They were not afraid to argue that it could change again in the present, spurred on, as they were, by Pope John XXIII, who, in his opening address at the council, called history "the great teacher of life," and suggested that the church "by making appropriate changes . . . will lead individuals, families, and peoples to turn their minds to heavenly things."[51]

This recognition of the church's movement through time culminated in *Lumen Gentium*'s penultimate chapter. The church is a pilgrim church, still "on the way" to the reign of God. But to speak of itself as a pilgrim is for the church to admit its own unfinished nature. It is to temper the triumphalism of the past. The council documents are marked by an epistemological humility, an openness to mystery that stands in stark contrast to the overly confident and always condemning language of past councils. The Dogmatic Constitution on the Church offers up a rich diversity of different images and metaphors for the church, each of which evokes some aspect of a reality that escapes easy definition. If *Lumen Gentium* ends with the church as pilgrim, it begins with the church as "mystery." In doing so the constitution "moved the council away from what councils were expected to do—define."[52] John O'Malley argues that Vatican II brought into existence a new style of conciliar discourse.[53] Leaving behind the terse, juridical, and punitive language of previous councils, Vatican II adopted a style that was invitational and expansive. It is the style of the patristic homily, not the neoscholastic textbook, a style of persuasion, not intimidation, of dialogue, not monologue. It was, in short, a more humble style. "To engage in persuasion is to some extent to put oneself on the same level as those being persuaded. Persuaders do not command from on high. Otherwise, they would not be persuading but dictating."[54] Persuasion is—the council seemed to realize—the only genre appropriate to speech about that profound mystery that gives meaning to the Christian life. Thus in the style of Vatican II we see modeled a style of church—an open church not so self-confident that it forgets it is "on the way" toward a mystery greater than our words can contain.

An open church is not only marked by an awareness of its own historicity and imbued with a certain humility regarding the claims it makes but it also recognizes the diversity internal to it. Karl Rahner famously observed that at Vatican II, the church began to live as a "world church," nudging Catholics out of centuries of monolithic Eurocentrism toward a truly global view—toward a Catholicism that would be decentralized and enculturated. The council was only the beginning, Rahner admitted. Despite the worldwide scope of its concerns and the diversity of its participants, Vatican II was very much a European gathering, driven by European questions and offering European answers. Still, in important ways, the council opened the door to pluralism within the church. Some of its earliest debates on the liturgy were debates about particularity and local adaptation. Out of these debates came the decision that best embodies the council's opening to diversity: the allowance for wider use of vernacular languages in the liturgy.[55] But this was only one of a number of openings toward local traditions and customs: "Even in the liturgy the church does not wish to impose a rigid uniformity in matters which do not affect the faith or the well-being of the entire community. Rather does it cultivate and foster the qualities and talents of the various races and nations."[56] In the text on the liturgy, we see the council making its way toward one of its great theological rediscoveries: its emphasis on the local church, the ecclesiological foundation of diversity.[57]

Finally, from its inception, the Second Vatican Council was a council of appreciative engagement with others outside of the church. In his speech on January 25, 1959, announcing his intention to call a council, John XXIII articulated two broad aims: first, to enlighten and edify Catholic Christians, and second, to extend "a renewed cordial invitation to the faithful of the separated communities to participate with us in this quest for unity and grace, for which so many souls long in all parts of the world."[58] This second, rather vague, goal suggested an ecumenical sensitivity that soon took on flesh in the role that Pope John accorded to the newly established Secretariat for Christian Unity, in his invitation to Protestant and Orthodox observers to join in the deliberations of Vatican II, and, ultimately, in the final text of the conciliar documents themselves. It was a dynamic of appreciative engagement that extended beyond other Christians to first Jews and then adherents of other religious traditions. In the closed church of the preconciliar period, who could have anticipated *Nostra Aetate*'s statement that the church "rejects nothing of what is true and holy in these religions," that the church has "a high regard for the manner of life and conduct, the precepts and doctrines" of these religions, "which, although differing in many ways from its own teaching, nevertheless often reflect a ray of that truth which enlightens all men and women"?[59] Or who could imagine, amidst the neoscholastic debates over church membership, the stunning, expanding circles of *Lumen Gentium*'s chapter 2, which reach out from

Catholics to catechumens, from Christians to Jews, from religious believers to all people, even those who do not know God? Ringing throughout the council documents is the category of dialogue, which reaches a kind of climax in *Gaudium et Spes'* stated hope for the church's dialogue with all of humanity.

Through the event that was the Second Vatican Council, the church began to actualize itself as an open church. Within a few years of the council, Karl Rahner recognized this shift, as well as the constant temptation (already visible in the early 1970s) to turn back:

> In future we must take the risk not only of a Church with "open doors," but of an "open Church." We cannot remain in the ghetto nor may we return to it. Anyone who experiences and endures the confusion, partly unavoidable, partly avoidable, in all dimensions of teaching and practice, which undoubtedly exists in the Church, is certainly tempted to long for the Church which older people among us knew under the four Pius's and up to the last Council. We are then tempted, in such movements as that "for Pope and Church," in what is in fact in the last resort a sterile pseudo-orthodoxy, to "purify" the Church as rapidly as possible and by administrative measures to draw clear frontiers, to "restore" the old order: in a word to enter on the march into the ghetto, even though the Church would then become, not the "little flock" of the gospel, but really a sect with a ghetto mentality.[60]

Rahner saw the council's move away from the myth of a changeless, uniform, and closed church as a move toward the church's own true nature. The model of the "open church," like that of the open narrative, is not a paradigm imposed on Christianity from outside. The vision of the open church embodied in the council—a church of openness to change, to new insight, to diversity within and difference without—is not simply an appeal to our postmodern appreciation for pluralism, a model attractive to our times. Rather it is a vision true to the church's essence. "The Church must positively will to remain open because only in this way can she be true to her own nature as the exodus, the people on pilgrimage towards the inconceivable mystery of God."[61] To be true to itself, the church must take the risk not just to be a church with "open doors," but to be an "open church"—one open to ongoing reform, internal diversity, and true freedom.[62]

Rahner rooted this vision of church in the deeper Christian commitment to the triune God and the role of the Spirit at work in the world. The church is an "open system." According to Rahner, an open system is any system or complex of realities that is defined by a point outside of the system itself. For the church, this defining point is the reign of God, the divine self-gift, the Spirit—what Rahner called, in its broadest sense, the "charismatic element" of the church.[63] Too often, Rahner admitted, the word "charismatic" evokes those supernatural gifts once wildly present at Corinth but later reserved to the saints. The charismatic is reduced to the odd and the unusual, the spectacular and the rare. We assume it refers to some extraordinarily gifted individual or sphere of freedom within the institutional church, a person or a movement that is tested by church authority and, by implication, subordinate to it. But for Rahner, the charismatic element is much wider and more primary. "When we use the term charismatic we are using a key word to stand for that ultimate incalculability which belongs to all the other elements in the Church in their mutual interplay. This means that the charismatic is, if we may so express it, transcendental in character, not one element in the system of the Church but a special characteristic of the system as a whole."[64] The charismatic element does not exist alongside the institutional element of the church; they are not two poles existing on the same plane. Nor is the charismatic a kind of exceptional principle offering the occasional break from routine. Rather the charismatic—as nothing less than the Spirit as ultimate source of the church's life—grounds and permeates every aspect of the church. It is the church's first and most ultimate characteristic.[65]

The church is an open church because, ultimately, it is defined by a point outside of itself—the transcendental presence of God, which we identify variously as the charismatic element, the Spirit, grace, the reign of God. This understanding of God's transcendental presence helps to explain what we mean when we describe God's call as an interruption. God interrupts not by parting the clouds and speaking from heaven. Vocation is not some "secret voice" or extrinsic directive demanding something arbitrary. Rather, God interrupts—God calls to us—when that silent mystery that always pulses beneath our lives bubbles up or bursts forth in our experience of encounter with the other. In a way, everything that has been said so far about alterity could be translated into this charismatic key, if we take "charismatic" in Rahner's sense of the Spirit as that transcendent principle that permeates all things—a presence that is always already present, waiting, inviting insight, breakthrough, interruption.[66] The Spirit works through the other to shake us out of our closed and self-assured stories, awakening us to a mystery deeper than any of our group projects or individual plans. Through the other, we hear. And the role of the church is to train our ear. The church is the place where we come to know the narrative of the interrupting God, the place where we practice meeting others, the place where we learn to listen for the voice speaking our vocation.

Open to Interruption

A basic critique of the open church can be summarized simply: "openness" is too open-ended. Chapter 6 will examine this critique in detail. Here we make just a start. Behind it is a legitimate concern that attention to the other leads to a diffusion of the self, that inclusivity waters down identity. Precisely in response to this concern, I have followed Boeve (and Rahner) in insisting that the open narrative is a demand of the Christian narrative itself. To be open to the other is to follow Jesus, for, at the heart of his story is an opening to the other in love. Alterity is not opposed to Christian identity but intrinsic to it. Therefore, in our attempt to appreciate the communal context of vocation, we have to recognize a powerful paradox: by sinking more deeply into the Christian narrative, Christians grow more open to the narratives of others.

The difficulty with "sinking more deeply into the Christian narrative" today is that this narrative is increasingly fragmented within postmodern consumer culture—frustrating its ability to share the story of Jesus in a way that is truly transformative. Here we return to the concern expressed in the book's introduction regarding the power of the paradigm of choice. Choice has become perhaps our primary lens on reality. Fueled by a consumer culture, choice transforms almost everything we encounter into a commodity. Vincent Miller argues that the global stretch of advanced capitalism, the ubiquity of advertising, and the commodification of culture itself has not only reshaped our world but it has also reshaped the way we look at the world.[67] In such an environment, religious believers are trained daily—in a way that is subtle but pervasive—to relate to their surroundings on the model of consumer choice. *Everything* becomes a commodity, even the beliefs and practices of our faith. In this commodified form, the Christian tradition loses the power to do what it ought to do: offer an orienting and coherent framework for life—a narrative of meaning. "The problem is that when people are trained to lift cultural/religious objects from their traditional contexts, they are less likely to be influenced by the other logics, values, and desires mediated by the religious traditions. Therefore they are unlikely to construct syntheses which enable them to develop forms of life that differ from the status quo."[68]

For centuries the Protestant doctrine of vocation struggled to resist its slow concession to the social status quo. In the mercantile enthusiasm of the Puritans, God's call was not so much integrated with the world of work as it was overwhelmed and absorbed by it. Today, the power of the market to co-opt extends beyond vocation to all aspects of Christian identity and practice. On the one hand, the modern market has made available to first world Christians the resources of their religion on an unprecedented scale. It has never been easier to access the riches of the tradition. Sitting at our laptops after dinner, we can browse the works of Teresa of Ávila or Thomas Aquinas, read serious biblical commentary, download podcasts of brilliant preachers, or buy popular books on theology written by accomplished scholars. On the other hand, the same processes that bring these resources to us also work to pull them apart from one another. The faith becomes fragmented. The overarching narrative and the rich internal complexity of the tradition are lost. Christianity appears to the spiritual consumer like a shelf full of stuff. "But for all the profundity and quality of this material, it leaves the spiritual consumer responsible for maintaining the discipline and sustaining their commitments. This spiritual consumer is constructed as an individual, in the single-family home, attempting to make sense of and to transform his or her life without the momentum provided by communal affiliation and support. One need not reduce the consumer's motives to selfishness to see the likelihood that such engagements with spiritual traditions are not likely to lead to long-term commitments."[69]

We have come to understand vocational discernment not as the discovery of some secret plan hidden in the mind of God but as a search for harmony between a particular decision and one's fundamental self-awareness before God. Thus for discernment to work depends on an honest sense of ourselves, a kind of inner freedom that only comes through an ongoing process of conversion and personal transformation that makes significant demands on the individual. Vocational discernment cannot be reduced to the moment of choice. It requires an inner openness to the will of God that takes some time to learn. And, like any extended process, it requires commitment.

Commitment is a struggle in our contemporary consumer culture. But, as Miller admits, the fault does not lie with choice itself. "Just as the freedom to choose a life partner does not automatically result in infidelity, choice in itself is not a sufficient cause for our broader lack of commitment."[70] The issue is more complicated. Not all spiritual seekers are narcissistic consumers looking to have their needs met. They turn to meditation, spiritual direction, or personal study of scripture, seeking God in all sincerity. The point that Miller wants to make is that, as good as such independent spiritual exercises are in themselves, they are extremely difficult to sustain over time. Torn out of their supporting communal infrastructures, commodified spiritual practices become the sole responsibility of the practitioner. She is left on her own to maintain a discipline that—because it involves conversion of heart and mind and life—is no easy task. Thus Miller pushes his argument beyond a superficial critique of religious consumerism or "Cafeteria Catholicism" to explore the deeper dynamics of consumer culture and the formative influence it has on us.

For Miller, the problem is not that we choose; the problem is that we are constantly encouraged to choose. Consumer culture fuels a form of never-ending desire. We are trained always to be looking for "the next thing." He writes, "The commonsense assumption about consumer desire—that it is desire for possession—might be consistent with religious commitment. Brand loyalty could correlate with denominational stability. As we saw in our discussion of seduction, however, from a thousand different directions we are constantly being tempted to consider something new. While individual manufacturers use advertising to cultivate brand loyalty and to channel consumption into integrated product lines, this takes place within the broader competition for consumer interest."[71] In our culture of consumer choice, it is not about "having" but about "getting." It is the actual process of the purchase, and not the enjoyment of the product, that lies at the heart of consumer culture. Once we get something, we are pushed to get something else. I buy my groceries, and immediately I am handed a stack of coupons prompting me to buy again. The dynamism of desire fueled by the imperative of economic growth and the urgency of advertising focuses us on the instant of consumption. This focus on the act of consumption is what wears down any effort at sustained commitment—spilling over from our economic lives to our spiritual lives. "Advertising encourages us to choose and to purchase, but not to keep and to use. Likewise, spiritually we are trained to seek, search, and choose but not to follow through and to commit."[72] If vocational discernment demands conversion as its prerequisite, if it demands a commitment to continued transformation, then we have to be honest about how difficult this really is. What Miller argues is that the difficulty comes not only from the fact that conversion and personal transformation is hard, which has always been the case. The difficulty also comes from the fact that consumer culture offers us very little practice at the kind of patience needed for personal transformation. In fact, consumer culture aggressively works against it.

All of this is not to say that the individual seeker cannot make his way, coming to hear and respond to the call of God. It is simply to highlight the challenges that our present context poses for the kind of sustained commitment to the life of discipleship that is the necessary condition for vocational discernment. What is the alternative to a commodified religiosity? In recent decades, a broad cross-section of theologians—mostly pastoral theologians, systematic theologians, and ethicists, many of them drawing on the narrative theology inspired by Barth and the philosophical framework offered by MacIntyre—have turned to the category of *practice* to talk about religious identity and continuity in an increasingly fragmented and commodified world. A keen observer of this trend, Robert Wuthnow embraces it, suggesting that a "practice-oriented spirituality" serves today as a rich alternative to the dwelling-oriented and seeking-oriented spiritualities that have so dominated the recent American religious landscape.[73] For both practitioners and theorists, it seems that directing our attention to concrete practices, such as private prayer and corporate worship, social service and active charity, offers the key toward that personal and social transformation made so difficult by consumer culture.

The language of practice allows a way to talk about how an individual narrative is drawn into a larger narrative, and how that larger story comes to shape the story of the individual. It helps to illumine the dynamic interplay between church community and subject. Near the end of his magisterial *A Secular Age*, Charles Taylor turns with some hope to practices: "Now if we don't accept the view that the human aspiration to religion will flag, and I do not, then where will the access lie to practice of and deeper engagement with religion? The answer is the various forms of spiritual practice to which each is drawn in his/her own spiritual life. These may involve meditation, or some charitable work, or a study group, or a pilgrimage, or some special form of prayer, or a host of such things."[74] Taylor points out that these kinds of personal practices have always been a part of historical Christianity, as "optional extras" for those already embedded in ordinary church practice. Today, however, it usually works in reverse. "First people are drawn to a pilgrimage, or a World Youth Day, or a meditation group, or a prayer circle; and then later, if they move along in the appropriate direction, they will find themselves embedded in ordinary practice."[75] The individualism of our present preoccupation with the spiritual quest need not be individuating.[76]

Christianity, as Louis Dupré reminds us, has always started with personal conversion of the heart. And it has inevitably drawn people into relationship with others. Even today, many people find their spiritual home in churches; their individual faith is not individualistic but rather finds form in a kind of "collective connection."[77] As Taylor argues, this movement from individual to community is not guaranteed, but it does not seem altogether exceptional even in today's consumer culture. The key, of course, is whether this "collective connection" becomes that form of sustained participation through which the individual not only joins the community but is also formed and transformed by it.

The notion of practices highlights the importance of individual agency ("this is something *I do*"). But the best accounts show a sensitivity to the way in which a genuine spiritual practice draws the individual out of her or himself and into something larger ("this is something *we do*"). This was one of the seminal insights of MacIntyre's discussion of practices, virtues, and tradition. Paraphrasing MacIntyre's own definition, the ethicist William Spohn described practices as "complex social activities that are intrinsically interesting and rewarding. They are rich human activities that draw us into themselves, thereby reorienting our initial intentions and motivations."[78] When we are deeply engaged in a practice, we "leave ourselves" and get lost in the practice itself. This is true when we play chess; it is true when we pray. The danger, of course, is that these practices—secular or spiritual—become ends in and of themselves. Then they become isolated and individualistic, exercises that become so engrossing or all-encompassing that they cut us off from others. Speaking specifically of spiritual practices, Spohn noted, "Problems arise when a lived spirituality is cut off from an adequate reflective framework, that is, from traditions and communities that could provide normative theological and ethical guidance. In their absence, spiritual practices are often justified by appeal to unexamined cultural commonplaces or narcissistic good feelings which are ripe for self-deception."[79] The danger is that there is no check or challenge to our own spiritual dysfunction, that the practice becomes affirming but never transforming. To avoid this individualistic interpretation of practices,

Craig Dykstra explains MacIntyre's crucial qualifier "social." What is meant here is not group activity. Indeed, what is conveyed is a deep embedment in tradition and community. "Practice is participation in a cooperatively formed pattern of activity that emerges out of a complex tradition of interactions among many people sustained over a long period of time."[80] A true practice cannot be abstracted from its past or from other people. It cannot be commodified. True spiritual practices work by drawing us out of ourselves and into a larger narrative of meaning, a larger community of concern.

Ultimately, Christian practices draw us into the narrative of Jesus. Terrence Tilley describes Christian discipleship as the practice of following Christ. "To be a disciple is to learn how to have faith in God by following Christ. Discipleship involves, indeed *is*, a way of life. This life is composed of various activities one learns how to engage in— prayer and worship; service with, to, and for others for the sake of righteousness and justice; reverence for all there is as God's gift; sustaining a community of disciples and so on."[81] Taking practice as his hermeneutical key, Tilley reconstructs christology around the reconciling practice of Jesus, embodied above all in Jesus' healing, teaching, forgiving, and table fellowship. Tilley signals the implications this "practical christology" has for the question of discernment: we discover God's will *in practice*. "As Christians, we discover God's will in the reconciling practices that constitute living in and living out the *basileia tou theou*. For in the practices of the Jesus-movement, we can recognize and display the overflowing love of God as present. We stop committing sins and refuse to give our allegiance to social and personal sin that blocks the realization of the reign of God. We live in and live out a tradition that seeks to overcome evil and sin not by 'overpowering' them but by reconciling sinners and saints, perpetrators and victims, the warriors and the vanquished, the exploiters and the exploited, insofar as that reconciliation is possible for those committed to living in and living out that tradition."[82]

By our participation in the reconciling practice of Jesus we come to that clarity that Rahner described as an honest awareness of our fundamental stance before God. This honesty, this clarity, this freedom helps us to better see what God is calling us to in any particular decision before us. To Tilley's reconciling practice—an image of drawing others together—I offer the complementary image of opening out and opening up to others. Drawing on Boeve, I see the practices of healing, teaching, forgiving, and fellowship as part of Jesus' critical-liberative praxis of the open narrative. It is through just such concrete practices of holding ourselves open to the other that we come to participate in the open narrative of Christ, and so open ourselves to God's call.

None of this can remain disembodied. Communal structures of support and accountability, a shared vocabulary, regular rituals, time with friends and a place for fellowship, tasks to accomplish together—this is the stuff of church. Participation is primarily an ecclesiological category. It is a doing-with and a being-with others. It is to "take part," to have a stake or a share in something. Bound up in the concept is an affirmation of the subject's initiative and agency. But this agency is combined with a greater emphasis on the role the subject plays within the larger context of the community. Religion or church is not simply a resource from which I draw; it is an arena within which I act. I take part in something larger than myself, and I do it with others.

Returning to Rahner's reflection on the charismatic, we come to see that a church understood as an open system—an open church—must at the same time be a participatory church. If the Spirit is the underlying dynamism of the church as a whole, then the church has to recognize that the Spirit works through every one of its members. The charismatic cannot be restricted to the occasional saint, nor can the Spirit's inspiration be reserved to the magisterium. Neither absolute monarchy nor totalitarian regime is an option. Such authoritarian models are contradicted by the very nature of the church and the breadth of the Spirit's work. For Rahner, the institutional element of the church is legitimate and necessary, but "it nevertheless remains encompassed by the charismatic movement of the Spirit in the Church, the Spirit who again and again ushers the Church as an open system into a future" that only the Spirit can see.[83] This more participatory model is not a regrettable situation, a penance that the church's leadership has to bear; rather, it is "a radical goal for the Church in the achievement of her own fulness."[84] An open, charismatic, participatory church is precisely what the church is meant to be. Nowhere in the Catholic magisterial tradition is this affirmed more clearly and consistently than at the Second Vatican Council, in the Constitution on the Sacred Liturgy's repeated call for "full, conscious and active participation" of all of the faithful in the work of God.[85]

If the church is to train believers into an openness that is not open-ended, then it needs to avoid a consumer model of membership and instead foster a participatory community in which believers work within a tradition that works on them, calling them beyond themselves through a process of transformation that takes time. Miller admits that encouraging broad participation among the faithful has never been Roman Catholicism's strong suit. But today, the rise of an educated laity and the corrosive effects of consumerism demand just this kind of encouragement. "In the past, clerics concerned about the excesses of popular religion could presume its unremitting vitality. Thus they could limit their responsibility to censoring, correcting, and controlling it."[86] Today, it is precisely the vitality of popular religion that can no longer be taken for granted. "Censoring an incorrigible culture is one task, preserving a vulnerable one is quite another."[87] Recognizing the fragmenting effects of postmodern consumer culture, the hierarchy has rightly turned its attention to Catholic identity. But its strategy for shoring up this identity—primarily through reasserting centralized clerical control and returning to closed narratives—seems sadly self-defeating. Bent on quieting dissent and deviation, church authorities insist on a narrow orthodoxy. But, in the present climate, disagreement is not nearly as deadly as disinterest. And the danger of new ideas pales in comparison to the danger of *no* ideas.

Conclusion

We human beings are perennially prone to self-deception. And one of the most costly mistakes of discernment is to set off in search of decision without conversion. Without conversion and ongoing transformation, it is all too easy to confuse who God wants me to be with who *I* want me to be. Ignatius's trust in the affections would be misguided without the purgative turning of the First Week of the *Exercises*. Rahner's search for harmony between "who I am" and "what I will do" would become a distracting echo chamber if one's fundamental life orientation remained skewed. Rahner recognized this. Ignatius recognized this. Over the centuries, the Christian tradition has called for conversion in a number of different ways. But how do we describe this conversion today? The present chapter has argued that the conversion called for at this present moment is the transformation that comes through an openness to the interruption of "the other." In order to hear the call of God, what we need most—as a church and as individuals—is to become open. For through openness to the other, we grow more and more open to *the* Other, the God who calls.

The church community can foster a "culture of vocation" today by being a place that schools its participants in receptivity to the other.

Such receptivity is more difficult than our broader culture likes to pretend. Too often we confuse openness with tolerance, or fall into a lazy inclusivity that keeps the other safely at a distance. Through our participation in the Christian community, we ought to be invited into something deeper. We ought to be drawn into the narrative of Jesus Christ—an open narrative that challenges us to move from acceptance to welcome, from acknowledgment to embrace, from coexistence to a level of engagement that leads us from individual presence to a more collective challenge of all the closed narratives that continue to oppress and exclude. In other words, to grow in discipleship of Jesus is not an exercise in ego enhancement or a shoring up of the boundaries of identity. Growing in discipleship is an opening to alterity, an imitation of Christ's slow and patient work of creating space for the neighbor. The church—the whole Christian community—facilitates this kind of growth when it fosters practices that draw its members into the practices that defined Jesus' life. As I will argue in the final chapter of this book, the most important of these practices (both in the Gospel and in our own time) are those that open us up to the other in need. In the *suffering* other we find a privileged place for conversion, and chapter 6 reflects on the profound implications of this "place" for a theology of vocation.

In the end, it is the narrative of Jesus Christ that guides the Christian narrative and the narratives of Christians. In his story, we find an alternative to that ever-present temptation amidst the shifting sands of postmodernity to close off and shut in, to seek security in certitude, to build walls around the truth rather than bridges toward it. Tempering our individual and corporate triumphalism helps us to hear. It schools us in receptivity to what others have to say, to what God is saying through others. Boeve concludes his volume *God Interrupts History* with the reminder that even Jesus was forced to recognize the inadequacy of all closed narratives.[88] When confronted by the Syrophoenician woman's plea for help, Jesus sends her away, saying "it is not fair to take the children's food and throw it to the dogs" (Mark 7:24-30; see Matt 15:21-28). But when the woman, desperate for her daughter, shouts back that even the dogs eat the children's scraps, Jesus is stopped short. His narrative about God is interrupted, broken open. And he learns to see God's love extending beyond the borders of Israel. In the faith of this woman—a non-Jew—God speaks. Through this other, God calls.

CHAPTER SIX

For Others

I will give you a talisman. Whenever you are in doubt, or when the self becomes too much with you, apply the following test.

Recall the face of the poorest and the weakest person whom you have seen, and ask yourself if the next step you contemplate is going to be of any use to that person. Will that person gain anything by it? Will it restore that person to control over his or her own life or destiny? In other words, will it lead to freedom for the hungry and spiritually starving millions?

Then you will find your doubts and your self melting away.

—*Mohandas Gandhi*[1]

We discover our vocations in response to the world. Mothers and fathers awaken to their calling by responding to the calls of their children. Teachers find theirs by responding to the questions of their students. Chapter 5 argued that God's call is mediated. But this mediation is not restricted to the channels of the church; it is not limited to some intratextuality of the Christian narrative. God's call comes to each of us through the total context of our social and historical existence, our "place of responsibility" in the world that Karl Barth believed constitutes each of us as a "unique opportunity." We live in the world, a world marked by genuine love, incredible beauty, and joy—as well as unbearable pain, deadly poverty, and violence. On the one hand, where we stand within this world of laughter and tears depends on factors beyond our control, the accidents of birth, environment, and experience. On the other hand, we are not condemned to circumstances. As free beings, each of us still chooses who we will be. Each of us asks, How will I act? What do I value? Where are my commitments? Whom do I love?

We shape our spot in the world by deciding what—and more important, *whom*—we are *for*. Dean Brackley writes, "Our surroundings shake us, sift us, and draw our vocation from us."[2] If so, then a lot depends on where we place ourselves.

We place ourselves. In his paradigm-shifting speech, "Toward a Theology of Liberation," delivered over forty years ago to a group of laity and clergy in Chimbote, Peru, Gustavo Gutiérrez offered up an enduring insight: our "place" in the world is not primarily where we *are*, but where we *go*.[3] Taking up the parable of the Good Samaritan, Gutiérrez reminds us that this story begins with the lawyer's question, "And who is my neighbor?" (Luke 10:29). It ends not with an answer but with another, quite different, question. After recounting the actions of the priest, the Levite, and the Samaritan, Jesus asks, "Which of these three was a neighbor?" Rather than point out our neighbor, Jesus shows us how *to be* a neighbor. To be a neighbor is to be the Samaritan, to go over to the one in need. It is to be in movement, to be in action for and toward and with another. Gutiérrez concludes that to "love thy neighbor" is not simply the command to care for those who are close. It is also the demand to love those who are distant—or rather, to go over, *to draw close*, to become a neighbor to those who suffer.

This final chapter considers the implications for our understanding of vocation when we, like the Samaritan, enter into the world of history's victims. What difference does it make to discernment when we place ourselves amidst those who suffer, particularly the poor? In recent decades, theologians of liberation like Gutiérrez—in Latin America and around the globe—have come to remind us of an ancient truth: the poor hold a privileged place in theological reflection and in Christian praxis. The "site" they occupy is sacred ground. This concern for the poor echoes across the tradition—from the words of the prophets to the preaching of Jesus to the proclamations of popes. It also speaks powerfully to the world today—a world divided, as Jon Sobrino puts it so starkly, between the wealthy who can take life for granted and the poor who cannot. For, however much they are hidden from view or deliberately avoided by those of us who *can* take life for granted, the massive and unjust suffering of the poor is what defines our global reality today. To ignore this fact in our treatment of vocation would be to ignore the world within which Christian discernment occurs.

Chapter 5 described how a recognition of the "other" has shaped our postmodern mentality. David Tracy acknowledges this fact, recognizing that the deepest need of the privileged and the powerful today is the need to face otherness and difference. But then he pointedly asks, "Where, in all the discussions of otherness and difference of the postmoderns as well as the moderns and the antimoderns, are the poor and the oppressed? These are the concrete others whose difference should make a difference."[4] Otherness remains abstract, and thus our reflections in chapter 5 remain unfinished, until we attend to the reality of billions of people—the majority of the world's population—who cannot take life for granted.

Chapter 6 argues that the poor and oppressed, the suffering and the forgotten, make a difference to a Christian theology of vocation. But what is this difference? It is not enough to say that all Christians are called to serve the poor—as true as this has always been. This chapter argues something more: it is precisely through presence with and on behalf of those who suffer that every Christian can come to a deeper recognition of her or his unique way of responding to God's call. The invitation to be with and for the poor is not the end of the discernment process. It is the beginning. For God speaks through the suffering of others. Defending this claim will require that we approach Christianity's "open narrative" with a deeper appreciation for what Johann Baptist Metz calls the "dangerous memory" of the Gospel; it will demand that we take the reality of history seriously; and it will invite us into the concept of solidarity in all its diverse and challenging forms. Ultimately, the call to be *for* others is always a call to be *with* others, particularly with those who suffer unjustly. For it is in the sad but sacred darkness of solidarity with the poor that our senses are heightened, and we come to hear more clearly the voice of God.

Suffering Interrupts

Vocation brings to the surface a deep and dynamic tension within the Christian life, namely, the tension between the comfort offered in the gospel message and its unrelenting challenge. God's call confirms who I am, but it also confronts who I am. It speaks to us where we are, but it also calls us to where we ought to be. Comfort and challenge run intertwined throughout the history of reflection on vocation, as the preceding chapters have shown. Identity and outreach, communion and mission, gift and task. An analogical imagination strives to hold these two poles together, seeking not a dialectical opposition but a creative tension. Every healthy treatment of vocation finds itself caught up in this tension, which is wonderfully evoked by Frederick Buechner's well-worn line, "The place God calls you to is the place where your deep gladness and the world's deep hunger meet."[5]

In the last chapter, we explored this basic tension through the model of the "open church." The open church is a community *confirmed* in its shared story of God's activity on behalf of humanity, a narrative centered around the life, death, and resurrection of Jesus Christ, a narrative that provides Christians with the primary framework for understanding and acting within the world. At the same time, the open church is a community *confronted* by "the other," a community called beyond the security of a sure and certain metanarrative, a community whose story is continually challenged by the needs and the narratives of others. Lieven Boeve, who helped frame our consideration of Christianity as an "open narrative," uses the language of interruption to speak of this confrontation. With it, he issues a warning against that ever-present temptation to close ourselves off to what God may be saying through the "interruption" of others—including the interruption of those who suffer.

Interruptions

The German Catholic theologian Johann Baptist Metz has taken these questions into the center of his theological project. The category of "interruption," used to such effect by Boeve, actually comes from Metz, who issued this one word as "the shortest definition of religion."[6] By defining religion as interruption, Metz wanted to make clear "that Christian faith can never slip unpunished into a sort of bourgeois religion, seamlessly woven into the prevailing culture and society, nor withdraw itself from or against its context. Such religion seeks a too-facile reconciliation, forgetting in the process the tragic suffering that confronts human existence."[7] For Metz, suffering interrupts. It disrupts any neat systematization of theology and every overly confident assertion about the way God works in the world. This conviction is powerfully illustrated by a story Metz shares from his own life, a story that gives a glimpse into his own vocational journey:

> Toward the end of the Second World War, when I was sixteen years old, I was taken out of school and forced into the army. After a brief period of training at a base in Würzburg, I arrived at the front, which by that time had already crossed the Rhine into Germany. There were well over a hundred in my company, all of whom were very young. One evening the company commander sent me with

a message to battalion headquarters. I wandered all night long through destroyed, burning villages and farms, and when in the morning I returned to the company I found only the dead, nothing but the dead, overrun by a combined bomber and tank assault. I could see only dead and empty faces, where the day before I had shared childhood fears and youthful laughter. I remember nothing but a wordless cry. Thus I see myself to this very day, and behind this memory all my childhood dreams crumble away. A fissure had opened in my powerful Bavarian-Catholic socialization, with its impregnable confidence. What would happen if one took this sort of remembrance not to the psychologist but into the Church? and if one did not allow oneself to be talked out of such unreconciled memories even by theology, but rather wanted to have faith with them and, with them, speak about God?[8]

The memory is worth citing at length, for it captures both the horror of history and Metz's own dogged effort not to let it slip away. In his tenacious refusal to turn away from the suffering of history—a history that continues into the present—Metz models a stance toward reality that will prove instructive for our own approach to the question of vocation.

As the quote above indicates, at the root of Metz's theology is a deep concern about the forgetfulness of modern society, in particular, its forgetfulness of history's victims. Metz was a student of Karl Rahner at the University of Innsbruck in the 1950s and, at the start of his career, he adopted Rahner's transcendental approach to theology. But after leaving Innsbruck for his own teaching post at Münster, Metz quickly moved away from the specific formulations and methodology of Rahner's system—even as he continued to affirm the underlying commitments of his theological mentor.[9] In the place of Rahner's transcendental analysis of the human subject, Metz developed a theological approach more consistently attentive to the ambiguities of humanity's social and historical existence, in other words, a theology more open to the interruptive memories of suffering.

It is the memory of the Holocaust—or, rather, the forgetting of the Holocaust—that haunts the heart of Metz's reflections. For him, this is the nadir of the West's historical amnesia. For all that he finds insightful and still significant in Rahner's work, Metz is painfully aware how little his German countryman mentioned the atrocity—the *Shoah*—that they both lived through. "Because of the way Auschwitz showed up—or did not show up—in theology, it became (slowly) clear to me how high the apathy content in theological idealism is, how incapable it is of taking on historical experiences—despite, or even because of, all its talk about history and historicity. It is clear that there is no meaning to history that one can save with one's back turned to Auschwitz, no truth to history that one can defend with one's back turned to Auschwitz, and no God of history whom one can worship with one's back turned to Auschwitz."[10] The crisis of religious faith in the contemporary world is not primarily that of secularization and unbelief, as Rahner's system presupposed. Instead, the crisis is that of horrific, inhuman suffering that is worldwide and only escalating. Metz would share Gustavo Gutiérrez's observation that the real challenge confronting Christian theology today is not that of the *nonbeliever*. The real challenge is that of the *nonperson*—the one that society defines as a nobody, the one whose survival is radically threatened by oppressive economic, political, and cultural structures that attack her very existence as a subject.

For Metz, the crisis is only deepened by a widespread indifference among those who could help. In the face of so much suffering, we shut down. We simply do not want to think about it. With increased education and instant communication, we are so much more aware of the world's pain than we have ever been. And yet, psychologically and spiritually, we are increasingly unable to face it. Catastrophes are reported on the radio "in between pieces of music." But we have become numb. "When atrocities happen it's like when the rain falls. No one shouts 'stop it!' anymore."[11] Metz sees this malady as a kind of malaise, a "weariness with being a subject." Being a subject means being able to take responsibility for oneself and for others. But we have become unwilling or unable to accept this responsibility. We retreat into our private realms of work and family—our callings—and let others worry about the social and political processes that determine life and death for millions.[12]

This crisis demands a new way of speaking theologically. It fuels an approach Metz calls "political theology," which takes up as its central concern the theodicy question—understood not as an existential issue but as a social, structural, and thus political one. How can we speak of God in the face of "the abysmal history of suffering in the world"?[13] In addressing this question, Metz stands against the prevailing currents of postmodern thought and process theology. As we saw in chapter 5, the postmodern concern for the other implies an ethic of resistance, a determinate claim that goes against the grain of postmodernity's own emphasis on indeterminateness. Metz sees this ambiguity clearly—fearful that the radical contextualization demanded by postmodernity too often leads modernity's "death of God" into a "death of the subject." For Metz, postmodernity risks losing the ability to take a stand for the subject. This is tragic because it is precisely the human subject that is in jeopardy.

For this reason, Metz steadfastly defends the gains that have come from modernity's turn to the subject, such as an emphasis on the dignity of the human person and the demands for justice that this dignity entails. (Karl Rahner, Metz would say, still has much to teach us.) The human subject still stands but always understood as a historical and social being, always related to the other both past and present. "Metz is as ferocious a critic as any of a concept of the subject which is atemporal, already constituted apart from or before social and historical relations, immune from the disruptive catastrophes that interrupt history. On the other hand, he recognizes the unparalleled critical and liberative power that the concept of the subject lends to Christian faith, as an instrument for articulating the biblical tradition of the unsated hunger and thirst for justice."[14] His theology, then, turns from the subject to the subject who suffers. In reply to postmodern relativism, he offers a passionate plea for a moral universalism that is rooted in the one authority recognized by all great cultures and religions: the authority of those who suffer. Metz writes, "I have worked to formulate a concept of theology that, while it recognizes the post-modernists' legitimate suspicion of universalistic approaches, does not collapse into a sheer relativization of cultural worlds. I have striven to do this by stressing a respect for and obedience to the authority of those who suffer. For me this authority is the only one in which the authority of the sovereign God is manifested in the world for all men and women."[15]

This authority speaks to us in the present, and it speaks to us from the past. Ultimately it is the memory of suffering that grounds a universal morality. And those who follow the crucified Christ witness to this *memoria passionis* in a special way. Here Metz's analysis becomes most explicitly and creatively Christian. The church is the bearer of the "dangerous memory" of the suffering, death, and resurrection of Jesus Christ. It is the authority of this suffering one that should speak to Christians. As his various writings reveal, for Metz, Christianity is a community of narrative and memory before it is an institution of rules and doctrine. At the heart of that narrative is the memory of Jesus. Metz cites an early noncanonical "saying" of Jesus—"Whoever is close to me, is close to the fire; whoever is far from me, is far from the Kingdom"— to communicate the apocalyptic urgency of this memory. "It is dangerous to be close to Jesus, it threatens to set us afire, to consume us."[16] The passion narrative is not an entertaining or edifying story. It is a disturbing one. It does not invite us to ponder; it calls us to follow.[17] Centuries of whitewashing this story, taming its memory, has washed out the discipleship it demands: "If the world hates you, be aware that it hated me before it hated you. . . . Remember the word that I said to you, 'Servants are not greater than their master.' If they persecuted me, they will persecute you" (John 15:18, 20). For Metz, the subversive, menacing memory of the cross opens us up to the ongoing crucifixions of history. We need to hear Jesus' cry from the cross, so that we can hear all those other cries from all those other crosses of history. The dangerous memory of Jesus' death shakes us, sifts us, and challenges us to turn to God and to the world in more open and honest ways.

And yet, for all the dark urgency of Metz's account, he clearly argues that the dangerous memories of suffering do not end in despair. For Metz these memories also hold open the possibility of hope, a solidaristic hope, a hope with and for others. They call forth a particular stance before God and the world that Metz calls "suffering unto God."[18] Though his theology is more about conveying a sense of crisis than it is about suggesting solutions—a dynamic seen most clearly in Metz's unapologetic embrace of apocalyptic[19]—still his sense of this stance proves fruitful for our reflection on vocation. As I will argue below, it is through our sensitivity to suffering that we develop a spirituality particularly well suited for discernment in troubled times.[20] But before exploring this spirituality, we must address a prior theological question. Metz's reflections on interruption have raised for us the possibility that God works in and through the negativity of history. How is it that God works through this negativity? What keeps such a claim from reducing the suffering other to an instrument of my own spiritual growth? Addressing this question involves, first, attending to the claim that God acts in and through history in general and, second, that God acts through the history of those who suffer in particular. For help in exploring these claims, we turn to those thinkers whom Metz saw as continuing and fulfilling his own theological agenda. We listen to representative voices of the theology of liberation.

Suffering and Salvation in History

Metz's theology communicates a sense of crisis that comes from the confrontation with violence and unjust suffering. He speaks of the "dangerous memory" of the cross and the interruption of Auschwitz. Whereas Boeve broadens the category of interruption in order to invite us to look out on the "colorful multiplicity" of postmodernity, Metz keeps our eyes firmly focused on the other who suffers. "Auschwitz" is not a symbol of universal misery or an evocative metaphor for evil. Rather, for Metz it is a concrete event, the real destruction of real people in history. And history (both past and present) is full of such events—the real suffering of real subjects who call out again and again, interrupting us with their cries.

God speaks to us in these cries. There is in this thesis a rather startling claim, dulled perhaps by its pious repetition: God calls us through the suffering of others. Our vocation is found in and through the world's pain. A first step in taking this claim seriously is to take *reality* seriously. We cannot understand how God speaks through the history of those who suffer if we do not first come to grasp how God speaks through history. History is reality, understood as the concrete unfolding of human life and freedom. And grappling with history, in many ways, defines the problematic of theology in our postmodern time. It is a kind of third wave, following the premodern emphasis on nature and the modern concern with the subject.[21] It reminds us that a theology of vocation cannot stay abstract, individual and internal. Its context cannot be reduced to an ideal narrative or idealized community. If we insist that God calls us for others—particularly those in need, those whose very existence is threatened—then we must face the mess and misery of concrete historical existence. And so, in order to take historical reality seriously, we turn from Metz to another student of Karl Rahner, the Basque theologian and Salvadoran martyr, Ignacio Ellacuría. Ellacuría's distinctive contribution to Latin American liberation theology represents the most fully developed and philosophically sophisticated attempt to ground theology and ethical praxis in historical reality. Thus his thought offers a rich resource for deepening our own understanding of the call to be with and for others.

Ignacio Ellacuría first became widely known outside of the political and ecclesiastical world of El Salvador with the news of his assassination in the early morning hours of November 16, 1989. As was later brought to light, Ellacuría was murdered, alongside five of his Jesuit housemates, their housekeeper and her fifteen-year-old daughter, by agents of the Salvadoran military. At the time, Ellacuría was professor and rector of the University of Central America, the author and editor of numerous publications, and an active participant in the public life of El Salvador—and it was largely for this political activity on behalf of the Salvadoran people that he was killed.[22] He left behind a body of work that took as its main concern the relationship between salvation and history. Ellacuría often repeated the central thesis of his theological project: salvation history is salvation *in* history.[23] This rather simple (and potentially misleading) statement rests on a complex philosophical and theological foundation. It, in turn, supports a theology of vocation committed to the conviction that the call of God comes in the cry of the poor.

Ellacuría's own historical context suggests his theological interest in history. For Ellacuría, to abstract from history is to become dangerously disconnected from reality—a reality in which innocent people are being killed and crying out to be saved. In the midst of political oppression, state-sanctioned violence, and inhuman poverty, Ellacuría argued that the question of salvation cannot be postponed for a future and far-off heaven. Salvation must touch people today. Their lives in history, their historical reality, matter. In order to make this case, Ellacuría developed a sophisticated philosophy of historical reality, drawing on Rahner and on the work of the great Basque philosopher Xavier Zubiri. Though Ellacuría was a student of Rahner at Innsbruck in the late 1950s and early 1960s, it was under Zubiri, while at the University of Madrid, that Ellacuría pursued his doctorate. This later work led Ellacuría to reread Rahner in light of Zubiri's philosophy of historical reality.[24]

Zubiri was a classically trained philosopher influenced by the phenomenologies of Edmund Husserl and Martin Heidegger. From the start, he shared with these thinkers a desire to free philosophy from an abstract idealism by focusing on the "things themselves." Gradually however, through his dialogue with psychology and contemporary science, Zubiri came to see that these phenomenologies continued to be constrained by Husserl's "epoche," which bracketed the question of the reality of the "phenomena" that we experience in the concrete, everyday world. Continuing the critique of an epistemology that prioritized conceptualization over sense experience, Zubiri sought to take phenomenology to the next level.[25] Thus he pushed beyond Heidegger's "being" (which remains abstract) to "reality"—the reality that we grasp through the dynamic act of our "sensing intelligence" (*inteligencia sentiente*).[26]

Ellacuría adopted Zubiri's philosophical realism and developed it through the category of history. For Ellacuría, reality is "historical reality," which integrates and subsumes the other types of reality—material, biological, personal, and social.[27] Inspired by the Second Vatican Council's call to read the "signs of the times" and challenged by the Latin American Bishops' call at Medellín to apply this reading to their own context, Ellacuría focused his life's work on understanding and realizing the history of salvation *in* the concrete historical reality of Latin America.[28] Ellacuría believed that it is only by locating concepts (such as salvation) within their specific and local historical context that their universal significance becomes clear. Ellacuría called this process of critical historical contextualization "historicization."[29] It is a process with two significant outcomes. First, historicization serves as a principle of "de-ideologization" that resists the abstraction of human concepts from the complex constellation of historical forces that shape them. It unmasks the way in which ideas and ideals are so often manipulated to serve particular social, political, and economic interests.[30] Second, this critical contextualization makes us acutely aware that such concepts are part of an ongoing historical process of which we are a part. We have responsibility within this process. Historicization thus involves a strong dimension of praxis.[31] To historicize salvation in Latin America is not only to ask what salvation means and how it functions in this particular historical situation but it is also to take responsibility to act within that situation.

For Ellacuría, we must take historical reality seriously. But what keeps this emphasis on history from devolving into a historical materialism? What keeps it from becoming a secular philosophy of history? Where, in all of this, is God? One of the early objections to liberation theology was that its emphasis on liberation from historical and political oppression tended to downplay liberation from personal sin. According to its critics, liberation theology had replaced God's grace with human effort, advocacy, and even political revolution. This concern was famously articulated in a 1984 Instruction issued by the Vatican's Congregation for the Doctrine of the Faith. In this cautionary document, concerns were raised about liberation theology's use of Marxist analysis, its ecclesiological presuppositions, and, especially, its temptation "to emphasize, unilaterally, the liberation from servitude of an earthly and temporal kind . . . to put liberation from sin in second place." The document went on: "To some it even seems that the necessary struggle for human justice and freedom in the economic and political sense constitutes the whole essence of salvation. For them, the gospel is reduced to a purely earthly gospel."[32]

Ellacuría took this charge seriously. Central to his theological project was his conviction that, while salvation comes in history, it cannot be reduced to the historical. Thus he acknowledged the danger of the reductionism warned about in the Instruction, even as he questioned the CDF's construal of liberation theology.[33] But he also warned against the opposite temptation. Certainly, theology must avoid a kind of monism that collapses the transcendent into history, but theology must also avoid a dualism that splits God off from the world. This later tendency Ellacuría saw as more pervasive and more pernicious than the first. It appears throughout the Christian tradition as an other-worldly spirituality masking itself as orthodoxy, dangerously ignoring the biblical witness of God's saving action in history.

What is needed, Ellacuría argued, is a proper understanding of transcendence, one that avoids both monism and dualism in its approach to the God-world relationship. Such a concept of transcendence "calls attention to a contextual structural difference without implying a duality," it "enables us to speak of an intrinsic unity without implying a strict identity."[34] Here Ellacuría's debt to Rahner comes through with astonishing clarity. In his distinction between the categorical and the transcendental, Rahner sought just such a unity-in-distinction. And in his conception of the supernatural existential, Rahner articulated a theology of grace that respects human freedom. What Ellacuría did was to historicize Rahner's supernatural existential. Robert Lassalle-Klein argues that this critical historical contextualization allowed Ellacuría to move beyond Rahner's focus on the individual human subject, thus locating this subject within a larger and more complex historical reality that is elevated and transformed by grace.[35] Citing Rahner, Ellacuría argued, "This openness which in every person is the transcendental openness that is elevated from a 'supernatural existential' (Rahner), is in the totality of history, the transcendental openness that is elevated from a gratuitous historicity."[36] To convey this sense of graced history, Ellacuría spoke of the *historical-theologal* structure of reality. By "theologal" he meant to name the transcendent God's presence *in* historical reality: God is present in reality not as one thing among others but as the very ground of all things. God is the power of reality; God is what makes reality real. In making this claim, Ellacuría advanced and developed Rahner's theology of grace through the categories of Zubiri's philosophical realism.

For Zubiri, the human encounter with reality signals to us that we are not the cause of our own existence but that, rather, existence itself is thrust upon us. We find ourselves "thrown among things." We discover ourselves as already existing.[37] This givenness—the gift—of existence reveals our dependence on what provides existence. Our existence is connected to our source as what continues to support us in existence. Zubiri introduced the word *religación* to name this fact of our being "re-connected" or "tied-back" to the source of our existence. Crucial to his account is that the source of our existence is not outside of our existence. The source of our existence is intrinsic to it. It is the very ground of existence itself. "We find ourselves linked to something which is not extrinsic, but which *antecedently makes us to be*."[38] Zubiri used the term *theologal* to name this "bonded" dimension of human existence, one that "involves, constitutively and formally, an inexorable confrontation with the ultimacy of the real, provisionally and nominally, that which we call God."[39] Thus the distinction between God and the world is not as banal as the distinction between two separate existing things (no matter how superior one might be to the other). The distinction is far more radical. It is the distinction between existing things and the very source of existence itself.[40] But it is this very distinction that keeps the two connected. Thus Zubiri's notion of *religación* would not support a detached mode of human existence. In this concept is a dynamism that drives us to encounter God precisely through our encounter with reality. Thus Zubiri could imagine a time when humans "will encounter [themselves] religated to God, not so as to flee from the world, and others, and themselves; but the other way around, in order to sustain and maintain themselves in being." *Religación* is not an escape but an imperative to encounter reality.[41]

All of this serves as the backdrop for Ellacuría's own rethinking of transcendence in what Kathryn Tanner calls a non-contrastive mode, one that sees in the God-world relationship *both* radical distinction *and* radical involvement.[42] After reviewing the mistaken assumption that transcendence implies separation, Ellacuría offered his own view:

> But there is a radically different way of understanding transcendence, more in line with the way reality and God's action are presented in biblical thinking. This is to see transcendence as something that transcends *in* and not as something that transcends *away from*; as something that physically impels to *more* but not by taking *out of*; as something that pushes *forward*, but at the same time *retains*. In this conception, when one reaches God historically—which is the same as reaching God personally—one does not abandon the human, does not abandon real history, but rather deepens one's roots, making more present and effective what was already effectively present.[43]

In the categories of *religación* and the theologal, Ellacuría found a language to communicate the deep Christian insight into transcendence-in-immanence that was the hallmark of Karl Rahner's theological vision. But what Ellacuría found in Zubiri was a way of articulating this insight that opened more naturally into historical process and human praxis, a move that marks the real genius of Ellacuría's own theological vision and the most helpful contribution to our own attempts to speak of God speaking in and through history.

In his essay "The Historicity of Christian Salvation," Ellacuría brought all of this down to earth with a question: "Who brought the people out of Egypt, Yahweh or Moses?"[44] Ellacuría's point was that the biblical authors were not particularly worried by the question. They simply took it for granted that God was the author of these saving deeds. *And* they took it for granted that Moses was the agent of God and that his historical actions were saving actions. The Bible offers a deeply non-dualistic, non-contrastive narrative. Ellacuría affirmed this vision in his often-repeated point that there are not two histories, a history of God and a history of humanity. "Rather there is a single historical reality in which both God and human beings intervene, so that God's intervention does not occur without some form of human participation, and human intervention does not occur without God's presence in some form."[45] The only way to say this coherently is by rejecting the zero-sum game of a contrastive account. God and human freedom are not competitive because they do not occupy the same plane. And, in fact, it is the more radical distinction between reality and ground of reality that allows for the profound intimacy of God in history.

History, then, is the special place of God's presence. Because history is reality as open to human action and freedom, history is the place where the creative and liberating future of God is most fully realized. "Thus history is the fullest place of transcendence, of a transcendence that does not appear mechanically, but only appears when history is made, and which irrupts in novel ways in the constant disestablishment of the determining process."[46] Ellacuría's thesis that "salvation history is salvation in history" sounds simplistic and reductionistic only if we forget his deep commitment to the theologal dimension of historical reality. It only makes sense as a Christian claim within the context of Ellacuría's non-contrastive account of the relationship between reality, on the one hand, and God as transcendent and ever-present source of reality, on the other. This account of salvation in history provides us with a theological foundation to explore the history that mattered most to Ellacuría: the history of unjust suffering embodied in the poor of El Salvador.

Before turning from a general consideration of history to a particular focus on the poor in history, we pause to assess the gains so far that Ellacuría's thought suggests for our understanding of vocation. Recall that one of the principal claims of this book is that the modern Catholic theology of vocation has been handicapped by a dualistic understanding of the nature-grace relationship. We have been trying to rethink vocation in light of the richer understanding of grace recovered by Catholic theology over the course of the twentieth century. Thus chapter 4 drew on the theology of Karl Rahner to reimagine the interior aspect of God's call in light of God's transcendental presence within the human subject. In this chapter, we turn from the human heart to human history. We ask how God's call might be understood, not in Rahner's language of the transcendental, but in Ellacuría's use of the theologal. Michael Lee insightfully observes that Ellacuría represents a second generation of grappling with the nature-grace dilemma.[47] Ellacuría picked up the debates of Rahner and de Lubac, and translated them into the idiom of history. In one essay, Ellacuría even suggested that what he meant by "salvation history" and "salvation in history" is what earlier theologians meant by "grace" and "nature."[48] And so, just as Rahner's notion of the transcendental allows us to speak of God's call in the depths of the heart, without appealing to some mysterious "secret voice"; likewise, Ellacuría's use of the theologal allows us to speak of God's call through the realities of history, without imagining it in terms of a miraculous intervention or divine sign. All of this helps us to speak more confidently of God's activity in history. However, the present chapter claims more than that God calls through history. It claims that God's call comes in a special way through the history of those who suffer, particularly those who suffer unjustly and in poverty. To this stronger claim we now turn.

Cry of the Crucified

From Zubiri, Ellacuría learned how to talk about God's transcendence as a transcendence *in* history. But history is ambiguous. It is the site of both the reign of God and the reign of sin—sin that is personal, social, and structural, sin that brings violence, dehumanization, and death. If it is true that God acts through the actions of humans, it is also true that not every human action is the act of God. In other words, oppression and liberation are not the same. Thus the believer faces a question: where in this history of sin and grace is the reign of God to be found?

The words of Jesus in Luke's gospel offer a clue: "Blessed are you who are poor, for yours is the kingdom of God."[49] Ellacuría argued that the poor represent the privileged place for encountering the reign of God in history. "The poor of Latin America are theological place insofar as they constitute the maximum and scandalous, prophetic and apocalyptic presence of the Christian God and, consequently, the privileged place of Christian praxis and reflection."[50] God reveals Godself—God speaks—in the poor. Ellacuría acknowledged that the word "poverty" often takes a broad scope, including various forms of oppression and marginalization, such as that based on race, gender, or culture. But his primary lens was socioeconomic. Insofar as other forms of oppression usually include a socioeconomic dimension, they are not excluded.[51] But for Ellacuría, the poor are first and foremost those deprived of basic material needs—a deprivation that brings death. As Gutiérrez puts it so directly, the poor are those who die before their time.

Ellacuría made a further point. The poor not only die, they are put to death. For Ellacuría poverty is dialectical: there are the poor because there are the rich. Thus poverty cannot be defined simply as the lack of material necessities. Indeed, if such a lack were universal, it would not be poverty according to Ellacuría's understanding. Nor is poverty simply the inequality between rich and poor. Poverty is a reality that is actively inflicted, and thus so is the death that comes with it. The poor are put to death by being deprived of what they need for life. This dialectical understanding was clearly shaped by Ellacuría's Salvadoran context, where people were, first, *made poor* by the plunder and exploitation of colonial powers and, later, *kept poor* by a violent military-political establishment serving an economic oligarchy. However, from this particular historical context, Ellacuría made a universal theological claim: "The death of the poor is the death of God, the ongoing crucifixion of the Son of God."[52] Not only are the poor put to death, they are put to death in a particular way: they are crucified. Thus Ellacuría's deep sense of God's presence in the poor—an intuition he saw so obviously affirmed by scripture, the magisterium, theologians, and ordinary believers—rests on an original theological principle: the poor are "the crucified people."

To speak of the poor as the crucified people immediately evokes the crucifixion of Jesus, a reality that Ellacuría argued must be historicized. In attempting just such a historically critical contextualization, Ellacuría distanced himself from traditional atonement theories, such as those that present the cross as an expiation for sin or a sacrificial offering to God. Beyond the problem these theories pose for our images of a loving God, Ellacuría saw in their neat logic the scandal of the cross reduced to a kind of natural necessity: this is what had to happen for sin to be forgiven and the world to be reconciled with God. Such ahistorical explanations are too tidy. They downplay the responsibility of those who killed Jesus, and they undermine our own responsibility to resist such sin in history. Needed is a less romanticized reading of the cross. As Ellacuría pointed out, Jesus did not seek death on the cross. Jesus sought to proclaim the reign of God. His death came as the result of this proclamation. Thus his death cannot be understood apart from his whole life, a life of love lived in a history marked by concrete personal and social structures of sin.

> The historic character of the death of Jesus entails, to begin with, that his death took place for historic reasons. New christologies are increasingly emphasizing this point. Jesus dies—is killed as both the four gospels and Acts so insist—because of the historic life he led, a life of deeds and words that those who represented and held the reins of the religious, socioeconomic and political situation could not tolerate. That he was regarded as a blasphemer, one who was destroying the traditional religious order, one who upset the social structure, a political agitator, and so forth, is simply to recognize from quite distinct angles that the activity, word, and very person of Jesus in the proclamation of the Reign were so assertive and so against the established order and basic institutions that they had to be punished by death.[53]

This historicized reading of the crucified Christ illuminates the reality of the crucified people. Jesus lived in history and was put to death in history. So too the poor live in history and are put to death in history. Just as Jesus' death should not be seen as a necessity following some hidden logic in the mind of God, neither should the death of the poor be seen in terms of natural necessity. This is not simply "the way it is." It is a sin. Calling this situation sin suggests causes, and invites investigation. Individual suffering is thus located within the larger context of a systemic evil that is actively imposed. As Kevin Burke argues, "The image of crucifixion evokes a profound sense of complexity and hidden complicity. These victims are not picked off randomly by snipers. They are systematically ground under by the vast, dull machinery and laby-rinthine workings of social, economic, political, and cultural systems. However, the systems are not imposed on history from outside history. Human choices construct them."[54] The sin behind this ongoing cru-cifixion cannot be spiritualized. The suffering and oppression of whole peoples and whole continents is a historical reality. It is the result of historical decisions and human actions.

It is the process of historicization that allowed Ellacuría to link Christ and the poor in a profound way. It enabled a theological as-sociation between the two realities—a christological connection—that undergirds his commitment to the special presence of God in the poor. On the one hand, the category of "the crucified peoples" allowed Ellacuría to uncover and condemn the sinful choices and sinful struc-tures that kill the body of Christ. On the other hand, it inspires a re-sponse. For if the cross of Christ calls for conversion and faithful discipleship, the ongoing crucifixion of the poor is the historical and continuing presence of that call, the extension of Christ's vocation—understood in the dual sense of his own personal response and the response he calls forth from us.

In the First Week of the *Spiritual Exercises*, Ignatius of Loyola asked the person making the retreat to kneel before the crucified Jesus and ask, "What have I done for Christ? What am I doing for Christ? What ought I do for Christ?" Ellacuría adapted this spiritual colloquy by inviting the believer to face the poor and the oppressed, and ask, "What have I done to crucify them? What am I doing in order to un-crucify them? What ought I do so that this people be raised?"[55] For Ellacuría, recognizing the reality of the crucified people leads to a notion of praxis that revolves around the question, how will I take the crucified people down from the cross? His extensive philosophical and theological work—on the nature of reality, historicization, the theologal—all came together in a claim about discipleship. Christians are called to follow Jesus. But this is not an abstract and ahistorical imitation. Rather, to follow (*seguir*) Jesus is to carry forward (*proseguir*) his historical mission. In other words, the question to ask is not, what would Jesus do? The question is, what *did* Jesus do? Through the process of historicization, we discover that Jesus proclaimed the reign of God and engaged in a ministry that had profound sociopolitical dimensions. It was a life of loving concern for the poor and the marginalized that challenged the oppressive structures of his day, engendered fierce opposition, and ultimately led to his death.

To be a disciple is to carry forward Jesus' mission in our own context. Discipleship is thus a historical continuation of a historical mission. Ellacuría called this a "progressive historicization," guided, he believed, by "the spirit of Christ who animates those who follow him."[56] Christology, for Ellacuría, is lived: "Consequently, Jesus' death is not the end of the meaning of his life, but the end of that pattern that must be repeated and followed in new lives with the hope of resurrection and thereby the seal of exaltation. . . . Therefore, his followers should not focus primarily on death as sacrifice, but on the life of Jesus, which will only really be his life if it leads to the same consequences as his life."[57] To imagine the same consequences for one's own life as those that followed on Jesus' life is to acknowledge the real danger of taking Jesus seriously. It articulates what Ellacuría's own life and death embodied.

The Crucified Bear Salvation

We might expect from Ellacuría just such a prophetic call to take up this struggle to liberate the poor. What we might not expect is the surprising—even scandalous, he admitted—claim that it is the poor who are the real liberators. The crucified people are not passive recipients of salvation-as-liberation. Instead they are the principal agents of Christ's salvation in the world. In Ellacuría's thought, salvation *for* the poor is inextricably bound up in the salvation that comes *from* the poor. This is the key insight behind his designation of the poor as the crucified peoples. For the primary analogue captured by this image is not between Christ and us. The primary analogue is between Christ and the poor. The poor are Christ crucified today. Thus it is the poor who—like Christ—bring salvation.

This scandalous claim has significant implications for our approach to vocation. If Ellacuría had simply ended with the call to serve the poor—to take the crucified people down from the cross—his theology would have added little to the process of vocational discernment beyond underscoring in stark terms the gospel imperative. But by linking salvation *for* the poor to salvation *from* the poor, Ellacuría pushed suffering toward solidarity. He invited a deeper reflection on how it is that each of us comes to know what each of us is called to do.

How is it, then, that the poor bring salvation? In short, the crucified people continue the saving action of Jesus by bearing the weight of the world's sin. In making this claim, Ellacuría avoided any kind of romanticization of poverty.[58] The poor mediate salvation not because they are more virtuous than the rest. Sin touches everyone. And victims of injustice are not immune from the impulse to dominate or seek revenge. Thus Ellacuría's account is more nuanced. In speaking of the salvific potential of the crucified people, he underscored the collective dimension of this historical reality, while still allowing for personal freedom. But he was not speaking of a collection of individual injuries; rather, the crucified people represent a communion of victims—a historical-theologal reality standing over and against the reality of sin. It is this communion that serves as the principle of universal salvation, and thus opens a window into vocation.[59]

Ellacuría turned to the Suffering Servant songs of Isaiah to develop the soteriological links between the crucified Christ and the crucified peoples. Christians have long associated Jesus with this mysterious servant of Yhwh, who was "wounded for our transgressions, crushed for our iniquities" (Isa 53:5). Ellacuría extended the image to the crucified of today. He argued that all who carry forward the mission of the servant—which is to bear the sins of others—are included within this rich biblical figure. Such is the solidarity of the communion of history's victims, within whom Jesus stands as head. The Suffering Servant "will be anyone unjustly crucified for the sins of human beings, because all of the crucified form a single unit, one sole reality, even though this reality has a head and members with different functions in the unity of expiation."[60] Like any group of human beings, the crucified people include many individual sinners. But as a whole, they bear the weight of sin they did not commit; thus they embody historically that death that bears salvation. And just as Yhwh brings forth for the servant the victory of justice, just as God raises Jesus from the dead, so too the Lord of history makes the crucified people both judge and savior in history.

As the final judgment scene in Matthew 25 so uncomfortably reminds us, salvation depends on how we treat the poor. But notice that the parable is not about salvation *for* the poor. It is about salvation that comes *from* the poor. It tells us that Christ becomes judge *in* the crucified peoples ("whatever you did for these least, you did for me"). This judgment is in fact salvation, "insofar as it unveils the sin of the world by standing up to it; insofar as it makes possible redoing what has been done badly; insofar as it proposes a new demand as the unavoidable route for reaching salvation."[61] To speak of the poor as judge and savior is indeed scandalous. But, as Ellacuría argued, the alternative is an ahistorical view of salvation in which both the historical life of Jesus and the historical lives of his followers are ultimately irrelevant, marginalized by the tidy logic of "sin-offense-victim-expiation-forgiveness."[62] Moreover, the scandal of claiming that salvation comes from the poor lies not in some downplaying of the salvific significance of Jesus Christ or a marginalization of the unique efficacy of Calvary. Ellacuría's notion of the theologal maintained the transcendent significance of Christ at the heart of the historical reality of the poor. Instead, the scandal is the scandal of the cross itself—that ultimate Christian scandal that sees victory coming through this failure, and life coming through this death. "The subject of liberation is, ideally, the one who himself is the greatest victim of domination, the one who really carries the cross of history, because this cross is the mockery, not of the one who suffers, but of the one who imposes it. It carries in itself a process of death that can and should give way to a distinct way of life."[63]

Ellacuría's notion of the crucified people as the principle of salvation returns to enrich the notion of discipleship and vocation. If we were to imagine salvation-liberation as simply *for* the poor, we could easily turn discipleship into a kind of detached charity from a distance, or advocacy from afar. But because salvation-liberation comes *from* the poor, discipleship cannot mean distance. The crucified people are carrying salvation. We need to catch up with them. We, like the Samaritan, have to cross over and place ourselves alongside the other in need. There we become a neighbor by loving our neighbor, and so find salvation. As I will argue below, vocational discernment does not end with a generic call to serve the poor. It begins with a decision to be in solidarity with the crucified people. To be called *for others* is to be *with others*, particularly with those who suffer.

From Suffering to Solidarity

The category of the "crucified people" invites reflection in two directions: What can we do for the poor? (How do we take the crucified people down from the cross?) And what can the poor do for us? (How does salvation come from this cross?) Yet we suspect there is something problematic about this way of framing the issue. It reinforces a separation—an "us-them" mentality—that is the root of the problem, not the way toward a solution. The whole force of Ellacuría's theology (and of liberation theology in general) pulls away from such separation and instead presses toward solidarity. Solidarity is often associated with activism and advocacy. But, in the pages that follow, I argue that it rests on a deeper spiritual disposition. Solidarity speaks to more than the question, what to do? More basically, it asks, who am I? More to the point, it asks, *whose* am I?[64] For whom does my heart break? With whom does my compassion lie? As Jon Sobrino, Ellacuría's close friend and colleague, points out, solidarity is a kind of dispossession, a process of turning oneself over to the other. Solidarity means *"letting oneself be affected* by the suffering of other human beings, sharing their pain and tragedy."[65] Thus, solidarity with the poor is, first and foremost, the act of placing oneself with the poor so that one might be "placed" by the poor, thus allowing oneself to be shaped and moved and motivated by the crucified people. If, as Luther argued so long ago, our surroundings are central to our vocation, today we ask, where do we need to be in order to hear God's call? The answer: at the foot of the cross.

At the Foot of the Cross

Ellacuría stated an obvious truth: "The 'where' from which one seeks to see decisively determines what one is able to see."[66] Where we place ourselves matters. Behind Ellacuría's claim lies his deep philosophical commitment to a kind of "localized" knowledge that stands as a compelling alternative to the monolith of modern reason, with its antiseptic scientific rationality and myth of pure objectivity. Drawing on Zubiri's notion of sensing-intelligence, Ellacuría argued that an engaged, participative, and historically situated way of apprehending the world is not some deficient kind of human knowing, overly subjective and unreliably arbitrary. Instead, such "placed" knowledge is a fuller and more complete way of approaching reality. It takes the real world of history more seriously than those philosophies that claim an objective "grasp" of the meaning of things. For Ellacuría, the function of intelligence "is not the comprehending of being or the capturing of meaning, but rather the apprehending and facing of reality."[67] Knowledge cannot be reduced to abstractions. And action is not simply the application of theory. Rather, through our complex encounter and engagement with reality, we come to know. From our particular place, we start to see.

Ellacuría articulated this perspective on "placed" knowledge with a threefold imperative: We must "realize the weight of reality." We must "shoulder the weight of reality." And we must "take charge of the weight of reality." [68] He learned from Zubiri the importance of "realizing the weight of reality." We have to face historical reality honestly, allowing ourselves to be confronted by its burdens and demands. But this apprehension (a "sensing intellection") is not detached reflection. Thus Ellacuría argued that we must "shoulder the weight of reality." By this he meant that knowledge of reality involves a fundamental choice about where we locate ourselves within it. This "place" is concrete and historical, including the various geographical, social, cultural, economic, and political dimensions of human existence. Though we are born into a particular constellation of contexts, still, Ellacuría argued, as free beings we place ourselves. We decide how we want to look out on the world. And thus we should place ourselves where we will best apprehend reality. Finally, this option for a particular place only becomes real as praxis, as a commitment not only to move to a particular place, but to move it, to actively engage and shape history. We are called "to take charge of the weight of reality."

Central to Ellacuría's conception is that these three levels of response—notional, ethical, and praxis—are dynamic and interrelated. They do not unfold in a temporal sequence but occur mutually and simultaneously. This is crucial to Ellacuría's engaged, participative theory of knowledge. It also helps correct some misunderstandings. "Theology does not first conceptualize a faith content, then take up an ethical stance on the basis of that conceptualization and, as a final step, adopt a pastoral praxis in response to these first two. Nor does it invert this schema—as some superficial explanations of liberation theology would have it—and begin with praxis, move to an ethical stance, and from there conceptualize the faith. Rather, Ellacuría's method starts from the integral human encounter with historical reality. When confronting the problems of living in and among realities, the three dimensions of human intellection—intelligent apprehension, ethical stance, and praxis—operate in dynamic tension."[69]

Within this frame of our fundamental encounter with reality, we come to see solidarity as both active and receptive: we move to those who suffer so that their suffering might move us. We place ourselves with the poor so that we might be placed by them. Doing so expands our frame of reference, affects our self-understanding and our values, and thus leads to a new consciousness and a new way of understanding the world. In short, solidarity with the poor positions us better to see. Here we get our best glimpse of God. "The where, the light, and the horizon in which one seeks God are of course precisely God, but God mediated in that place chosen by God, which is the poor of the earth."[70] In the crucified people, we come before the crucified Christ himself.

Thus we choose to stand at the foot of this cross because, to put it bluntly, it offers the best view.

Matthew Ashley invites us to consider how Ellacuría's notion of engaged, historically localized knowing was informed by his encounter with the *Spiritual Exercises* of Ignatius of Loyola.[71] As we recall, the method of the *Exercises* is to invite the retreatant to imagine himself or herself within the narrative of Christ in the Gospels. The goal is to incarnate the will of God through a concrete decision within one's own life. Thus the process involves a rich intersection of Jesus' history and the retreatant's own history, all within the context of the one salvation history of God. We only come to know ("realizing") God's will within the context of our unique historical reality ("shouldering") and with a commitment to enact it in the concrete ("taking charge"). It is precisely this kind of historically localized—"placed"—knowledge that Ellacuría sought to conceptualize in his philosophical work.[72] And it was the epistemology behind his ethics. Thus Ellacuría continued a long spiritual trajectory, taking up the quite traditional Christian themes of cross, discernment, and the poor, and carrying them forward in the process of historicization. Ashley reaches back beyond Ignatius, finding in the Franciscan Bonaventure a motto for this spirituality of liberation: "there is no other path but through the burning love of the Crucified."[73] Today, the burning love of the crucified is embodied in the poor. For a spirituality of liberation, there is no other path than the one walked in solidarity with the crucified people.

The Option for the Poor

Ellacuría and other liberation theologians have explained this path to solidarity most consistently and most powerfully through the category of "the preferential option for the poor." The phrase itself first entered into official Catholic teaching at the Latin American bishops' conference in Puebla in 1979, where the bishops presented it in continuity with the groundbreaking statements of the same conference a decade earlier: "With renewed hope in the vivifying power of the Spirit, we are going to take up once again the position of the Second General Conference of the Latin American episcopate in Medellín, which adopted a clear and prophetic option expressing preference for, and solidarity with, the poor. . . . We affirm the need for conversion on the part of the whole church to a preferential option for the poor, an option aimed at their integral liberation."[74]

Gustavo Gutiérrez points out that this preferential option can be traced back beyond Medellín, all the way to the prophets of ancient Israel. But he connects its modern reemergence to the event of the Second Vatican Council—seeing its inspiration in the words of Pope John XXIII that "the church is, and wants to be, the church of all people and especially the church of the poor" and underscoring the opening lines of the council's Pastoral Constitution on the Church in the Modern World (*Gaudium et Spes*): "The joys and hopes, the grief and anguish of the people of our time, especially of those who are poor or afflicted, are the joys and hopes, the grief and anguish of the followers of the Christ as well."[75] For Gutiérrez, *preferential* does not mean exclusive, *option* does not mean optional, and *poor* cannot be equated simply with economics. Rather, the preferential option for the poor speaks of the demand placed on all Christians to turn first in special concern and solidarity toward the world's "little ones" as a concrete expression of God's universal love for all humanity.

But who are the poor? And what does this preferential option look like? What is the specific shape this solidarity is to take? As Ellacuría insisted, the poor have as their primary, though not exclusive, referent a material deprivation that denies life. For Gutiérrez, the economic aspect of poverty is key; still, for him, poverty cannot be reduced to it. Gutiérrez's early writing gestured to a broader understanding by the use of terms such as "nonpersons" and "insignificant ones." Over the course of his career he addressed more explicitly other forms of marginalization (such as that based on race, gender, and culture) that threaten the personhood of human beings.[76] However, this broadening never led to a spiritualization of poverty. If anything, Gutiérrez intensifies his account by defining poverty in terms of *death*. "The world of the poor is a universe in which the socio-economic aspect is basic but not all-inclusive. In the final analysis, poverty means death: lack of food and housing, the inability to attend properly to health and education needs, the exploitation of workers, permanent unemployment, the lack of respect for one's human dignity, and unjust limitations placed on personal freedom in the areas of self-expression, politics, and religion. Poverty is a situation that destroys peoples, families, and individuals; Medellín and Puebla called it 'institutionalized violence.'"[77] For Gutiérrez, poverty is the negation of life; it is a contradiction to the will-to-life of the Creator God. Such a theological expansion should not weaken the theologian's commitment to analyzing the economic and social mechanisms that marginalize and oppress. Instead it is "to grasp poverty's cruel and deep

meaning: its radical rejection of life, the gift of God, as this life is manifested in the narrative of creation."[78]

Bound up in Gutiérrez's account is the twofold concern we saw in
Ellacuría's notion of the crucified people: first, that poverty refers to a
condition affecting not only individuals but also whole groups of human
society; second, that this condition results from human actions and decisions. Contrary to the biblical worldview, much of Christian history has
operated on the assumption that poverty is a given, a fact of life flowing
from the sin of Adam but now floating free of human choices. Today,
due to a growing awareness of the complex complicity of our global
economic and political systems, we see that poverty is not a matter of
fate: "it is a condition, not a destiny; an injustice, not a misfortune."[79]
Poverty means death; more specifically, it means being put to death—or
as Ellacuría repeatedly insisted, it means being crucified.

However, as Gutiérrez emphasizes repeatedly, "being poor" is not
only a matter of deprivation. It is not only a situation of death but also
a way of—and a way toward—life. "Being poor is also a way of feeling,
knowing, reasoning, making friends, loving, believing, suffering, celebrating, and praying."[80] The poor represent not merely a collection of
victims but a communion of persons—far from perfect, and full of all
the grace and sin that marks any human community. Yet the poor all
fall under the shadow of the struggle for basic human survival, the fact
that they cannot take life for granted. Under this shadow, the poor
constitute "a world." Like Ellacuría, we find in Gutiérrez a complex
appreciation for this world that lays the foundation for any adequate
treatment of solidarity. For it is this world that all Christians are called
to enter into. "Commitment to the poor means entering into their
universe (or in some cases remaining in it but now with a clearer awareness) and living in it. It means regarding it no longer as a place of work
but as a place of residence. It means not going into this world for a few
hours in order to bear witness to the gospel, but rather emerging from
it each morning to proclaim the good news to every human being."[81]

What does this commitment look like in the concrete? What is the
shape of solidarity? When Gutiérrez says that we must enter into the
world of the poor and emerge from it each morning, is he speaking
about literal, geographic residence? Here the option for the poor runs
up against its most formidable First-World challenge: what does this
mean *for me*? And in responding to this question, Gutiérrez offers a
nuanced perspective. Solidarity cannot remain a shadow. It must be
real, historical, embodied, lived out in praxis. But there is a spectrum

of such concrete acts of love and ways of being in the world. Most fundamentally, when Gutiérrez talks about the preferential option, he is talking about a commitment, a commitment that includes both a presence to the poor and a protest against poverty. It has to do with "a lifestyle"—we might say a way of life and a way of looking at life—and "not with sporadic acts of proximity or assistance to the poor."[82] Rather than responding with a few good deeds, the option for the poor is a more fundamental way of disposing oneself—of opening oneself—by placing oneself in the place of the poor.

To place ourselves in the place of the poor is not primarily a physical or physiological exercise. Place has to do, first of all, with perspective, commitment, and concern. In reflecting on the proper "place" to do theology, Jon Sobrino offers some insight. For Sobrino, the place where theology is done can be understood in a number of different ways: physical/institutional environment, geographical/social situation, and historical/cultural location. All of these are important to consider and have an impact on the way theology is done, but none of them is the "fundamental place" of theology. Liberation theology insists that its fundamental place "must be that historical reality in which we can find a maximum of Truth and the Absolute and that contains both the greatest demands to act within history and the greatest promise of salvation."[83] Sharing so much with his friend Ellacuría, Sobrino concludes that this fundamental place is found within the world's suffering—which he calls "the most real world." For Sobrino, this does not mean finding a concrete place in the world that happens to be suffering but rather, finding a place within the very suffering of the world. "Place" refers not to a geographical location but to the hermeneutical situation that influences how one looks at and acts within the world. It is "much more a *quid* than an *ubi*"—more *what* than *where*.[84] Sobrino, who at great risk to his own life returned to the University of Central America to teach after the assassination of his housemates, is not naïve about the relationship between the *quid* and the *ubi* of commitment. Certain physical and social "places" make it either more difficult or more easy to enter into the world of the poor. As Ellacuría reminds us, "realizing" the weight of reality is intricately intertwined with our particular position and praxis within this reality. Sobrino would agree. There is no observation deck looking out over the history of suffering. We are all engaged participants. Still, that does not mandate for any one individual a particular way of participating in the preferential option for the poor.

There is no way to say, concretely, what solidarity looks like for all people. Most popular treatments of the preferential option for the poor start with this fact. They proclaim the profound demands of the preferential option, but then too quickly move on to a variety of ways an individual might respond—with little time spent in the space between these two poles.[85] Here the preferential option dissipates, as a number of "options" are ticked off: direct service, regular personal contact with the homeless or hungry, efforts to raise consciousness in our churches and our communities, donating money, political advocacy, living more simply, and so on. All of these activities are good and ought to be encouraged. However, there is always a danger that such advice is taken as the end of solidarity, rather than as its beginning. Never should such recommendations become so detached from a deeper reflection on the reality of suffering, its sources, and our own life commitments, that acting on them serves simply to assuage our consciences. Of course, our solidarity with the poor depends on the different circumstances of our lives. This has to be recognized. But how are we to affirm it in such a way that our "different circumstances" do not become an excuse for avoiding the challenging demands placed before us by the reality of the poor? The tension that we traced back to Luther remains alive today: when do we remain in our calling and when do we depart from it?

As noted above, solidarity cannot remain a shadow. Concrete acts of love are needed. And there is a spectrum of such acts. But whenever such acts of solidarity work only to reduce guilt or whenever they end with a self-satisfied sense that "I do care," then such acts in fact work against solidarity. They keep the reality of the poor safely at a distance. For nothing muffles the cry of the crucified more than the content conviction that "I'm doing my part." What is needed instead is a praxis of solidarity that draws us deeper into the world of the poor in such a way that we grow ever more troubled by it. Volunteering at the soup kitchen does not get us off the hook. It ought to hook us, drawing us more deeply into the place of the poor as a place of ongoing and growing commitment and concern. When concrete acts of love like these unsettle us, and continue to unsettle us, then they appropriately serve as the beginning of solidarity. Then we start to share the pain of those who suffer. Then we no longer enter the world of the poor for a few hours to preach the gospel. Instead we begin to stand alongside the poor, and emerge from this shared world each morning to proclaim the scandalous but good news that God is present here.

Gutiérrez recognizes full well that the situation of the poor will almost certainly overstrain our human capacity for solidarity. The will to live in the world of the poor can only follow an asymptotic curve: "a constantly closer approach that can, however, never reach the point of real identification with the life of the poor."[86] This should not discourage us but instead invite us to adopt an appropriate posture of humility toward the preferential option. In this posture of humility, which Gutiérrez associates with a "poverty of spirit," we catch a glimpse of the fundamentally spiritual nature of solidarity. This spirituality of solidarity can never become spiritualized; it can never be detached from concrete praxis. Still, it evokes something deeper than a laundry list of volunteer opportunities or good causes to care about. It speaks to a basic spiritual stance that makes possible the link between concern and embodied commitment. What I want to suggest is that in this poverty of spirit lies the key to the contemporary conversion so crucial to vocational discernment today.

Cry with the Crucified

The preferential option for the poor rests on a fundamental spiritual disposition, what I have called a spirituality of solidarity. As noted above, by stressing the spiritual dimension of solidarity, the last thing we want to do is to spiritualize it, to reduce the option for the poor to the well-paved path of good intentions or a heartfelt concern for the "less fortunate." Such spiritualizing is the constant temptation for those of us whose hearts are moved by injustice and suffering but whose lives are not. To speak of a spirituality of solidarity is not to evade the difficult question of what to do, but to approach it head-on, step-by-step. Indeed, if we are ever going to make the move in our own lives from a moral concern for the poor to a living out of this concern through concrete commitments, if we are ever to discover what God is calling us to through "the world's deep hunger," then we have to pay attention to our underlying spiritual disposition. For the biggest barrier to solidarity lies within us. Even good people are not immune to the resistance and resentment that wells up when we are reminded of the reality of the poor. (Why is this my problem? I didn't cause it.) Even those who genuinely care can be easily overwhelmed by the sheer scope of suffering. (What can one person do?) The "Third World" thus becomes an abstraction, and the numbers numb. I am tempted to turn away, to focus my energies where I have more control: my own work, my own family, my own life, my own calling. Metz saw in contemporary culture a growing apathy, a "weariness with being a subject," that causes us to pull back from history and society—ceding responsibility for all of these problems to someone else. Not to avoid these concerns but precisely to meet them, Metz turned to the language of spirituality. And so we return to his mystical-political theology, which shares so many of the same concerns as Ellacuría, Sobrino, and Gutiérrez.

We actualize the option for the poor in our own lives through a spirituality in which we place ourselves among those who suffer and thus share in their own stance before God. We cry with the crucified. Metz calls this a spirituality of *Leiden an Gott*, "suffering unto God." Suffering unto God describes a particular kind of complaint or lament in which the suffering one turns the question of suffering back on God, passionately and expectantly. This is the stance taken by Job in the Hebrew Bible. It is found powerfully in Jesus' cry from the cross: "My God, my God, why have you forsaken me?" In such a stance, suffering is neither ignored nor explained away. Instead, suffering is met with a kind of resistance, a protest, a remembering. As Metz explains, "The language of this God mysticism is not primarily one of consoling answers to experiences of suffering; rather, it is much more a language of passionate requestioning that arises out of suffering, a requestioning of God, full of highly charged expectation."[87]

Traditional theodicies try to explain away suffering, or justify God in the face of it. Metz rejects all such attempts. The suffering other cannot be folded into a system, conveniently assimilated into some larger story, lost in its long paragraphs. For Metz, suffering must unsettle us. It must interrupt. The "dangerous memories" of history's victims should disturb our modern consciousness, calling us out of ourselves and into solidarity with all those who suffer and who suffer unjustly. When Job's friends speak, their theodicies add insult to injury. But the real violence they achieve is to further isolate Job. In defending their God, they distance their friend. They are so comfortable in their convictions that they refuse to be disturbed by Job's pain. For Metz, the Christian call is to join Job—to adopt his stance, and not that of his friends. In other words, solidarity comes not by sitting alongside God and looking down on the suffering one, beneficently bestowing our ideas and agenda. Solidarity comes by standing alongside the suffering one and looking up to God, crying out to heaven with the crucified. For in the face of so much misery, the only faithful response is Job's passionate complaint, Why God? Why?

The gains of this understanding slowly come into view. By approaching solidarity as a basic spiritual stance (before it is a concrete action plan), we open up space within ourselves to admit, it is okay not to have it all figured out. It is alright to feel overwhelmed by the world's pain. We *should* be unsettled by all of this. It means we are paying attention. It means we are present to it. Indeed, Metz calls this fundamental spiritual stance "a mysticism of open eyes." It is an awareness, a wakefulness, an unblinking attention to the suffering of others that pulls us into their world and pushes us toward action. "It is a mysticism that especially makes visible all invisible and inconvenient suffering, and—convenient or not—pays attention to it and takes responsibility for it, for the sake of a God who is a friend to human beings."[88]

Metz links this mysticism of open eyes, this spirituality of *Leiden an Gott*, to a classic theme within the history of Christian spirituality, just glimpsed in Gutiérrez: poverty of spirit. Metz addressed this beatitude over the course of his career, confessing that meditation on it "permeates my theological biography."[89] Traditionally, poverty of spirit was understood as an indifference to the goods of the world that flowers into a more fundamental indifference, which is nothing less than total openness to the will of God. Early in his career Metz adopted this theme of indifference but transposed it into an existential, historical, and more active key: poverty of spirit is the obedient taking up of one's finite, historically situated existence as the path to self-realization.[90] Like his mentor Rahner, Metz explained that this detachment is not the source of apathy toward the world. Rather, it is the motivation for a fuller and freer engagement within it.[91] Metz's view, however, shifted over time, as the tragic realities of this world entered more forcefully into his theology. In his later work, he came to speak of spiritual poverty in terms of suffering in history and suffering unto God. He did so by turning to the theodicy of ancient Israel.

To Metz, biblical Israel appears as a people with a particular sensitivity for theodicy.[92] But it is a peculiar kind of sensitivity. What sets Israel—this "small, culturally rather insignificant and politically voiceless desert people"—apart from all its neighbors is its almost total inability to explain away its suffering.[93] This was Israel's particular poverty: its failure to mythologize or idealize away its pain. Israel never quite succeeded in distancing itself from "the contradictions, the terrors and chasms in its life."[94] It had little talent for forgetting, little aptitude for "automatic, idealistic processing of its disappointments."[95]

Israel simply could not be consoled, and so its prophets turned to God in prayer and in protest—demanding and awaiting an answer in hope. Metz sees this poverty as a strength, the great contribution of Israel's spiritual vision. Israel remained always a "landscape of cries." Its faith "did not so much lead to answers for the suffering it experienced; rather it expressed itself above all as a questioning arising out of suffering, as an incessant turning of its questions back to—Yahweh."[96] This was Israel's poverty of spirit, the lens for Metz's later appropriation of this first of the beatitudes.

Over the course of the history of Christian mysticism, poverty of spirit served as a crucial touchstone in the process of discernment, thus touching directly on our concerns about vocation. In the Christian tradition, the process of aligning one's own will to the will of God— through a variety of methods and against a variety of backdrops— involves a surrender, an offering, a disciplined indifference to one's own wants or the lures of the world. The danger, however, is that such indifference leans toward detachment from the world and denigration of it—a distancing from the material realm that we might expect given the church's incubation in the nursery of Greek dualism. Yet the imperative of love always cuts against such a distancing indifference to the needs of others. We recall Rahner's defense of his own spiritual heritage, arguing that Ignatian "indifference" (*indiferencia*) need not feed an apathy but rather ought to free the Christian for a fuller engagement in the world: "Out of such an attitude of *indiferencia* there springs of itself the perpetual readiness to hear a new call from God to tasks other than those previously engaged in, continually to decamp from those fields where one wanted to find God and to serve him; there springs the will to be at hand like a servant always ready for new assignments; the courage to accept the duty of changing oneself and of having nowhere a permanent resting-place as in a restless wandering towards the restful God; the courage to regard no way to him as being *the* way, but rather to seek him on all ways."[97]

What Rahner's words lift into view is one of the side effects of the indifference associated with poverty of spirit—a side effect even more significant in such world-affirming spiritualities as the Ignatian contemplation in action: indifference invites an openness to the will of God that is open-ended. This is both its great contribution, and its great ambiguity. As Rahner's article insists, we must remain open to *anything*. But the question stalking vocation over the centuries returns: Can God call us to *anything*? Can *any* occupation be a calling? Is there not a temptation today, particularly for the comfortable and the privileged, to see such affirmations as simply blessing the status quo, or reinscribing in religious language a culture of consumer choice? Do we too easily translate the demand for a spiritual openness to any path into the assumption that every path opens to the spiritual? We do not have to read far to realize that Ignatius's spirituality and Rahner's system resist such a directionless indifference. But Metz confronts it head-on when he associates the key to his theological vision—a spirituality of suffering unto God—with Israel's poverty of spirit.

Poverty of spirit is not an indifferent openness, an unspecified surrender to the will of God—whatever that may be. Instead it is an openness that is oriented. Discipleship matters, and not every point of view is the same. We are called to take the perspective of Israel in exile, of Job, of the prophets, of countless others over the course of history who suffer unjustly. To return to Ellacuría, we take the perspective of the crucified people. We take their perspective and take up their cry. We cry *with* the crucified—a cry that is both sob and shout, both compassion and protest. Ellacuría suggested that the phrase "poor in spirit" be understood as "poor *with* spirit." By this, he meant to stress that this beatitude marks the place of commitment for the Christian—where we "shoulder the weight" of reality.[98] The radical openness to God's call that Rahner describes speaks a profound truth, but it presupposes a conversion that cannot rest with the easy consolation that Israel so consistently avoided. In the face of profound and ongoing suffering in history, a spirituality of solidarity speaks not the comforting last words of Jesus in Luke's gospel, "Father, into your hands I commend my spirit." Instead, it cries out with the Jesus of Mark, "My God, my God, why have you forsaken me?"[99] When we share such a stance, discipleship cannot be deferred. Spirituality spills into action. When we cry with the crucified—there is no other path than through this burning love—we become who we are truly meant to be, and we come to see that, whatever we do, we do it to take the crucified people down from the cross. Summing up Metz's *Leiden an Gott*, Matthew Ashley concludes, "This is a stance, finally, in which we are ourselves transformed since it challenges us to enlarge the horizon of our hopes and actions to include the crucified peoples, both past and present, without whom we ourselves cannot fully become and remain subjects. It is a spirituality, rooted in biblical narratives, nourished in individual and liturgical prayer, certainly giving rise to thought, but only fully actualized in action on behalf of others."[100]

Conclusion: Discipleship and Discernment

How does all of this help make the connection to concrete choices and particular ways of responding to God's call to be *for* others? In short, what difference does this make to vocation? These questions invite us to pull together the various strands that together constitute the argument of this book. We have moved from God to the human person to the church community to the world in need. The end result is not a "how-to" manual or handbook for discernment but a healthy way of thinking about ourselves, among others and before God, as called.

Over the course of the preceding chapters, we have come to see that vocation is not a detailed blueprint imposed on my life from above. It is not a hidden plan silently stored away, shared with some through a secret voice. Rather, my vocation is right there in front of me. It *is* me—my life lived out in harmony with the gift of grace, which is nothing other than God's loving presence within. Thus discernment is a process of reflecting on my fundamental identity before God. Each of us decides what to do by placing particular possibilities for life before this fundamental sense of ourselves, listening for either resonance or dissonance. Harmony between the two helps us know what we are called to do.

The trouble is that we can be more or less aware of who we are before God. According to Rahner, our fundamental "sense" of ourselves is ordinarily implicit in human consciousness. And when we try to interpret this fundamental orientation, we often get it wrong. As fallen creatures, we "see" ourselves through a glass darkly. The genius that Rahner discovered in the *Spiritual Exercises* of Ignatius is the way in which it lays out a method to help individuals grow in honest awareness of their own transcendental orientation before God. People can be led to see themselves more openly and more immediately—freed from the self-serving ideas and agendas that so often get in the way. When Rahner identified Ignatius's obscure category of "consolation without preceding cause" as the key to the whole process, he highlighted the importance of an unobstructed view. For Rahner, consolation without cause occurs when God's presence within us—that always present, silent presence—moves into conscious focus *without being clouded by concepts*. Though he strained to say how we can "experience" this without the mediation of categories, he held to his deep conviction that such immediacy to the love of God within us helps us to better see ourselves, and thus our vocations.

When Rahner was pressed by critics that his interpretation gave too little attention to the specificity of the Christian narrative, Rahner admitted that Christ does not appear as prominently in his essays as he appears in the *Exercises*. But he argued that Christ is still there. And he made a telling connection to the cross. According to Rahner, Ignatian discernment "works" because it recognizes that an authentic vocational choice (the "election") can only be made when an individual is freed (by God's grace) from any particular attachment to the object of that choice, and "has thus achieved openness to immediacy to God as the sole focus of his existence."[101] Ignatius did not leap right to vocational decision making. He fostered a process of purification of the affections and conversion of the heart that allows one to see oneself as one truly is: a child of God. Rahner continued: "This detachment, not merely theoretical but existential, from a particular finite value, from a good in the existential realm, is in all truth, whether one reflects on it or not, a participation in Christ's death." The only one who can really choose freely is the person whom God frees from the enslaving tyranny of intramundane "principalities and powers."[102] This freedom is a conversion. This detachment is a dying, a sharing in the cross of Christ. What I have argued above is that the kind of conversion demanded by our postmodern and deeply pained world is a conversion as extro-version—a turning outward, an opening up to the other, particularly the other who suffers. And, as Rahner reminds us, the classic locus for such conversion is the cross.

Within the context of his existential and transcendental system, Rahner read the death of Christ through the lens of the subject: death is the "end" of human life that marks both its finality and its goal, the culmination of what it means to be a person.[103] But what if we were to read the death of Christ not through the death of the *subject* or the *self* but through the death of the *other*? Then we see the crucified people. Then conversion finds form as a turning outward, a turning toward that suffering other. The spirituality demanded in such a world is not that of a directionless detachment but an oriented openness—a spirituality of solidarity.

What is the prerequisite for discernment today? Precisely in order to affirm the fundamental insight of Rahner on discovering the particular will of God, we can expand his treatment of conversion with the help of the historically conscious and praxis-oriented theologies laid out in this chapter. What we need to be freed from today is not just the opacity of our concepts (Rahner's apophatic mysticism), but that particular form of delusion that comes from our rationalizations and resentments, our ignorance and indifference in the face of the poor. Such a conversion opens up a long road. And so we start with a small step: allowing ourselves to be troubled. Like ancient Israel, we refuse to explain away the pain. We refuse to make sense of all this suffering too quickly. We allow ourselves to be bothered by the way the world is running. With such a poverty of spirit, we will not easily be consoled. And because we are not easily consoled, not easily comforted by our rationalizations and self-serving explanations, we will be drawn into a continual process of conversion. If we hold ourselves open to another's pain, we cannot stop. And thus through small steps we come to stand with those who suffer, turning with them to God, demanding and expecting a response. Since solidarity—real solidarity—cannot but spill out into action, we slowly come to see that the response we expect from God is the one that God answers through us—through our choices, our lives, our vocations.

And that, in the end, is the good news of being called by God *for* others. Actualizing our discipleship through a spirituality of solidarity helps us to discover our true selves: I am not only a child of God, I am among the children of God. As Jesus' actions insist, we are all terribly tied together. This recognition lies behind the deep-seated joy in the accounts of Gutiérrez, Ellacuría, and other theologians of liberation, who see in the poor not only death but also life—the place of Christ's salvation in the present. With such solidarity, we continue the historical mission of Jesus. And so we are set free to live with the kind of freedom we see Jesus living out in the gospels. As saints over the centuries have testified, there is tremendous light in the darkness of the poor, great hope amidst so much hopelessness. Jon Sobrino articulates well this wisdom, embodied in the martyrs among whom he lived. Speaking of Ellacuría and his other housemates, Sobrino concludes:

> They also leave us good news, a gospel. On this sinful and sense-less earth it is possible to live like human beings and like Christians. We can share in that current of history that Paul calls life in the Spirit and life in love, in that current of honesty, hope, and commitment that is always being threatened with suffocation but that time and again bursts forth from the depths like a true miracle of God. Joining this current of history, which is that of the poor, has its price, but it encourages us to go on living, working, and believing, it offers meaning and salvation. This is what I believe these new martyrs bequeath to us. With it we can go on walking through history, humbly, as the prophet Micah says, amid suffering and darkness, but with God.[104]

We walk in the dark . . . but with others . . . but with God. And within this darkness, we come to hear more clearly what it is that God is calling us toward. What is it that I am to do with my "one wild and precious life"? The answer is not evident at the start of solidarity. But through the conversion it works, we grow more and more open to others, and so grow more and more open to *the* Other. Through discipleship, we learn to discern.

Conclusion

As noted in the book's introduction, the broadening of the language of vocation that followed the Second Vatican Council has not resolved many of the difficult theological questions surrounding this key category. Indeed, the expansion may have only intensified these questions—for no longer do they concern an elite few but rather they touch on the life of every believer. Thus, much of *Awakening Vocation* has been spent exploring the various theological contexts within which the concept of vocation functions and finds meaning. What are our underlying assumptions about God and ourselves, about the church and the world? And what do these assumptions mean for the way we understand God's call in our lives? What I have done in these pages, then, is not so much shine a spotlight on vocation as slowly turn up the houselights, illuminating the theological drama unfolding around our central character. Or, to return to our guiding metaphor, my goal has been to gently open up the blinds, in order to let in the morning sun, light up the room, and wake up an idea.

I have argued that an intellectually credible, pastorally relevant, and personally meaningful theology of vocation comes into view when vocation is seen in light of a theology of grace that affirms God's pervasive presence in the world. Not an extrinsic force operating on us from above, grace is the gift of God's own self that extends across all of human history and into every human heart. God permeates all of creation as both the ground of existence and the invitation to the fullness of life. Within this world of grace, God's call—my vocation—cannot be reduced to some static state of life or secret voice. My vocation is *me*. It is my life lived out in concert with the gift of grace, God's loving presence within. Thus to discover my vocation is to hear a certain harmony between who I am as a child of God and how I live in the world, with and for others. To repeat a point I made earlier, what faith-filled people are saying when they say that they "have been called" to this or to that is not that they have found some hidden plan but that they have felt a profound resonance between their deepest sense of themselves before God and a particular path forward.

This image of forward movement—the *whither* of vocation—appears again and again in the pages above. It serves as a unifying thread running throughout the book, offering both a distinctively Catholic contribution to contemporary theological discussions of vocation and, I argue, a helpful way of framing the question of vocational discernment.

When Martin Luther launched the modern history of reflection on vocation, he meant to underscore the concrete context within which the Christian is called to "love thy neighbor." No need to run off to the monastery, Luther argued; we serve God best where we are, in the particular state of life (*Stand*) already allotted to us by divine providence. Rooted in the medieval notion of *Stand* and developed within a theology of creation and providence, the Protestant doctrine of vocation came to emphasize a calling as the place *from which* we respond to God and serve others. It has stressed the *whence*. Catholic reflection on vocation, on the other hand, remained inspired by the early monastic call to a new way of life. It developed not within a theology of creation but within a theology of grace. Thus the Catholic tradition has spoken of vocation not so much as the place *from which* we respond but as the place *to which* God calls. It has stressed the *whither*. Over the course of the long modern period, Catholics writing on vocation were preoccupied with the call to religious life and priesthood. Thus their emphasis was on choosing and changing one's state of life. In contrast, Protestants often returned to St. Paul's exhortation to "abide in your calling." Believing that the various realms and functions of society were God-given, Protestant preaching tended to emphasize not the call to change but the importance of living out one's faith wherever one found oneself.

More recently, Protestant theologians have pointed out the danger of such an easy acquiescence to the social status quo. They have asked: In our increasingly instrumentalized, commodified, and militarized world—a world so profoundly split between the rich and the poor—can such a conception of vocation continue? Is such a view of calling too quick to confirm one's place in the world, in society, in a certain occupation or line of work? Is it capable of confronting our fallen condition, our unjust economic structures, our comfort in conforming to a dehumanizing system? And they have offered their own prophetic responses, rooted in the primacy of the Gospel and the dialectical sensibility of Protestant thought. But the great Reformed critic, Karl Barth, recognized that there was something in the Catholic *whither* that could not be easily dismissed. He argued that the Protestant tradition of call had a positive effect in breaking vocation free from the confines of the monastery. But along the way, "Protestantism . . . lost sight of the divine grandeur and purity of this *klesis*, which were always in some sense retained even by monasticism."[1]

Of course, Catholics have had their own problems with vocation. Locked in its clerical quarters and frustrated by a dualistic theology of grace, the modern Catholic theology of vocation slipped into quiet irrelevance. For centuries, as priest theologians struggled to catalogue the qualities of a vocation, few lay Catholics would have imagined the word even applied to them. Now, with Vatican II's affirmation of the universal call to holiness, Catholicism has entered into a new era of vocational expansion. This era has been marked by a profound affirmation of the baptismal dignity of all believers and a deep recognition of the sanctity of ordinary, everyday life in the world. This shift is welcome and absolutely foundational, for the basis of Christian identity and discipleship lies in the gift of God's grace that is extended to all. But what will be the lasting legacy of this broadening of vocation? Will it end with the affirmation of our common baptismal dignity? Or will it also challenge all of the baptized to respond to the radical demands that this dignity entails? Alongside the comfort of the Gospel message comes its unrelenting *call*. Yes, we are called to be ourselves—we are confirmed in our own graced identity, our unique context and constitution. And yes, we are called beyond ourselves—we are challenged to respond to Christ, to the needs of others, to our own need for conversion. If we recognize that grace is not separate from nature but rather wrapped up in it, then we start to see that these two dimensions of vocation are not at odds. They go together. By responding to Christ's call to move beyond who we are, we come to see who we *really* are. The call beyond ourselves helps us to discover our *true* selves.

What *Awakening Vocation* suggests, then, is a way to reimagine the "Catholic whither," such that vocation might reemerge as meaningful language for fostering the life of faith today. This *whither* can no longer be reduced to the flight that distorted the monastic impulse and that led to centuries of exclusive focus on the religious and priestly vocations. Instead of being called out of a sinful world, we are called into a suffering one. Instead of being called to some special state of life, we are called to the other in need. The *whither* of vocation is neither an abstract role nor a particular career; it is—first and foremost—presence to the suffering, the oppressed, the marginalized, and the forgotten. Luther used the biblical category of *klesis* to argue that we must serve the neighbor whom we meet where we are, in the daily exercise of our callings. It was a challenge to love those who are close. But as Gustavo Gutiérrez reminds us, the Gospel also challenges us to love those who appear distant. Like the Good Samaritan, we are called to "love thy neighbor" by becoming a neighbor, by going over and drawing close to the abused and neglected one on the side of the road. This movement toward the other is what I described above as a spirituality of solidarity—a fundamental stance of openness that draws us into the world of history's victims, the place where we learn to cry with the crucified people. This is the *whither* of Christ's call today.

If that were all to be said, we could only despair under the paralyzing demands of a universalist ethic. Thus the real test of a theology of vocation comes in discernment. What does this mean *for me*? As *Awakening Vocation* has argued, a spirituality of solidarity is not the end of the discernment process; it is the beginning. It is the start of a journey of learning how to listen, a practice of presence and openness to others that trains us, over time, in openness to God's special and particular call in our lives. Alongside the practices of prayer and worship, service and advocacy, fellowship and forgiveness, the practice of solidarity works on us. It chips away at all those self-centered and alienating delusions that have such a hold on us. Slowly, solidarity helps us to see ourselves more honestly, and thus hear our callings more clearly. If we expect a quick and easy answer to the question, what am I to do with my life? we will be disappointed. For discernment demands nothing less than the long and difficult path of discipleship.

But the great good news of the Christian call is that following Jesus frees us. As disciples we discover ourselves—our true selves, our unique, unfinished, and incredibly beautiful selves. It is not just an idea that is awakened. *We* are awakened. We wake up and step out into a great procession, joining a sea of unique and beautiful selves surging forward into the reign of God. To live one's life as a response to God's call is a pilgrimage, a shared journey of faith, solidarity, and transformation in the light of Christ—the marks of a very different kind of quest.

Notes

Introduction—pages xi–xviii

1. Mary Oliver, "The Summer Day," in *New and Selected Poems* (Boston: Beacon Press, 1992), 94. Reprinted with permission. Thanks to John Neafsey for pointing me to Oliver's poem. See John Neafsey, *A Sacred Voice Is Calling: Personal Vocation and Social Conscience* (Maryknoll, NY: Orbis, 2006).

2. *Lumen Gentium* 40, in *Vatican Council II: The Basic Sixteen Documents*, ed. Austin Flannery, OP (Northport, NY: Costello Publishing, 1996). Unless otherwise noted, all quotations from the council texts are taken from this edition.

3. Recent years have seen a renewed interest in vocation in North America, sparked in part by the Lilly Endowment's Programs for the Theological Exploration of Vocation. Launched in 1999, the primary aim of PTEV has been to encourage religiously affiliated colleges and universities to integrate reflection on vocation into their various educational efforts. PTEV has sparked a number of initiatives, scholarly research, and two helpful anthologies, *Callings: Twenty Centuries of Christian Wisdom on Vocation*, ed. William C. Placher (Grand Rapids, MI: Eerdmans, 2005); and *Leading Lives That Matter: What We Should Do and Who We Should Be*, eds. Mark R. Schwehn and Dorothy C. Bass (Grand Rapids, MI: Eerdmans, 2006). For background, resources, and an extended bibliography, see www.ptev.org. For an example of recent theological work on vocation across various Christian traditions, see *Revisiting the Idea of Vocation: Theological Explorations*, ed. John C. Haughey (Washington, DC: Catholic University of America Press, 2004); Douglas J. Schuurman, *Vocation: Discerning Our Callings in Life* (Grand Rapids, MI: Eerdmans, 2004); and *Christ at Work: Orthodox Christian Perspectives on Vocation*, ed. Ann Mitsakos Bezzerides (Brookline, MA: Holy Cross Orthodox Press, 2006).

4. Robert Wuthnow, *After Heaven: Spirituality in America Since the 1950s* (Berkeley: University of California Press, 1998), 2.

5. Wade Clark Roof, *Spiritual Marketplace* (Princeton: Princeton University Press, 1999), 86.

6. See the helpful discussion in Charles Taylor, *A Secular Age* (Cambridge, MA: Harvard University Press, 2007), 505–35.

7. I draw this wonderful image from Dean Brackley, *The Call to Discernment in Troubled Times: New Perspectives on the Transformative Wisdom of Ignatius of Loyola* (New York: Crossroad, 2004), 127–28. Brackley cites John Paul II, The Splendor of Truth (*Veritatis Splendor*) (Washington, DC: USCCB Publishing, 1993) 52.

Chapter One—pages 3–46

1. I Henry IV, act 1, scene 2, lines 102–5, in *William Shakespeare: The Complete Works*, eds. Stanley Wells and Gary Taylor (Oxford: Clarendon Press, 1986), 513.

2. Max Weber, *The Protestant Ethic and the Spirit of Capitalism*, trans. Talcott Parsons (London: Unwin Hyman, 1930, orig. 1904–5).

3. For example, Weber did not insist on logical or theological causal connections. What he wanted to explore were the psychological links between a particular religious worldview and a new attitude toward economic activity. See Paul Marshall, *A Kind of Life Imposed on Man: Vocation and Social Order from Tyndale to Locke* (Toronto: University of Toronto Press, 1996), 7. Marshall provides a helpful "bibliography of bibliographies" of the voluminous literature on Weber's thesis at p. 103, n. 3.

4. Charles Taylor, *Sources of the Self: The Making of the Modern Identity* (Cambridge, MA: Harvard University Press, 1989), 211.

5. "Call" is also used in the New Testament in a more generic sense, for example, to call by name, to call upon, to invite, and so on. For a concise summary of the biblical material, see Marshall, *A Kind of Life*, 12–14.

6. For example, Rom 1:6-7; 8:30; 1 Cor 1:9; 1:26; Gal 1:6, 15; 1 Thess 2:22; 5:25; 2 Thess 2:14. See Marshall, *A Kind of Life*, 13; William A. Beardslee, *Human Achievement and Divine Vocation in the Message of Paul* (London: SCM Press, 1961).

7. Such as Paul's conviction that he had been called to be an apostle. See Rom 1:1; 1 Cor 1:1.

8. A. J. Droge, "Call Stories," in *The Anchor Bible Dictionary*, vol. 1, ed. David Noel Freedman (New York: Doubleday, 1992), 821–23.

9. This view is articulated by Yves Congar in the original edition of his classic *Lay People in the Church: A Study for a Theology of Laity*, revised ed., trans. Donald Attwater (Westminster, MD: The Newman Press, 1965), 3. The original appeared as *Jalons pour une théologie du laïcat* (Paris: Cerf, 1953).

10. Ignace de la Potterie, "L'origine et le sens primitif du mot 'laïc,'" *Nouvelle Revue Théologique* 80 (1958): 840–53, cited in Giovanni Magnani, "Does the So-Called Theology of the Laity Possess a Theological Status?" in *Vatican II: Assessment and Perspectives*, vol. 1, ed. René LaTourelle (New York: Paulist Press, 1988): 568–633, at 572. In his 1964 revised edition of *Jalons*, Congar accepts la Potterie's argument; see *Lay People in the Church*, 3–4.

11. Taylor, *Sources of the Self*, 220.

12. David G. Hunter, *Marriage, Celibacy, and Heresy in Ancient Christianity: The Jovinianist Controversy* (Oxford: Oxford University Press, 2007), 243.

13. Augustine, "Sermon 104: Discourse on Martha and Mary, as Representing Two Kinds of Lives," par. 4, in *The Works of Saint Augustine: A Translation for the*

21st Century, vol. 3/4, ed. John E. Rotelle (New York: New City Press, 1992), 81–87, at 83–84. See J. Matthew Ashley, "Contemplation in the Action of Justice: Ignacio Ellacuría and Ignatian Spirituality," in *Love That Produces Hope: The Thought of Ignacio Ellacuria*, eds. Kevin F. Burke and Robert Lassalle-Klein (Collegeville, MN: Liturgical Press, 2006), 144–65, at 150–52.

14. See David N. Power, "Church Order," in *The New Dictionary of Sacramental Worship*, ed. Peter E. Fink (Collegeville, MN: Liturgical Press, 1990), 212–33, at 217.

15. Ann W. Astell, "Introduction," in *Lay Sanctity, Medieval and Modern: A Search for Models*, ed. Ann W. Astell (Notre Dame, IN: University of Notre Dame Press, 2000), 1–26, at 8. See Richard Kieckhefer, "Imitators of Christ: Sainthood in the Christian Tradition," in *Sainthood: Its Manifestations in World Religions*, ed. Richard Kieckhefer and George D. Bond (Berkeley: University of California Press, 1988), 1–42.

16. See André Vauchez, *The Laity in the Middle Ages: Religious Beliefs and Devotional Practices*, ed. Daniel E. Bornstein, trans. Margery J. Schneider (Notre Dame, IN: University of Notre Dame Press, 1993), 41.

17. Astell, "Introduction," 6. See John R. Sommerfeldt, "The Social Theory of Bernard of Clairvaux," in *Studies in Medieval Cistercian History*, Cistercian Studies Series, no. 13 (Spencer, MA: Cistercian Publications, 1971), 35–48; Georges Dumézil, *The Three Orders: Feudal Society Imagined*, trans. Arthur Goldhammer (Chicago: University of Chicago Press, 1980).

18. Cited in Congar, *Lay People in the Church*, 11.

19. See Congar, *Lay People in the Church*, 86, n. 1.

20. See Vauchez, *The Laity in the Middle Ages*, 185–90.

21. Karl Holl, "The History of the Word Vocation (*Beruf*)," trans. Heber F. Peacock, *Review and Expositor* 55 (1958): 126–54, at 129. This influential overview was originally published as "Die Geschichte des Wortes Beruf," in *Gesammelte Aufsätze zur Kirchengeschichte*, vol. 3 (Tübingen: Mohr, 1928), 189–219.

22. Holl, "The History of the Word Vocation," 136.

23. "Sermon 2," in *Meister Eckhart: The Essential Sermons, Commentaries, Treatises, and Defense*, trans. Edmund Colledge and Bernard McGinn (New York: Paulist Press, 1981), 177–81, at 178. See also "Sermon 86," in *Meister Eckhart: Teacher and Preacher*, ed. Bernard McGinn (New York: Paulist Press, 1986), 338–45. Eckhart's preference for Martha over Mary was not completely unprecedented. In the eleventh century, Robert of La Chaise-Dieu placed Martha before Mary, and Bernard of Clairvaux argued that the true contemplative is the one who desires to serve those who love God. Nor was Eckhart alone in the late medieval reconfiguration of this text. The Dominican Johann Tauler argued that Jesus' rebuke of Martha was "not because of the things she did, for these were good and sanctified; but because of the ways in which she did them, with too much worry and anxiety" (cited in Marshall, *A Kind of Life*, 22). See Giles Constable, "The Interpretation of Mary and Martha," in *Three Studies in Medieval Religious and Social Thought* (Cambridge: Cambridge University Press, 1995), 1–141, at 116. A helpful commentary is Amy Hollywood, "Preaching as Social Practice in Meister

Eckhart," in *Mysticism and Social Transformation*, ed. Janet Ruffing (Syracuse, NY: Syracuse University Press), 76–90.

24. Eckhart, "Sermon 86," 340.

25. Ashley, "Contemplation in the Action of Justice," 152.

26. Ashley, "Contemplation in the Action of Justice," 150.

27. Martin Luther, "To the Christian Nobility of the German Nation Concerning the Reform of the Christian Estate," in *Luther's Works*, vol. 44, ed. James Atkinson (Philadelphia: Fortress Press, 1966), 115–217, at 123.

28. See Gary D. Badcock, *The Way of Life: A Theology of Christian Vocation* (Grand Rapids, MI: Eerdmans, 1998), 33.

29. Luther, "To the Christian Nobility," 127.

30. Luther, "To the Christian Nobility," 129.

31. Martin Luther, "The Judgment of Martin Luther on Monastic Vows," in *Luther's Works*, vol. 44, ed. James Atkinson (Philadelphia: Fortress Press, 1966), 243–400. Note that it is not monastic life as such that is Luther's concern, but the problem posed by the vows themselves. Gustaf Wingren points out that Luther's doctrine of vocation "presupposes that the monastic ideal has already been overthrown from within" (Gustaf Wingren, *Luther on Vocation*, trans. Carl C. Rasmussen [Philadelphia: Muhlenberg Press, 1957], viii).

32. Martin Luther, "Commentary on 1 Corinthians 7," in *Luther's Works*, vol. 28, ed. Hilton C. Oswald (Saint Louis: Concordia Publishing, 1973), 1–56, at 47.

33. Martin Luther, "The Babylonian Captivity of the Church," in *Luther's Works*, vol. 36, ed. Adbel Ross Wentz and Helmut Lehmann (Philadelphia: Fortress Press, 1959), 78.

34. Martin Luther, "Lectures on Galatians," in *Luther's Works*, vol. 26, ed. Jaroslav Pelikan (Saint Louis: Concordia Publishing, 1963), 1–461, at 217.

35. Martin Luther, "The Estate of Marriage," in *Luther's Works*, vol. 45, ed. Walther I. Brandt (Philadelphia: Muhlenberg Press, 1962), 11–49, at 40.

36. Luther, "Commentary on 1 Corinthians 7," 39. See Marshall, *A Kind of Life*, 22; Weber, *The Protestant Ethic*, 207–11.

37. After 1522, Luther used *Stand* interchangeably with *Befehl* (duty), *Amt* (office), and *Beruf* (calling). See Marshall, *A Kind of Life*, 23.

38. Luther may have pressed Paul too far here. Many biblical scholars today point out that if Paul intended *klesis* in 1 Cor 7:20 to refer to the external condition or "station" of life, he would have been using the word in a sense used nowhere else in his writing, or in the rest of the New Testament for that matter. Indeed, it would be a use without parallel in the Greek of that period. More likely, Paul used *klesis* here in a way parallel to other uses, as the calling to be Christian, thus exhorting Christians to remain in their calling *as Christians*. Given the eschatological context of the letter, Paul's point here was to emphasize that either circumcision (vv. 18-19) or one's state in life (vv. 21-24) is ultimately unimportant in light of the call to discipleship in Christ. On this exegetical debate, see Marshall, *A Kind of Life*, 13–14; Weber, *The Protestant Ethic*, 207–11; Karl Barth, *Church Dogmatics*, vol. III/4 (Edinburgh: T & T Clark, 1961), 600–605; Charles K. Barrett, *A Commentary on the First Epistle to the Corinthians* (London: Adam & Charles Black, 1968), 169–70.

39. Wingren, *Luther on Vocation*, 10.

40. Wingren, *Luther on Vocation*, 65.

41. Martin Luther, *Luther's Church Postil: Gospels: Advent, Christmas and Epiphany Sermons*, ed. John Nicholas Lenker (Minneapolis: Lutherans in All Lands Co., 1905), 282.

42. Wingren, *Luther on Vocation*, 5–8.

43. Preaching on Christmas morning, Luther reminded his listeners that, after meeting the baby Jesus, the shepherds did not run off to the monastery, "they do not don monk's garb, they do not shave their heads, neither do they change their clothing, schedule, food, drink, nor any external work. They return to their place in the fields to serve God there!" Martin Luther, "The Gospel for the Early Christmas Service," in *Luther's Works*, vol. 52, ed. Hans J. Hillerbrand (Philadelphia: Fortress Press, 1974), 32–40, at 37.

44. See William C. Placher, ed., *Callings: Twenty Centuries of Christian Wisdom on Vocation* (Grand Rapids, MI: Eerdmans, 2005), 207.

45. Wingren, *Luther on Vocation*, 172.

46. Wingren, *Luther on Vocation*, 72.

47. John Calvin, *Institutes of the Christian Religion*, 3.11.6, ed. John T. McNeill (Philadelphia: Westminster Press, 1960).

48. Calvin, *Institutes of the Christian Religion*, 3.11.6.

49. John Calvin, *A Commentary on the Harmony of the Evangelists*, vol. 2, trans. William Pringle (Grand Rapids, MI: Eerdmans, 1949), 142–43.

50. Calvin, *Institutes of the Christian Religion*, 1.16.3.

51. Calvin, *Institutes of the Christian Religion*, 3.11.6.

52. Ernst Troeltsch, *The Social Teaching of the Christian Churches*, trans. Olive Wyon (New York: Harper & Row, 1960, orig. 1911), 611.

53. Lee Hardy, *The Fabric of This World: Inquiries into Calling, Career Choice, and the Design of Human Work* (Grand Rapids; MI: Eerdmans, 1990), 66. In his exegesis of the parable of the talents (Matt 25:14-30), Calvin avoids the allegorical interpretation of the coins as spiritual gifts. For Calvin, these talents are historical, concrete, and directly related to one's vocation. In fact, his reinterpretation helped shape the modern meaning of the word "talent." See Marshall, *A Kind of Life*, 25.

54. Marshall, *A Kind of Life*, 26.

55. William Tyndale, "Parable of the Wicked Mammon," in *Doctrinal Treatises and Portions of Holy Scripture* (Cambridge: Parker Society, 1848), 102, cited in Marshall, *A Kind of Life*, 31. The passage was later quoted by William Perkins. See Taylor, *Sources of the Self*, 224.

56. See Taylor, *Sources of the Self*, 222–23.

57. Cited in Taylor, *Sources of the Self*, 224.

58. Marshall, *A Kind of Life*, 34.

59. Marshall, *A Kind of Life*, 35.

60. William Perkins, *A Treatise of the Vocations* (London: John Haviland, 1631). Reproduced, with substantially modified spelling and punctuation, in William Perkins, "A Treatise of the Vocations," in *Callings: Twenty Centuries of Christian Wisdom on Vocation*, ed. William C. Placher (Grand Rapids, MI: Eerdmans, 2005), 262–73.

61. Perkins, "A Treatise of the Vocations," 264.

62. Perkins, "A Treatise of the Vocations," 263.

63. Perkins, "A Treatise of the Vocations," 271.

64. Perkins, "A Treatise of the Vocations," 272.

65. Perkins, "A Treatise of the Vocations," 269.

66. Perkins, "A Treatise of the Vocations," 269.

67. Perkins, "A Treatise of the Vocations," 269.

68. Perkins, "A Treatise of the Vocations," 267.

69. Marshall, *A Kind of Life*, 46.

70. Marshall, *A Kind of Life*, 45.

71. Cited in Marshall, *A Kind of Life*, 48.

72. Cited in Marshall, *A Kind of Life*, 48.

73. We see this secularization of the calling today in the many ways that the word "vocation" is simply equated with work or career without any specific religious association, for example, "vocational counseling," "vocational colleges," etc.

74. John Calvin, "On What the Libertines Understand by the Vocation of Believers, and How Under This Guise They Excuse Every Form of Villainy," in *Treatise Against the Anabaptists and Against the Libertines*, ed. Benjamin Wirt Farley (Grand Rapids, MI: Baker Academic, 1982), 276–81, at 277. See Douglas J. Schuurman, *Vocation: Discerning Our Callings in Life* (Grand Rapids, MI: Eerdmans, 2004), 97.

75. Jacques Ellul, "Work and Calling," in *Callings!*, ed. James Y. Holloway and Will D. Campbell (New York: Paulist Press, 1974), 18–44, at 19.

76. Ellul, "Work and Calling," 25.

77. Stanley Hauerwas, "Work as Co-Creation: A Critique of a Remarkably Bad Idea," in *Co-Creation and Capitalism: John Paul II's* Laborem Exerces, ed. John W. Houck and Oliver F. Williams (Washington, DC: University Press of America, 1983), 42–58, at 48. As the title suggests, Hauerwas is directing his comments not to the Protestant doctrine of vocation, but to the Catholic social teaching tradition, articulated particularly in Pope John Paul II's encyclical on human work.

78. Indeed, Volf begins *Work in the Spirit* by claiming that the "dead hand of 'vocation' needed to be lifted from the Christian idea of work"—an expression he later admitted put it "too starkly." See Miroslav Volf, *Work in the Spirit: Toward a Theology of Work* (Oxford: Oxford University Press, 1991), vii; id., "Eschaton, Creation, and Social Ethics," *Calvin Theological Journal* 30 (1995): 130–43, at 131.

79. Volf, *Work in the Spirit*, 107–9.

80. Volf, *Work in the Spirit*, 107.

81. Volf, *Work in the Spirit*, 107–8. See Jürgen Moltmann, "The Right to Work," in *On Human Dignity: Political Theology and Ethics* (Philadelphia: Fortress Press, 1984), 47.

82. Volf has been accused of overstating the contrast between protology and eschatology, and thus between vocation and gift. But in *Work in the Spirit*, he searches for continuity between the two, arguing that the protological and eschatological are not alternatives but instead complement each other. Still, there is a definite priority here. The doctrine of creation "as such is an insufficient basis

for developing a theology of work. It needs to be placed in the broad context of the (partial) realization and of the expectation of the new creation" (*Work in the Spirit*, 101). For Volf, the eschatological can include and support the protological in a way that the protological cannot include the eschatological. See the exchange: Lee Hardy, "Review of *Work in the Spirit: Toward a Theology of Work*," *Calvin Theological Journal* 28 (1993): 191–96; Volf, "Eschaton, Creation, and Social Ethics"; Douglas J. Schuurman, "Creation, Eschaton, and Social Ethics: A Response to Volf," *Calvin Theological Journal* 30 (1995): 144–58.

83. "If anyone says the married state is to be preferred to that of virginity or celibacy, and that it is no better or more blessed to persevere in virginity or celibacy than to be joined in marriage: let him be anathema" (*Doctrina de sacramento matrimonii*, canon 10 [Session 24, November 11, 1563], in *Decrees of the Ecumenical Councils*, vol. 2, ed. Norman P. Tanner [London/Washington, DC: Sheed & Ward/ Georgetown University Press, 1990], 755).

84. Charles Taylor traces this impulse for reform back to the Fourth Lateran Council and its 1215 decree mandating yearly auricular confession for all Catholics. Taylor contends that by requiring everyone to confess, the council was in effect saying that *everyone* could and should aspire to holiness. See Charles Taylor, *A Secular Age* (Cambridge, MA: Belknap Press, 2007), 68; see also 64, 243, 265.

85. Francis de Sales, *Introduction to the Devout Life*, trans. John K. Ryan (New York: Doubleday/Image Books, 1950), 33.

86. Francis, *Introduction*, 44.

87. For example, the Jesuit Pierre Coton's *L'intérieure occupation d'une âme dévote* anticipated the *Introduction* by several years. See Henri Bremond, *A Literary History of Religious Thought in France*, vol. 2, trans. K. L. Montgomery (New York: MacMillan, 1930, orig. 1916), 76.

88. Etienne-Jean Lajeunie, *Saint François de Sales: L'homme, La Pensée, l'action*, vol. 2 (Paris: Guy Victor, 1966), 221.

89. Francis, *Introduction*, 40.

90. Francis, *Introduction*, 41.

91. Francis, *Introduction*, 68.

92. Bremond, *A Literary History of Religious Thought in France*, vol. 1, 296.

93. Michael J. Buckley, "Seventeenth-Century French Spirituality: Three Figures," in *Christian Spirituality: Post-Reformation and Modern*, eds. Louis Dupré and Don E. Saliers (New York: Crossroad, 1989), 28–68, at 33.

94. Francis, *Introduction*, 43.

95. Francis is an examplar of what Henri Bremond called the "devout humanism" of the seventeenth century. See the discussion by Louis Dupré in "Ignatian Humanism and Its Mystical Origins," *Communio* 18 (1991): 164–82.

96. Buckley, "Seventeenth-Century French Spirituality," 35.

97. The experience was recounted in detail by Jeanne de Chantal in testimony given as part of the canonization process for Francis. See *St. Francis de Sales: A Testimony by St. Chantal*, ed. Elizabeth Stopp (Hyattsville, MD: Institute of Salesian Studies, 1967), 44–45.

98. Buckley, "Seventeenth-Century French Spirituality," 35.

99. Francis de Sales, *Treatise on the Love of God*, trans. Henry Benedict Mackey (Westminster, MD: Newman, 1942), 56–57. For a creative comparative study of Francis's *Treatise*, see Francis X. Clooney, *Beyond Compare: St. Francis de Sales and Sri Vedanta Desika on Loving Surrender to God* (Washington, DC: Georgetown University Press, 2008).

100. Buckley, "Seventeenth-Century French Spirituality," 40.

101. Louis Dupré, *Passage to Modernity: An Essay in the Hermeneutics of Nature and Culture* (New Haven, CT: Yale University Press, 1993), 227.

102. Francis, *Introduction*, 193. See Richard Strier, "Sanctifying the Aristocracy: 'Devout Humanism' in François de Sales, John Donne, and George Herbert," *The Journal of Religion* 69 (1989): 36–58.

103. Francis, *Introduction*, 34.

104. Francis, *Introduction*, 82.

105. Francis, *Treatise*, 14.

106. The Visitation Sisters began as a community of women engaged in limited works of charity in society. But Francis eventually bowed to pressure from the archbishop of Lyons and discontinued these apostolic works, adopting the full cloister in 1618. See Robert W. Richgels, "François De Sales, Holiness in the Lay Life, and Counter-Reformation Clericalism," *Journal of Religious Studies* 12 (1985): 65–75, at 74–75.

107. See Wendy M. Wright and Joseph F. Powers, "Introduction," in *Francis de Sales, Jane de Chantal: Letters of Spiritual Direction*, trans. Péronne Marie Thibert (New York: Paulist Press, 1988), 54–55.

108. Dupré, *Passage to Modernity*, 228–29. Dupré argues further that Francis never succeeded in clarifying the relationship between free will and grace, succumbing instead to the questionable theory of Molina in which God "grants efficacious grace to those whom he foresees will respond to it, thus assuming a time sequence in God who first wants to save all people, then, in a second moment, grants grace only to those who will adequately respond to it" (*Passage to Modernity*, 283, n. 10).

109. "Uncompromising in his refusal to present as one what in the theology of his time appeared inherently divided, Luther converted the religious tension into the very essence of a new Christian piety. His appears the most religiously authentic of all attempts toward a reintegration. But a theology that fails to overcome the dialectical opposition between a totally corrupt nature and a divine justification must fall short of solving the particular problem afflicting the religious consciousness of the modern age, namely, the separation of nature from grace" (Dupré, *Passage to Modernity*, 208–9).

110. Henri Godin and Yvan Daniel, *France, pays de mission?* (Paris: Les editions ouvriès, 1943). See Maisie Ward, *France Pagan? The Mission of Abbé Godin* (New York: Sheed & Ward, 1949).

111. It was this fragmentation that Leo XIII's *Rerum Novarum* (1891) sought to address through an affirmation of the right of workers. By applying Catholic teaching to concrete social conditions, Leo XIII forcefully inserted the church into the secular arena and inspired the great social encyclicals of the twentieth century.

112. Yves M.-J. Congar, "My Path-Findings in the Theology of Laity and Ministries," *The Jurist* 32 (1972): 169–88, at 172.

113. Pius XI, "Discourse to Italian Catholic Young Women," *L'Osservatore Romano* (March 21, 1927): 14.

114. Gérard Philips, "Dogmatic Constitution on the Church: History of the Constitution," in *Commentary on the Documents of Vatican II*, vol. 1, ed. Herbert Vorgrimler (New York: Herder and Herder, 1967), 130.

115. Paul Lakeland, *The Liberation of the Laity: In Search of an Accountable Church* (New York: Continuum, 2002), 88.

116. See Congar's early articles on the laity, "Sacerdoce et laïcat dans l'Église," *Vie Intellectuelle* 14 (1946): 6–39; and "Pour une théologie du laïcat," *Études* 256 (1948): 42–54, 194–218; as well as his major work, *Jalons pour une théologie du laïcat*.

117. Congar, *Lay People in the Church*, 24. The quote comes from the 1964 addendum to his original work, in which he defended and qualified his position in light of subsequent critiques.

118. Congar, *Lay People in the Church*, 19 (emphasis in original).

119. Congar, *Lay People in the Church*, 66.

120. Congar, *Lay People in the Church*, 84.

121. Congar, *Lay People in the Church*, 92.

122. The full text reads, "Here (in this context) the Holy Synod understands by the word *laity* the faithful who are incorporated into the people of God by baptism but, living in the world, are solely guided by the general norms of Christian life. The Synod is therefore concerned with those faithful who have not been called from the people of God to the hierarchy of sacred orders or to a religious state approved by the Church, but who must strive after christian sanctity for the glory of God in their own special way, including secular activity. Actively engaged in the concerns of this world, but led by the spirit of the gospel, they courageously fight the evil of this world and even sanctify the world so to speak from within through their christian calling" (cited in Edward Schillebeeckx, *The Definition of the Christian Layman* [Chicago: Franciscan Herald Press, 1970], 14).

123. The text continues, "The Synod is therefore concerned with those who are actively engaged in the affairs of this world, but led by the spirit of the gospel, strenuously oppose worldly desires and even sanctify the world so to speak from within through their christian calling" (cited in Schillebeeckx, *The Definition of the Christian Layman*, 17).

124. See Schillebeeckx, *The Definition of the Christian Layman*, 18.

125. See Philips, "Dogmatic Constitution on the Church: History of the Constitution," 120.

126. *Lumen Gentium* 31. Author's translation.

127. *Lumen Gentium* 31, translation from *The Documents of Vatican II*, ed. Walter M. Abbott (New York: Guild Press, 1966), 57 (emphasis added).

128. John XXIII, *Mater et Magistra* 255, cited in Friedrich Wulf, "Introductory Remarks on Chapters V and VI," in *Commentary on the Documents of Vatican II*, vol. 1, ed. Herbert Vorgrimler (New York: Herder and Herder, 1967), 258.

129. *Lumen Gentium* 39.

130. *Lumen Gentium* 30. See discussion in Ferdinand Klostermann, "The Laity," in *Commentary on the Documents of Vatican II*, vol. 1, ed. Herbert Vorgrimler (New York: Herder and Herder, 1967), 235.

131. Cited in Joseph A. Komonchak, "Clergy, Laity, and the Church's Mission in the World," *The Jurist* 41 (1981): 422–47, at 430.

132. Kenan Osborn argues that Vatican II presents the lay vocation as one particular vocation within the people of God. See *Ministry: Lay Ministry in the Roman Catholic Church, Its History and Theology* (New York: Paulist Press, 1993), 599.

133. See John Paul II, The Lay Members of Christ's Faithful People (*Christifideles Laici*) (Washington, DC: USCCB Publishing, 1988); id., I Will Give You Shepherds: On the Formation of Priests in the Circumstances of the Present Day (*Pastores Dabo Vobis*) (Washington, DC: USCCB Publishing, 1992); id., The Consecrated Life (*Vita Consecrata*) (Washington, DC: USCCB Publishing, 1996).

134. John Paul II, *Vita Consecrata* 31.

135. Magnani, "Does the So-Called Theology of the Laity Possess a Theological Status?" 600–601 (emphasis in original).

136. See *Optatam Totius* 10; *Lumen Gentium* 44.

137. John Paul II, *Vita Consecrata* 32 (emphasis in original). See the discussion of "objective superiority" in Peter C. Phan, "Possibility of a Lay Spirituality: A Re-examination of Some Theological Presuppositions," *Communio* 10 (1983): 378–95.

138. Komonchak, "Clergy, Laity, and the Church's Mission in the World," 431.

139. A similar difference can be seen in the way Vatican II dealt with the issue of priesthood. For Luther, an affirmation of the biblical notion of the "priesthood of all believers" meant a deconstruction of the ministerial priesthood of the ordained. Vatican II did not set the two in opposition but affirmed both of these priesthoods as distinct ways of participating in the one priesthood of Christ. See *Lumen Gentium* 10.

Chapter Two—pages 47–90

1. Author's translation.

2. Joseph Lahitton, *La Vocation Sacerdotale* (Paris: Lethielleux, 1909). The second edition (Paris: Beauchesne, 1913) was significantly revised. The book ultimately went into a seventh edition (1931).

3. See John W. O'Malley, *Trent and All That: Renaming Catholicism in the Early Modern Era* (Cambridge, MA: Harvard University Press, 2000); John W. O'Malley, ed., *Catholicism in Early Modern History: A Guide to Research* (St. Louis: Center for Reformation Research, 1988).

4. Thomas F. O'Meara, *Theology of Ministry*, rev. ed. (New York: Paulist Press, 1999), 115.

5. In the early church the people played an important role in choosing their leaders. But in the face of the Reformers' insistence on the role of the local community, Trent taught that ordination does not require either the consent of

the people or the confirmation of civil authority. Those who assume the offices of ministry only on those grounds—that is, without hierarchical approval—are "thieves and robbers who have not entered by the sheepgate" (Council of Trent, 23rd Session [July 15, 1563], in *Decrees of the Ecumenical Councils*, vol. 2, ed. Norman P. Tanner [London/Washington, DC: Sheed & Ward/Georgetown University Press, 1990], 743). On the role of the community in early ordination, see Yves Congar, "Ordination *invitus, coactus* de l'église antique au canon 214," *Revue des Sciences Philosophiques et Théologiques* 50 (1966): 169–97.

6. John W. O'Malley, "Spiritual Formation for Ministry: Some Roman Catholic Traditions—Their Past and Present," in *Theological Education and Moral Formation*, ed. Richard John Neuhaus (Grand Rapids, MI: Eerdmans, 1992), 79–111, at 82.

7. Bonaventure's influential *Legenda maior* presents the life of Francis within a highly developed spiritual theology moving the reader through the three stages of the spiritual life: purgation, illumination, and perfection. Text and notes found in *Bonaventure: The Soul's Journey into God, The Tree of Life, The Life of St. Francis*, trans. Ewert Cousins (New York: Paulist Press, 1978).

8. O'Malley, "Spiritual Formation for Ministry," 82. See Ugolino di Monte Santa Maria, *The Little Flowers of St. Francis of Assisi*, trans. W. Heywood (New York: Vintage Books, 1998).

9. John W. O'Malley, "Priesthood, Ministry and Religious Life: Some Historical and Historiographical Considerations," *Theological Studies* 49 (1988): 223–57, at 232. See Donald Edward Heintschel, *The Medieval Concept of an Ecclesiastical Office* (Washington, DC: Catholic University of America, 1956). Lawrence C. Landini, *The Causes of the Clericalization of the Order of Friars Minor (1209–1260) in the Light of Early Franciscan Sources* (Chicago: n.p., 1968) argues that both external and internal factors forced the Franciscans to adopt more clerical structures.

10. See L. Sempé, "Vocation," in *Dictionnaire de Théologie Catholique*, vol. 15, eds. A. Vacant et al. (Paris: Librairie Letouzey et Ané, 1950), 3148–81, at 3162–64.

11. *Contra Retrahentes*, in *Opuscula Theologica*, vol. 2 (Rome: Marietti, 1954), 173. English translation adapted from Thomas Aquinas, *An Apology for the Religious Orders*, trans. John Procter (London: Sands & Co., 1902), 426–27.

12. Aquinas defends religious life in three polemical treatises: *Contra impugnantes Dei cultum et religionem* (1256), *De perfectione spiritualis vitae* (1269–70), and *Contra doctrinam retrahentium a religione* (1271), cited above. They are collected in *An Apology for the Religious Orders*. See also *Summa Theologiae* II-II, qq. 179–89, in Thomas Aquinas, *Summa Theologiae*, vols. 46 and 47 (New York: McGraw-Hill, 1964). A helpful summary of Aquinas's role in the debates of 1269–71 is found in James A. Weisheipl, *Friar Thomas D'Aquino: His Life, Thought, and Work* (Garden City, NY: Doubleday and Company, 1974), 263–72. See also Decima Douie, *The Conflict Between the Seculars and the Mendicants at the University of Paris in the 13th Century* (London: Blackfriars, 1954); and Yves Congar's important essay, "Aspects ecclésiologiques de la querelle entre mendiants et séculiers dans la seconde moitié du XIIIe siècle et le début du XIVe," *Archives d'Histoire Doctrinale et Littéraire du Moyen Age* 28 (1961): 35–151.

13. Sempé, "Vocation," 3167.

14. The best source for information on Ignatius's early life is his own autobiography, dictated to Luís Gonçalves da Câmara in 1553 and 1555. Citation taken from "The Autobiography," in *Ignatius of Loyola: The Spiritual Exercises and Selected Works*, ed. George E. Ganss (New York: Paulist Press, 1991), 68. See also Cándido de Dalmases, *Ignatius of Loyola, Founder of the Jesuits: His Life and Work*, trans. Jerome Aixalá (St. Louis: The Institute of Jesuit Sources, 1985); and John W. O'Malley, *The First Jesuits* (Cambridge, MA: Harvard University Press, 1993), 23–50.

15. O'Malley, *The First Jesuits*, 25.

16. *Exercises*, n. 4. Quotations from the *Spiritual Exercises* are taken from the translation by George E. Ganss and found in *Ignatius of Loyola: The Spiritual Exercises and Selected Works*, ed. George E. Ganss (New York: Paulist Press, 1991). References are to paragraph number.

17. *Exercises*, n. 1.

18. See Paul Shore, "The *Vita Christi* of Ludolph of Saxony and its Influence on the *Spiritual Exercises* of Ignatius of Loyola," *Studies in the Spirituality of Jesuits* 30 (1998): 1–32; Ewert H. Cousins, "Franciscan Roots of Ignatian Meditation," in *Ignatian Spirituality in a Secular Age*, ed. George P. Schner (Waterloo, ON: Wilfrid Laurier University Press, 1984), 51–64; id., "The Humanity and the Passion of Christ," in *Christian Spirituality: High Middle Ages and Reformation*, ed. Jill Raitt (New York: Crossroad, 1987), 375–91; id., "Francis of Assisi: Christian Mysticism at the Crossroads," in *Mysticism and Religious Traditions*, ed. Steven Katz (New York: Oxford University Press, 1983), 163–91.

19. Cited in Ganss, ed., *Ignatius of Loyola: The Spiritual Exercises and Selected Works*, 22.

20. See, for example, *Exercises*, nn. 2, 66–70, and 214.

21. The concern to distinguish true from false spirits at work in the soul spans the history of Christian thought, rooted as it is in the fundamental ambiguity of religious experience. Paul reminds the Thessalonians to "test everything" (1 Thess 5:19-22), while the First Letter of John counsels, "Beloved, do not believe every spirit, but test the spirits to see whether they are from God; for many false prophets have gone out into the world" (1 John 4:1) (Michael J. Buckley, "Discernment of Spirits," in *The New Dictionary of Catholic Spirituality*, ed. Michael Downey [Collegeville, MN: Liturgical Press, 1993], 274–81). For a penetrating analysis that locates the discernment of spirits within a larger epistemological and mystical framework, see Mark A. McIntosh, *Discernment and Truth: The Spirituality and Theology of Knowledge* (New York: Crossroad, 2004). On Ignatius, see Jules J. Toner, *A Commentary on Saint Ignatius' Rules for the Discernment of Spirits: A Guide to the Principles and Practice* (Saint Louis: The Institute of Jesuit Sources, 1982); Timothy M. Gallagher, *The Discernment of Spirits: An Ignatian Guide for Everyday Living* (New York: Crossroad, 2005); id., *Spiritual Consolation: An Ignatian Guide for the Greater Discernment of Spirits* (New York: Crossroad, 2007).

22. John W. O'Malley, "Early Jesuit Spirituality: Spain and Italy," in *Christian Spirituality: Post-Reformation and Modern*, eds. Louis Dupré and Don E. Saliers (New York: Crossroad, 1989), 3–27, at 6.

23. Buckley, "Discernment of Spirits," 280. See also id., "The Structure of the Rules for Discernment," in *The Way of Ignatius Loyola: Contemporary Approaches to the Spiritual Exercises*, ed. Philip Sheldrake (Saint Louis: The Institute of Jesuit Sources, 1991), 219–37. Ignatius indicated a twofold progression in the opening paragraph of the *Exercises*, in which he defined "Spiritual Exercises" as all those methods and meditations that serve as a means of "preparing and disposing our soul to rid itself of all its disordered affections and then, after their removal, of seeking and finding God's will in the ordering of our life for the salvation of our soul" (*Exercises*, n. 1).

24. *Exercises*, n. 15.

25. O'Malley, *The First Jesuits*, 43.

26. *Exercises*, n. 14.

27. *Exercises*, nn. 352–70. John O'Malley argues that the "Rules" articulate an attitude to church teaching generally presumed in the sixteenth century. In their attention to the more institutional aspects of religion they balance out the rest of the text. "They are thus a manifesto of Ignatius's own orthodoxy, frequently impugned precisely on this score." As basically an "antidote" to dangerous ideas, they are important but not integral to the text (O'Malley, *The First Jesuits*, 49–50).

28. *Exercises*, n. 170.

29. O'Malley, "Early Jesuit Spirituality," 17.

30. Charles Taylor notes the impact in the late sixteenth and early seventeenth centuries of a "neo-Stoic" mode of thinking that emphasized methodic self-mastery and discipline as a way toward reforming militaries, civil administrations, trade and labor, health conditions, and even piety (*Sources of the Self: The Making of the Modern Identity* [Cambridge, MA: Harvard University Press, 1989], 159). On these movements, see Gerhard Oestreich, *Neo-Stoicism and the Early Modern State* (Cambridge: Cambridge University Press, 1983); Marc Raeff, *The Well-Ordered Police State* (New Haven: Yale University Press, 1983); and, classically, Michel Foucault, *Discipline and Punish: The Birth of the Prison*, trans. Alan Sheridan (New York: Vintage Books, 1995).

31. Louis Dupré, *Passage to Modernity: An Essay in the Hermeneutics of Nature and Culture* (New Haven: Yale University Press, 1993), 225. See also id., "Ignatian Humanism and Its Mystical Origins," *Communio* 18 (1991): 164–82.

32. The phrase is Dupré's. See *Passage to Modernity*, 167–89.

33. Dupré, *Passage to Modernity*, 225.

34. Dupré, *Passage to Modernity*, 225.

35. Gaston Fessard argues that the *Exercises* are most basically a method for gaining true freedom. See *La dialectique des Exercises spirituels de saint Ignace de Loyola* (Paris: Aubier, 1956).

36. *Exercises*, nn. 23, 235.

37. Dupré, *Passage to Modernity*, 226.

38. *Constitutions*, n. 288, in *Ignatius of Loyola: The Spiritual Exercises and Selected Works*, ed. George E. Ganss (New York: Paulist Press, 1991), 292.

39. O'Malley, *The First Jesuits*, 127–33.

40. O'Malley, *The First Jesuits*, 158.

41. This brief background relies on John W. O'Malley, "Diocesan and Religious Models of Priestly Formation: Historical Perspectives," in *Priests: Identity and Ministry*, ed. Robert J. Wister (Wilmington, DE: Michael Glazier, 1990), 54–70, at 56.

42. The implementation of Trent's decree was uneven at best, and was largely ignored in many places for decades. It was not until 1696, for example, that a diocesan seminary was established in Paris and attendance made mandatory for ordination. See Joseph M. White, "How the Seminary Developed," in *Reason for the Hope: The Futures of Roman Catholic Theologates*, by Katarina Schuth (Wilmington, DE: Michael Glazier, 1989), 11–28. A classic study is Antoine Degert, *Histoire des séminaires Français jusqu'á la Révolution* (Paris: Beauchesne, 1912), 2 vols. The central conciliar statement is Council of Trent, 23rd Session (July 15, 1563), Reform Decree, chap. 18, in Tanner, *Decrees of the Ecumenical Councils*, 2:750–53.

43. O'Malley, "Spiritual Formation for Ministry," 85–86.

44. According to Jordan Aumann, "Nevertheless, the Christocentric spirituality of the French school was diffused so widely that for all practical purposes Catholic spirituality in modern times could be characterized as French spirituality" (*Christian Spirituality in the Catholic Tradition* [London: Sheed & Ward, 1985], 218). The best comprehensive study of the French School is Yves Krumenacker, *L'école française de spiritualité: Des mystiques, des fondateurs, des courants et leurs interprètes* (Paris: Cerf, 1998). Krumenacker builds on the work of Henri Bremond, *A Literary History of Religious Thought in France*, vol. 3, trans. K. L. Montgomery (New York: MacMillan, 1930); Pierre Pourrat, *La Spiritualité chrétienne*, vol. 3 (Paris: Lecoffre, 1925); and Louis Cognet, *Les origines de la spiritualité française au XVIIe siècle* (Paris: La Colombe, 1949).

45. On Bérulle's life see Jean Dagens, *Bérulle et les origines de la restauration catholique (1575–1611)* (Paris: Desclée de Brouwer, 1952); and Bremond, *A Literary History of Religious Thought in France*, 3:1–222.

46. Madame Barbe Acarie—later Blessed Marie de la Incarnation—was the wife of a French aristocrat and the mother of six who gathered around her some of the major spiritual figures of the day, including Bérulle, the Jesuits Etienne Binet and Pierre Coton, the Sorbonne theologian André Duval, Dom Beaucousin, and Francis de Sales. The group was deeply influenced by the Puritan convert and later Capuchin William Fitch, better known as Benoît de Canfield, who articulated a spirituality based on the progressive identification of one's individual will with the will of God. See Michael J. Buckley, "Seventeenth-Century French Spirituality: Three Figures," in *Christian Spirituality: Post-Reformation and Modern*, eds. Louis Dupré and Don E. Saliers (New York: Crossroad, 1989), 28–68, at 28–32; Louis Cognet, *La spiritualité moderne* (Paris: Aubier, 1966), 233–73.

47. "Discourse on the State and Grandeurs of Jesus" 2.2, in *Bérulle and the French School: Selected Writings*, ed. William M. Thompson (New York: Paulist Press, 1989), 116–17.

48. Bérulle, *De l'adoration de Dieu* 3.1210, cited in Buckley, "Seventeenth-Century French Spirituality," 49.

49. Buckley, "Seventeenth-Century French Spirituality," 48.

50. Fernando Guillén Preckler, *"État" chez le Cardinal de Bérulle: Théologie et spiritualitédes "états" bérulliens* (Rome: Gregorian University, 1974), 143. Cited in William Thompson, "Introduction," in *Bérulle and the French School*, 42.

51. "It follows that contemplation of the states of Jesus belongs to the very heart of Christian life. The faithful are called to participate in the mysteries of the Incarnation, not as these were visible in the earthly life of Jesus but as they are eternalized in his ever-present states. In a theology of grace, this view entails the consequence that men's participation in Christ is effected in their interiorization of the external mysteries. The faithful share the states of Jesus, experiencing in themselves the same interior attitudes in which Jesus lived his mysteries" (George H. Tavard, "The Christology of the Mystics," *Theological Studies* 42 [1981]: 561–79, at 575).

52. Buckley, "Seventeenth-Century French Spirituality," 51.

53. In his 1664 biography of Vincent de Paul, Louis Abelly offered a classic summary of this widespread assessment. See *The Life of the Venerable Servant of God, Vincent de Paul*, vol. 1, ed. John E. Rybolt, trans. William Quinn (New York: New City Press, 1993), 1–34. See also Louis Cognet, "Ecclesiastical Life in France," in *The Church in the Age of Absolutism and Enlightenment*, eds. Hubert Jedin and John Dolan (New York: Crossroad, 1981), 3–106; and Degert, *Histoire des séminaires français jusqu'à la Révolution*.

54. Cited in Thompson, "Introduction," 11, from André Dodin, ed., *Entrétiens spirituels aux missionaires* (Paris: Seuil, 1960), 502.

55. Cited in Thompson, "Introduction," 56. On the influence of Bérulle's "high" theology of the priesthood, see Paul Cochois, *Bérulle et l'École Française* (Paris: Éditions du Seuil, 1963), 12–33; and Michel Dupuy, *Bérulle et le sacerdoce: Étude historique et doctrinale* (Paris: Lethielleux, 1969).

56. Bérulle, "Pièce 891: A Letter on the Priesthood," in *Bérulle and the French School*, 183–85.

57. Bremond, *A Literary History of Religious Thought in France*, 3:393. An excellent biography is Michel Dupuy, *Se laisser à l'Esprit. L'Itinéraire spirituel de Jean-Jacques Olier* (Paris: Cerf, 1982).

58. Olier, "Introduction to the Christian Life and Virtues," in *Bérulle and the French School*, 274. See Thompson, "Introduction," 38. The language of the "heart" will erupt in the writings of John Eudes and in his work promoting devotion to the Sacred Heart of Jesus.

59. Jean-Jacques Olier, *Mémoires autographes*, vol. 2 (Paris: Sulpician Archives, 1642–52), 427.

60. For Olier, a true vocation was marked by three things: first, the movement of God within the soul manifested in a strong and constant inclination toward the priesthood; second, an inclination toward the functions of the ministry; and third, a proper intention in entering the ministry.

61. Jean-Jacques Olier, *De l'État ecclésiastique*, n. 1, cited in Gilles Chaillot, Paul Cochois, and Irénée Noye, *Traité des saints ordres (1676) comparé aux écrits authentiques de Jean-Jacques Olier (d. 1657)* (Paris: Compagnie de Saint-Sulpice,

1984), 106. *De l'État ecclésiastique* was discovered among the books in the personal library of Louis Tronson (1622–1700), the third superior general of the Society of Saint-Sulpice. This draft text appears to be Olier's attempt to prepare a spiritual guide for seminary candidates and their teachers.

62. Chaillot, Cochois, and Noye argue that the *Traité* (1676) was the work of Louis Tronson, who compiled the treatise from various writings of Olier and, in the process, significantly altered Olier's own emphases. Four important shifts reveal how the *Traité* diverges from Olier's writings: (1) the *Traité* emphasizes the ordained priesthood as a "religious state"—superior to those in religious vows—largely seen in terms of cultic functions, thus losing Olier's more apostolic vision; (2) the *Traité* underscores ascetical practices for the priest, giving a more negative assessment of creation and a more otherworldly spirituality; (3) Olier saw the bishop as the fullness of the priesthood, but the *Traité* lifts up the priest over all else, including the bishop; (4) finally, whereas Olier locates the holiness of the priest within the call to holiness of all the baptized, the *Traité* leaves out the references to the faithful. See Chaillot et al., *Traité des saints ordres*, xxiii-xlviii. A good summary is found in Kenan B. Osborne, *Priesthood: A History of the Ordained Ministry in the Roman Catholic Church* (New York: Paulist, 1988), 285–88. See also Thompson, "Introduction," 61–63; Krumenacker, *L'école française de spiritualité*, 423–37.

63. Chaillot et al., *Traité des saints ordres*, 107–8. While Olier's text suggests three marks of a true vocation, the *Traité* includes four: (1) purity of life, (2) disdain for the world, (3) a constant and deep inner inclination to this state, and (4) the aptitude and disposition needed to carry out the duties of this ministry. The addition of the first and second marks clearly reflects Tronson's more ascetic and otherworldly ideal. See Chaillot et al., *Traité des saints ordres*, 97–110.

64. Buckley, "Seventeenth-Century French Spirituality," 52.

65. Buckley, "Seventeenth-Century French Spirituality," 52.

66. Given Augustine's attention to the interior life, it is no coincidence that the early modern era saw a resurgence of Augustinian spirituality across denominational divides. See Taylor, *Sources of the Self*, 141.

67. See Taylor, *Sources of the Self*, 156–58; Etienne Gilson, *The Christian Philosophy of Saint Augustine*, trans. L. E. M. Lynch (New York: Random House, 1960), 41–43.

68. Dupré, *Passage to Modernity*, 3.

69. In the sixteenth century, the Louvain theologian Baius would attempt to argue from Augustine that, since innocence was a "natural state," the union of our first parents with God did not require grace. But for Augustine, the concept of "human nature" and the term "natural" refer not to some abstract reality imagined apart from grace but to the concrete human creature who exists *already touched by God's grace*. The original state of innocence is already a gift from God; it is already a grace. See Louis Dupré, "Introduction to the 2000 Edition," in Henri de Lubac, *Augustinianism and Modern Theology*, trans. Lancelot Sheppard (New York: Crossroad, 2000), x.

70. Dupré, *Passage to Modernity*, 170.

71. Dupré points out that Aristotle's concept of nature was often developed according to organic metaphors, giving it a flexibility that Aquinas could exploit, but that later interpreters lost. See Dupré, *Passage to Modernity*, 174.

72. Cited in Dupré, "Introduction to the 2000 Edition," xiii–xiv.

73. Dupré, "Introduction to the 2000 Edition," xii.

74. "It is clear that the same effect is ascribed to a natural cause and to God, not as though part were effected by God and part by the natural agent; but the whole effect proceeds from each, yet in different ways, just as the whole of one and the same effect is ascribed to the instrument, and again the whole is ascribed to the principal agent" (Aquinas, *Summa contra Gentiles* III.70, in *Basic Writings of Saint Thomas Aquinas*, vol. 2, trans. Anton C. Pegis [New York: Random House, 1945], 130). See Dupré, *Passage to Modernity*, 177.

75. Dupré, *Passage to Modernity*, 174.

76. Henri de Lubac, *Surnaturel: Etudes historiques* (Paris: Aubier, 1946), 262, cited in Dupré, "Introduction to the 2000 Edition," xiv.

77. The impact of *Surnaturel* on Catholic understandings of the nature-grace relationship is hard to overstate. The book linked together several earlier historical studies by de Lubac. For an overview, see Stephen J. Duffy, *The Graced Horizon: Nature and Grace in Modern Catholic Thought* (Collegeville, MN: Liturgical Press, 1992), 66–84. On the reactions of de Lubac's contemporaries, see the series of articles by Philip J. Donnelly, "On the Development of Dogma and the Supernatural," *Theological Studies* 8 (1947): 471–91; id., "Discussions on the Supernatural Order," *Theological Studies* 9 (1948): 213–49; id., "A Recent Critique of P. de Lubac's *Surnaturel*," *Theological Studies* 9 (1948): 554–60; id., "The Gratuity of the Beatific Vision and the Possibility of a Natural Destiny," *Theological Studies* 11 (1950): 374–404. Two English texts, recently reissued, offer a summary of de Lubac's argument in *Surnaturel*, which was never translated in its entirety into English. See de Lubac, *Augustinianism and Modern Theology*; and id., *The Mystery of the Supernatural*, trans. Rosemary Sheed (New York: Crossroad, 1998, orig. 1965).

78. This basic historical argument was not original to de Lubac. In an earlier work, Henri Bouillard had laid out the differences in the theology of grace found in Aquinas and in his later commentators. See Henri Bouillard, *Conversion et grâce chez St. Thomas d'Aquin* (Paris: Aubier, 1944). De Lubac lists a number of exegetes who had previously pointed out the ways in which Cajetan diverged from Aquinas. See *Augustinianism and Modern Theology*, 114–15.

79. See Michael J. Buckley, *At the Origins of Modern Atheism* (New Haven: Yale University Press, 1987). De Lubac himself was deeply concerned about what he saw as the exile of faith from life. Writing in the midst of a Europe suffering a second world war in as many generations, de Lubac argued that the blame for the cultural alienation of Christianity could not be laid solely at the feet of atheistic philosophies or nationalistic ideologies. The theologians bore some responsibility.

80. "The doctrine of grace, as set forth in classrooms [sic] and textbooks, was reduced to an uninviting short chapter on what had come to be called 'sanctifying grace' and long chapters dealing with the endless disputes on the subject of 'actual

grace.' The divine indwelling, no longer the indwelling of the Blessed Trinity, was lost sight of as the living ground and source of created grace. Instead, it was turned into an immediate consequence, a necessary fruit of infused grace—an extremely impoverished understanding, indeed, of what Scripture teaches" (Peter F. Fransen, *The New Life of Grace*, trans. Georges Dupont [New York: Desclee, 1969], 96).

81. Paul D. Holland, "Vocation," in *The New Dictionary of Theology*, eds. Joseph Komonchak, Mary Collins, Dermot Lane (Collegeville, MN: Liturgical Press, 1987), 1087–92, at 1091.

82. Alphonsus de Liguori, *The Great Means of Salvation and Perfection*, vol. 3 of *The Complete Works of Saint Alphonsus de Liguori: The Ascetical Works*, ed. Eugene Grimm (Brooklyn, NY: Redemptorist Fathers, 1927), 491–98.

83. Liguori, *The Great Means*, 381.

84. Liguori, *The Great Means*, 384.

85. Liguori, *The Great Means*, 384–85.

86. Liguori, *The Great Means*, 390.

87. Liguori, *The Great Means*, 488 (italics in original).

88. Scavini's *Theologia moralis universa ad mentem S. Alphonsi* (1841) went through sixteen editions over the course of the nineteenth century. Gasparri's reputation as professor of canon law at the Institut Catholique in Paris, cardinal secretary of state, and principal author of the 1917 Code of Canon Law gave his own *Tractatus canonicus de Sacra Ordinatione* (1893–94) enormous influence well into the twentieth century.

89. See Degert, *Histoire des séminaires français jusqu'à la Révolution*, 2:365. Lahitton relied on Degert's account, as did John Blowick, *Priestly Vocation* (Dublin: M. H. Gill and Son, 1932). Blowick followed Lahitton's argument closely, but somewhat tendentiously, expanding on Lahitton's historical survey.

90. Cited in Degert, *Histoire des séminaires français jusqu'à la Révolution*, 2:361; and reproduced in Blowick, *Priestly Vocation*, 22.

91. Cited in Charles A. Schleck, *The Theology of Vocations* (Milwaukee, WI: Bruce Publishing, 1963), 180.

92. Council of Trent, 23rd Session (July 15, 1563), in *Decrees of the Ecumenical Councils*, 2:743.

93. *Catechism of the Council of Trent for Parish Priests*, trans. John A. McHugh and Charles J. Callan (New York: Joseph F. Wagner, 1934), 318–19.

94. For Godeau, this attraction meant that the candidate "feels himself from day to day in the depths of his soul more strongly inclined to the ecclesiastical profession; feels himself quite suddenly set free from the uneasiness and irresolution by which he had been previously tormented and that not by any idea of his own worthiness but by a sweet acquiescence in the will of God and by the efficacy of his interior voice" (cited in Degert, *Histoire des séminaires français jusqu'à la Révolution*, 2:368–69, and reproduced in Blowick, *Priestly Vocation*, 26).

95. Cited in Blowick, *Priestly Vocation*, 55.

96. Cited in Blowick, *Priestly Vocation*, 55–56.

97. Louis Branchereau, *De la Vocation Sacerdotale* (Paris: Vic & Amat, 1896), 184. Another pure example of this Sulpician trajectory is Henri-Joseph Icard,

Traditions de la Compagnie des prêtres de Saint-Sulpice pour la direction des grands séminaires (Paris: Librairie Victor LeCoffre, 1886), esp. 281–97, 331–59.

98. Branchereau, *De la Vocation Sacerdotale*, 223–42.

99. Lahitton quickly followed his 1909 *La Vocation Sacerdotale* with a second volume advancing the same basic argument, *Deux conceptions divergentes de la vocation sacerdotale* (Paris: Lethielleux, 1910). See Raymond Darricau, "Un débat sur la vocation au début du XXe siècle: L'Affaire Lahitton (1909–1912)," in *La vocation religieuse et sacerdotale en France: XVII-XIX Siècles* (Angers: Université d'Angers, 1979), 65–77.

100. Joseph Lahitton, *La Vocation Sacerdotale: Traité théorique et pratique*, 4th ed. (Paris: Beauchesne, 1914), 7. Unless otherwise noted, translations are from this fourth edition, which reflects a number of revisions from the first edition.

101. Lahitton, *La Vocation Sacerdotale*, 147.

102. First edition cited in Philip Endean, *Karl Rahner and Ignatian Spirituality* (Oxford: Oxford University Press, 2001), 105–6.

103. In the second edition, Lahitton wrote, "This work, as the title indicates, has as its main concern the priestly vocation. No doubt it would not be difficult to find in it general principles applying just as well to other states of life, and, more particularly, to religious profession. Nevertheless, the plan here has been to speak directly of the priestly vocation" (cited in Endean, *Karl Rahner and Ignatian Spirituality*, 106, n. 22).

104. For a helpful overview of this debate, including bibliographical information on reviews and responses to *La Vocation Sacerdotale*, see Darricau, "Un débat sur la vocation au début du XXe siècle," 70–73.

105. The core of Merry del Val's letter reads, "The work of the outstanding man, Canon Joseph Lahitton, is in no way to be condemned. In fact it is to be praised highly when he says that: (1) No one ever has any right to ordination prior to the free choice of the bishop. (2) The requisite on the part of the one to be ordained, which we call priestly vocation, does not at all consist—at least necessarily and ordinarily—in a certain interior attraction of the subject or in an invitation of the Holy Spirit to enter the priesthood. (3) On the contrary, in order that one may be rightly called by the bishop, nothing further is required beyond the right intention, together with that suitability which is founded upon those gifts of nature and grace and confirmed by goodness of life and sufficiency of learning, which give well-founded hope that he will be able to fulfill the duties of the priestly state properly and observe the obligations of that state in a holy manner" (*Acta Apostolicae Sedis* 4 [1912]: 485). The entire letter is reprinted in the front of the fourth edition of Lahitton's *La Vocation Sacerdotale*, x–xi.

106. See Edward Farrell, *The Theology of Religious Vocation* (Saint Louis: B. Herder Book Co., 1951), 20–28; and Schleck, *The Theology of Vocations*, 177–79. Karl Rahner raised a similar concern, calling Lahitton's position an overcorrection (see chap. 4 of this volume). Following "l'affaire Lahitton," magisterial statements avoided emphasizing attraction but nevertheless reaffirmed the notion of the "inner call" to the priesthood. This development reached a culmination in Pius XII's 1956 apostolic constitution *Sedes Sapientiae*. The text, meant to provide

general principles for those involved in the cultivation and formation of religious and priestly vocations, began by reflecting on how "by an interior and, as it were, mystic colloquy, Christ the Redeemer has inspired souls who are especially dear to Him with the invitation . . . *Come, follow me*." The letter goes on to describe vocation as made up of two essential elements, the one divine, the other ecclesiastical. The divine element is described as a kind of grace bestowed on the individual. The ecclesiastical element is presented in terms of the line from the tridentine catechism, "they are said to be called by God, who are called by the lawful ministers of the church" (Pius XII, "The Apostolic Constitution: *Sedes Sapientiae,*" *Pope Speaks* 3 [1956–57], 287–98, at 287–88).

Chapter Three—pages 93–124

1. Hermann Hesse, *The Glass Bead Game*, trans. Richard and Clara Winston (New York: Holt, Rinehart and Winston, 1969), 58.

2. Martin Luther, "The Bondage of the Will," in *Luther's Works*, vol. 33, ed. Philip S. Watson (Philadelphia: Fortress Press, 1972), 291.

3. Alphonsus de Liguori, *The Great Means of Salvation and Perfection*, vol. 3 of *The Complete Works of Saint Alphonsus de Liguori: The Ascetical Works*, ed. Eugene Grimm (Brooklyn, NY: Redemptorist Fathers, 1927), 501.

4. Liguori, *The Great Means*, 424.

5. Liguori, *The Great Means*, 381–82 (emphasis in original). Later, while speaking of the priestly vocation, Liguori again cited Romans 8:30, stating, "Thus to vocation succeeds justification, and to justification, glory; that is, the attainment of eternal life. He, then, who does not obey the call of God, shall neither be justified nor glorified" (*The Great Means*, 502).

6. See the helpful discussion in Paul Marshall, *A Kind of Life Imposed on Man: Vocation and Social Order from Tyndale to Locke* (Toronto: University of Toronto Press, 1996), 67–84.

7. On the relationship between the two men, see John W. Hart, *Karl Barth vs. Emil Brunner: The Formation and Dissolution of a Theological Alliance, 1916–1936* (New York: Peter Lang, 2001). An in-depth study of the theologies of vocation in Barth and Brunner can be found in Michael R. Wassenaar, *Four Types of Calling: The Ethics of Vocation in Kierkegaard, Brunner, Scheler and Barth* (PhD dissertation, Yale University, 2009), 82–131, 182–233.

8. Emil Brunner, *The Divine Imperative*, trans. Olive Wyon (Philadelphia: Westminster Press, 1947, orig. 1932), 200.

9. Brunner, *The Divine Imperative*, 202–3 (emphasis in original).

10. Brunner, *The Divine Imperative*, 203.

11. Brunner, *The Divine Imperative*, 203. Brunner addressed the space for reform more fully at *The Divine Imperative*, 249–60.

12. Karl Barth, "Vocation," in *Church Dogmatics*, vol. III/4, trans. A. T. Mackay et al. (Edinburgh: T & T Clark, 1961), 602.

13. Barth, *Church Dogmatics* III/4, 600.

14. Barth, *Church Dogmatics* III/4, 641.

15. Barth, *Church Dogmatics* III/4, 644.

16. Barth, *Church Dogmatics* III/4, 645.

17. Barth, *Church Dogmatics* III/4, 598. On the distinction, see Rhys Kuzmic, "*Beruf* and *Berufung* in Karl Barth's *Church Dogmatics*: Toward a Subversive Klesiology," *International Journal of Theology* 7 (2005): 262–78.

18. Barth, *Church Dogmatics* III/4, 602. Barth cited Max Weber, K. L. Schmidt, A. de Quervain, and, in particular, Karl Holl, whom Barth saw as the end point of this faulty interpretation of vocation. See Karl Holl, "The History of the Word Vocation (*Beruf*)," trans. Heber F. Peacock, *Review and Expositor* 55 (1958): 126–54, originally published as "Die Geschichte des Wortes Beruf," in *Gesammelte Aufsätze zur Kirchengeschichte*, vol. 3 (Tübingen: Mohr, 1928), 189–219.

19. Hans Urs von Balthasar, *The Theology of Karl Barth*, trans. John Drury (New York: Holt, Rinehart and Winston, 1971), 156.

20. Thomas Aquinas, *Summa Theologiae* I.23.1, in *St. Thomas Aquinas Summa Theologica*, trans. English Dominicans, vol. 1 (Notre Dame, IN: Ave Maria Press, 1981), 126.

21. As indicated in chapter 2, Aquinas's theology would hardly support such a subordination of God's saving work, or such a simple split between nature and grace. The same could not always be said about his later interpreters.

22. "When beliefs about providence stem from Christ rather than move to him, providence becomes, not the immanent movement of created powers, but those arrangements of the world that reflect God's prior intentions for the world in Christ, arrangements that reflect God's primary intention to draw the world towards him" (Kathryn Tanner, "Creation and Providence," in *The Cambridge Companion to Karl Barth*, ed. John Webster [Cambridge: Cambridge University Press, 2000], 111–26, at 111–12). See Horton Davies, *The Vigilant God: Providence in the Thought of Augustine, Aquinas, Calvin, and Barth* (New York: Peter Lang, 1992), 127–62.

23. See Henri Rondet, "Predestination: Concept and History of the Problem," in *Sacramentum Mundi: An Encyclopedia of Theology*, vol. 5, ed. Karl Rahner (New York: Herder and Herder, 1970), 88.

24. Aquinas agreed with Augustine that God predestines those ordained to eternal salvation and reprobates (or condemns) those who turn aside from that end. But Aquinas's more positive view of human nature as graced accorded a clearer role to human freedom. Moreover, he underscored the fact that there is a qualitative difference between predestination and reprobation. In the life of the elect, God's predestination is the cause of both the present grace they enjoy and the future glory they will attain. For the damned, God's reprobation is the cause of their future punishment, but not the cause of their present sin. Sin rests squarely on the shoulders of the human agent. See Aquinas, *Summa Theologiae* I.23.3.

25. Luther had in mind either Ezekiel 33:11 or 18:23. See Luther, "The Bondage of the Will," 138.

26. Luther, "The Bondage of the Will," 139.

27. Luther, "The Bondage of the Will," 62–63. See Bernard McGinn, "*Vere tu*

es Deus absconditus: The Hidden God in Luther and Some Mystics," in *Silence and the Word: Negative Theology and Incarnation*, eds. Oliver Davies and Denys Turner (Cambridge: Cambridge University Press, 2002), 94–114.

28. Brian A. Gerrish, "'To the Unknown God': Luther and Calvin on the Hiddenness of God," *The Journal of Religion* 53 (1973): 263–92, at 268.

29. Luther, "The Bondage of the Will," 139.

30. Luther, "The Bondage of the Will," 140.

31. Luther, "The Bondage of the Will," 139.

32. Luther, "The Bondage of the Will," 140.

33. Luther, "The Bondage of the Will," 146. Earlier Luther wrote, "Thus he does not will the death of a sinner, according to his word; but he wills it according to that inscrutable will of his" (Luther, "The Bondage of the Will," 140).

34. Luther, "The Bondage of the Will," 190.

35. Gerrish, "'To the Unknown God,'" 274.

36. Luther, "The Bondage of the Will," 190.

37. This point is clarified in François Wendel, "Justification and Predestination in Calvin," in *Readings in Calvin's Theology*, ed. Donald K. McKim (Grand Rapids: Baker Book House, 1984), 160–61; and Edward A. Dowey, *The Knowledge of God in Calvin's Theology* (New York: Columbia University Press, 1952), 213–14. See William C. Placher, *The Domestication of Transcendence: How Modern Thinking About God Went Wrong* (Louisville: Westminster John Knox Press, 1996), 60–64.

38. John Calvin, *Institutes of the Christian Religion*, trans. Ford Lewis Battles (Philadelphia: Westminster, 1960), 3.23.1.

39. Joseph L. Mangina, *Karl Barth: Theologian of Christian Witness* (Louisville: Westminster John Knox Press, 2004), 68–69.

40. Placher, *The Domestication of Transcendence*, 61.

41. Calvin, *Institutes* 3.21.1.

42. Gerrish, "'To the Unknown God,'" 281.

43. Gerrish, "'To the Unknown God,'" 283. See Calvin, *Institutes* 1.17.10–11.

44. John Calvin, "Commentaries on the Second Epistle of Peter," in *Calvin's Commentaries*, vol. 22, trans. John Own (Grand Rapids, MI: Baker, 1981), 419.

45. Gerrish, "'To the Unknown God,'" 285.

46. Michael J. Buckley, "Seventeenth-Century French Spirituality: Three Figures," in *Christian Spirituality: Post-Reformation and Modern*, eds. Louis Dupré and Don E. Saliers (New York: Crossroad, 1989), 28–68, at 35.

47. Buckley, "Seventeenth-Century French Spirituality," 35.

48. Paul Tillich named three types of anxiety that correspond to three periods of Western history. Ontic anxiety, concerned with fate and death, was predominant at the end of ancient civilization. Moral anxiety, marked by the fear of guilt and condemnation, colored the end of the Middle Ages. Our own time, the end of the modern period, is characterized by spiritual anxiety, the danger of emptiness and meaninglessness. See *The Courage To Be* (New Haven: Yale University Press, 1952), 40–63.

49. Charles Taylor, *Sources of the Self: The Making of the Modern Identity* (Cambridge, MA: Harvard University Press, 1989), 18.

50. Mangina, *Karl Barth*, 6. See Karl Barth, *Church Dogmatics*, vol. II/1, eds. G. W. Bromiley and T. F. Torrance (Edinburgh: T & T Clark, 1956), 93–97.

51. Barth, *Church Dogmatics* II/1, 183.

52. Barth, *Church Dogmatics* II/1, 188.

53. Barth, *Church Dogmatics* II/1, 542.

54. Barth, *Church Dogmatics* II/1, 542.

55. Daniel J. Peterson, "Speaking of God after the Death of God," *Dialog: A Journal of Theology* 44 (2005): 207–26, at 212.

56. Barth, *Church Dogmatics* II/2, 65–66.

57. Barth, *Church Dogmatics* II/2, 66.

58. Barth, *Church Dogmatics* II/2, 76.

59. Daniel W. Hardy, "Karl Barth," in *The Modern Theologians: An Introduction to Christian Theology Since 1918*, 3rd ed., ed. David F. Ford (Malden, MA: Blackwell, 2005), 21–42, at 32. Barth developed his theology of election within his treatment of the doctrine of God in volume II/2 of *Church Dogmatics*.

60. Barth, *Church Dogmatics* II/2, 3.

61. Barth, *Church Dogmatics* II/2, 104.

62. Mangina, *Karl Barth*, 69.

63. Barth, *Church Dogmatics* II/2, 63.

64. Barth, *Church Dogmatics* II/2, 76–77.

65. Bruce McCormack, "Grace and Being: The Role of God's Gracious Election in Karl Barth's Theological Ontology," in *The Cambridge Companion to Karl Barth*, ed. John Webster (Cambridge: Cambridge University Press, 2000), 92–110, at 97.

66. Von Balthasar, *The Theology of Karl Barth*, 157.

67. Barth, *Church Dogmatics* II/2, 103–16.

68. McCormack, "Grace and Being," 100.

69. McCormack, "Grace and Being," 98.

70. Barth, *Church Dogmatics* II/2, 13.

71. Mangina, *Karl Barth*, ix.

72. Barth, *Church Dogmatics* II/2, 52.

73. Mangina, *Karl Barth*, 69.

74. Barth, *Church Dogmatics* II/2, 3.

75. Barth, *Church Dogmatics* III/4, 634.

76. Barth, *Church Dogmatics* III/4, 598.

77. It is under the doctrine of creation (*Church Dogmatics*, vol. 3) that Barth considers calling in terms of human vocation. Under the doctrine of reconciliation (vol. 4), Barth takes up calling in terms of the divine summons—in more direct dialogue with his christology. See "The Vocation of Man," in *Church Dogmatics* IV/3.2, 481–680.

78. Barth, *Church Dogmatics* III/4, 598.

79. Barth, *Church Dogmatics* III/4, 599–600.

80. Barth, *Church Dogmatics* III/4, 565.

81. Barth, *Church Dogmatics* III/4, 569.

82. Barth, *Church Dogmatics* III/4, 603.

83. Barth, *Church Dogmatics* III/4, 604. Here Barth used *klesis* to refer to the divine summons (*Berufung*): "*Klesis* is the call of God. It comes from heaven and therefore from above. There can be no changing this. It is not to be co-ordinated with a human vocation and finally circuitously identified with the inner call. It is not the underlining or repeating of something old which men have already perceived and affirmed. It is always a new thing which God wants of man" (ibid., 603).

84. Barth, *Church Dogmatics* III/4, 575.

85. Barth, *Church Dogmatics* III/4, 634–36.

86. Barth, *Church Dogmatics* III/4, 636.

87. Barth, *Church Dogmatics* III/4, 607.

88. Barth, *Church Dogmatics* III/4, 636. See also ibid., 606.

89. Rowan Williams, *A Ray of Darkness: Sermons and Reflections* (Cambridge: Cowley Publications, 1995), 147.

90. Frederick Buechner, *Wishful Thinking: A Seeker's ABC* (San Francisco: HarperSanFrancisco, 1993), 119.

91. "Barth himself goes to the other pole and almost lifts callings beyond any historical context. . . . How does the calling relate to history, and how does history relate to the created order? When Barth speaks of this 'transitory' order he is surely right to resist the implied baptism of specific historical circumstances; but what of the fact that we live our lives in just these specific historical situations and no other?" (Marshall, *A Kind of Life*, 125–26).

92. Brunner, *The Divine Imperative*, 615.

Chapter Four—pages 125–158

1. Gerard Manley Hopkins, "As kingfishers catch fire."

2. Thomas Merton, "Things in Their Identity," in *Seeds of Contemplation* (New York: Dell, 1949), 26.

3. Jean-Paul Sartre, "Existentialism is a Humanism," in *Existentialism from Dostoevsky to Sartre*, ed. Walter Kaufmann (New York: Meridian Books, 1975), 345–69, at 356–57. Avery Dulles highlights the Sartre lecture in his "Finding God's Will: Rahner's Interpretation of the Ignatian Election," *Woodstock Letters* 94 (1965): 139–52, at 139.

4. Sartre, "Existentialism Is a Humanism," 355.

5. In a different context and toward a different end, Karl Rahner pointed out that "it is only very indirectly or not at all that the Church can dissuade from a mistaken choice of profession or marriage, although this can be much more devastating than a sin, against which she does protest" (see "Principles and Prescriptions," in *The Dynamic Element in the Church*, trans. W. J. O'Hara [New York: Herder and Herder, 1964], 13–41, at 39).

6. See David Tracy, *The Analogical Imagination: Christian Theology and the Culture of Pluralism* (New York: Crossroad, 1981).

7. See Philip Endean, *Karl Rahner and Ignatian Spirituality* (Oxford: Oxford University Press, 2001), 103–6; Herbert Vorgrimler, *Understanding Karl Rahner:*

An Introduction to His Life and Thought (New York: Crossroad, 1986), 52. Rahner made explicit reference to Lahitton in a lengthy footnote in his important 1956 essay on discernment, "The Logic of Concrete Individual Knowledge in Ignatius Loyola," in *The Dynamic Element in the Church*, 98–100; as well as in "Being Open to God as Ever Greater," *Theological Investigations*, vol. 7, trans. David Bourke (New York: Herder and Herder, 1971), 25–46, at 42; and "On the Question of a Formal Existential Ethic," in *Theological Investigations*, vol. 2, trans. Karl-H. Kruger (Baltimore: Helicon Press, 1963), 217–34, at 233. For Hürth's view, see Franz Hürth, "Zur Frage nach dem Wesen des Berufs," *Scholastik* 3 (1928): 94–102.

8. Joseph Lahitton, *La Vocation Sacerdotale* (Paris: Lethielleux, 1909), 31–33, cited in Endean, *Karl Rahner and Ignatian Spirituality*, 104.

9. Rahner, "On the Question of a Formal Existential Ethic," 233.

10. "Rahner—convinced that Ignatius and other mystical writers had truly experienced God—began to examine the 'conditions for the very possibility' of such experience. He did so first in an apparently only historical way . . . and then in a more systematic and explicitly transcendental way" (James A. Wiseman, "'I Have Experienced God': Religious Experience in the Theology of Karl Rahner," *American Benedictine Review* 44 [1993]: 22–57, at 28). Rahner's early thoughts on the *unmittelbare Gotteserfahrung* of the mystics can be glimpsed in the footnotes and commentary he added to Marcel Viller's history of early Christian spirituality. See *Aszese und Mystik in der Väterzeit*, ed. Karl Heinz Neufeld (Freiburg: Herder, 1989). For a nuanced treatment, see Endean, *Karl Rahner and Ignatian Spirituality*, 12–67.

11. In a different context, Rahner acknowledged the difficulties that come in trying to understand the individual experience of God within the context of a deficient and dualistic theology of grace: "One would have to ask whether the experimental contact with grace in infused contemplation . . . is compatible with the theological data concerning the nature of grace, whether, in other words, a true experiencing of grace, in the strict sense of a grasping of the experienced reality in its proper intelligibility and its own being, is reconcilable with the fact that grace is necessarily and invariably also uncreated grace . . . and whether such an experience would not be conceptually identical with the Beatific Vision. Theologically, therefore, the question would have to be posed, whether and how there can be any middle term between faith and immediate vision of God, and if not, how then mystical experience should be conceived so that it remains really genuine and yet falls unmistakably into the sphere of faith" (Karl Rahner, "Ignatian Mysticism of Joy in the World," in *Theological Investigations*, vol. 3, trans. Karl-H. and Boniface Kruger [Baltimore: Helicon Press, 1967], 277–93, at 279).

12. As we will see below, Rahner saw this insight as Ignatius of Loyola's most important contribution to Western spirituality. See Rahner, "The Logic of Concrete Individual Knowledge in Ignatius Loyola," 104.

13. See the nuanced assessment of visionary phenomena in Karl Rahner, *Visions and Prophecies*, trans. Charles Henkey and Richard Strachan (New York: Herder and Herder, 1963).

14. Karl Rahner, *Foundations of Christian Faith: An Introduction to the Idea of Christianity*, trans. William V. Dych (New York: Crossroad, 1978), 20.

15. This metaphor of the horizon—coming from Rahner himself—is beautifully evoked by Elizabeth A. Johnson in *Quest for the Living God: Mapping Frontiers in the Theology of God* (New York: Continuum, 2007), 34.

16. Rahner, *Foundations of Christian Faith*, 21.

17. See "Experience," in Karl Rahner and Herbert Vorgrimler, *Theological Dictionary* (New York: Herder and Herder, 1965), 162.

18. Rahner, *Foundations of Christian Faith*, 226.

19. Karl Rahner, "The Concept of Mystery in Catholic Theology," in *Theological Investigations*, vol. 4, trans. Kevin Smyth (Baltimore: Helicon, 1966), 36–73. See James J. Bacik, *Apologetics and the Eclipse of Mystery: Mystagogy According to Karl Rahner* (Notre Dame, IN: University of Notre Dame Press, 1980).

20. Stephen J. Duffy, "Experience of Grace," in *The Cambridge Companion to Karl Rahner*, eds. Declan Marmion and Mary E. Hines (Cambridge: Cambridge University Press, 2005), 43–62, at 44. See id., *The Graced Horizon: Nature and Grace in Modern Catholic Thought* (Collegeville, MN: Liturgical Press, 1992).

21. Karl Rahner, "Some Implications of the Scholastic Concept of Uncreated Grace," in *Theological Investigations*, vol. 1, trans. Cornelius Ernst (Baltimore: Helicon Press, 1961), 319–46, at 341.

22. Peter Fransen, *The New Life of Grace*, trans. Georges Dupont (New York: Desclee Co., 1969), 100.

23. Rahner, *Foundations of Christian Faith*, 121.

24. Rahner, "Some Implications of the Scholastic Concept of Uncreated Grace," 336.

25. Karl Rahner, "Ignatius of Loyola Speaks to a Modern Jesuit," in *Ignatius of Loyola*, trans. Rosaleen Ockenden (London: Collins, 1978), 19. Translation from Endean, *Karl Rahner and Ignatian Spirituality*, 44.

26. Rahner, "Ignatius of Loyola Speaks," 15.

27. Karl Rahner, *Is Christian Life Possible Today?*, trans. Salvator Attanasio (Denville, NJ: Dimension Books, 1984), 65.

28. Pius XII's encyclical *Humani Generis* stated, "others corrupt the 'gratuity' of the supernatural order, since they hold that God could not create beings endowed with intellect without ordering and calling them to the beatific vision" (cited in David Coffey, "The Whole Rahner on the Supernatural Existential," *Theological Studies* 65 [2004], 95–118, at 99). Many saw this charge directed at de Lubac. He himself denied that it was intended for him. See Henri de Lubac, *The Mystery of the Supernatural*, trans. Rosemary Sheed (New York: Crossroad, 1998), 50, 80. See also Duffy, *The Graced Horizon*, 50–65.

29. The term first appeared in "Eine Antwort," *Orientierung* 14 (1950): 141–45, which was republished in modified form as "Über das Verhältnis von Natur und Gnade," *Schriften zur Theologie* 1 (Einsiedeln: Benziger, 1954), 323–45. English translation: "Concerning the Relationship Between Nature and Grace," in *Theological Investigations*, vol. 1, trans. Cornelius Ernst (Baltimore: Helicon Press, 1961), 297–317.

30. Rahner directed his response in this early article to another article, written by an anonymous "D"—whom David Coffey identifies as the French Jesuit Emile Delaye. See David Coffey, "Some Resources for Students of *la nouvell théologie*," *Philosophy and Theology* 11 (1999): 381–94, at 399–402. D's article appeared as "Ein Weg zur Bestimmung des Verhältnisses von Natur und Gnade," *Orientierung* 14 (1950): 138–41. An English translation is available in the Coffey article cited above.

31. Coffey, "The Whole Rahner on the Supernatural Existential," 99.

32. The classic text is Martin Heidegger, *Being and Time*, trans. John Macquarrie and Edward Robinson (New York: Harper & Row, 1962).

33. The offer of God's self-communication touches every human person "as an existential of their concrete existence" (Rahner, *Foundations of Christian Faith*, 127).

34. Rahner, *Foundations of Christian Faith*, 127.

35. Karl Rahner, "The Individual in the Church," in *Nature and Grace*, trans. Dinah Wharton (New York: Sheed & Ward, 1963), 51–83, at 57–58.

36. Rahner, "The Individual in the Church," 58.

37. Karl Rahner, "The Significance in Redemptive History of the Individual Member of the Church," in *The Christian Commitment: Essays in Pastoral Theology*, trans. Cecily Hastings (New York: Sheed & Ward, 1963), 75–113, at 85.

38. Rahner, *Foundations of Christian Faith*, 126. See ibid., 116–37.

39. Endean, *Karl Rahner and Ignatian Spirituality*, 102.

40. Karl Rahner, *Karl Rahner in Dialogue: Conversations and Interviews 1965–1982*, eds. Paul Imhof and Hubert Biallowons, trans. Harvey D. Egan (New York: Crossroad, 1986), 191. About this passage Matthew Ashley comments, "Yet, its rhetorical power notwithstanding, it is by no means easy to give this claim a more specific content, and lacking that it is often more parenetically asserted than systematically mined for insights into Rahner's contribution to theology" ("Review of *Karl Rahner and Ignatian Spirituality*," *Spiritus* 2 [2002]: 112–15, at 112). As Ashley's review reveals, the work of Philip Endean is one attempt to provide just such specific content. Endean questions whether Ignatius was as central to Rahner's thought as Rahner later claimed. He argues that Rahner's transcendental theological system served as the lens through which Rahner read Ignatius, a lens that caused Rahner to read into Ignatius Rahner's own presuppositions. Still, Endean admits that Ignatius offered a decisive psychological and spiritual impetus to Rahner's work. See Endean, *Karl Rahner and Ignatian Spirituality*, 241. On the Ignatian roots of Rahner's spirituality, see also Harvey D. Egan, *The Spiritual Exercises and the Ignatian Mystical Horizon* (Saint Louis: Institute of Jesuit Sources, 1976); id., *Karl Rahner: Mystic of Everyday Life* (New York: Crossroad, 1998); Declan Marmion, *A Spirituality of Everyday Faith: A Theological Investigation of the Notion of Spirituality in Karl Rahner* (Louvain: Peeters Press, 1998); George Vass, *The Mystery of Man and the Foundations of a Theological System: Understanding Karl Rahner*, 2 vols. (London: Sheed & Ward, 1985).

41. Karl Rahner, *Faith in a Wintry Season: Conversations and Interviews with Karl Rahner in the Last Years of His Life*, ed. Paul Imhof and Hubert Biallowons, translation ed. Harvey D. Egan (New York: Crossroad, 1990), 104.

42. When he died, Rahner left on his desk an unfinished open letter, which repeated a common complaint: "I am of the opinion—though this is not to be taken as definitive—that we Jesuits, down the history of our theology (and probably also of our praxis), have not been very Ignatian at all" (Karl Rahner, "A Letter to a Young Jesuit in the Charismatic Renewal," *Centrum Ignatianum Spiritualitatis* 15 [1984]: 131–34, at 133).

43. Karl Rahner, "Modern Piety and the Experience of Retreats," in *Theological Investigations*, vol. 16, trans. David Morland (New York: Crossroad, 1983), 135–55, at 138–39.

44. *Exercises*, n. 15, in *Ignatius of Loyola: The Spiritual Exercises and Selected Works*, ed. George E. Ganss (New York: Paulist Press, 1991).

45. Rahner, "Modern Piety," 141.

46. The *Exercises* clearly specify that the object of election must be indifferent or good in and of itself; it cannot contradict church teaching. Thus Ignatius presumed that the retreatant is already working within the orbit of universal norms proposed by the church. The real issue is discovering God's particular will within this arena (*Exercises*, n. 170). Rahner argued that the proper response to a problematic "essentialist" ethic that relies exclusively on universal norms is not a "situation ethic" that ignores these norms. Instead he suggested an "existentialist" ethic as a complementary moral logic, one that would attend to the question of particular imperatives in a way that did not simply reduce them to the application of universal norms to a concrete situation. At the end of his seminal essay, Rahner noted the implications of this existentialist ethic on several other theological topics, including the interpretation of the *Exercises* and vocational discernment. See Rahner, "On the Question of a Formal Existential Ethic," 217–34. His dictionary article on vocation likewise makes this link: "The further discussion of vocation merges into that of the knowledge of particular obligations, as distinguished from knowledge of the general norms that limit the field of what is right in particular cases but cannot clearly define it. It is the problem of 'individual ethics' (Existential ethics)" (Karl Rahner and Herbert Vorgrimler, *Theological Dictionary*, ed. Cornelius Ernst, trans. Richard Strachan [New York: Herder and Herder, 1965], 484).

47. Rahner, "Modern Piety," 141. In a note, Rahner adds, "Ignatius developed a logic of existential decision by means of his rules of choice, which had not existed in this form before, despite the traditional doctrine of the discernment of spirits. Since then, there has never been sufficient theological study of the real meaning and presuppositions of this Ignatian innovation. Its importance remains valid today, but it must be removed from the context of the choice of a vocation in the Church and clearly expressed in terms of its general significance for human existence."

48. First published as "Die ignatianische Logik der existentiellen Erkenntnis: Über einige theologische Probleme in den Wahlregeln der Exerzitien des Heiligen Ignatius," in *Ignatius von Loyola: Seine geistliche Gestalt und sein Vermächtnis (1556–1956)*, ed. Friedrich Wulf (Würzburg: Echer, 1956), 343–405.

49. *Exercises*, nn. 175–78.

50. Rahner, "The Logic of Concrete Individual Knowledge in Ignatius Loyola," 116.

51. We should say, the goodness of the choice *for the individual*. It bears repeating that Ignatius had already limited the possible objects of the election to things that are either indifferent or good in and of themselves. The question, then, is which decision is good for this particular person at this particular time. Rahner, "The Logic of Concrete Individual Knowledge in Ignatius Loyola," 118.

52. *Exercises*, n. 32.

53. Rahner, "The Logic of Concrete Individual Knowledge in Ignatius Loyola," 120–21.

54. *Exercises*, n. 330. The concept of "consolation without preceding cause" occurs in two places in the *Exercises*, here as the second rule for the Second Week, and a few paragraphs later, in the eighth rule (n. 336).

55. Francisco de Suárez, *Tractatus de Religione Societatis Jesu* (Bruxellis: Greuse, 1857), 510, cited in Egan, *The Spiritual Exercises and the Ignatian Mystical Horizon*, 32.

56. Rahner, "The Logic of Concrete Individual Knowledge in Ignatius Loyola," 131.

57. A summary of four recent views, including a critical appraisal of Rahner, can be found in Jules J. Toner, *A Commentary on Saint Ignatius' Rules for the Discernment of Spirits* (Saint Louis: Institute of Jesuit Sources, 1982), 291–313. See also Egan, *The Spiritual Exercises and the Ignatian Mystical Horizon*, 31–65; Endean, *Karl Rahner and Ignatian Spirituality*, 127–82; Dulles, "Finding God's Will," 139–52. A summary of the 1956 article can be found in "The Ignatian Process for Discovering the Will of God in an Existential Situation," in *Ignatius of Loyola: His Personality and Spiritual Heritage (1556–1956)*, ed. Friedrich Wulf (Saint Louis: Institute of Jesuit Sources, 1977), 280–89.

58. Rahner, "The Logic of Concrete Individual Knowledge in Ignatius Loyola," 145–46.

59. Rahner, "The Logic of Concrete Individual Knowledge in Ignatius Loyola," 134.

60. Rahner, "The Logic of Concrete Individual Knowledge in Ignatius Loyola," 123. By introducing a more nuanced view of human consciousness, Rahner believed that he had made space for a genuine experience of grace that does not contradict the teaching of Trent, namely, that no one can know with absolute certainty whether he or she is among the predestined. See Karl Rahner, "Religious Enthusiasm and the Experience of Grace," in *Theological Investigations*, vol. 16, trans. David Morland (New York: Crossroad, 1983), 35–51, at 36.

61. Endean argues that Rahner's remarks on the consolation without cause need to be tempered by reading them within the context of his epistemology, rather than seeing them as an exception to his general account (*Karl Rahner and Ignatian Spirituality*, 133). Others highlight the tension between this account and his specific comments on Ignatian discernment. See Martin Maier, "La Théologie des Exercices de Karl Rahner," *Recherces de science rélieuse* 79 (1991): 535–60, at 552; and Matthew Ashley, *Interruptions: Mysticism, Politics, and Theology in*

the Work of Johann Baptist Metz (Notre Dame, IN: University of Notre Dame Press, 1998), 182–83. Still others reject Rahner's exegesis of Ignatius in toto (e.g., Toner, *A Commentary on Saint Ignatius' Rules for the Discernment of Spirits*, 301–13). Rahner himself acknowledged that his particular exegetical arguments were not decisive, admitting that he was not providing a full historical study but only seeking a "stimulus" for his own thought.

62. Rahner, "The Logic of Concrete Individual Knowledge in Ignatius Loyola," 149.

63. *Exercises*, n. 336.

64. Rahner, "The Logic of Concrete Individual Knowledge in Ignatius Loyola," 149.

65. Rahner, "The Logic of Concrete Individual Knowledge in Ignatius Loyola," 135.

66. Endean, *Karl Rahner and Ignatian Spirituality*, 102.

67. Rahner, "The Logic of Concrete Individual Knowledge in Ignatius Loyola," 156–57.

68. Rahner, "The Logic of Concrete Individual Knowledge in Ignatius Loyola," 158.

69. Rahner, "The Logic of Concrete Individual Knowledge in Ignatius Loyola," 159.

70. Rahner, "The Logic of Concrete Individual Knowledge in Ignatius Loyola," 166.

71. Rahner, "The Logic of Concrete Individual Knowledge in Ignatius Loyola," 166.

72. Karl Rahner, "Ignatian Spirituality and Devotion to the Heart of Jesus," in *Mission and Grace*, vol. 3, trans. Cecily Hastings (London: Sheed & Ward, 1966, German original 1955), 176–210.

73. Rahner, "Ignatian Spirituality and Devotion to the Heart of Jesus," 204–5.

74. Rahner, "Ignatian Spirituality and Devotion to the Heart of Jesus," 205.

75. Rahner, "Ignatian Spirituality and Devotion to the Heart of Jesus," 205–6.

76. Rahner, *Faith in a Wintry Season*, 95.

77. Dulles, "Finding God's Will," 149–50.

78. Coffey, "The Whole Rahner on the Supernatural Existential," 95–118.

79. Karl Rahner, "Questions of Controversial Theology on Justification," in *Theological Investigations*, vol. 4, trans. Kevin Smyth (Baltimore: Helicon Press, 1966), 189–218, at 218.

80. Thomas Merton, "Things in Their Identity," in *Seeds of Contemplation* (Norfolk, CT: New Directions, 1949), 24–30, at 26–27 (emphasis in original).

81. Karl Rahner, "The Theological Concept of Concupiscentia," in *Theological Studies*, vol. 1, trans. Cornelius Ernst (Baltimore: Helicon Press, 1961), 347–82.

82. Rahner, *Foundations of Christian Faith*, 106–15.

83. Rahner, *Foundations of Christian Faith*, 111.

84. Rahner, "Modern Piety," 141 (emphasis added).

85. Duffy, "Experience of Grace," 58.

86. Merton, "Things in Their Identity," 28.

87. Duffy, *The Graced Horizon*, 99.

88. Karl Rahner, "The *Exercises* Today," in *Christian at the Crossroads* (New York: Seabury Press, 1975), 72.

89. Karl Rahner, "Christian Living Formerly and Today," in *Theological Investigations*, vol. 7, trans. David Bourke (New York: Herder and Herder, 1971), 3–24, at 15. Also id., "The Spirituality of the Church of the Future," in *Theological Investigations*, vol. 20, trans. Edward Quinn (New York: Crossroad, 1981), 143–53, at 149. See Harvey Egan, "'The Devout Christian of the Future Will . . . be a "Mystic."' Mysticism and Karl Rahner's Theology," in *Theology and Discovery: Essays in Honor of Karl Rahner, S.J.*, ed. William J. Kelly (Milwaukee, WI: Marquette University Press, 1980), 139–58.

90. Rahner, "The Spirituality of the Church of the Future," 149. See Louis Dupré, "Spiritual Life and the Survival of Christianity: Reflections at the End of the Millennium," *Cross Currents* 48 (Fall 1998): 381–90.

Chapter Five—pages 159–192

1. John Paul II, I Will Give You Shepherds: On the Formation of Priests in the Circumstances of the Present Day (*Pastores Dabo Vobis*) (Washington, DC: USCCB Publishing, 1992) 35.

2. J. R. R. Tolkien, *The Two Towers*, vol. 2 of The Lord of the Rings Series (Boston: Houghton Mifflin Co., 1988), 321.

3. Alasdair MacIntyre, *After Virtue: A Study in Moral Theory*, 2nd ed. (Notre Dame, IN: University of Notre Dame Press, 1984), 204.

4. MacIntyre, *After Virtue*, 206.

5. MacIntyre, *After Virtue*, 205.

6. MacIntyre, *After Virtue*, 211.

7. MacIntyre, *After Virtue*, 213.

8. MacIntyre, *After Virtue*, 216.

9. MacIntyre, *After Virtue*, 220.

10. MacIntyre, *After Virtue*, 220.

11. MacIntyre, *After Virtue*, 221.

12. It may be more appropriate to speak of Christian narrative*s* or tradition*s*, in the plural, in order to better capture the complex diversity across various Christian churches and within each church. Indeed, as earlier chapters have demonstrated, even subsets within "the Christian tradition," such as the Ignatian spiritual tradition, are themselves internally diverse. In what follows, "the Christian narrative" and "the Christian tradition" will be used to signify the unitary whole of the two-millennial-old movement initiated by Jesus of Nazareth, but always accompanying this claim to unity is a recognition of the almost infinite strands of tradition that constitute it.

13. A classic work on biblical hermeneutics is Hans W. Frei, *The Eclipse of Biblical Narrative: A Study in Eighteenth and Nineteenth Century Hermeneutics* (New Haven, CT: Yale University Press, 1974). An alternative, less dialectical, approach to narrative is that of Paul Ricoeur. See id., "The Narrative Function," in *Hermeneutics*

and the Human Sciences, ed. John B. Thompson (Cambridge: Cambridge University Press, 1981), 274–96; id., *Time and Narrative*, trans. K. McLaughlin and D. Pellauer (Chicago: University of Chicago Press, 1984); Gary Comstock, "Truth or Meaning: Ricoeur versus Frei on Biblical Narrative," *Journal of Religion* 66 (1986): 117–40. For an overview of narrative theology, see Michael Goldberg, *Theology and Narrative: A Critical Introduction*, 2nd ed. (Philadelphia: Trinity Press International, 1991); Stanley Hauerwas and L. Gregory Jones, *Why Narrative? Readings in Narrative Theology* (Grand Rapids, MI: Eerdmans, 1989); Keith E. Yandell, ed., *Faith and Narrative* (Oxford: Oxford University Press, 2001). Two Catholic contributions to this conversation are Robert A. Krieg, *Story Shaped Christology: The Role of Narrative in Identifying Jesus Christ* (New York: Paulist Press, 1988); and Terrence W. Tilley, *Story Theology* (Wilmington, DE: Michael Glazier, 1985).

14. George Hunsinger, *How to Read Karl Barth: The Shape of His Theology* (New York: Oxford University Press, 1991), 46.

15. Hunsinger, *How to Read Karl Barth*, 47.

16. Frei, *The Eclipse of Biblical Narrative*, 220.

17. Frei, *The Eclipse of Biblical Narrative*, 130.

18. James Fodor, "Postliberal Theology," in *The Modern Theologians: An Introduction to Christian Theology since 1918*, ed. David F. Ford (Malden, MA: Blackwell, 2005), 229–48, at 234.

19. George A. Lindbeck, *The Nature of Doctrine: Religion and Theology in a Postliberal Age* (Philadelphia: Westminster Press, 1984).

20. For a representative selection, see John Berkman and Michael Cartwright, eds., *The Hauerwas Reader* (Durham, NC: Duke University Press, 2001).

21. Gerard Mannion explains the term "neoexclusivism" in *Ecclesiology and Postmodernity: Questions for the Church in Our Time* (Collegeville, MN: Liturgical Press, 2007), 43–74.

22. Lieven Boeve, *Interrupting Tradition: An Essay on Christian Faith in a Postmodern Context* (Louvain: Peeters Press, 2003), 24.

23. Jean-François Lyotard, *The Postmodern Condition—A Report on Knowledge*, trans. Régis Durand (Manchester: Manchester University Press, 1984), xxiv.

24. Boeve, *Interrupting Tradition*, 79.

25. Boeve, *Interrupting Tradition*, 61.

26. Boeve, *Interrupting Tradition*, 94.

27. Boeve, *Interrupting Tradition*, 62.

28. Boeve, *Interrupting Tradition*, 90–91.

29. Boeve, *Interrupting Tradition*, 99.

30. Lieven Boeve, "Beyond the Modern-Anti-Modern Dilemma: *Gaudium et Spes* and Theological Method in a Postmodern Context," *Horizons* 34 (2007): 292–305, at 302 (emphasis in original).

31. Boeve, "Beyond the Modern–Anti-Modern Dilemma," 303.

32. Boeve, *Interrupting Tradition*, 106 (emphasis in original).

33. Boeve, *Interrupting Tradition*, 131, citing L. Aerts (emphasis in original).

34. Boeve, *Interrupting Tradition*, 120.

35. Boeve, *Interrupting Tradition*, 134.

36. Boeve, *Interrupting Tradition*, 131.

37. Boeve, *Interrupting Tradition*, 133. See Edward Schillebeeckx, *Jesus: An Experiment in Christology*, trans. Hubert Hoskins (New York: Crossroad, 1995), 256–71.

38. David Tracy, *On Naming the Present: Reflections on God, Hermeneutics, and Church* (Maryknoll, NY: Orbis, 1994), 16–17. Citing Emmanuel Levinas, Tracy calls this "the secret flaw" of postmodern thought.

39. See Lieven Boeve, *God Interrupts History: Theology in a Time of Upheaval* (New York: Continuum, 2007).

40. See chapter 2.

41. Louis Dupré, "Alternatives to the Cogito," *Review of Metaphysics* 40 (1987): 687–716, at 711. See "Seeking Christian Interiority: An Interview with Louis Dupré," *The Christian Century* (July 16–23, 1997): 654–60, revised and published in essay form in Louis Dupré, "Spiritual Life and the Survival of Christianity: Reflections at the End of the Millennium," *Cross Currents* 48 (1998): 381–90.

42. MacIntyre, *After Virtue*, 263.

43. Dupré, "Alternatives to the Cogito," 716.

44. Dupré, "Seeking Christian Interiority," 655.

45. Boeve, *Interrupting Tradition*, 87.

46. Boeve, *Interrupting Tradition*, 88.

47. Boeve, *Interrupting Tradition*, 95.

48. See Lieven Boeve, "The Sacramental Interruption of Rituals of Life," *Heythrop Journal* 44 (2003): 401–17, at 412. Boeve draws the category from Metz, adding to Metz's concern for the interruption forced by the encounter with suffering his own recognition of the interruption brought on by the postmodern "other." See Lieven Boeve, "The Shortest Definition of Religion: Interruption," *Communio Viatorum* 46 (2004): 299–322; id., *God Interrupts History*, 203–6.

49. Lewis S. Mudge, *The Church as Moral Community: Ecclesiology and Ethics in Ecumenical Debate* (New York: Continuum, 1998), 77–79.

50. John Courtney Murray, "This Matter of Religious Freedom," *America* 112 (January 9, 1945): 40–43, at 43.

51. Cited in John W. O'Malley, *What Happened at Vatican II* (Cambridge, MA: Harvard University Press, 2008), 38.

52. John W. O'Malley, "Vatican II: Did Anything Happen?" *Theological Studies* 67 (2006): 3–33, at 25.

53. See O'Malley, "Vatican II: Did Anything Happen?" 21–31; id., *What Happened at Vatican II*; id., "The Style of Vatican II," *America* 188 (February 24, 2003): 12–15.

54. O'Malley, *What Happened at Vatican II*, 48.

55. *Sacrosanctum Concilium* 36, 63.

56. *Sacrosanctum Concilium* 37.

57. See *Lumen Gentium* 26; *Christus Dominus* 11; also Jean-Marie Tillard, *L'Église Locale: Ecclésiologie de communion et catholicité* (Paris: Cerf, 1995); Joseph A. Komonchak, "The Local Church and the Church Catholic: The Contemporary Theological Problematic," *The Jurist* 52 (1992): 416–47; and Christopher Ruddy,

The Local Church: Tillard and the Future of Catholic Ecclesiology (New York: Crossroad, 2006).

58. Cited in O'Malley, *What Happened at Vatican II*, 17. The speech came, significantly, in a ceremony to mark the end of the Octave for Christian Unity.

59. *Nostra Aetate* 2.

60. Karl Rahner, *The Shape of the Church to Come*, trans. Edward Quinn (New York: Seabury Press, 1974), 93.

61. Karl Rahner, "Observations on the Factor of the Charismatic in the Church," *Theological Investigations*, vol. 12, trans. David Bourke (New York: Seabury Press, 1974), 81–97, at 93–94.

62. See Rahner, *The Shape of the Church to Come*, 93–101.

63. Rahner, "Observations on the Factor of the Charismatic," 89.

64. Rahner, "Observations on the Factor of the Charismatic," 94.

65. Rahner, "Observations on the Factor of the Charismatic," 97.

66. Thanks to Richard Lennan for his keen insight on this point, and to Chris Pramuk for the language to articulate it.

67. Vincent J. Miller, *Consuming Religion: Christian Faith and Practice in a Consumer Culture* (New York: Continuum, 2003).

68. Miller, *Consuming Religion*, 210.

69. Miller, *Consuming Religion*, 142.

70. Miller, *Consuming Religion*, 141.

71. Miller, *Consuming Religion*, 141.

72. Miller, *Consuming Religion*, 142.

73. Robert Wuthnow, *After Heaven: Spirituality in America since the 1950s* (Berkeley: University of California Press, 1998).

74. Charles Taylor, *A Secular Age* (Cambridge, MA: Harvard University Press, 2007), 515.

75. Taylor, *A Secular Age*, 516.

76. Taylor, *A Secular Age*, 516.

77. Taylor, *A Secular Age*, 516.

78. William C. Spohn, *Go and Do Likewise: Jesus and Ethics* (New York: Continuum, 1999), 43.

79. Spohn, *Go and Do Likewise*, 35.

80. Craig Dykstra, "Reconceiving Practice," in *Shifting Boundaries: Contextual Approaches to the Structure of Theological Education*, eds. Barbara G. Wheeler and Edward Farley (Louisville: Westminster John Knox Press, 1991), 35–66, at 43.

81. Terrence W. Tilley, *The Disciples' Jesus: Christology as Reconciling Practice* (Maryknoll, NY: Orbis, 2008), 14. Tilley's work represents a sustained Catholic engagement with the questions of narrative and practice. The trajectory of his thought can be traced through id., *Story Theology*; id., *Postmodern Theologies* (Maryknoll, NY: Orbis, 1995); id., *The Wisdom of Religious Commitment* (Washington, DC: Georgetown University Press, 1995); id., *Inventing Catholic Tradition* (Maryknoll, NY: Orbis, 2000); id., *History, Theology and Faith: Dissolving the Modern Problematic* (Maryknoll, NY: Orbis, 2004).

82. Tilley, *The Disciples' Jesus*, 228–29.

83. Rahner, "Observations on the Factor of the Charismatic," 97.

84. Karl Rahner, "On the Structure of the People of the Church Today," in *Theological Investigations*, vol. 12, trans. David Bourke (New York: Seabury Press, 1974), 218–28, at 222–23. See Richard Lennan, *The Ecclesiology of Karl Rahner* (Oxford: Oxford University Press, 1995), 215.

85. *Sacrosanctum Concilium* 14.

86. Miller, *Consuming Religion*, 211.

87. Miller, *Consuming Religion*, 211.

88. Boeve, *God Interrupts History*, 206.

Chapter Six—pages 193–229

1. *The Collected Works of Mahatma* Gandhi, vol. 89 (Ahmedabad: Navajivan Pub., 1983), 125, cited in *Mohandas Gandhi: Essential Writings*, ed. John Dear (Maryknoll, NY: Orbis, 2002), 190–91.

2. Dean Brackley, *The Call to Discernment in Troubled Times: New Perspectives on the Transformative Wisdom of Ignatius of Loyola* (New York: Crossroad, 2004), 59.

3. Gustavo Gutiérrez, "Toward a Theology of Liberation (July 1968)," in *Liberation Theology: A Documentary History*, ed. Alfred T. Hennelly (Maryknoll, NY: Orbis, 1990), 62–76. Gutiérrez has returned repeatedly to this image over the course of his career, recently in "The Option for the Poor Arises From Faith in Christ," *Theological Studies* 70 (2009): 317–26, at 318. See Maureen O'Connell's insightful use of the Samaritan story in *Compassion: Loving Our Neighbor in an Age of Globalization* (Maryknoll, NY: Orbis, 2009).

4. David Tracy, *On Naming the Present: Reflections on God, Hermeneutics, and Church* (Maryknoll, NY: Orbis, 1994), 21.

5. Frederick Buechner, *Wishful Thinking: A Theological ABC* (New York: Harper & Row, 1973), 95.

6. Johann Baptist Metz, *Faith in History and Society: Toward a Practical Fundamental Theology*, trans. J. Matthew Ashley (New York: Crossroad, 2007), 158.

7. Lieven Boeve, *God Interrupts History: Theology in a Time of Upheaval* (New York: Continuum, 2007), 203. See also id., "The Shortest Definition of Religion: Interruption," *Communio Viatorum* 46 (2004): 299–322, at 315.

8. Johann Baptist Metz, "In Place of a Foreword: On the Biographical Itinerary of My Theology," in *A Passion for God: The Mystical-Political Dimension of Christianity*, trans. J. Matthew Ashley (New York: Paulist Press, 1998), 1–5, at 1–2.

9. J. Matthew Ashley argues convincingly that the discontinuities between the thought of Metz and Rahner rest on deeper continuities. Ultimately, the differences can be traced not to differing theological or philosophical commitments but to different spiritualities. See *Interruptions: Mysticism, Politics, and Theology in the Work of Johann Baptist Metz* (Notre Dame, IN: University of Notre Dame Press, 1998).

10. Johann Baptist Metz, "On the Way to a Postidealist Theology," in *A Passion for God*, 39–40.

11. Metz, *Faith in History and Society*, 157. Metz is quoting Bertolt Brecht.

12. J. Matthew Ashley, "Johann Baptist Metz," in *The Blackwell Companion to Political Theology*, eds. Peter Scott and William T. Cavanaugh (Malden, MA: Blackwell Publishing), 241–55, at 251.

13. Johann Baptist Metz, "Suffering unto God," trans. J. Matthew Ashley, *Critical Inquiry* 20 (1994): 611–22, at 612. See also id., "Theology as Theodicy?" in *A Passion for God*, 54–71.

14. Ashley, *Interruptions*, 198.

15. Metz, "In Place of a Foreword," 4.

16. Metz, "On the Way to a Postidealist Theology," 47–48.

17. Metz, "On the Way to a Postidealist Theology," 48.

18. The translation is Ashley's, who captures in English the dynamic nature of the relationship between humanity and God evoked by Metz's phrase *Leiden an Gott*. See Ashley, *Interruptions*, 127–29, 153–63, 218 n. 31.

19. Discussion of Metz's treatment of time, though central to his project, would take us too far afield here. See the seminal article by J. Matthew Ashley, "Apocalypticism in Political and Liberation Theology: Toward an Historical *Docta Ignorantia*," *Horizons* 27 (2000): 22–43; also the exchange between Ashley and David Tracy in *The Option for the Poor in Christian Theology*, ed. Daniel G. Groody (Notre Dame, IN: University of Notre Dame Press, 2007), 119–54. Helpful context is provided in Walter Lowe, "Prospects for a Postmodern Christian Theology: Apocalyptic Without Reserve," *Modern Theology* 15 (1999): 17–24; Stephen D. O'Leary, *Arguing the Apocalypse: A Theory of Millennial Rhetoric* (New York: Oxford University Press, 1994); Christopher Pramuk, "Apocalypticism in a Catholic Key: Lessons from Thomas Merton," *Horizons* 36 (2009): 1–30.

20. See Brackley, *The Call to Discernment in Troubled Times*.

21. Michael E. Lee, *Bearing the Weight of Salvation: The Soteriology of Ignacio Ellacuría* (New York: Crossroad, 2009), 64.

22. See the opening account in Kevin F. Burke, *The Ground Beneath the Cross: The Theology of Ignacio Ellacuría* (Washington, DC: Georgetown University Press, 2000). On Ellacuría's life, see Teresa Whitfield, *Paying the Price: Ignacio Ellacuría and the Murdered Jesuits of El Salvador* (Philadelphia: Temple University Press, 1994); Jon Sobrino et al., *Companions of Jesus: The Jesuit Martyrs of El Salvador* (Maryknoll, NY: Orbis, 1990). On the events surrounding his death, see Martha Doggett, *Death Foretold: The Jesuit Murders in El Salvador* (Washington, DC: Georgetown University Press, 1993); The United Nations, "From Madness to Hope: The 12-Year War in El Salvador," *Report of the Commission on the Truth for El Salvador* (April 1, 1993); Robert Lassalle-Klein, "The Jesuit Martyrs of the University of Central America—Why Were They Killed?" *Explore* 13 (2009): 4–13. On Ellacuría's theology, see Burke, *The Ground Beneath the Cross*; Kevin F. Burke and Robert Lassalle-Klein, eds., *Love That Produces Hope: The Thought of Ignacio Ellacuría* (Collegeville, MN: Liturgical Press, 2006); and Lee, *Bearing the Weight of Salvation*.

23. This formulation, often repeated, first appears in *Freedom Made Flesh: The Mission of Christ and His Church*, trans. John Drury (Maryknoll, NY: Orbis, 1976), 15.

24. For Rahner's influence on Ellacuría, see Martin Maier, "Karl Rahner: The Teacher of Ellacuría," trans. Anna Bonta and Kevin Burke, in *Love That Produces Hope*, 128–43; Jon Sobrino, "Karl Rahner and Liberation Theology," *The Way* 43 (2004): 53–66; Robert Lassalle-Klein, "Rethinking Rahner on Grace and Symbol: New Proposals from the Americas," in *Rahner Beyond Rahner: A Great Theologian Encounters the Pacific Rim*, ed. Paul Crowley (Kansas City: Sheed & Ward, 2005), 87–99.

25. See the introduction to Zubiri's three-volume magnus opus, Xavier Zubiri, *Inteligencia sentiente: Inteligencia y realidad*, vol. 1 (Madrid: Alianza Editorial, 1980), 11–12. The influence of Zubiri on Ellacuría is explored in Robert Lassalle-Klein, "Ignacio Ellacuría's Debt to Xavier Zubiri: Critical Principles for a Latin American Philosophy and Theology of Liberation," in *Love That Produces Hope*, 88–127; Georges De Schrijver, "The Distinctive Contribution of Ignacio Ellacuría to a Praxis of Liberation: 'Shouldering the Burden of Reality,'" trans. Manuel R. Pajarillo, *Louvain Studies* 25 (2000): 312–35.

26. De Schrijver puts it more forcefully: "Zubiri decided thus to take the path of '*sentir*'—attentiveness through feelings—a form of knowledge evoked by the encounter with real things that have their own value-laden qualities. What matters in *sentir* is not so much the correlation between consciousness and given things, but reality itself, and the way it insists on acquiring 'actuality' or sensible 'presence' in the sentient intellect (*inteligencia sentiente*). This seems like a subtle nuancing of the phenomenological approach, but in fact, it is its reversal. Phenomenologists move from consciousness toward objects in order to replenish consciousness. Enriched by the conquered booty, they then simply return to consciousness for storage. But Zubiri calls attention to a reality that imposes itself upon our sentient intelligence and whose givenness is much richer than anything we could put together with our thought forms" ("The Distinctive Contribution of Ignacio Ellacuría to a Praxis of Liberation," 313).

27. Ignacio Ellacuría, "El objeto de la filosofia," in *Filosofia de la realidad histórica* (San Salvador: UCA Editores, 1990), 43–44. See Lassalle-Klein, "Ignacio Ellacuría's Debt to Xavier Zubiri," 107.

28. See *Gaudium et Spes* 4; Second General Conference of Latin American Bishops, "The Church in the Present-Day Transformation of Latin America in the Light of the Council," in *Liberation Theology: A Documentary History*, ed. Alfred T. Hennelly (Maryknoll, NY: Orbis, 1990), 89–119.

29. Robert Lassalle-Klein shows that there are two meanings of the term "historicization" in Ellacuría. The first refers to the transformative power human praxis has over the natural dimensions of reality. The second refers to the critical contextualization described here. See Lassalle-Klein, "Ignacio Ellacuría's Debt to Xavier Zubiri," 88–127.

30. Ellacuría pointed out, for example, how the concept of private property as a basic human right has, in his own Salvadoran context, been used to legitimize a system that attacks human dignity and denies most Salvadorans the right to own property. See Ignacio Ellacuría, "The Historicization of the Concept of Property," trans. Phillip Berryman, in *Towards a Society That Serves its People: The*

Intellectual Contribution of El Salvador's Murdered Jesuits, eds. John Hassett and Hugh Lacey (Washington, DC: Georgetown University Press, 1991), 105–37, at 106–9; J. Matthew Ashley, "Ignacio Ellacuría and the *Spiritual Exercises* of Ignatius Loyola," *Theological Studies* 61 (2000): 16–39, at 24.

31. Ellacuría speaks of praxis as "historical praxis," thus locating human activity within a broader field. It can neither be reduced to an atomistic action or a collective process. "Ellacuría's understanding of praxis protects the integrity of personal action, but places the human person in a wider net of mutual interrelatedness" (Lee, *Bearing the Weight of Salvation*, 112).

32. Congregation for the Doctrine of the Faith, "Instruction on Certain Aspects of the 'Theology of Liberation,'" in *Liberation Theology: A Documentary History*, 393–414, at 393, 400. This collection also includes an earlier, more balanced, assessment of liberation theology produced by the International Theological Commission, "Declaration on Human Development and Christian Salvation," in *Liberation Theology: A Documentary History*, 205–19.

33. Ellacuría's response to the Vatican Instruction agreed that the positions of this "hypothetical theology of liberation" that the CDF rejects ought in fact to be rejected, but he saw the Vatican's presentation as a caricature of what liberation theologians were in fact saying. See "Estudio teológico-pastoral de la 'Instrucción sobre algunos aspectos de la teología de la liberación,'" *Revista Latinoamericana de Teología* n. 2 (1984): 155–56.

34. Ignacio Ellacuría, "The Historicity of Christian Salvation," trans. Margaret D. Wilde, in *Mysterium Liberationis: Fundamental Concepts of Liberation Theology*, eds. Ignacio Ellacuría and Jon Sobrino (Maryknoll, NY: Orbis, 1993), 251–89, at 254.

35. Lassalle-Klein, "Rethinking Rahner on Grace and Symbol," 87–99. Lassalle-Klein notes his debt to Martin Maier for this insight, as well as how he advances it. See id., "Jesus of Galilee and the Crucified People: The Contextual Christology of Jon Sobrino and Ignacio Ellacuría," *Theological Studies* 70 (2009): 347–76, at 350 n. 10.

36. Ignacio Ellacuría, "Historia de la salvación," *Revista Latinoamericano de teología* 28 (1993): 8, cited in Lassalle-Klein, "Rethinking Rahner on Grace and Symbol," 92.

37. Zubiri, *Nature, History, God*, trans. Thomas B. Fowler, Jr. (Washington, DC: University Press of America, 1981), 323. The following remarks rely on Michael E. Lee's helpful discussion in "Liberation Theology's Transcendent Moment: The Work of Xavier Zubiri and Ignacio Ellacuría as Noncontrastive Discourse," *Journal of Religion* 83 (2003): 226–43.

38. Zubiri, *Nature, History, God*, 327.

39. Cited in Lee, *Bearing the Weight of Salvation*, 54.

40. See Robert Sokolowski, *The God of Faith and Reason: Foundations of Christian Theology* (Washington, DC: Catholic University of America Press, 1995); David B. Burrell, *Freedom and Creation in Three Traditions* (Notre Dame, IN: University of Notre Dame Press, 1993). As Michael Lee puts it, "Ellacuría may speak coherently about the liberating God of Exodus because he speaks

properly (noncontrastively) about the creating God of Genesis" (Lee, "Liberation Theology's Transcendent Moment," 228).

41. Cited in Lee, "Liberation Theology's Transcendent Moment," 231–32.

42. "Far from appearing to be incompatible with it, a non-contrastive transcendence of God suggests an extreme of divine involvement with the world" (Kathryn Tanner, *God and Creation in Christian Theology* [New York: Blackwell, 1988], 46). See Lee, "Liberation Theology's Transcendent Moment," 228.

43. Ellacuría, "The Historicity of Christian Salvation," 254–55.

44. Ellacuría, "The Historicity of Christian Salvation," 254.

45. Ellacuría, "The Historicity of Christian Salvation," 254.

46. Ellacuría, "The Historicity of Christian Salvation," 259.

47. Lee, *Bearing the Weight of Salvation*, 6, 10, 39, 64, 71.

48. Ignacio Ellacuría, "Historia de la salvación y salvación en la historia," *Escritos teológicos*, vol. 1 (San Salvador: UCA Editores, 2000), 519, cited in Lee, *Bearing the Weight of Salvation*, 171, n. 87.

49. Luke 6:20. I draw this transition and the following reflections from the concise treatment of Burke, "Christian Salvation and the Disposition of Transcendence: Ignacio Ellacuría's Historical Soteriology," in *Love That Produces Hope*, 174–75.

50. Ignacio Ellacuría, "Los pobres, 'lugar teológico' en América Latina," *Conversión de la Iglesia al Reino de Dios: Para anunciarlo y realizarlo en la historia* (Santander: Editorial Sal Terrae, 1984), 163, cited in Burke, "Christian Salvation and the Disposition of Transcendence," 174.

51. See the discussion in Lee, *Bearing the Weight of Salvation*, 86.

52. Ellacuría, "The Historicity of Christian Salvation," 276.

53. Ignacio Ellacuría, "The Crucified People," trans. Phillip Berryman and Robert R. Barr, in *Mysterium Liberationis: Fundamental Concepts of Liberation Theology*, eds. Ignacio Ellacuría and Jon Sobrino (Maryknoll, NY: Orbis, 1993), 580–603, at 588.

54. Burke, *The Ground Beneath the Cross*, 181.

55. Ignacio Ellacuría, "Las iglesias latinoamericanas interpelan a la Iglesia de España," *Sal Terrae* 826 (1982): 219–30, at 230, cited in Lee, *Bearing the Weight of Salvation*, 73–74. See Ignatius of Loyola, *Spiritual Exercises*, n. 53, in *Ignatius of Loyola: The Spiritual Exercises and Selected Works*, ed. George E. Ganss (New York: Paulist Press, 1991), 138.

56. Ignacio Ellacuría, "Lectura Latinoamerican de los *Ejercicios Espirituales* de san Ignacio," *Revista Latinoamericana de Telogía* (1991), 111–47, at 127, cited in Ashley, "Ignacio Ellacuría and the *Spiritual Exercises*," 29.

57. Ellacuría, "The Crucified People," 589.

58. Likewise, in speaking of the dialectical notion of sin, Ellacuría avoided a Manichean division of the world into those who are crucified and those who crucify: "While maintaining the universal pattern of people crucifying others in order to live themselves, the subsystems of crucifixion that exist in both groups, oppressors and oppressed, should also be examined" (Ellacuría, "The Crucified People," 591).

59. Burke, *The Ground Beneath the Cross*, 181.

60. Ellacuría, "The Crucified People," 598.

61. Ellacuría, "The Crucified People," 603.

62. Ellacuría, "The Crucified People," 588.

63. Ignacio Ellacuría, "Función liberadora de la filosofía," in *Veinte años de historia en El Salvador (1969–1989): Escritos políticos*, vol. 1 (San Salvador: UCA Editores, 1993), 119–20, cited in Lee, *Bearing the Weight of Salvation*, 91.

64. See Walter Brueggemann, "Covenanting as Human Vocation: A Discussion of the Relation of Bible and Pastoral Care," *Interpretation* 33 (1979): 115–29.

65. Jon Sobrino, *Where Is God? Earthquake, Terrorism, Barbarity, and Hope*, trans. Margaret Wilde (Maryknoll, NY: Orbis, 2004), 19.

66. Ellacuría, "The Historicity of Christian Salvation," 285.

67. Ignacio Ellacuría, "Hacia una fundamentación filosófica del método teológico Latinoamericano," in *Liberación y cautiverio: debates en torno al metodo de la teología en América Latina*, ed. E. Ruiz Maldonado (Mexico City: Comité Organizador, 1975), 609–35, at 625; also in *Estudios Centroamericanos* nn. 322–23 (1975): 409–25. Cited in Burke, *The Ground Beneath the Cross*, 43.

68. This framework is articulated most clearly in Ellacuría, "Hacia una fundamentación filosófica del método teológico Latinoamericano." The translation is that of Kevin Burke. On the issues involved in this translation, see Burke, *The Ground Beneath the Cross*, 114–16, n. 7. Recently, Jon Sobrino has approved his own translation of these three famous phrases: "grasping what is at stake in reality," "assuming responsibility for reality and paying the price for it," and "taking charge of reality" (Jon Sobrino, "Jesus of Galilee From the Salvadoran Context: Compassion, Hope, and Following the Light of the Cross," trans. Robert Lassalle-Klein with J. Matthew Ashley, *Theological Studies* 70 [2009]: 437–60, at 449). The following summary relies on Burke, "Christian Salvation and the Disposition of Transcendence," 171.

69. Burke, "Christian Salvation and the Disposition of Transcendence," 171–72.

70. Ellacuría, "The Historicity of Christian Salvation," 285.

71. Ashley, "Ignacio Ellacuría and the *Spiritual Exercises*," 30–37.

72. Ashley, "Ignacio Ellacuría and the *Spiritual Exercises*," 34.

73. Ashley, "Apocalypticism in Political and Liberation Theology," 41.

74. CELAM III, "Puebla Final Document, 'A Preferential Option for the Poor,'" n. 1.1, in *Liberation Theology: A Documentary History*, 254.

75. See Gustavo Gutiérrez, "Introduction to the Revised Edition: Expanding the View," in *A Theology of Liberation: History, Politics, and Salvation*, rev. ed., trans. Caridad Inda and John Eagleson (Maryknoll, NY: Orbis, 1988), xxv–xxviii. Gutiérrez notes that although the issue of the poor was present in the council debates and final documents, it did not predominate.

76. See Gutiérrez, "The Option for the Poor Arises From Faith in Christ," 322.

77. Gutiérrez, "Introduction to the Revised Edition: Expanding the View," xxi.

78. Gustavo Gutiérrez, "Memory and Prophecy," in *The Option for the Poor in Christian Theology*, ed. Daniel G. Groody (Notre Dame, IN: University of Notre Dame Press, 2007), 17–38, at 28.

79. Gutiérrez, "Memory and Prophecy," 25.

80. Gustavo Gutiérrez, *We Drink From Our Own Wells: The Spiritual Journey of a People*, trans. Matthew J. O'Connell (Maryknoll, NY: Orbis, 1984), 125. "The poor person is someone brimming over with capacities and possibilities, whose culture has its own values, derived from racial background, history and language" (Gutiérrez, "The Task and Content of Liberation Theology," trans. Judith Condor, in *The Cambridge Companion to Liberation Theology*, ed. Christopher Rowland, 2nd ed. [Cambridge: Cambridge University Press, 2007], 19–38, at 25).

81. Gustavo Gutiérrez, *The Truth Shall Make You Free*, trans. Matthew J. O'Connell (Maryknoll, NY: Orbis, 1990), 10. Compare Gutiérrez, *We Drink From Our Own Wells*, 125.

82. Gutiérrez, "Memory and Prophecy," 30.

83. Jon Sobrino, "Theology in a Suffering World: Theology as *Intellectus Amoris*," trans. José Pedrozo and Paul F. Knitter, in *The Principle of Mercy: Taking the Crucified People from the Cross* (Maryknoll, NY: Orbis, 1994), 27–46, at 31.

84. Sobrino, "Theology in a Suffering World," 32.

85. As an exception to this rule, see the marvelously concise and deeply reflective introduction: Peter J. Henriot, *Opting for the Poor: A Challenge For North Americans* (Washington, DC: Center of Concern, 1990).

86. Gutiérrez, *We Drink From Our Own Wells*, 126.

87. Metz, "Suffering unto God," 621.

88. Metz, "A Passion for God: Religious Orders Today," in *A Passion for God*, 163.

89. Metz, "A Passion for God: Religious Orders Today," 157. On the evolution of Metz's thinking on spiritual poverty, see Ashley, "Introduction: Reading Metz," in *A Passion for God*, 19–20; id., *Interruptions*, 95, 127–28, 160–61, 180–81.

90. See Johann Baptist Metz, *Poverty of Spirit*, trans. John Drury (New York: Newman Press, 1968).

91. See Karl Rahner, "The Ignatian Mysticism of Joy in the World," in *Theological Investigations*, vol. 3, trans. Karl-H. and Boniface Kruger (Baltimore: Helicon Press, 1967), 277–93. See chapter 4 of this volume.

92. Metz, "Suffering unto God," 614.

93. Metz, "A Passion for God: Religious Orders Today," 157.

94. Metz, "Theology as Theodicy?" 65.

95. Metz, "A Passion for God: Religious Orders Today," 158.

96. Metz, "Theology as Theodicy?" 66.

97. Rahner, "The Ignatian Mysticism of Joy in the World," 291.

98. Ellacuría, "Las bienaventuranzas," in *Escritos teológicos*, vol. 2 (San Salvador: UCA Editores, 2000), 435. See Lee, *Bearing the Weight of Salvation*, 124.

99. See Ashley, *Interruptions*, 245 n. 59.

100. Ashley, *Interruptions*, 163.

101. Karl Rahner, "Comments by Karl Rahner on Questions Raised by Avery Dulles," trans. James M. Quigley, in *Ignatius of Loyola: His Personality and Spiritual Heritage 1556–1956* (Saint Louis, MO: Institute of Jesuit Sources, 1977), 290–93, at 292.

102. Rahner, "Comments by Karl Rahner on Questions Raised by Avery Dulles," 292.

103. Karl Rahner, *On the Theology of Death*, trans. C. H. Henkey and W. J. O'Hara (New York: Herder and Herder, 1965); Philip Endean, *Karl Rahner and Ignatian Spirituality* (Oxford: Oxford University Press, 2001), 190–94.

104. Jon Sobrino, "Companions of Jesus," trans. Dinah Livingstone, in *Companions of Jesus: The Jesuit Martyrs of El Salvador* (Maryknoll, NY: Orbis, 1990), 3–56, at 55. See Ashley, "Apocalypticism in Political and Liberation Theology," 43.

Conclusion—pages 230–233

1. Karl Barth, *Church Dogmatics*, vol. III/4, trans. A. T. Mackay, et al. (Edinburgh: T & T Clark, 1961), 602.

Bibliography

Ashley, J. Matthew. "Apocalypticism in Political and Liberation Theology: Toward an Historical *Docta Ignorantia.*" *Horizons* 27 (2000): 22–43.

——. "Ignacio Ellacuría and the *Spiritual Exercises* of Ignatius Loyola." *Theological Studies* 61 (2000): 16–39.

——. *Interruptions: Mysticism, Politics, and Theology in the Work of Johann Baptist Metz.* Notre Dame, IN: University of Notre Dame Press, 1998.

Astell, Ann W., ed. *Lay Sanctity, Medieval and Modern: A Search for Models.* Notre Dame, IN: University of Notre Dame Press, 2000.

Badcock, Gary D. *The Way of Life: A Theology of Christian Vocation.* Grand Rapids, MI: Eerdmans, 1998.

Barth, Karl. "Vocation." In *Church Dogmatics*, III/4:595-647, translated by A. T. Mackay et al. Edinburgh: T & T Clark, 1961.

Bezzerides, Ann Mitsakos. *Christ at Work: Orthodox Christian Perspectives on Vocation.* Brookline, MA: Holy Cross Orthodox Press, 2006.

Boeve, Lieven. *God Interrupts History: Theology in a Time of Upheaval.* New York: Continuum, 2007.

——. *Interrupting Tradition: An Essay on Christian Faith in a Postmodern Context.* Louvain: Peeters Press, 2003.

Brackley, Dean. *The Call to Discernment in Troubled Times: New Perspectives on the Transformative Wisdom of Ignatius of Loyola.* New York: Crossroad, 2004.

Burke, Kevin F. *The Ground Beneath the Cross: The Theology of Ignacio Ellacuría.* Washington, DC: Georgetown University Press, 2000.

Burke, Kevin F., and Robert Lassalle-Klein, eds. *Love That Produces Hope: The Thought of Ignacio Ellacuría.* Collegeville, MN: Liturgical Press, 2006.

Calvin, John. *Institutes of the Christian Religion.* Edited by John T. McNeill. Philadelphia: Westminster Press, 1960.

Congar, Yves. *Lay People in the Church: A Study for a Theology of Laity*, revised edition. Translated by Donald Attwater. Westminster, MD: The Newman Press, 1965.

Dupré, Louis. "Ignatian Humanism and Its Mystical Origins." *Communio* 18 (1991): 164–82.

———. *Passage to Modernity: An Essay in the Hermeneutics of Nature and Culture.* New Haven, CT: Yale University Press, 1993.

———. "Spiritual Life and the Survival of Christianity: Reflections at the End of the Millennium." *Cross Currents* 48 (1998): 381–90.

Egan, Harvey D. *The Spiritual Exercises and the Ignatian Mystical Horizon.* Saint Louis, MO: Institute of Jesuit Sources, 1976.

Ellacuría, Ignacio. *Freedom Made Flesh: The Mission of Christ and His Church.* Translated by John Drury. Maryknoll, NY: Orbis, 1976.

Ellacuría, Ignacio, and Jon Sobrino, eds. *Mysterium Liberationis: Fundamental Concepts of Liberation Theology.* Maryknoll, NY: Orbis, 1993.

Endean, Philip. *Karl Rahner and Ignatian Spirituality.* Oxford: Oxford University Press, 2001.

Groody, Daniel G., ed. *The Option for the Poor in Christian Theology.* Notre Dame, IN: University of Notre Dame Press, 2007.

Gutiérrez, Gustavo. *A Theology of Liberation: History, Politics, and Salvation,* revised edition. Translated by Caridad Inda and John Eagleson. Maryknoll, NY: Orbis, 1988.

Haughey, John C., ed. *Revisiting the Idea of Vocation: Theological Explorations.* Washington, DC: Catholic University of America Press, 2004.

Hennelly, Alfred T., ed. *Liberation Theology: A Documentary History.* Maryknoll, NY: Orbis, 1990.

Holl, Karl. "The History of the Word Vocation (*Beruf*)." Translated by Heber F. Peacock. *Review and Expositor* 55 (1958): 126–54.

Holland, Paul D. "Vocation." In *The New Dictionary of Theology,* edited by Joseph Komonchak, Mary Collins, and Dermot Lane, 1087–92. Collegeville, MN: Liturgical Press, 1987.

Ignatius of Loyola. *Ignatius of Loyola: The Spiritual Exercises and Selected Works.* Edited by George E. Ganss. New York: Paulist Press, 1991.

John Paul II. The Consecrated Life/*Vita Consecrata.* Washington, DC: USCCB Publishing, 1996.

———. I Will Give You Shepherds: On the Formation of Priests in the Circumstances of the Present Day/*Pastores Dabo Vobis.* Washington, DC: USCCB Publishing, 1992.

———. The Lay Members of Christ's Faithful People/*Christifideles Laici.* Washington, DC: USCCB Publishing, 1988.

Lahitton, Joseph. *La Vocation Sacerdotale.* Paris: Lethielleux, 1909.

Lee, Michael E. *Bearing the Weight of Salvation: The Soteriology of Ignacio Ellacuría.* New York: Crossroad, 2009.

Liguori, Alphonsus de. *The Great Means of Salvation and Perfection,* vol. 3 of *The Complete Works of Saint Alphonsus de Liguori: The Ascetical Works.* Edited by Eugene Grimm. Brooklyn, NY: Redemptorist Fathers, 1927.

Luther, Martin. "The Bondage of the Will." In *Luther's Works*, 33:3–295, edited by Philip S. Watson. Philadelphia: Fortress Press, 1972.

———. "Commentary on 1 Corinthians 7." In *Luther's Works*, 28:1–56, edited by Hilton C. Oswald. Saint Louis: Concordia Publishing, 1973.

———. "The Estate of Marriage." In *Luther's Works*, 45:11–49, edited by Walther I. Brandt. Philadelphia: Muhlenberg Press, 1962.

———. "The Judgment of Martin Luther on Monastic Vows." In *Luther's Works*, 44:243–400, edited by James Atkinson. Philadelphia: Fortress Press, 1966.

MacIntyre, Alasdair. *After Virtue: A Study in Moral Theory*, second edition. Notre Dame, IN: University of Notre Dame Press, 1984.

Marshall, Paul. *A Kind of Life Imposed on Man: Vocation and Social Order from Tyndale to Locke*. Toronto: University of Toronto Press, 1996.

McIntosh, Mark A. *Discernment and Truth: The Spirituality and Theology of Knowledge*. New York: Crossroad, 2004.

Merton, Thomas. "Things in Their Identity." In *Seeds of Contemplation*, 24–40. New York: Dell, 1949.

Metz, Johann Baptist. *Faith in History and Society: Toward a Practical Fundamental Theology*. Translated by J. Matthew Ashley. New York: Crossroad, 2007.

———. *A Passion for God: The Mystical-Political Dimension of Christianity*. Translated by J. Matthew Ashley. New York: Paulist Press, 1998.

———. *Poverty of Spirit*. Translated by John Drury. New York: Newman Press, 1968.

Miller, Vincent J. *Consuming Religion: Christian Faith and Practice in a Consumer Culture*. New York: Continuum, 2003.

Neafsey, John. *A Sacred Voice Is Calling: Personal Vocation and Social Conscience*. Maryknoll, NY: Orbis, 2006.

O'Connell, Maureen. *Compassion: Loving Our Neighbor in an Age of Globalization*. Maryknoll, NY: Orbis, 2009.

O'Malley, John W. *The First Jesuits*. Cambridge, MA: Harvard University Press, 1993.

———. *What Happened at Vatican II*. Cambridge, MA: Harvard University Press, 2008.

Placher, William C., ed. *Callings: Twenty Centuries of Christian Wisdom on Vocation*. Grand Rapids, MI: Eerdmans, 2005.

Rahner, Karl. *Foundations of Christian Faith: An Introduction to the Idea of Christianity*. Translated by William V. Dych. New York: Crossroad, 1978.

———. "Ignatian Mysticism of Joy in the World." In *Theological Investigations*, 3:277–93, translated by Karl-H. Kruger and Boniface Kruger. Baltimore: Helicon Press, 1967.

———. "Ignatian Spirituality and Devotion to the Heart of Jesus." In *Mission and Grace*, 3:176–210, translated by Cecily Hastings. London: Sheed & Ward, 1966.

———. "Ignatius of Loyola Speaks to a Modern Jesuit." In *Ignatius of Loyola*, 9–38, translated by Rosaleen Ockenden. London: Collins, 1978.

———. "The Individual in the Church." In *Nature and Grace*, 51–83, translated by Dinah Wharton. New York: Sheed & Ward, 1963.

———. "The Logic of Concrete Individual Knowledge in Ignatius Loyola." In *The Dynamic Element in the Church*, 84–170, translated by W. J. O'Hara. New York: Herder and Herder, 1964.

———. "Modern Piety and the Experience of Retreats." In *Theological Investigations*, 16:135–55, translated by David Morland. New York: Crossroad, 1983.

———. "Observations on the Factor of the Charismatic in the Church." In *Theological Investigations*, 12:81–97, translated by David Bourke. New York: Seabury Press, 1974.

———. "On the Question of a Formal Existential Ethics." In *Theological Investigations*, 2:217–34, translated by Karl-H. Kruger. Baltimore: Helicon Press, 1963.

———. "The Significance in Redemptive History of the Individual Member of the Church." In *The Christian Commitment: Essays in Pastoral Theology*, 75–113, translated by Cecily Hastings. New York: Sheed & Ward, 1963.

Sales, Francis de. *Introduction to the Devout Life.* Translated by John K. Ryan. New York: Doubleday/Image Books, 1950.

———. *Treatise on the Love of God.* Translated by Henry Benedict Mackey. Westminster, MD: Newman, 1942.

Schleck, Charles A. *The Theology of Vocations.* Milwaukee, WI: Bruce Publishing, 1963.

Schuurman, Douglas J. *Vocation: Discerning Our Callings in Life.* Grand Rapids, MI: Eerdmans, 2004.

Schwehn, Mark R., and Dorothy C. Bass, eds. *Leading Lives That Matter: What We Should Do and Who We Should Be.* Grand Rapids, MI: Eerdmans, 2006.

Sempé, L. "Vocation." In *Dictionnaire de Théologie Catholique*, 15:3148–81, edited by A. Vacant et al. Paris: Librairie Letouzey et Ané, 1950.

Sobrino, Jon et al., *Companions of Jesus: The Jesuit Martyrs of El Salvador.* Maryknoll, NY: Orbis, 1990.

Taylor, Charles. *A Secular Age.* Cambridge, MA: Harvard University Press, 2007.

———. *Sources of the Self: The Making of the Modern Identity.* Cambridge, MA: Harvard University Press, 1989.

Thompson, William M., ed. *Bérulle and the French School: Selected Writings.* New York: Paulist Press, 1989.

Tilley, Terrence W. *The Disciples' Jesus: Christology as Reconciling Practice.* Maryknoll, NY: Orbis, 2008.

Tracy, David. *On Naming the Present: Reflections on God, Hermeneutics, and Church.* Maryknoll, NY: Orbis, 1994.

Troeltsch, Ernst. *The Social Teaching of the Christian Churches*. Translated by Olive Wyon. New York: Harper & Row, 1960.

Volf, Miroslav. *Work in the Spirit: Toward a Theology of Work*. Oxford: Oxford University Press, 1991.

Wassenaar, Michael R. *Four Types of Calling: The Ethics of Vocation in Kierkegaard, Brunner, Scheler and Barth*. PhD dissertation, Yale University, 2009.

Weber, Max. *The Protestant Ethic and the Spirit of Capitalism*. Translated by Talcott Parsons. London: Unwin Hyman, 1930.

Wingren, Gustaf. *Luther on Vocation*. Translated by Carl C. Rasmussen. Philadelphia: Muhlenberg Press, 1957.

Wuthnow, Robert. *After Heaven: Spirituality in America Since the 1950s*. Berkeley: University of California Press, 1998.

Index

sanctifying, 79, 132–39, 154,
250n80
as supernatural, 27, 74, 78–80,
89, 90, 136
theology of, 38, 74–80, 90, 104,
123–24, 128–39, 141–42, 152,
156–57, 230–32
Gratian, 9
Greek philosophy, 7–8, 11, 74–75,
224
Gregory Nazianzen, St., 81
Gregory of Nyssa, St., 129
Gregory the Great, St., 8
Gurnall, William, 23
Gutiérrez, Gustavo, 194, 198, 208,
217–19, 221, 222, 223, 228, 233,
268n3

Hall, Joseph, 20
Hallier, François, 81, 83, 84
Hardy, Lee, 238n53
Hauerwas, Stanley, 24–25, 167,
239n77
Haughey, John C., 234n3
Heidegger, Martin, 136–37, 202
Henriot, Peter J., 274n85
Hesse, Hermann, 93
hiddenness, divine, 94–95, 101–11
history, theology of, 197–207, 209,
219
holiness
of church, 40, 43
hierarchy of, 6–11, 27–28,
42–43, 45, 99, 110
of laity, 9–10, 29, 31–33, 37–40,
240n84
and monasticism, 7–9, 13–14, 50
of priests, 67–68
Puritan conception, 20–21, 23
universal call to, xi, xvii, 27–45,
90, 159, 232
Holl, Karl, 10, 254n18
Holocaust, 197–98

Holy Spirit, 25–26, 40, 52, 88, 134,
182–83, 190
Homobonus, St., 11
Hopkins, Gerard Manley, 125
Hume, David, 163
Hürth, Franz, 128
Husserl, Edmund, 202

Ignatius of Loyola, St.
on the affections, 56–58, 60, 89,
143–44, 191, 246n23
on consolation, 57–58, 143–47,
156
on discernment, xv, 55–60,
70–71, 89, 141–44, 160, 174
early life, 53–54
on grace, 59–61, 74, 89
Ignatian spirituality, 53–61
Spiritual Exercises, 55–61,
62–63, 65, 70–71, 89, 140–58,
159, 191, 210, 216, 226,
246n23, 261n46
See also discernment of spirits;
Society of Jesus
indifference, 160, 223–25
interruption, 171–73, 175–79, 184,
191–92, 196-200, 201, 266n48
Israel, 217, 223–25, 228

Jacopoda da Voragine, 53
Jansenius, 78
Jerome, St., 8
Jesuits. *See* Society of Jesus
Jesus Christ
call of, 6, 120
life of, 55–57, 158, 172–73, 189,
192
on love of neighbor, 44, 194
priesthood of, 68
and salvation, 102–3, 106, 133
spiritual "states" of, 66–69,
248n51
suffering and death. *See* cross
resurrection, 172